THE COMPLETE CHESS WORKOUT

EVERYMAN CHESS

Richard Palliser

First published in 2007 by Gloucester Publishers plc (formerly Everyman Publishers plc),
Northburgh House, 10 Northburgh Street, London EC1V 0AT

First published 2007 by Gloucester Publishers plc

British Library Cataloguing-in-Publication Data
A catalogue record for this book is available from the British Library.

ISBN 978 185744 532 9

Distributed in North America by The Globe Pequot Press, P.O Box 480,
246 Goose Lane, Guilford, CT 06437-0480.

All other sales enquiries should be directed to Everyman Chess, Northburgh House,
10 Northburgh Street, London EC1V 0AT
tel: 020 7253 7887 fax: 020 7490 3708
email: info@everymanchess.com
website: www.everymanchess.com

EVERYMAN CHESS SERIES (formerly Cadogan Chess)
Chief advisor: Byron Jacobs
Commissioning editor: John Emms
Assistant editor: Richard Palliser

Typesetting and editing by First Rank Publishing, Brighton.
Cover design by Horatio Monteverde.
Printed and bound in America by Versa Press.

Contents

Introduction

Spending as little as 10-15 minutes a day on one's tactical ability really can reap dividends. I can certainly testify to that myself and it's always very welcome to see a pupil regularly trying to solve a number of tactical exercises: not only do they become more tactically alert, but they also improve their clock handling and gain in confidence.

During the past decade some quite challenging puzzle books have appeared, aimed chiefly at the level of the stronger club player and above. These are a most welcome development, but are perhaps not the best tactical training for less experienced players or even average club players. Some attempted solving of very tough positions is a good thing, especially if the solution is then studied in some detail, but such works are unlikely to provide the budding student with a grounding in the fundamentals of tactical and attacking play.

Wanting to produce a book that would improve the tactical knowledge of the average player led me to drawing up categories of both the more common attacking motifs (bishop sacrifices on h7 and knight sacrifices on f7 being two main examples) and the less usual (such as a queen sacrifice on h6). Thus there are a number of examples of each key theme in this work which should, I hope, help to cement these important ideas into the reader's subconscious, thereby improving both their attacking and defensive ability.

One cannot, of course, blindly attack in every game: the right conditions to attack must be present, such as a chip in the opposition king's pawn wall or the ability to quickly transfer many of one's pieces to the attacking zone. Many of the puzzles in this work deal with attacking scenarios and should help the reader to further appreciate just when and why an attack is likely to work.

What, though, of the many games in which we don't get to attack? In these tactical play is no less likely to occur and it's important to always be alert to tactical opportunities. One very handy way of not letting these pass by is to keep in mind John Nunn's very useful mnemonic: LPDO ('loose pieces drop off'). Indeed, it's very noticeable just how many tactics are to do with a piece being undefended or poorly defended. The reader will become fully aware of the concept of LPs while working through the large chapter on attacking motifs, but so important is the topic that I've also included a later chapter devoted to both it and the related theme of overloading a defensive piece.

To remind the reader that tactics are present throughout the game, there are also chapters devoted to tactics in both the opening and the endgame, while the fiendish puzzles of Chapter Six should challenge even the very tactically able. I've also aimed to make things a little trickier throughout for the reader by not following the common practice of sorting each chapter by difficulty. Instead the order is much more like the tactical opportunities that occur in our games, being random (sorting alphabetically by tournament location is about as random as one can get!) and thereby simple tactics follow quite challenging ones and vice versa. Do be aware too that by no means every combination mates in style or wins heavy material; just as in real life, many of the puzzles included here only lead to the win of a pawn, while a few even see the side to move scrambling a draw through some tactical device or other.

I couldn't resist including a few classic favourites among the 1,200 puzzles, but even those with an excellent knowledge of the classics should find the majority of the positions included new. No less than 585 of the puzzles are from games played in 2007 and I've also drawn heavily on unpublished games collections: chiefly my own I'm afraid, but I'm also very grateful to a number of people who sent or supplied games: Chris Duggan, Scott Fraser, Paul Hopwood, Neville Pearce, Kieran Smallbone, Norman Stephenson, Sean Terry (editor of the excellent Oxford City CC magazine, *DisInformator*), and Tim Turner.

I hope that this work will improve the tactical eye of the reader, while also reminding them of the many beautiful possibilities thrown up by our favourite royal game.

Richard Palliser,
York,
September 2007

1: Warming Up

Even those fairly new to the game should find the following hundred puzzles quite solvable. Just remember that you're not always looking to force mate; quite often the solution is just a little tactic to pick up a pawn or two.

1) □ A.Andres Gonzalez ■ J.De la Villa Garcia
Abierto 2006

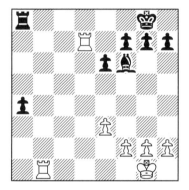

White to Play

2) □ A.Yermolinsky ■ T.Kurosaki
Agoura Hills 2007

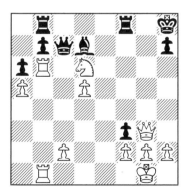

White to Play

3) □ B.Esen ■ T.Demirel
Ankara 2007

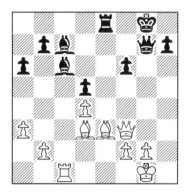

White to Play

4) □ A.Mortola ■ P.Scanferla
Arvier 2007

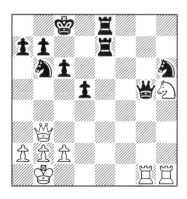

Black to Play

5) □ **A.Fedorov** ■ **Z.Mamedjarova**
Baku 2007

White to Play

6) □ **A.Khudaverdieva** ■ **N.Miezis**
Baku 2007

Black to Play

7) □ **C.Baudson** ■ **L.Gil**
Balagne 2007

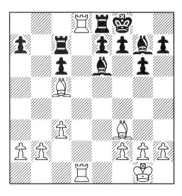

White to Play

8) □ **L.Damjanovic** ■ **A.Panic**
Belgrade 2007

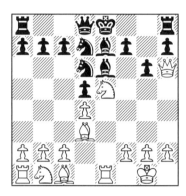

White to Play

9) □ **R.Mitrovic** ■ **M.Mihajlovic**
Belgrade 2007

Black to Play

10) □ **J.Emms** ■ **G.Burgess**
British League 1999

White to Play

11) □ **M.Quinn** ■ **M.Lyell**
British League 2000

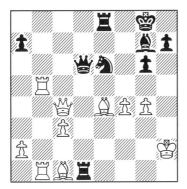

Black to Play

12) □ **M.Simons** ■ **R.Noyce**
British League 2000

White to Play

13) □ **M.Soszynski** ■ **J.Stevenson**
British League 2007

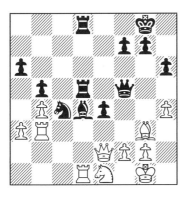

Black to Play

14) □ **Al.Ivanov** ■ **V.Sanduleac**
Bucharest 2007

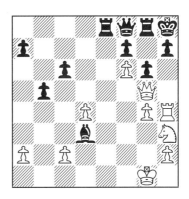

White to Play

15) □ **L.Vadja** ■ **K.Haznedaroglu**
Budapest 2007

White to Play

16) □ **M.Galyas** ■ **W.Wilke**
Budapest 2007

White to Play

17) □ **S.Farago** ■ **Hj.Gretarsson**
Budapest 2007

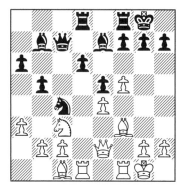

Black to Play

18) □ **Y.Drozdovskij** ■ **V.Georgiev**
Cappelle la Grande 2007

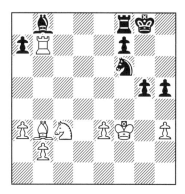

White to Play

19) □ **T.Rrhioua** ■ **C.Debray**
Champs sur Marne 2007

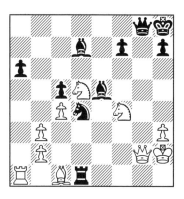

Black to Play

20) □ **L.Hylands** ■ **M.Uddin**
Cheltenham 2007

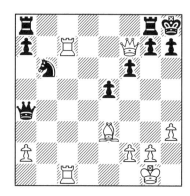

White to Play

21) □ **A.Riazantsev** ■ **B.Galstian**
Chelyabinsk 2007

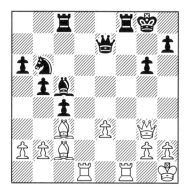

White to Play

22) □ **M.Abdul** ■ **N.Murshed**
Dhaka 2007

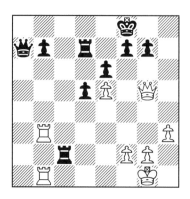

White to Play

23) □ **S.Reefat** ■ **M.Abdul**
Dhaka 2007

White to Play

26) □ **A.Savickas** ■ **A.Hunt**
Dresden 2007

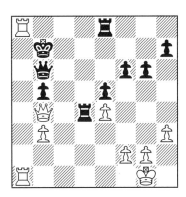

White to Play

24) □ **A.Graf** ■ **A.Gasthofer**
Dresden 2007

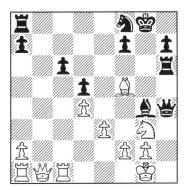

Black to Play

27) □ **M.Erdogdu** ■ **A.David**
Dresden 2007

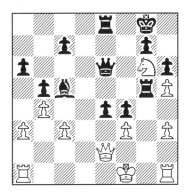

Black to Play

25) □ **A.Hafenstein** ■ **R.Brunello**
Dresden 2007

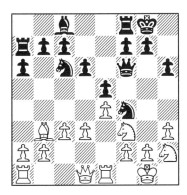

Black to Play

28) □ **R.Vaganian** ■ **S.Siebrecht**
Dresden 2007

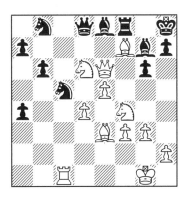

White to Play

29) □ **V.Durarbeyli** ■ **B.Damljanovic**
Dresden 2007

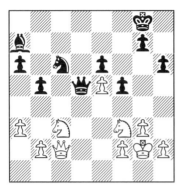

Black to Play

30) □ **V.Shalimov** ■ **A.Bagrationi**
Evpatoria 2007

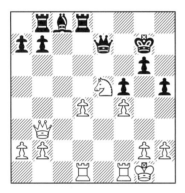

White to Play

31) □ **Y.Gozzoli** ■ **E.Reinhart**
French League 2007

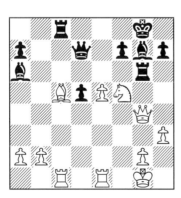

White to Play

32) □ **B.Holland** ■ **R.Rough**
Gibraltar 2007

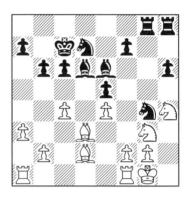

Black to Play

33) □ **M.Garcia** ■ **H.Strand**
Gibraltar 2007

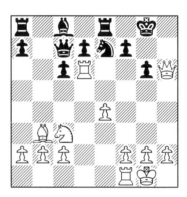

White to Play

34) □ **M.Helin** ■ **L.Manetto**
Gibraltar 2007

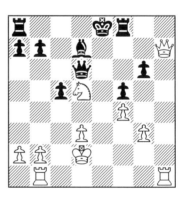

White to Play

35) ☐ **O.Vea** ■ **H.Rasch**
Gibraltar 2007

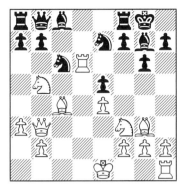

White to Play

36) ☐ **P.Wallace** ■ **A.Dekker**
Gibraltar 2007

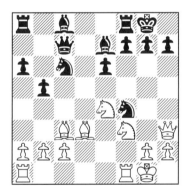

White to Play

37) ☐ **R.Westra** ■ **R.Palliser**
Goole (rapid) 1999

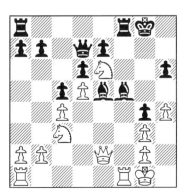

White to Play

38) ☐ **C.Wilman** ■ **A.Tate**
Hamilton 2005

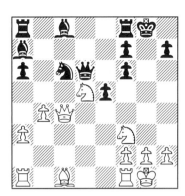

White to Play

39) ☐ **G.Salimbeni** ■ **N.Hutchinson**
Hastings 2006

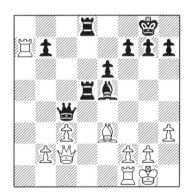

Black to Play

40) ☐ **D.Schut** ■ **L.Bensdorp**
Hilversum 2007

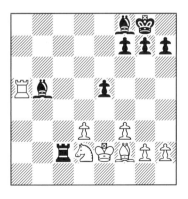

Black to Play

41) ☐ **M.Bogorads** ■ **D.Jahr**
Hockenheim 2007

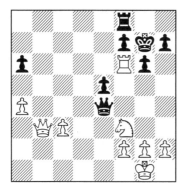

White to Play

42) ☐ **O.Gladyszev** ■ **S.Kidambi**
Isle of Man 2005

Black to Play

43) ☐ **S.Siebrecht** ■ **A.Szieberth**
Isle of Man 2006

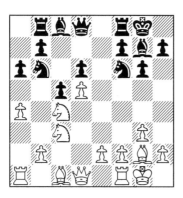

White to Play

44) ☐ **Y.Zimmerman** ■ **P.Adams**
Isle of Man 2005

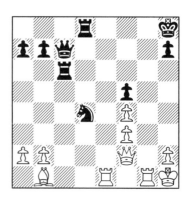

White to Play

45) ☐ **A.May** ■ **H.Hecht**
Islington 1971

Black to Play

46) ☐ **A.Nikolaeva** ■ **O.Vozovic**
Kharkiv 2007

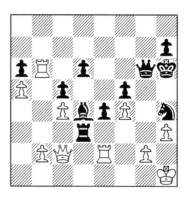

Black to Play

47) □ **S.Vysochin** ■ **V.Sergeev**
Kyiv 2007

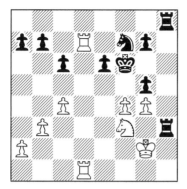

White to Play

50) □ **M.Alonso Contreras** ■ **D.Trujillo Delgado**
La Laguna 2007

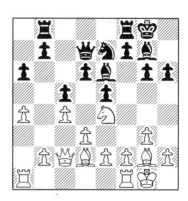

White to Play

48) □ **V.Balanovskij** ■ **I.Kusnetsov**
Kyiv 2007

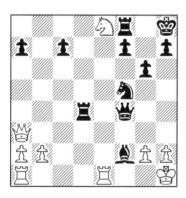

Black to Play

51) □ **A.Moreto Quintana** ■ **V.Koziak**
La Rode 2007

Black to Play

49) □ **B.Kurajica** ■ **C.Schneider Sanchez**
La Laguna 2007

White to Play

52) □ **O.Hindle** ■ **P.Puig Puildo**
Lucerne 1963

White to Play

53) □ **C.Ficco** ■ **M.Godena**
Lugano 2007

Black to Play

54) □ **R.Martin del Campo** ■ **L.Alonso Arteaga**
Merida 2006

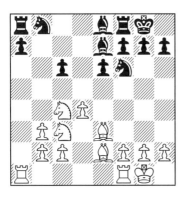

White to Play

55) □ **A.Kosten** ■ **C.Marchal**
Metz 2007

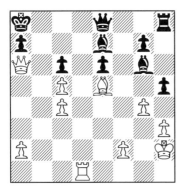

White to Play

56) □ **A.Touret** ■ **V.Petkov**
Metz 2007

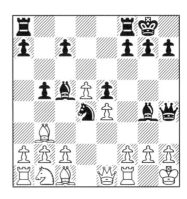

Black to Play

57) □ **N.Guliyev** ■ **V.Schweitzer**
Metz 2007

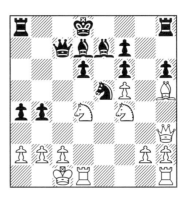

White to Play

58) □ **A.Chudinovskih** ■ **O.Nikolenko**
Moscow 2007

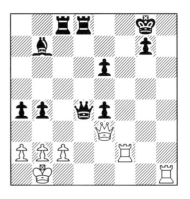

White to Play

59) □ **A.Okara** ■ **M.Yuganova**
Moscow 2007

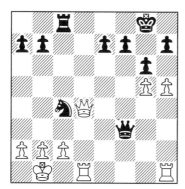

White to Play

60) □ **A.Venevtsev** ■ **M.Mozharov**
Moscow 2007

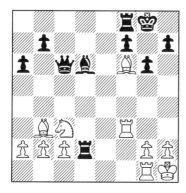

Black to Play

61) □ **D.Bronstein** ■ **A.Koblencs**
Moscow 1945

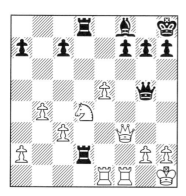

White to Play

62) □ **E.Lasker** ■ **M.Steinitz**
Moscow 1896

White to Play

63) □ **A.Aguilar** ■ **M.Leskovar**
Necochea 2007

Black to Play

64) □ **'Andrei21'** ■ **R.Palliser**
online blitz 2007

White to Play

65)　□ **R.Palliser** ■ **'Perparim3'**
online blitz 2007

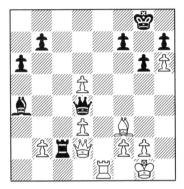

White to Play

68)　□ **A.Chua** ■ **Z.Izoria**
Parsippany 2007

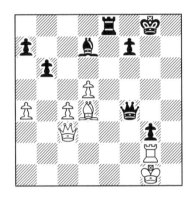

Black to Play

66)　□ **D.Bruce** ■ **R.Palliser**
Oxford 2003

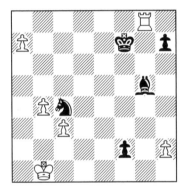

White to Play

69)　□ **B.Katz** ■ **R.Tomasko**
Parsippany 2007

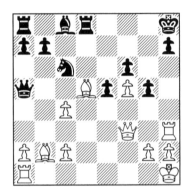

White to Play

67)　□ **K.Smallbone** ■ **S.Terry**
Oxford 1999

White to Play

70)　□ **V.Hylapov** ■ **L.Lintchevski**
Peterhof 2007

White to Play

71) ☐ **A.Nickel** ■ **L.Deruda**
Porto Mannu 2007

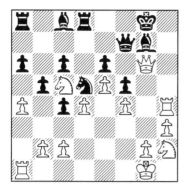

White to Play

72) ☐ **R.Markus** ■ **D.Doric**
Rijeka 2006

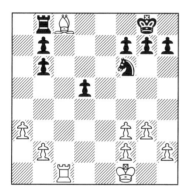

White to Play

73) ☐ **P.Hempson** ■ **R.Palliser**
Rotherham (rapid) 2007

Black to Play

74) ☐ **A.Volokitin** ■ **E.Bareev**
Russian Team Championship 2007

White to Play

75) ☐ **D.Tyomkin** ■ **V.Gaprindashvili**
Saint Vincent 2005

White to Play

76) ☐ **A.Rodriguez** ■ **A.Needleman**
San Luis 2007

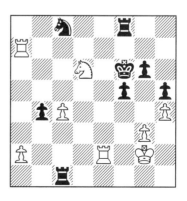

White to Play

77) □ **F.Corrales** ■ **F.De la Paz**
Santa Clara 2007

Black to Play

78) □ **A.Morozevich** ■ **S.Movsesian**
Sarajevo 2007

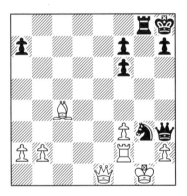

Black to Play

79) □ **C.Ward** ■ **R.Palliser**
Scarborough 2001

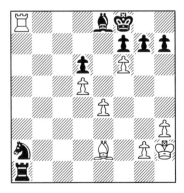

White to Play

80) □ **R.Palliser** ■ **J.Houska**
Scarborough 2004

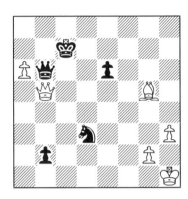

White to Play

81) □ **A.Gavrilov** ■ **R.Perez Garcia**
Seville 2007

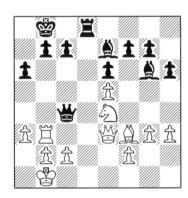

White to Play

82) □ **K.Ambartsumova** ■ **J.Kochetkova**
Sochi 2007

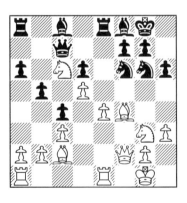

White to Play

83) □ **A.Bogdanov** ■ **F.Rodkin**
St Petersburg 2006

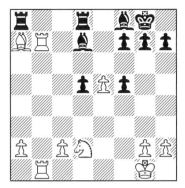

Black to Play

84) □ **A.Eliseev** ■ **V.Kurilov**
St Petersburg 2007

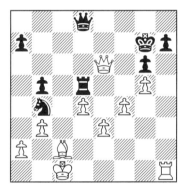

White to Play

85) □ **A.Guzenko** ■ **S.Klobukov**
St Petersburg 2007

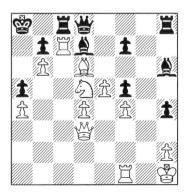

White to Play

86) □ **A.Lomako** ■ **T.Airapetian**
St Petersburg 2007

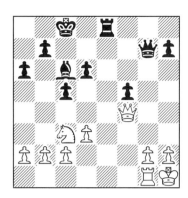

Black to Play

87) □ **A.Vunder** ■ **M.Zacurdajev**
St Petersburg 2007

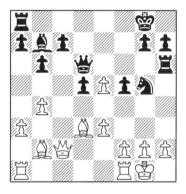

Black to Play

88) □ **R.Palliser** ■ **D.Seymour**
Stockton on Tees simul 2005

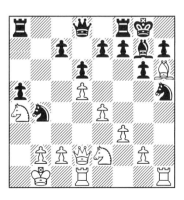

White to Play

89) □ **R.Zimmermann** ■ **J.Lener**
Teplice 2007

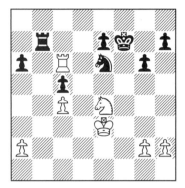

White to Play

90) □ **A.Mordue** ■ **S.Dilleigh**
Torquay 2006

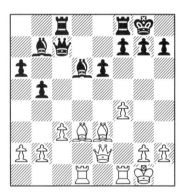

White to Play

91) □ **I.Starostits** ■ **R.Bezler**
Triesen 2007

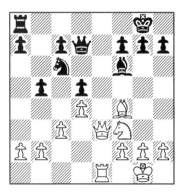

White to Play

92) □ **P.San Segundo Carrillo** ■ **R.Wojtaszek**
Turin 2006

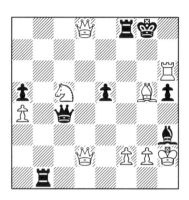

Black to Play

93) □ **A.Karpov** ■ **M.Stojanovic**
Valjevo 2007

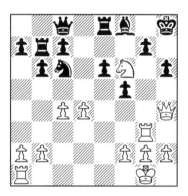

White to Play

94) □ **L.Golovin** ■ **V.Ivanov**
Voronezh 2007

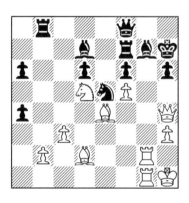

White to Play

95) □ **A.Walas** ■ **G.Gajewski**
Warsaw (rapid) 2006

Black to Play

96) □ **B.Rhodes** ■ **P.Hopwood**
York 1995

Black to Play

97) □ **M.Rogerson** ■ **R.Palliser**
York 2007

Black to Play

98) □ **P.Cloudsdale** ■ **P.Hopwood**
York 2001

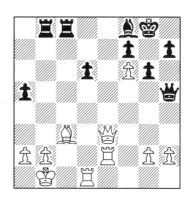

Black to Play

99) □ **P.Hopwood** ■ **E.Lockwood**
York 1995

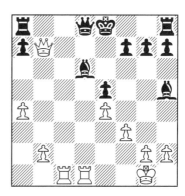

White to Play

100) □ **L.Pecnik** ■ **B.Galoic**
Zagreb 2007

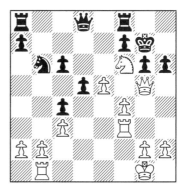

White to Play

2: Attack!

We now reach the meat and bones of this work. Most players love to attack, and solving the puzzles in this large chapter should help to hone both your attacking and defensive technique. I've tried to include several examples of all the main mating motifs to help fix these in the reader's mind, but once again do be aware that by no means every solution will force mate; quite often the defender can prevent your main attacking threats at the cost of a pawn or the exchange.

101) ☐ **V.Pupols** ■ **R.Adamson**
Agoura Hills 2007

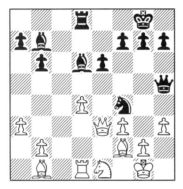

Black to Play

103) ☐ **G.Fontein** ■ **M.Euwe**
Amsterdam 1939

Black to Play

102) ☐ **A.Yusupov** ■ **A.Reuss**
Altenkirchen 2005

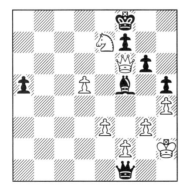

White to Play

104) ☐ **I.Campbell** ■ **P.Beggi**
Arvier 2007

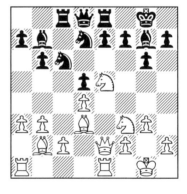

White to Play

105) □ **W.De Marco** ■ **V.Bashkite**
Arvier 2007

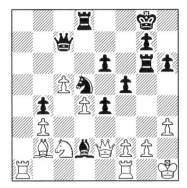

Black to Play

108) □ **N.Skalkotas** ■ **V.Kotrotsos**
Athens 2007

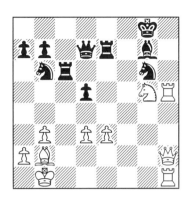

White to Play

106) □ **I.Moiseenko** ■ **A.Ismagambetov**
Astana 2007

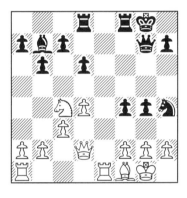

Black to Play

109) □ **Ni Hua** ■ **R.Palliser**
Athens 2001

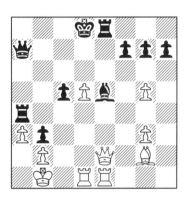

Black to Play

107) □ **M.Zacarias** ■ **C.Valiente**
Asuncion 2006

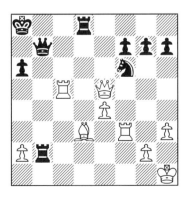

White to Play

110) □ **F.Hoelzl** ■ **H.Knoll**
Austrian League 2007

White to Play

111) □ **H.Teske** ■ **M.Stangl**
Austrian League 2007

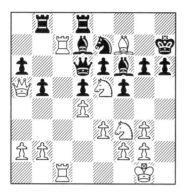

White to Play

112) □ **P.Popovic** ■ **J.Pinter**
Austrian League 1997

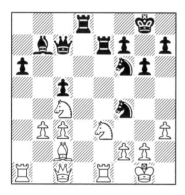

Black to Play

113) □ **M.Narciso Dublan** ■ **H.Mecking**
Ayamonte 2006

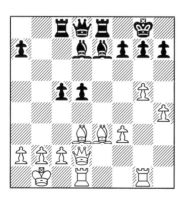

White to Play

114) □ **V.Korchnoi** ■ **A.Karpov**
Baguio City 1978

Black to Play

115) □ **T.Mamedjarova** ■ **A.Naiditsch**
Baku 2007

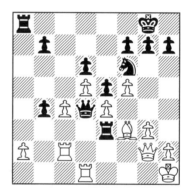

Black to Play

116) □ **A.Horvath** ■ **L.Seres**
Balatonlelle 2006

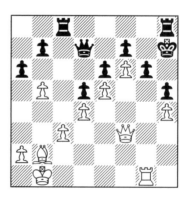

White to Play

117) □ **D.Berczes** ■ **T.Roussel Roozmon**
Balatonlelle 2007

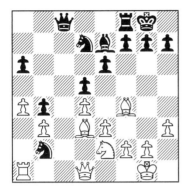

White to Play

118) □ **I.Molano Lafuente** ■ **M.Conde Chijeb**
Barcelona 2007

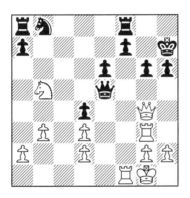

White to Play

119) □ **X.Colom Andres** ■ **M.Zohaib Hassan**
Barcelona 2007

Black to Play

120) □ **B.Alshoha** ■ **A.El Kawabia**
Beirut 2007

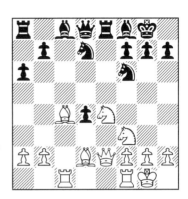

White to Play

121) □ **K.Leenhouts** ■ **C.Sielecki**
Belgian League 2007

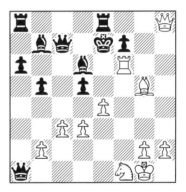

White to Play

122) □ **P.Motwani** ■ **E.Wiersma**
Belgian League 2007

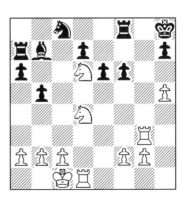

White to Play

123) □ **S.Hautot** ■ **M.Saltaev**
Belgian League 2007

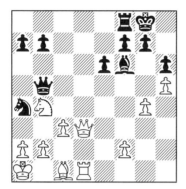

Black to Play

126) □ **I.Martic** ■ **R.Irizanin**
Belgrade 2007

White to Play

124) □ **D.Radulovic** ■ **B.Lajthajm**
Belgrade 2007

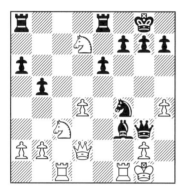

Black to Play

127) □ **J.Vasic** ■ **V.Zivkovic**
Belgrade 2006

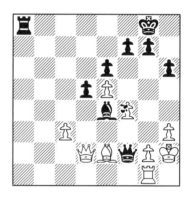

Black to Play

125) □ **D.Rajkovic** ■ **B.Tadic**
Belgrade 2007

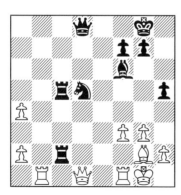

Black to Play

128) □ **S.Ostojic** ■ **V.Conic**
Belgrade 2007

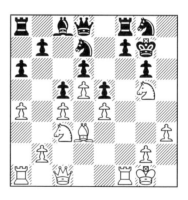

White to Play

129) ☐ J.Blackburne ■ J.Schwarz
Berlin 1881

White to Play

130) ☐ L.Vadja ■ B.Ivkov
Bern 2006

White to Play

131) ☐ D.Marholev ■ L.Morelle
Bethune 2006

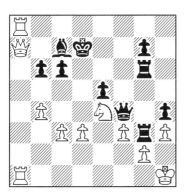

White to Play

132) ☐ R.Palliser ■ R.Callis
Beverley 2000

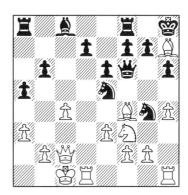

White to Play

133) ☐ I.Matijasevic ■ I.Bender
Bizovac 2007

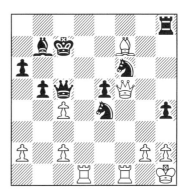

Black to Play

134) ☐ V.Prlac ■ P.Szakolczai
Bizovac 2007

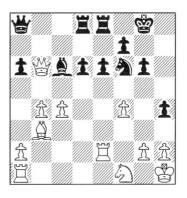

Black to Play

135)   □ **G.Rigg** ■ **A.Masters**
Blackpool 2007

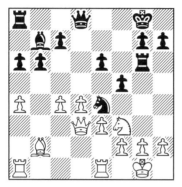

Black to Play

136)   □ **J.Wheeler** ■ **J.Dore**
Blackpool 1956

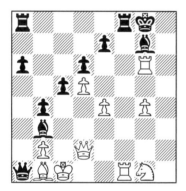

White to Play

137)   □ **L.Barden** ■ **B.H.Wood**
Blackpool 1956

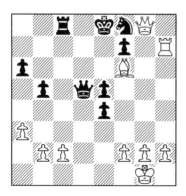

White to Play

138)   □ **S.Haslinger** ■ **D.Gormally**
Blackpool 2003

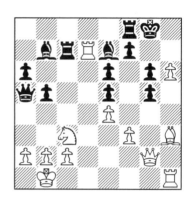

White to Play

139)   □ **A.Franco** ■ **P.Rodriguez**
Bogota 2006

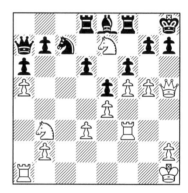

White to Play

140)   □ **W.Burt** ■ **N.Dennis**
Bourne End (rapid) 2002

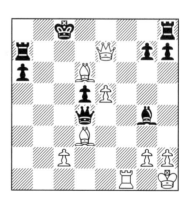

White to Play

141) □ **A.Ibbotson** ■ **P.Hopwood**
Bradford 2001

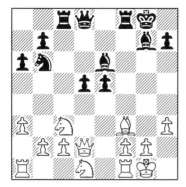

Black to Play

142) □ **A.Byron** ■ **N.Hosken**
British League 2006

White to Play

143) □ **A.Hagesaether** ■ **A.Greet**
British League 2005

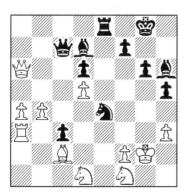

Black to Play

144) □ **A.Kosten** ■ **B.Hague**
British League 2007

White to Play

145) □ **A.Law** ■ **J.Gallagher**
British League 1999

Black to Play

146) □ **C.Waters** ■ **R.Richmond**
British League 1999

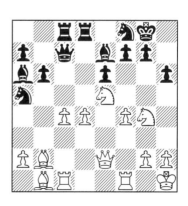

White to Play

147) ☐ **D.Coleman** ■ **L.D'Costa**
British League 2003

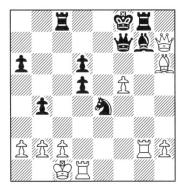

White to Play

148) ☐ **D.Ledger** ■ **J.Burnett**
British League 2002

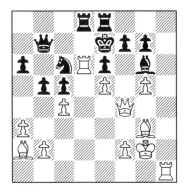

White to Play

149) ☐ **D.Shaw** ■ **Low Ying Min**
British League 2005

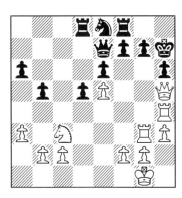

White to Play

150) ☐ **D.Wise** ■ **J.Blackburn**
British League 2002

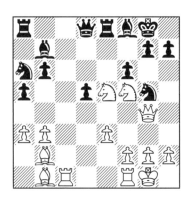

White to Play

151) ☐ **Dal.James** ■ **D.Anderton**
British League 2005

Black to Play

152) ☐ **G.Buckley** ■ **N.Mitchem**
British League 2004

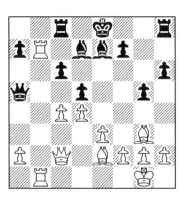

White to Play

153) □ **G.Flear** ■ **S.Ansell**
British League 2003

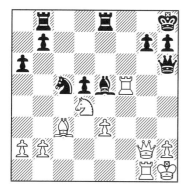

White to Play

154) □ **H.Hoffmann** ■ **S.Munson**
British League 2006

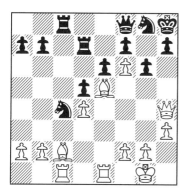

White to Play

155) □ **I.Upton** ■ **P.Brown**
British League 2000

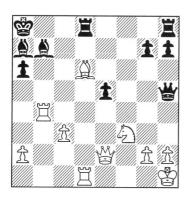

White to Play

156) □ **J.Bourne** ■ **K.Gregory**
British League 2007

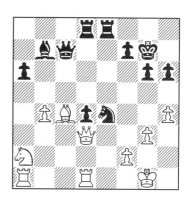

Black to Play

157) □ **J.Emms** ■ **D.Ledger**
British League 2006

White to Play

158) □ **J.Foster** ■ **J.Parmar**
British League 2005

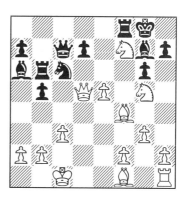

White to Play

159) □ **J.Gilbert** ■ **Gr.Morris**
British League 2006

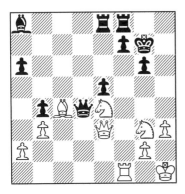

White to Play

162) □ **J.Sherwin** ■ **B.Hague**
British League 2004

Black to Play

160) □ **J.Mestel** ■ **A.Hynes**
British League 2004

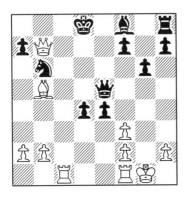

White to Play

163) □ **K.Smallbone** ■ **D.Gunter**
British League 2002

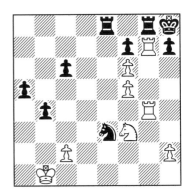

White to Play

161) □ **J.Rudd** ■ **K.Arakhamia Grant**
British League 2007

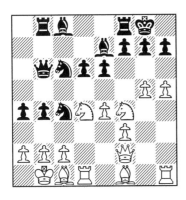

Black to Play

164) □ **L.D'Costa** ■ **P.Wells**
British League 2003

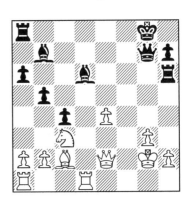

Black to Play

165)   □ **L.Trent** ■ **D.Tan**
British League 2003

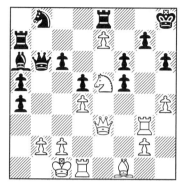

White to Play

168)   □ **M.Rich** ■ **S.Barrett**
British League 2004

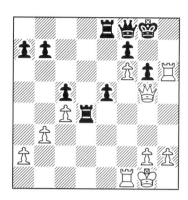

White to Play

166)   □ **M.Adams** ■ **M.Hennigan**
British League 2001

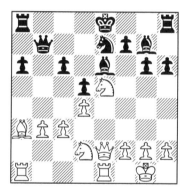

White to Play

169)   □ **M.Simons** ■ **H.Richards**
British League 2002

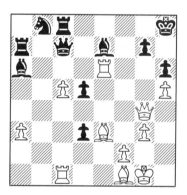

White to Play

167)   □ **M.Adams** ■ **R.Bates**
British League 2005

White to Play

170)   □ **N.Povah** ■ **J.Sisask**
British League 2004

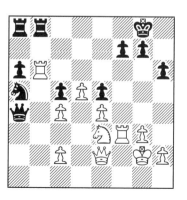

White to Play

171)   □ **O.Cooley** ■ **J.Moore**
British League 2000

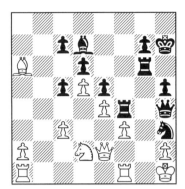

Black to Play

172)   □ **P.Helbig** ■ **R.Palliser**
British League 2005

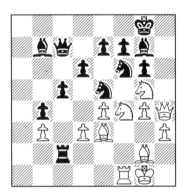

White to Play

173)   □ **P.Valden** ■ **K.Smallbone**
British League 2005

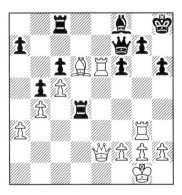

Black to Play

174)   □ **R.Bates** ■ **D.Mason**
British League 2006

White to Play

175)   □ **R.De Coverly** ■ **N.Frost**
British League 2000

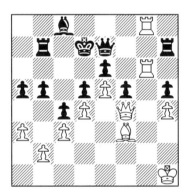

White to Play

176)   □ **R.Eames** ■ **M.Simmons**
British League 2005

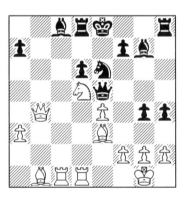

White to Play

177) ☐ **R.Edwards** ■ **S.Lalic**
British League 2000

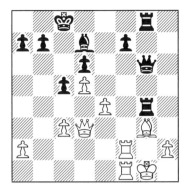

Black to Play

178) ☐ **R.Granat** ■ **J.Bentley**
British League 2004

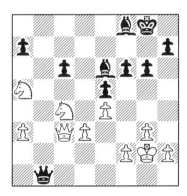

Black to Play

179) ☐ **R.Palliser** ■ **H.Hunt**
British League 1999

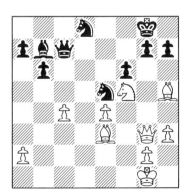

White to Play

180) ☐ **R.Palliser** ■ **M.Broomfield**
British League 2003

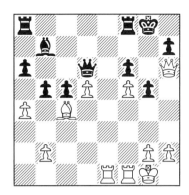

White to Play

181) ☐ **R.Webb** ■ **P.Townsend**
British League 1999

White to Play

182) ☐ **R.Willis** ■ **N.Twitchell**
British League 2007

White to Play

183) ☐ **S.Bibby** ■ **D.Johnston**
British League 2001

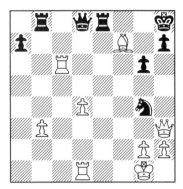

Black to Play

184) ☐ **S.Macak** ■ **J.Rowson**
British League 2007

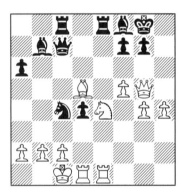

Black to Play

185) ☐ **T.Cox** ■ **G.Dickson**
British League 2004

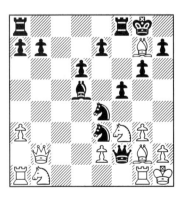

Black to Play

186) ☐ **V.Bologan** ■ **J.Lautier**
British League 2005

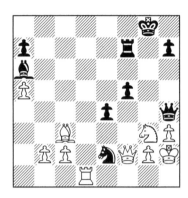

White to Play

187) ☐ **K.Smallbone** ■ **M.Cupal**
Brno 2004

White to Play

188) ☐ **D.Milanovic** ■ **G.Grigore**
Bucharest 2007

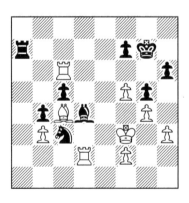

White to Play

189) □ **V.Barnaure** ■ **C.Nanu**
Bucharest 2007

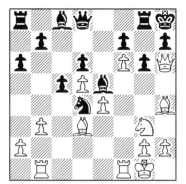

White to Play

190) □ **B.Lengyel** ■ **To Nhat Minh**
Budapest 2007

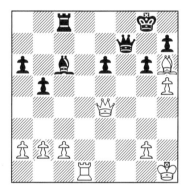

White to Play

191) □ **D.Bronstein** ■ **P.Keres**
Budapest 1950

White to Play

192) □ **M.Ignacz** ■ **K.Niemi**
Budapest 2007

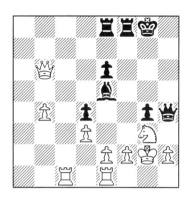

Black to Play

193) □ **S.Collins** ■ **A.Illner**
Budapest 2007

White to Play

194) □ **L.Szabo** ■ **A.Bisguier**
Buenos Aires 1955

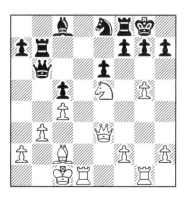

White to Play

195) □ **A.Karpov** ■ **V.Hort**
Bugojno 1978

White to Play

196) □ **A.Mendelson** ■ **R.Quinn**
Bunratty 2007

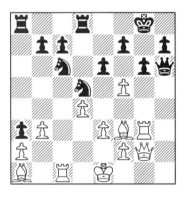

Black to Play

197) □ **A.Peile** ■ **N.Miller**
Bunratty 2002

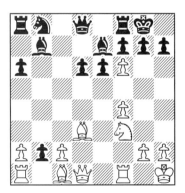

White to Play

198) □ **V.Sauvonnet** ■ **Ni Hua**
Calvi 2007

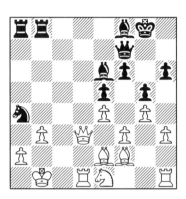

Black to Play

199) □ **A.Kovalev** ■ **H.Stevic**
Calvia 2004

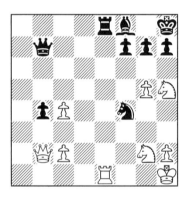

White to Play

200) □ **E.Arlandi** ■ **A.Kveinys**
Calvia 2004

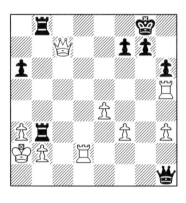

Black to Play

201) □ **Z.Almasi** ■ **L.Winants**
Calvia 2004

Black to Play

202) □ **A.Maz Machado** ■ **E.Fernandez Romero**
Campillos 2007

Black to Play

203) □ **D.Recuero Guerra** ■ **E.Valero Cano**
Campillos 2007

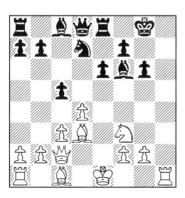

White to Play

204) □ **F.Tahirov** ■ **A.Shirov**
Canada de Calatrava (rapid) 2007

Black to Play

205) □ **N.Guliyev** ■ **S.Mamedyarov**
Canada de Calatrava (rapid) 2007

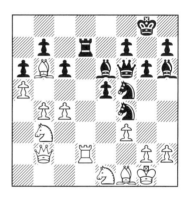

Black to Play

206) □ **O.Gritsak** ■ **E.Bacrot**
Canada de Calatrava (rapid) 2007

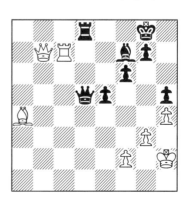

White to Play

207) □ D.Smerdon ■ H.Cunanan
Canberra 2007

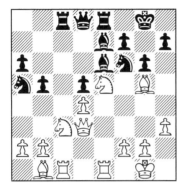

White to Play

208) □ I.Saric ■ M.Gurevich
Cannes 2007

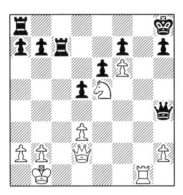

White to Play

209) □ M.Libens ■ F.Fargere
Cannes 2007

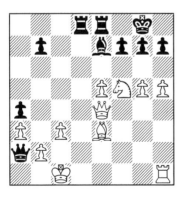

Black to Play

210) □ N.Arsenault ■ E.Pepino
Cannes 2007

White to Play

211) □ P.Van Hoolandt ■ E.El Gindy
Cannes 2007

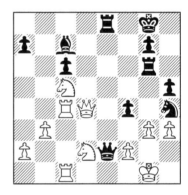

Black to Play

212) □ R.Hrzica ■ J.Armas
Cannes 2007

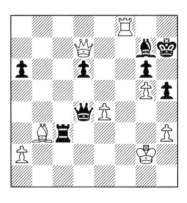

White to Play

213) □ **S.Collas** ■ **P.Lebel**
Cannes 2007

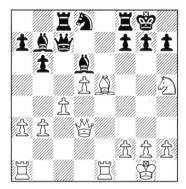

White to Play

214) □ **Zhao Xue** ■ **S.Karjakin**
Cap d'Agde (rapid) 2006

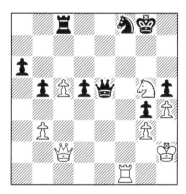

White to Play

215) □ **D.Arutinian** ■ **O.Danielian**
Cappelle la Grande 2007

White to Play

216) □ **J.Friedel** ■ **L.Cyborowski**
Cappelle la Grande 2007

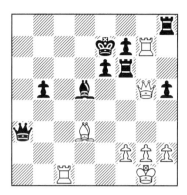

White to Play

217) □ **C.Keller** ■ **S.Slukova**
Champs sur Marne 2007

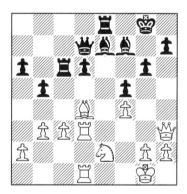

White to Play

218) □ **E.White** ■ **D.Curnow**
Cheltenham 2007

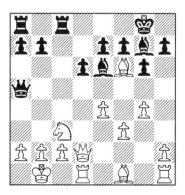

Black to Play

219) □ **E.Romanov** ■ **L.Mkrtchian**
Chelyabinsk 2007

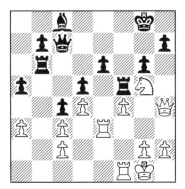

White to Play

220) □ **A.Almeida Saenz** ■ **M.Gagunashvili**
Chicago 2007

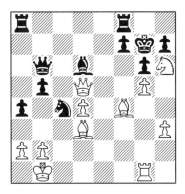

White to Play

221) □ **S.Bercys** ■ **A.Simutowe**
Chicago 2007

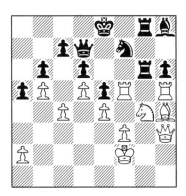

White to Play

222) □ **H.Agustsson** ■ **K.Madland**
Copenhagen 2006

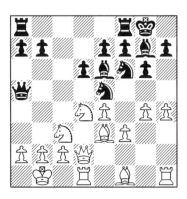

Black to Play

223) □ **D.Path** ■ **F.Rayner**
Cork 2005

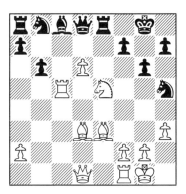

White to Play

224) □ **M.Bartel** ■ **S.Cicak**
Cork 2005

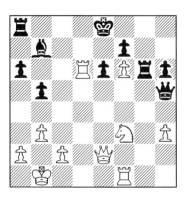

White to Play

225) □ **P.Cafolla** ■ **B.Socko**
Cork 2005

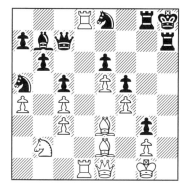

Black to Play

226) □ **R.Almond** ■ **C.Rossi**
Cork 2005

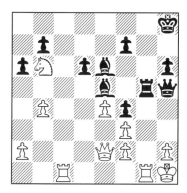

Black to Play

227) □ **T.Hickey** ■ **N.Ahern**
Cork 2005

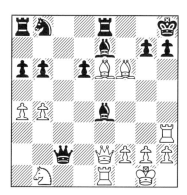

White to Play

228) □ **V.Cmilyte** ■ **J.Benjamin**
Cork 2005

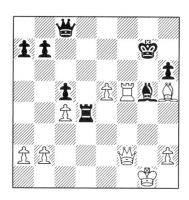

White to Play

229) □ **V.Kotronias** ■ **G.Sarakauskas**
Cork 2005

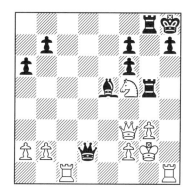

White to Play

230) □ **V.Kotronias** ■ **J.Benjamin**
Cork 2005

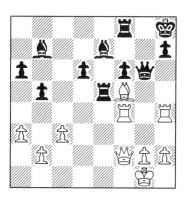

Black to Play

231) □ Z.Gymesi ■ A.Fox
Cork 2005

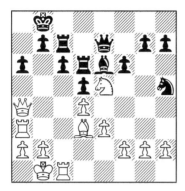

White to Play

232) □ J.Rudd ■ A.Khantuev
Coulsdon 2007

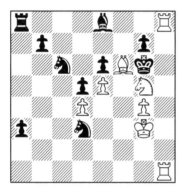

White to Play

233) □ N.Tavoularis ■ I.Snape
Coulsdon 2007

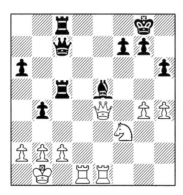

Black to Play

234) □ M.Ivic ■ D.Pavasovic
Croatian Team Championship 2007

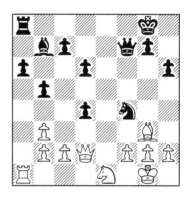

Black to Play

235) □ M.Ivic ■ M.Medic
Croatian Team Championship 2007

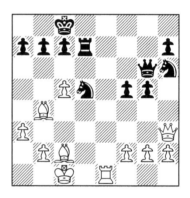

White to Play

236) □ M.Zovko ■ G.Mohr
Croatian Team Championship 2007

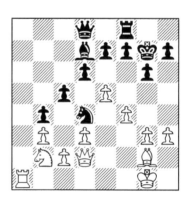

Black to Play

237) □ **I.Naumkin** ■ **M.Abatino**
Cutro 2007

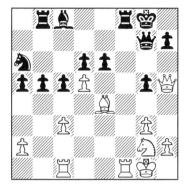

White to Play

238) □ **T.Cheval** ■ **P.Gerfault**
d'Angers 2007

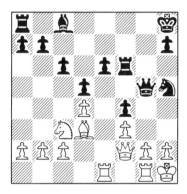

Black to Play

239) □ **B.Cooper** ■ **D.Scott**
Didcot 2005

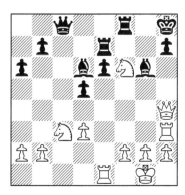

White to Play

240) □ **S.Megaranto** ■ **C.Batchuluun**
Doha (rapid) 2006

White to Play

241) □ **P.Catt** ■ **H.Lockwood**
Doncaster 2006

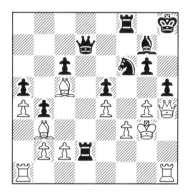

Black to Play

242) □ **V.Topalov** ■ **A.Naiditsch**
Dortmund 2005

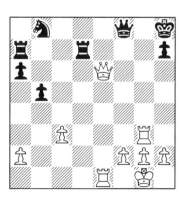

White to Play

243) □ A.Ardeleanu ■ G.Kachieshvili
Dresden 2007

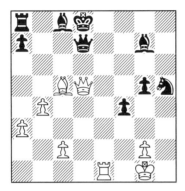

White to Play

244) □ A.Naiditsch ■ J.Gustafsson
Dresden 2007

Black to Play

245) □ A.Naiditsch ■ P.Sowray
Dresden 2007

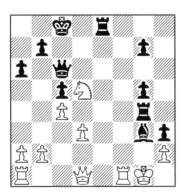

Black to Play

246) □ E.Korbut ■ L.Javakhishvili
Dresden 2007

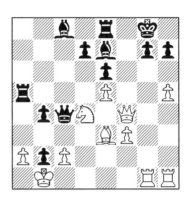

White to Play

247) □ E.Levushkina ■ H.Vogel
Dresden 2007

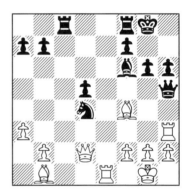

Black to Play

248) □ E.Najer ■ V.Neverov
Dresden 2007

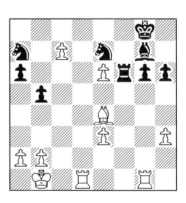

White to Play

249) □ **E.Zweschper** ■ **H.Hanemann**
Dresden 2007

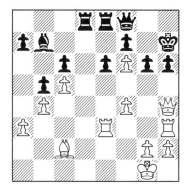

White to Play

252) □ **I.Zakurdjaeva** ■ **E.Paehtz**
Dresden 2007

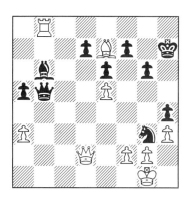

White to Play

250) □ **F.Handke** ■ **F.Dinger**
Dresden 2007

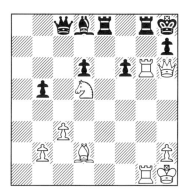

White to Play

253) □ **J.Geske** ■ **A.Ardeleanu**
Dresden 2007

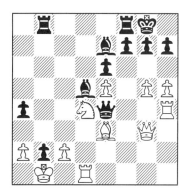

Black to Play

251) □ **G.Beckhuis** ■ **K.Jakubowski**
Dresden 2007

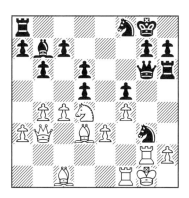

Black to Play

254) □ **J.Zawadzka** ■ **A.Stefanova**
Dresden 2007

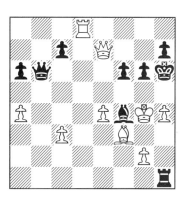

Black to Play

255) ☐ **K.Arakhamia Grant** ■ **E.Levushkina**
Dresden 2007

White to Play

256) ☐ **M.Roos** ■ **J.Stocek**
Dresden 2007

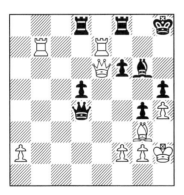

Black to Play

257) ☐ **M.Schulz** ■ **G.Marville**
Dresden 2007

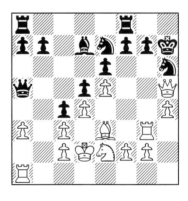

White to Play

258) ☐ **M.Womacka** ■ **S.Kaphle**
Dresden 2007

White to Play

259) ☐ **N.Pert** ■ **A.Aleksandrov**
Dresden 2007

White to Play

260) ☐ **P.Bobras** ■ **E.Can**
Dresden 2007

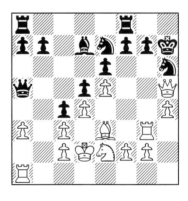

White to Play

261) □ **S.Azarov** ■ **T.Sanikidze**
Dresden 2007

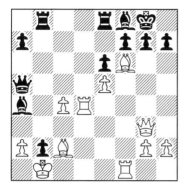

White to Play

262) □ **S.Bakker** ■ **L.Gutman**
Dresden 2007

Black to Play

263) □ **V.Neverov** ■ **R.Strohhaeker**
Dresden 2007

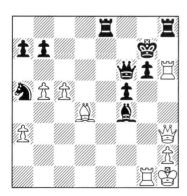

Black to Play

264) □ **Z.Mamedjarova** ■ **K.Nemcova**
Dresden 2007

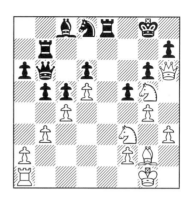

White to Play

265) □ **A.Iljin** ■ **K.Sakaev**
Dresden (rapid) 2007

White to Play

266) □ **K.Georgiev** ■ **B.Socko**
Dresden (rapid) 2007

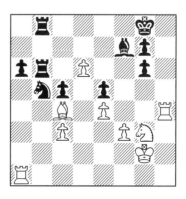

White to Play

267) □ H.Melkumyan ■ T.L.Petrosian
Dubai 2007

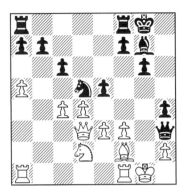

Black to Play

270) □ D.Stellwagen ■ M.Bosboom
Dutch League 2006

White to Play

268) □ S.Mamedyarov ■ M.Al Modiahki
Dubai 2004

White to Play

271) □ D.Van Kerkhof ■ M.Piket
Dutch League 2007

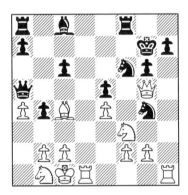

White to Play

269) □ J.Burnett ■ R.Palliser
Durham 2002

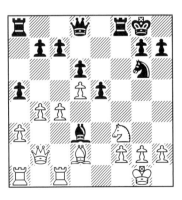

Black to Play

272) □ F.Nijboer ■ M.Hoffmann
Dutch League 2006

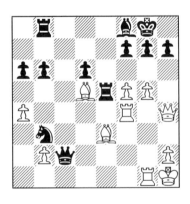

White to Play

273) □ **L.Winants** ■ **M.Okkes**
Dutch League 2006

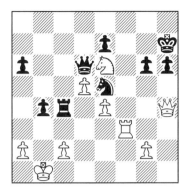

White to Play

274) □ **E.Ferry** ■ **K.Ruxton**
Edinburgh 2007

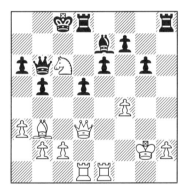

Black to Play

275) □ **H.Brechin** ■ **J.Aagaard**
Edinburgh 2007

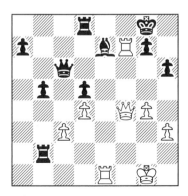

White to Play

276) □ **B.Mudongo** ■ **S.Andriasian**
Ekaterinburg 2007

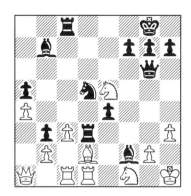

Black to Play

277) □ **T.Sabure** ■ **E.Danielian**
Ekaterinburg 2007

Black to Play

278) □ **O.Korneev** ■ **C.Landenbergue**
Elgoibar 2006

White to Play

279) □ E.Rozentalis ■ M.Adams
Elista 1998

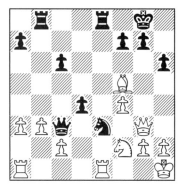

Black to Play

280) □ I.Sudakova ■ O.Guseva
Elista 2002

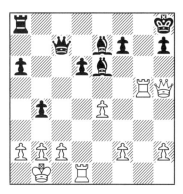

White to Play

281) □ D.Garcia Ilundain ■ A.Miles
Escaldes 1998

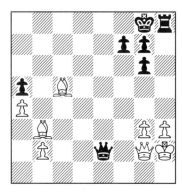

Black to Play

282) □ O.Gritsayeva ■ A.Kolomiets
Evpatoria 2007

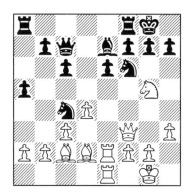

White to Play

283) □ P.Golubka ■ A.Bagrationi
Evpatoria 2007

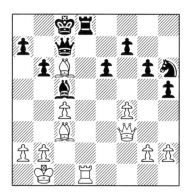

White to Play

284) □ V.Galakhov ■ A.Olishevsky
Evpatoria 2007

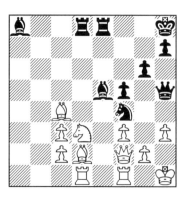

Black to Play

285) □ **Jo.Hall** ■ **A.Brusey**
Exmouth 2007

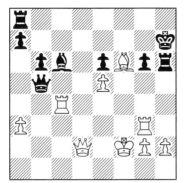

White to Play

288) □ **V.Marincas** ■ **L.Csilcser**
Felix Spa 2007

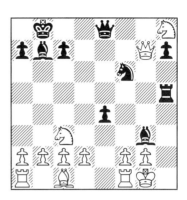

Black to Play

286) □ **G.Mateuta** ■ **V.Iovan**
Felix Spa 2007

White to Play

289) □ **E.Hintikka** ■ **T.Paakkonen**
Finnish League 2006

Black to Play

287) □ **N.Ristic** ■ **I.Adam**
Felix Spa 2007

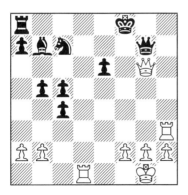

White to Play

290) □ **T.Sammalvuo** ■ **V.Maki**
Finnish League 2007

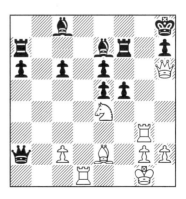

White to Play

291) □ **O.Hindle** ■ **J.Van Oosterom**
Flushing 1962

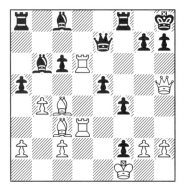

White to Play

292) □ **T.Taylor** ■ **P.Vavrak**
Foxwoods 2007

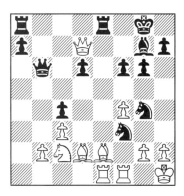

Black to Play

293) □ **W.Schukowski** ■ **C.Jacob**
Frankfurt 2006

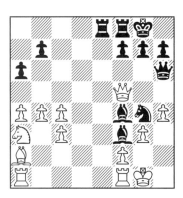

Black to Play

294) □ **A.Wirig** ■ **M.Kazhgaleyev**
French League 2003

Black to Play

295) □ **I.Nataf** ■ **J.Riff**
French League 2006

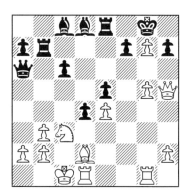

White to Play

296) □ **M.Apicella** ■ **N.Giffard**
French League 2003

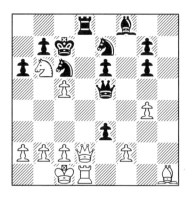

White to Play

297) □ **S.Pucher** ■ **J.Lautier**
French League 2007

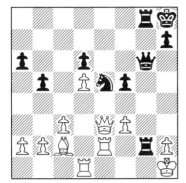

Black to Play

298) □ **E.Pospisil** ■ **M.Mroziak**
Frydek Mistek 2007

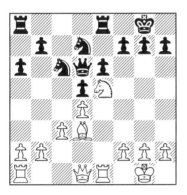

White to Play

299) □ **K.Motuz** ■ **P.Petran**
Frydek Mistek 2007

Black to Play

300) □ **V.Talla** ■ **K.Motuz**
Frydek Mistek 2007

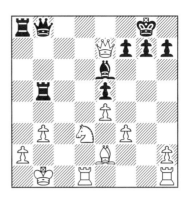

Black to Play

301) □ **A.Morozevich** ■ **K.Georgiev**
Fuegen 2006

White to Play

302) □ **A.Naiditch** ■ **S.Mamedyarov**
Fuegen 2006

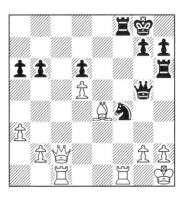

Black to Play

303) □ **A.Greet** ■ **G.Pitl**
Gausdal 2007

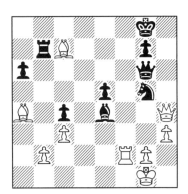

White to Play

304) □ **P.Jagstaidt** ■ **A.Zozulia**
Geneva 2007

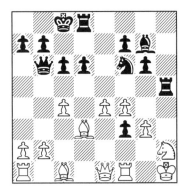

Black to Play

305) □ **F.Gehringer** ■ **I.Rausis**
Gerlingen 2007

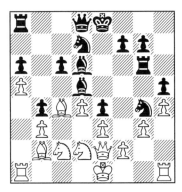

Black to Play

306) □ **D.Baramidze** ■ **P.H.Nielsen**
German League 2006

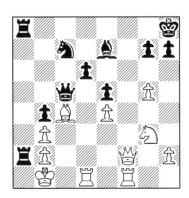

Black to Play

307) □ **D.Navara** ■ **R.Rabiega**
German League 2006

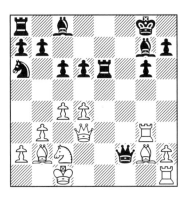

Black to Play

308) □ **J.Fischer** ■ **V.Beim**
German League 2006

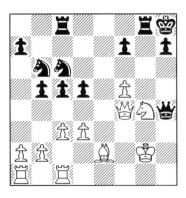

Black to Play

309) □ **J.Nunn** ■ **C.Pritchett**
German League 1985

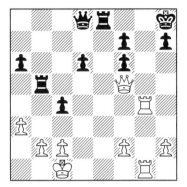

White to Play

310) □ **J.Werle** ■ **R.Mainka**
German League 2007

Black to Play

311) □ **L.Vogt** ■ **O.Teschke**
German League 2007

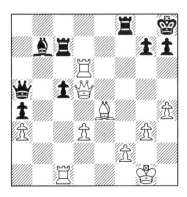

White to Play

312) □ **L.Zesch** ■ **P.Acs**
German League 2006

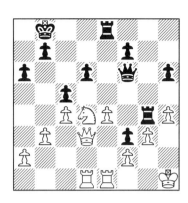

Black to Play

313) □ **M.Borriss** ■ **L.Nisipeanu**
German League 2007

Black to Play

314) □ **S.B.Hansen** ■ **J.Wintzer**
German League 2006

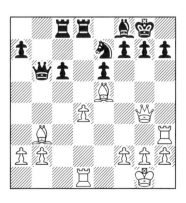

White to Play

315) □ S.Ernst ■ S.Loeffler
German League 2006

White to Play

316) □ T.Luther ■ A.Sokolov
German League 2007

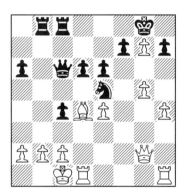

Black to Play

317) □ Z.Ribli ■ K.Muranyi
German League 2007

White to Play

318) □ F.Caruana ■ M.Adams
Gibraltar 2007

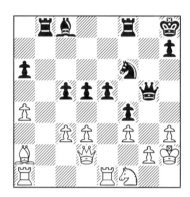

Black to Play

319) □ F.Poggio ■ R.Livesey
Gibraltar 2007

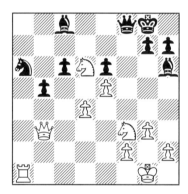

White to Play

320) □ H.Rasch ■ E.Schiller
Gibraltar 2007

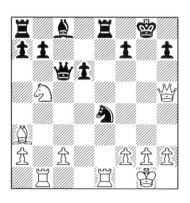

White to Play

321) □ I.Krush ■ K.Ruxton
Gibraltar 2007

White to Play

322) □ I.Rogers ■ R.Ris
Gibraltar 2007

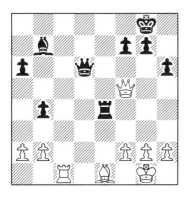

Black to Play

323) □ J.Dworakowska ■ P.Cramling
Gibraltar 2007

Black to Play

324) □ J.Hickman ■ S.Menon
Gibraltar 2007

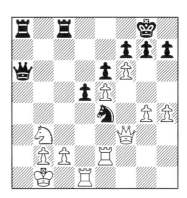

Black to Play

325) □ K.Lahno ■ N.Malmdin
Gibraltar 2007

White to Play

326) □ N.Arsenault ■ R.Ris
Gibraltar 2007

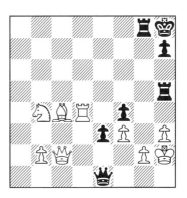

Black to Play

327) □ R.Wade ■ C.Horton
Gibraltar 2007

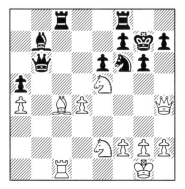

White to Play

330) □ V.Korchnoi ■ I.Krush
Gibraltar 2007

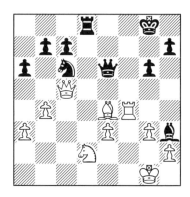

White to Play

328) □ S.Kristjansson ■ C.Salgado Allaria
Gibraltar 2007

Black to Play

331) □ G.Popilski ■ I.Porat
Givataim 2007

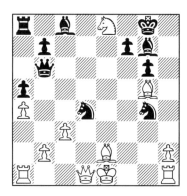

Black to Play

329) □ V.Korchnoi ■ I.Krush
Gibraltar 2007

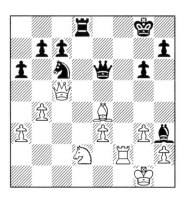

Black to Play

332) □ P.Hopwood ■ M.Mackenzie
Glasgow 2004

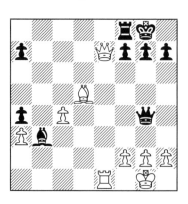

White to Play

333) □ **I.Robertson** ■ **I.Stokes**
Glenrothes 2005

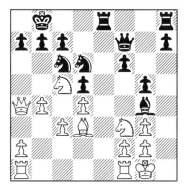

White to Play

334) □ **A.Bodnaruk** ■ **V.Gunina**
Gorodets 2006

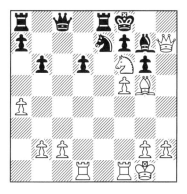

White to Play

335) □ **T.Seeman** ■ **R.Akesson**
Gothenburg 2006

White to Play

336) □ **W.Unzicker** ■ **D.Bronstein**
Gothenburg 1955

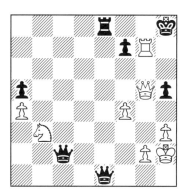

Black to Play

337) □ **D.McGowan** ■ **L.MacGregor**
Grangemouth 2006

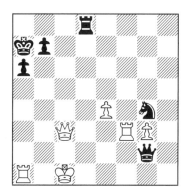

White to Play

338) □ **O.Adda** ■ **E.Janev**
Grenoble 2007

Black to Play

339) □ **R.Di Paolo** ■ **J.Olivier**
Grenoble 2007

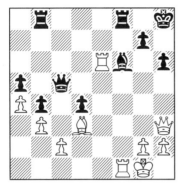

White to Play

342) □ **V.Slovineau** ■ **S.Rukminto**
Halkidiki 2007

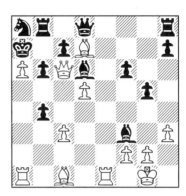

White to Play

340) □ **P.Holt** ■ **R.Palliser**
Guernsey 1995

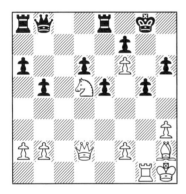

White to Play

343) □ **M.Rogerson** ■ **R.Palliser**
Harrogate 2006

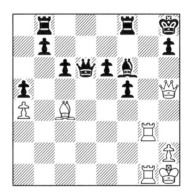

White to Play

341) □ **C.Dorrington** ■ **S.Williams**
Halifax (rapid) 2004

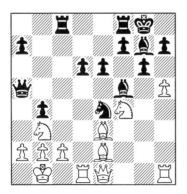

Black to Play

344) □ **K.Smallbone** ■ **M.Brazier**
Hastings 2002

White to Play

345) ☐ **M.Taimanov** ■ **R.Persitz**
Hastings 1955

White to Play

346) ☐ **N.Short** ■ **P.Biyiasis**
Hastings 1979

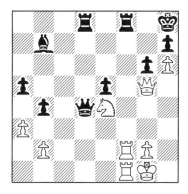

White to Play

347) ☐ **S.Mulligan** ■ **D.Foord**
Hastings 2007

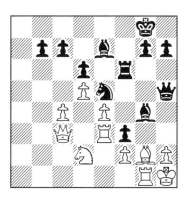

Black to Play

348) ☐ **H.Westerinen** ■ **B.Larsen**
Havana 1967

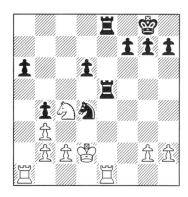

Black to Play

349) ☐ **S.Siebrecht** ■ **J.Diaz Diaz**
Havana 2007

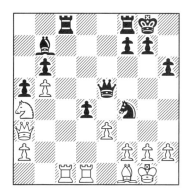

Black to Play

350) ☐ **J.Turner** ■ **K.Smallbone**
Hereford 2000

White to Play

351) □ R.Palliser ■ J.Horner
Heywood 2006

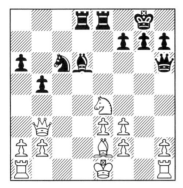

Black to Play

352) □ C.Otten ■ M.Bensdorp
Hilversum 2007

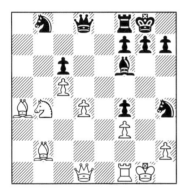

Black to Play

353) □ G.Grotenhuis ■ E.L'Ami
Hilversum 2006

Black to Play

354) □ Peng Zhaoqin ■ P.Van Nies
Hilversum 2007

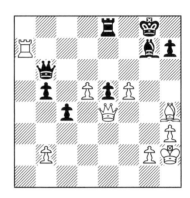

White to Play

355) □ H.Schmoll ■ B.Giacomelli
Hockenheim 2007

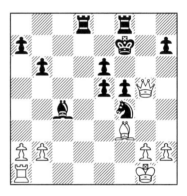

Black to Play

356) □ L.Van Wely ■ P.Acs
Hoogeveen 2002

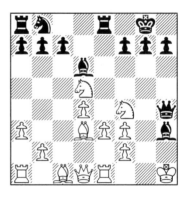

Black to Play

357) □ **A.Caveney** ■ **R.Tia**
Houston 2006

Black to Play

358) □ **A.Hunt** ■ **R.Palliser**
Hove 1997

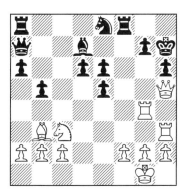

White to Play

359) □ **T.Harper** ■ **R.Palliser**
Hull 1999

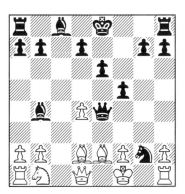

Black to Play

360) □ **E.Fomichenko** ■ **A.Anibar**
Illes Medes 2007

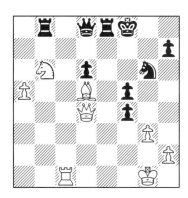

White to Play

361) □ **M.Pruja** ■ **A.Muratet**
Illes Medes 2006

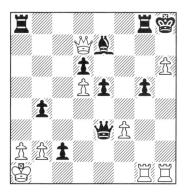

Black to Play

362) □ **R.Gerber** ■ **M.Bartel**
Illes Medes 2007

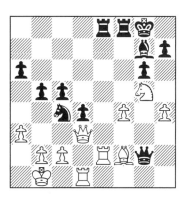

Black to Play

363) ☐ **A.Zapata** ■ **G.Welling**
Isle of Man 2002

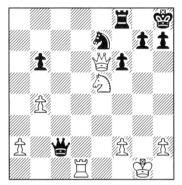

White to Play

364) ☐ **D.Howell** ■ **P.Wells**
Isle of Man 2005

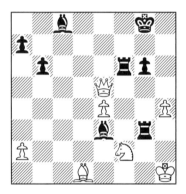

Black to Play

365) ☐ **J.Lutton** ■ **R.Palliser**
Isle of Man 2002

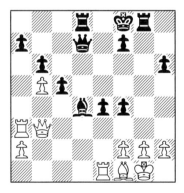

Black to Play

366) ☐ **L.Kritz** ■ **D.Kolbus**
Isle of Man 2005

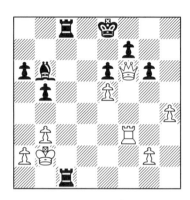

Black to Play

367) ☐ **M.Devereaux** ■ **T.Lunn**
Isle of Man 2006

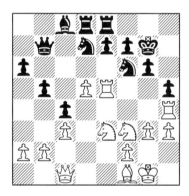

White to Play

368) ☐ **M.Ferguson** ■ **T.Eggleston**
Isle of Man 2006

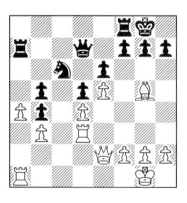

White to Play

369) □ O.Korneev ■ M.Devereaux
Isle of Man 2006

Black to Play

372) □ V.Ikonnikov ■ R.Palliser
Isle of Man 2005

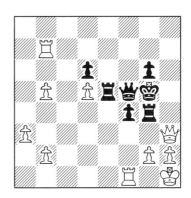

Black to Play

370) □ R.Palliser ■ V.Malakhatko
Isle of Man 2005

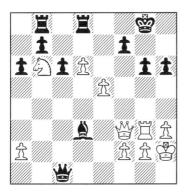

White to Play

373) □ V.Sareen ■ S.Lohou
Isle of Man 2005

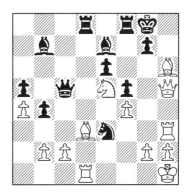

White to Play

371) □ R.Van Kemenade ■ M.Dougherty
Isle of Man 2002

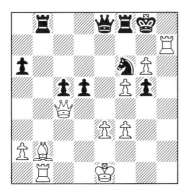

White to Play

374) □ Y.Kuzubov ■ H.Wademark
Isle of Man 2005

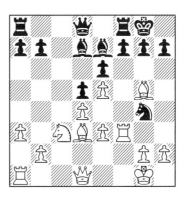

White to Play

375) □ **Y.Kuzubov** ■ **R.Palliser**
Isle of Man 2006

White to Play

376) □ **Y.Yakovich** ■ **G.Sarakauskas**
Isle of Man 2006

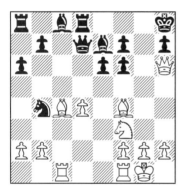

White to Play

377) □ **G.Dickson** ■ **G.Botterill**
Islington 1971

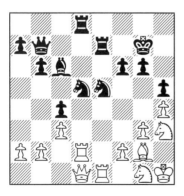

Black to Play

378) □ **M.Lambshire** ■ **R.Keely**
Islington 1971

White to Play

379) □ **P.Scott** ■ **P.Simonds**
Islington 1971

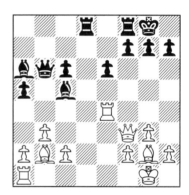

White to Play

380) □ **S.Webb** ■ **R.Bellin**
Islington 1971

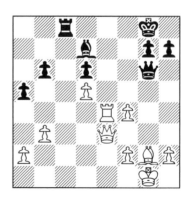

Black to Play

381) ☐ **J.Emms** ■ **L.Fressinet**
Istanbul 2000

White to Play

382) ☐ **M.Adams** ■ **M.Maki Uuro**
Izmir 2004

White to Play

383) ☐ **M.Lucey** ■ **N.Miller**
Kidlington 2003

Black to Play

384) ☐ **S.James** ■ **R.Lobo**
Kidlington 2007

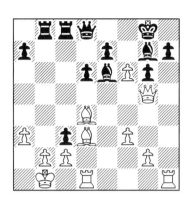

White to Play

385) ☐ **W.Burt** ■ **R.Dams**
Kidlington 2006

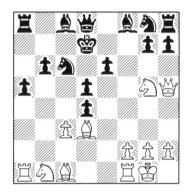

White to Play

386) ☐ **B.Spassky** ■ **V.Korchnoi**
Kiev 1968

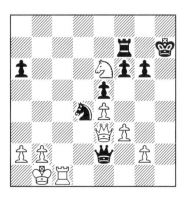

White to Play

387) □ **M.Novik** ■ **K.Sakaev**
Kirishi (rapid) 2007

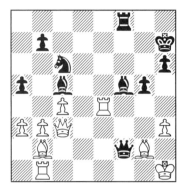

Black to Play

388) □ **M.Darban** ■ **S.Paridar**
Kish 2005

Black to Play

389) □ **F.Schellmann** ■ **K.Kachiani**
Koenigshofen 2007

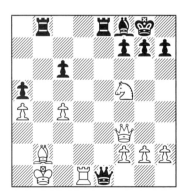

Black to Play

390) □ **T.Henrichs** ■ **M.Prusikin**
Königshofen 2007

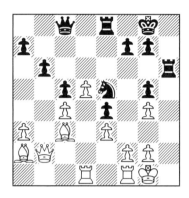

Black to Play

391) □ **A.Malienko** ■ **P.Kruglyakov**
Kyiv 2007

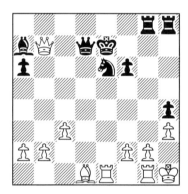

White to Play

392) □ **V.Kovalenko** ■ **A.Chistiakov**
Kyiv 2007

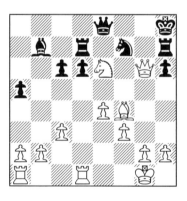

White to Play

393) □ A.Perez Celis ■ F.Mingorance Torres
La Laguna 2007

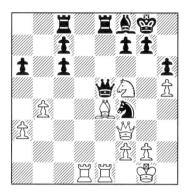

White to Play

396) □ J.Slaby ■ L.Mendoza
La Laguna 2007

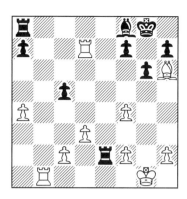

White to Play

394) □ C.Damaso Tacoronte ■ C.Campos Vera
La Laguna 2007

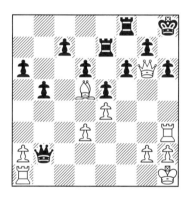

White to Play

397) □ R.Gimeno Higueras ■ J.Radulski
La Roda 2007

Black to Play

395) □ H.Marrero Falcon ■ B.Vega Gutierrez
La Laguna 2007

White to Play

398) □ A.Yermolinsky ■ C.Onyekwere
Las Vegas 2006

White to Play

399) □ **K.Cottrell** ■ **M.Aigner**
Las Vegas 2007

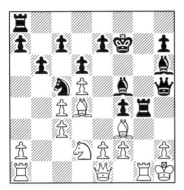

Black to Play

402) □ **R.Palliser** ■ **C.McNab**
Leeds (rapid) 1999

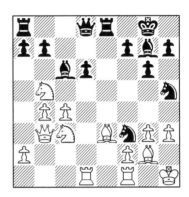

Black to Play

400) □ **P.Hopwood** ■ **G.Conroy**
Leeds 2001

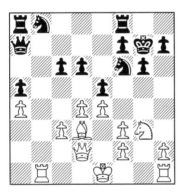

White to Play

403) □ **L.Van Wely** ■ **E.L'Ami**
Leeuwarden 2004

Black to Play

401) □ **R.Palliser** ■ **S.Ansell**
Leeds 2005

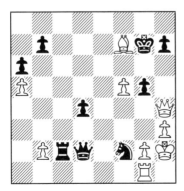

White to Play

404) □ **R.Palliser** ■ **D.Prole**
Leicester 1995

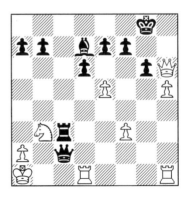

Black to Play

405) □ S.Gordon ■ P.Hopwood
Leicester 1998

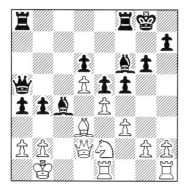

Black to Play

406) □ T.Bailey ■ R.Palliser
Leicester 1994

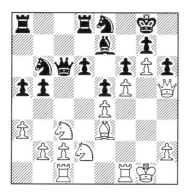

White to Play

407) □ A.Karpov ■ M.Taimanov
Leningrad 1977

Black to Play

408) □ I.Bondarevsky ■ M.Botvinnik
Leningrad 1941

Black to Play

409) □ G.Miralles ■ M.Thesing
Lenk 2007

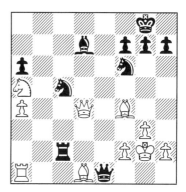

Black to Play

410) □ P.Garcia Castro ■ J.Arizmendi Martinez
Leon 2006

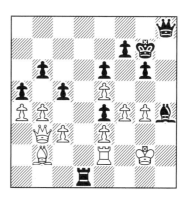

Black to Play

411) □ **A.Neiksans** ■ **H.Stefansson**
Liepaya (rapid) 2004

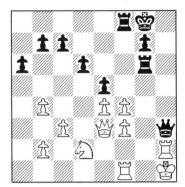

Black to Play

412) □ **A.Karpov** ■ **V.Salov**
Linares 1993

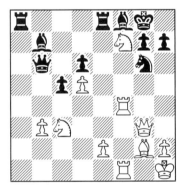

White to Play

413) □ **A.Shirov** ■ **V.Kramnik**
Linares 1997

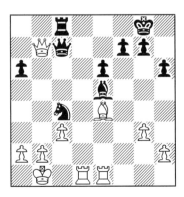

Black to Play

414) □ **E.Kulovana** ■ **A.Berescu**
Litomysl 2006

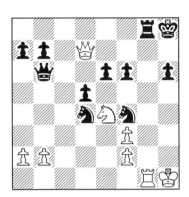

White to Play

415) □ **M.Blecha** ■ **A.Berescu**
Litomysl 2006

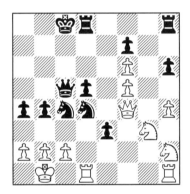

Black to Play

416) □ **M.Krupa** ■ **P.Giuriati**
Litomysl 2007

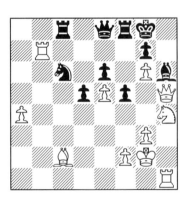

White to Play

417) □ **B.Addison** ■ **R.Palliser**
Liverpool 1999

Black to Play

418) □ **A.Rubinstein** ■ **Hirschbein**
Lodz 1927

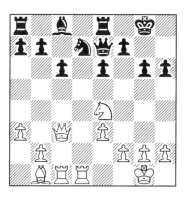

White to Play

419) □ **D.King** ■ **C.Crouch**
London 1977

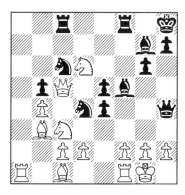

Black to Play

420) □ **D.Rowe** ■ **O.Boytsun**
London 2007

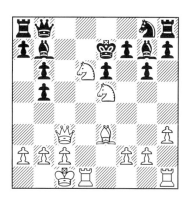

White to Play

421) □ **G.Steinkuehler** ■ **J.Blackburne**
London 1863

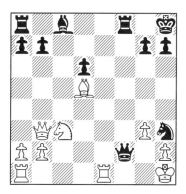

Black to Play

422) □ **J.Leake** ■ **J.Emms**
London 2006

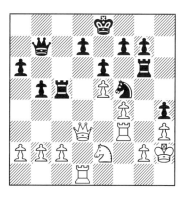

Black to Play

423) ☐ **J.Mackinnen** ■ **J.Emms**
London 2007

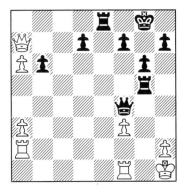

Black to Play

424) ☐ **J.Spreeuw** ■ **J.Emms**
London 2007

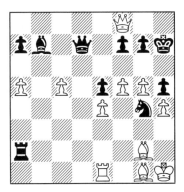

White to Play

425) ☐ **M.Adams** ■ **A.Hon**
London 1992

White to Play

426) ☐ **M.Cresswell** ■ **R.Wigbout**
London 2005

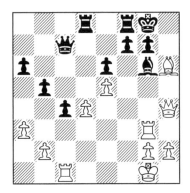

White to Play

427) ☐ **R.Bellin** ■ **A.Hanreck**
London 1977

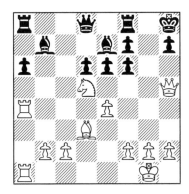

White to Play

428) ☐ **R.Kieran** ■ **K.Smallbone**
London 2002

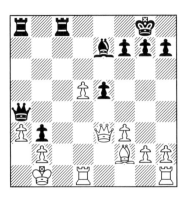

Black to Play

429) ☐ **R.Schulder** ■ **S.Boden**
London 1860

Black to Play

430) ☐ **V.Menchik** ■ **G.Thomas**
London 1932

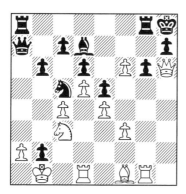

White to Play

431) ☐ **W.Steinitz** ■ **S.Rosenthal**
London 1883

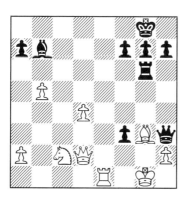

Black to Play

432) ☐ **I.Andrenko** ■ **O.Kalinina**
Lviv 2007

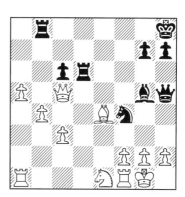

Black to Play

433) ☐ **L.Butkiewicz** ■ **T.Van der Veen**
Maastricht 2007

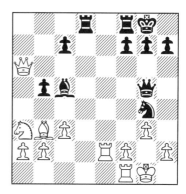

Black to Play

434) ☐ **P.Saligo** ■ **P.Taverniers**
Maastricht 2007

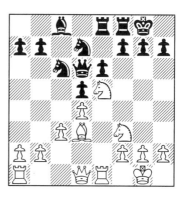

White to Play

435) □ **D.M.Martin** ■ **H.Hernandez Carmenates**
Madrid 2007

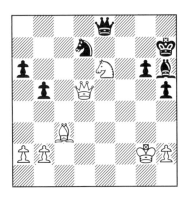

White to Play

436) □ **R.Mateo** ■ **H.Hernandez Carmenates**
Madrid 2007

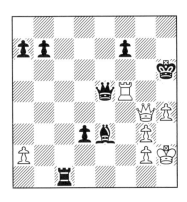

Black to Play

437) □ **V.Knox** ■ **B.Pytel**
Manchester 1981

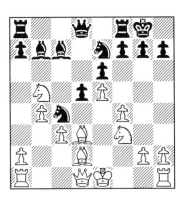

White to Play

438) □ **P.Konguvel** ■ **A.Del Valle Cirera**
Manresa 2004

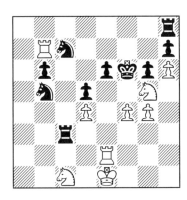

White to Play

439) □ **M.Ripari** ■ **J.Cori**
Mar del Plata 2007

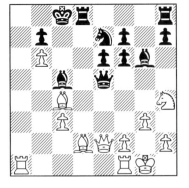

White to Play

440) □ **R.Hungaski** ■ **O.Di Diego**
Mar del Plata 2007

White to Play

441) ☐ **F.Frink** ■ **J.Horyna**
Marianske Lazne 2007

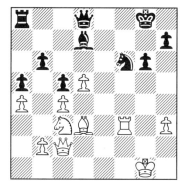

White to Play

444) ☐ **L.Milman** ■ **J.Fang**
Mashantucket 2005

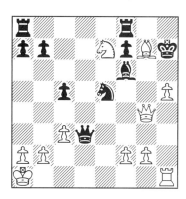

White to Play

442) ☐ **F.Stross** ■ **P.Benes**
Marianske Lazne 2007

White to Play

445) ☐ **B.Zivkovic** ■ **P.Bodiroga**
Mataruska Banja 2007

Black to Play

443) ☐ **V.Hruby** ■ **B.Baum**
Marianske Lazne 2007

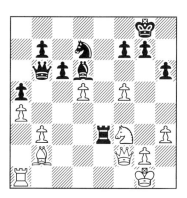

Black to Play

446) ☐ **V.Malakhatko** ■ **D.Hartmann**
Metz 2007

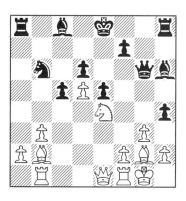

White to Play

447) ☐ **M.Leon Hoyes** ■ **O.Sanchez Enriquez**
Mexico City 2007

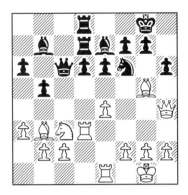

White to Play

448) ☐ **F.N.Stephenson** ■ **P.Rowntree**
Middlesbrough 2007

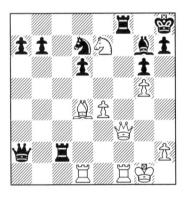

White to Play

449) ☐ **K.Zakoscielna** ■ **B.Siembab**
Mielno 2007

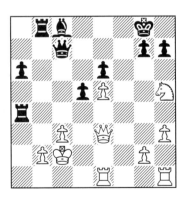

Black to Play

450) ☐ **P.Bobras** ■ **M.Kanarek**
Mielno 2007

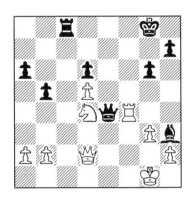

Black to Play

451) ☐ **F.N.Stephenson** ■ **A.Greet**
Millfield 2000

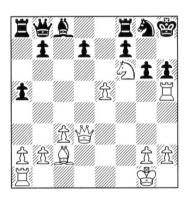

White to Play

452) ☐ **A.Hellenschmidt** ■ **I.Sakayev**
Mineola 2006

White to Play

453) □ **N.Maiorov** ■ **A.Aleksandrov**
Minsk 2007

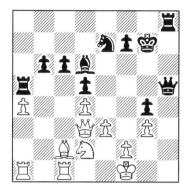

Black to Play

456) □ **A.Perez** ■ **F.Vallejo Pons**
Mondariz 1996

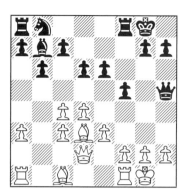

Black to Play

454) □ **M.Botvinnik** ■ **N.Padevsky**
Monaco 1969

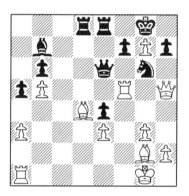

White to Play

457) □ **F.Handke** ■ **A.Kosten**
Montpellier 2006

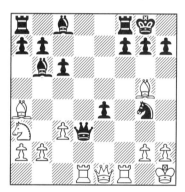

Black to Play

455) □ **P.Svidler** ■ **A.Morozevich**
Monaco (blindfold) 2007

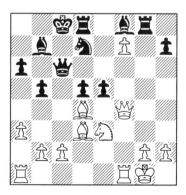

Black to Play

458) □ **T.Roussel Roozmon** ■ **A.Moiseenko**
Montreal 2004

Black to Play

459) □ **L.Aronian** ■ **M.Carlsen**
Morelia 2007

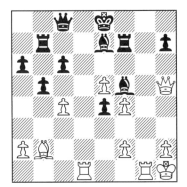

Black to Play

460) □ **M.Carisen** ■ **V.Topalov**
Morelia 2007

Black to Play

461) □ **U.Capo Vidal** ■ **F.Magana**
Morelia 2007

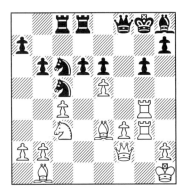

White to Play

462) □ **A.Gavrilov** ■ **O.Yuzhakov**
Moscow 2007

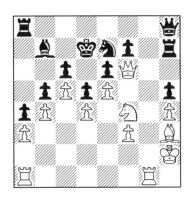

White to Play

463) □ **A.Karpov** ■ **V.Korchnoi**
Moscow 1974

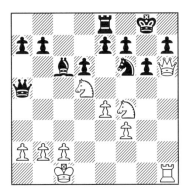

White to Play

464) □ **B.Jobava** ■ **J.Ehlvest**
Moscow 2007

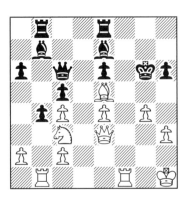

White to Play

465) ☐ **B.Savchenko** ■ **C.Balogh**
Moscow 2007

Black to Play

466) ☐ **C.Torre Repetto** ■ **F.Sämisch**
Moscow 1925

White to Play

467) ☐ **D.Bronstein** ■ **A.Kotov**
Moscow 1946

White to Play

468) ☐ **D.Bronstein** ■ **E.Geller**
Moscow 1961

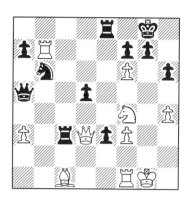

White to Play

469) ☐ **D.Markosian** ■ **A.Bodnaruk**
Moscow 2006

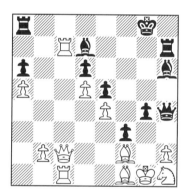

Black to Play

470) ☐ **D.Skurikhin** ■ **A.Samedov**
Moscow 2007

White to Play

471) ☐ E.Alekseev ■ S.Novikov
Moscow 2007

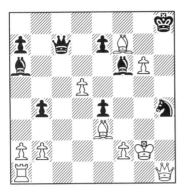

White to Play

472) ☐ G.Kaidanov ■ V.Anand
Moscow 1987

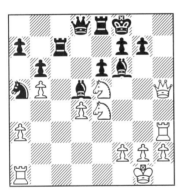

White to Play

473) ☐ I.Khairullin ■ S.Vijayalakshmi
Moscow 2007

White to Play

474) ☐ I.Lysyj ■ J.Ehlvest
Moscow 2007

White to Play

475) ☐ J.Ulko ■ A.Zontakh
Moscow 2007

White to Play

476) ☐ N.Kharmunova ■ A.Gavrilov
Moscow 2007

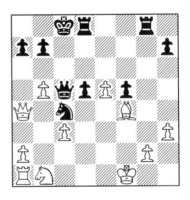

Black to Play

477) ☐ **R.Vaganian** ■ **G.Sargissian**
Moscow 2005

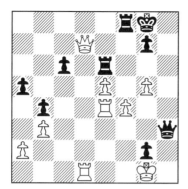

Black to Play

478) ☐ **S.Ionov** ■ **A.Kremenietsky**
Moscow 2007

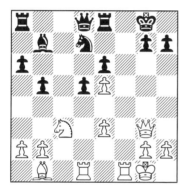

White to Play

479) ☐ **M.Botvinnik** ■ **V.Smyslov**
Moscow 1958

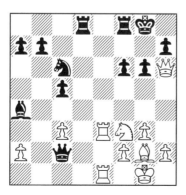

White to Play

480) ☐ **Y.Balashov** ■ **K.Ambartsumova**
Moscow 2007

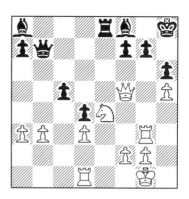

White to Play

481) ☐ **Y.Yakovich** ■ **A.Naiditsch**
Moscow 2007

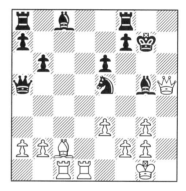

White to Play

482) ☐ **G.Kasparov** ■ **V.Anand**
Moscow (rapid) 1996

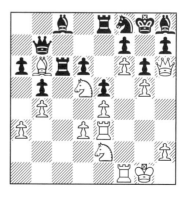

White to Play

483) □ **V.Okhotnik** ■ **C.Marzolo**
Nancy 2007

White to Play

484) □ **D.Marciano** ■ **E.Prie**
Narbonne 1997

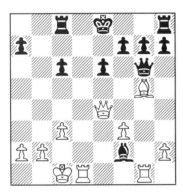

White to Play

485) □ **D.Contin** ■ **L.Perdomo**
Necochea 2007

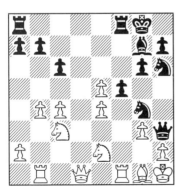

Black to Play

486) □ **J.Cubas** ■ **A.Shcherbine**
Necochea 2007

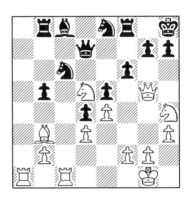

White to Play

487) □ **D.Barua** ■ **A.Dreev**
New Delhi 2007

Black to Play

488) □ **K.Shashikant** ■ **E.Hossain**
New Delhi 2007

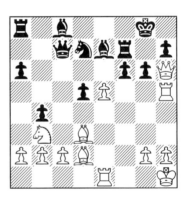

White to Play

489) ☐ **N.Marache** ■ **P.Morphy**
New Orleans simul 1857

Black to Play

490) ☐ **L.Evans** ■ **A.Bisguier**
New York 1958

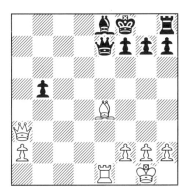

White to Play

491) ☐ **L.Evans** ■ **B.Zuckerman**
New York 1966

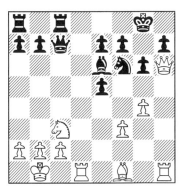

White to Play

492) ☐ **V.Kotronias** ■ **D.King**
New York 1990

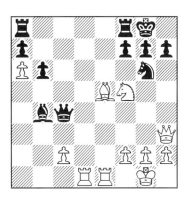

White to Play

493) ☐ *X3D Fritz* ■ **G.Kasparov**
New York 2003

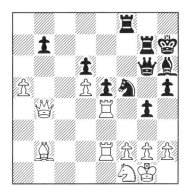

White to Play

494) ☐ **R.Palliser** ■ **D.Eggleston**
Newcastle (rapid) 2005

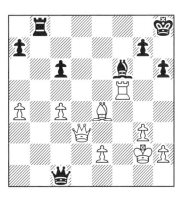

White to Play

495) □ **S.Gordon** ■ **R.Palliser**
Newport Pagnell (rapid) 2007

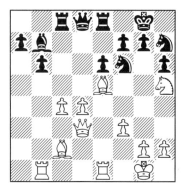

White to Play

496) □ **E.Tomashevsky** ■ **I.Popov**
Nojabrsk 2005

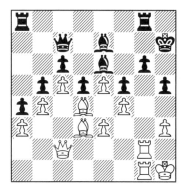

White to Play

497) □ **J.Skoberne** ■ **V.Hari**
Nova Gorica 2002

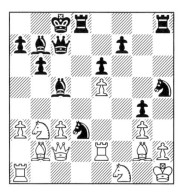

Black to Play

498) □ **P.Kokol** ■ **M.Varini**
Nova Gorica 2007

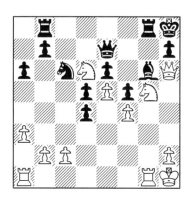

White to Play

499) □ **S.Jeric** ■ **J.Gombac**
Nova Gorica 2007

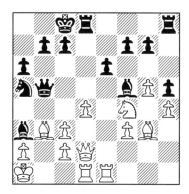

Black to Play

500) □ **S.Radosavljevic** ■ **D.Marholev**
Novi Becej 2007

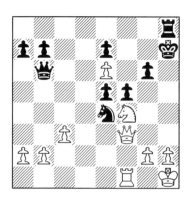

White to Play

501) □ **J.Mason** ■ **I.Gunsberg**
Nuremberg 1883

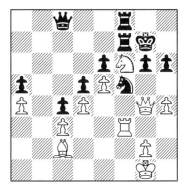

White to Play

502) □ **A.Blagidze** ■ **L.Stein**
Odessa 1960

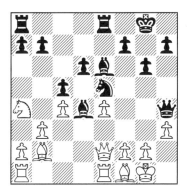

Black to Play

503) □ **'Aak'** ■ **R.Palliser**
online blitz 2006

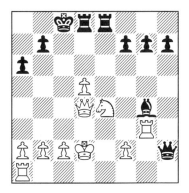

Black to Play

504) □ **'La_Vie_en_rose'** ■ **R.Palliser**
online blitz 2006

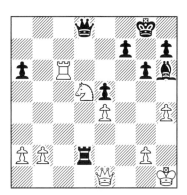

White to Play

505) □ **G.Gamzardia** ■ **R.Palliser**
online blitz 2007

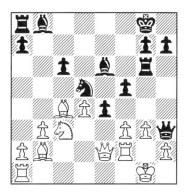

Black to Play

506) □ **H.Nakamura** ■ **R.Har Zvi**
online blitz 2007

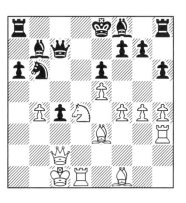

White to Play

507) ☐ J.Sammour Hasbun ■ T.L.Petrosian
online blitz 2007

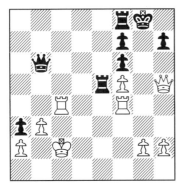

White to Play

508) ☐ R.Palliser ■ 'Diliman12'
online blitz 2007

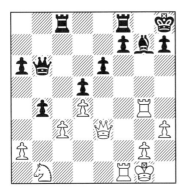

White to Play

509) ☐ R.Palliser ■ 'Maratonac'
online blitz 2007

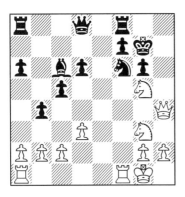

White to Play

510) ☐ R.Palliser ■ 'NoMore'
online blitz 2006

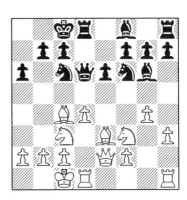

White to Play

511) ☐ R.Palliser ■ 'Quike'
online blitz 2006

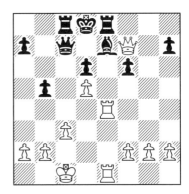

White to Play

512) ☐ J.Kochetkova ■ A.Lomako
Orel 2006

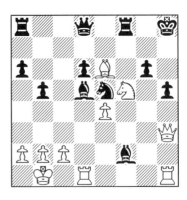

White to Play

513) □ **J.Reipsch** ■ **K.Zuse**
Osterburg 2006

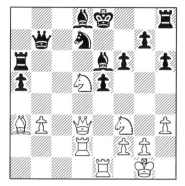

White to Play

516) □ **C.Timmins** ■ **C.Crouch**
Oxford 2004

White to Play

514) □ **T.Henrichs** ■ **H.Namyslo**
Osterburg 2006

White to Play

517) □ **D.Bruce** ■ **G.Pafura**
Oxford 2004

Black to Play

515) □ **A.Khantuev** ■ **K.Smallbone**
Oxford 2004

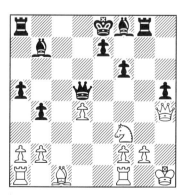

Black to Play

518) □ **K.Smallbone** ■ **I.Marshall**
Oxford 2002

Black to Play

519) □ **L.Podgornei** ■ **W.Burt**
Oxford 2002

Black to Play

520) □ **M.Perryman** ■ **M.Brown**
Oxford 2004

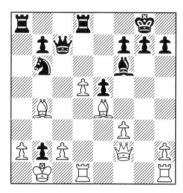

Black to Play

521) □ **R.Palliser** ■ **A.Summerscale**
Oxford 2002

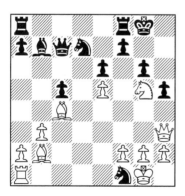

White to Play

522) □ **W.Burt** ■ **S.King**
Oxford 2005

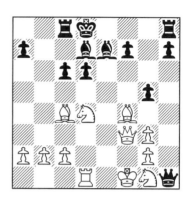

White to Play

523) □ **D.Bruce** ■ **R.Palliser**
Oxford (blitz) 2003

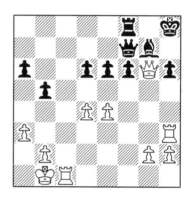

White to Play

524) □ **J.Yates** ■ **M.Rose**
Oxford (blitz) 2005

White to Play

525) □ K.Riley ■ W.Burt
Oxford (blitz) 2003

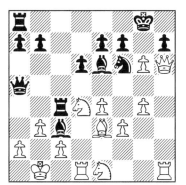

Black to Play

528) □ R.Palliser ■ N.Miller
Oxford simul 2003

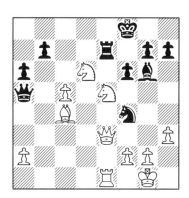

White to Play

526) □ J.Speelman ■ W.Burt
Oxford simul 2006

Black to Play

529) □ M.Lostuzzi ■ A.Spada
Palermo 2007

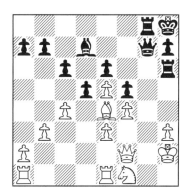

Black to Play

527) □ R.Palliser ■ K.Henbest
Oxford simul 2006

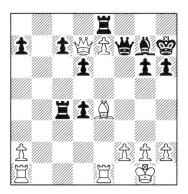

White to Play

530) □ J.Schulten ■ L.Kieseritzky
Paris 1844

Black to Play

531) □ **J.Margiotta** ■ **M.Chen**
Parsippany 2007

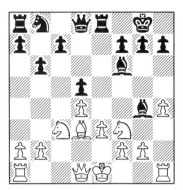

White to Play

532) □ **A.Donskov** ■ **E.Prokuronov**
Peterhof 2007

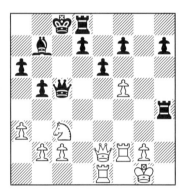

Black to Play

533) □ **A.Malofeev** ■ **S.Fedoseev**
Peterhof 2007

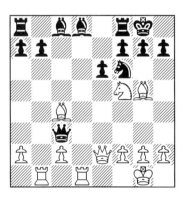

White to Play

534) □ **M.Mustaps** ■ **N.Somova**
Peterhof 2007

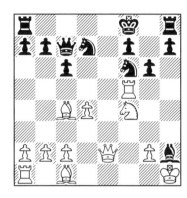

White to Play

535) □ **V.Fedoseev** ■ **V.Khamidulin**
Peterhof 2007

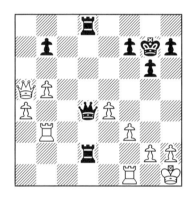

Black to Play

536) □ **D.Strenzwilk** ■ **M.Thaler**
Philadelphia 2006

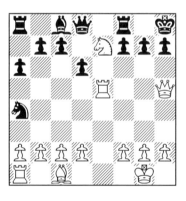

White to Play

537) □ **R.Dimitrov** ■ **E.Janev**
Plovdiv 2007

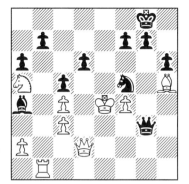

Black to Play

540) □ **M.Brugo** ■ **B.Grosse Honebrink**
Porto Mannu 2007

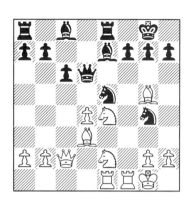

Black to Play

538) □ **I.Sokolov** ■ **V.Bologan**
Poikovsky 2006

Black to Play

541) □ **J.Erneker** ■ **V.Meijers**
Prague 2007

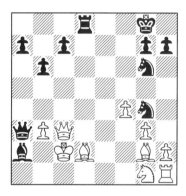

Black to Play

539) □ **V.Bologan** ■ **D.Jakovenko**
Poikovsky 2007

Black to Play

542) □ **V.Babula** ■ **P.Blatny**
Prague 2007

White to Play

543) ☐ I.Padurariu ■ M.Tutulan
Predeal 2007

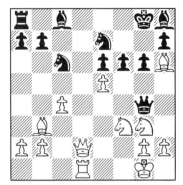

White to Play

544) ☐ R.Palliser ■ D.G.Ellison
Preston 2006

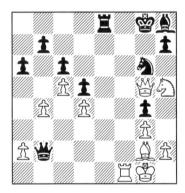

White to Play

545) ☐ A.Bak ■ R.Palliser
Pudsey 2007

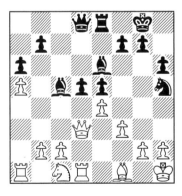

Black to Play

546) ☐ D.Rogic ■ M.Bulatovic
Pula 2007

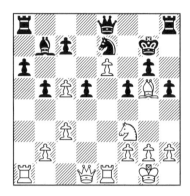

White to Play

547) ☐ J.Plenca ■ I.Saric
Pula 2007

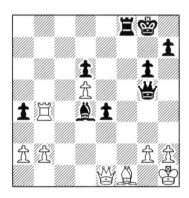

Black to Play

548) ☐ R.Vaganian ■ J.Gallagher
Pula 1997

Black to Play

549) □ **C.Sandipan** ■ **L.Nisipeanu**
Pune 2006

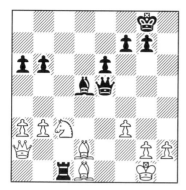

Black to Play

552) □ **M.Borriss** ■ **R.Palliser**
Rethymnon 2003

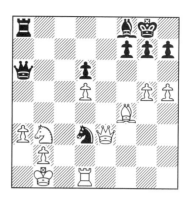

Black to Play

550) □ **G.Kasparov** ■ **V.Chuchelov**
Rethymnon 2003

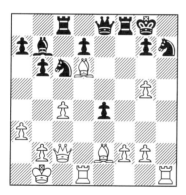

White to Play

553) □ **R.Palliser** ■ **S.Zhigalko**
Rethymnon 2003

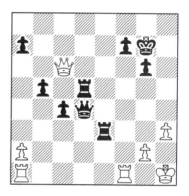

Black to Play

551) □ **J.Parker** ■ **K.Rasmussen**
Rethymnon 2003

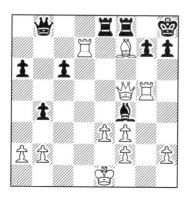

White to Play

554) □ **N.Miller** ■ **H.Murray-Smith**
Richmond (rapid) 2002

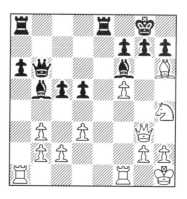

White to Play

555) □ **D.Bronstein** ■ **N.Krogius**
Riga 1958

White to Play

556) □ **C.Voicu** ■ **D.Taras**
Romanian Team Championship 2006

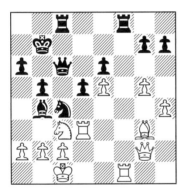

Black to Play

557) □ **R.Palliser** ■ **M.Surtees**
Rotherham (rapid) 2007

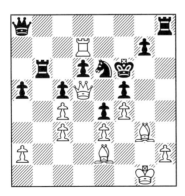

White to Play

558) □ **A.Goloshchapov** ■ **I.Belov**
Russian Team Championship 2007

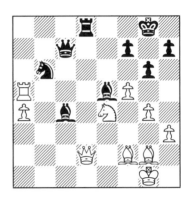

White to Play

559) □ **D.Bocharov** ■ **A.Babiy**
Russian Team Championship 2004

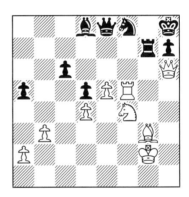

White to Play

560) □ **I.Nepomniachtchi** ■ **I.Kurnosov**
Russian Team Championship 2007

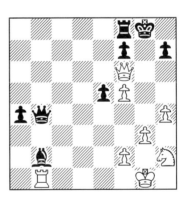

White to Play

561) ☐ **S.Rublevsky** ■ **V.Bologan**
Russian Team Championship 2005

Black to Play

562) ☐ **V.Bologan** ■ **E.Van Haastert**
Saint Vincent 2005

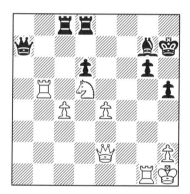

White to Play

563) ☐ **A.Shabalov** ■ **I.Krush**
San Diego 2004

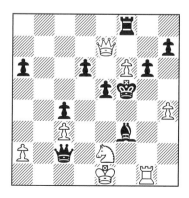

White to Play

564) ☐ **M.Colautti** ■ **L.Burijovich**
San Luis 2007

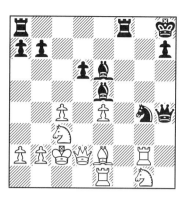

Black to Play

565) ☐ **J.Garro Beraza** ■ **E.Estevez Pegenaute**
San Sebastian 2007

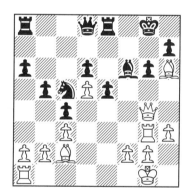

White to Play

566) ☐ **J.Garro Beraza** ■ **J.Kuende Gorostidi**
San Sebastian 2007

Black to Play

567) □ J.Yrjola ■ J.Riesco Lekuona
San Sebastian 2007

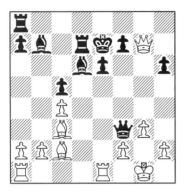

White to Play

568) □ L.Schrocker ■ G.Stahlberg
Santiago 1946

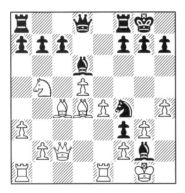

Black to Play

569) □ J.Dominguez ■ E.Iturrizaga
Santo Domingo 2007

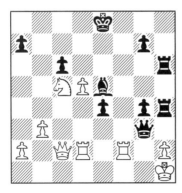

Black to Play

570) □ M.Leon Hoyes ■ J.Dominguez
Santo Domingo 2007

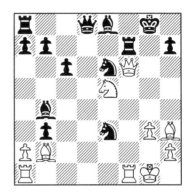

White to Play

571) □ T.Rodrigues ■ R.Molina
Santos 2007

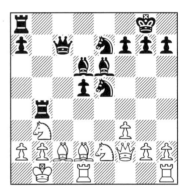

Black to Play

572) □ A.Graf ■ M.Carlsen
Sanxenxo 2004

White to Play

573) ☐ **R.R.Castineira** ■ **J.Caselas Cabanas**
Sanxenxo 2007

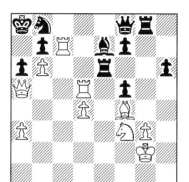

White to Play

574) ☐ **M.Santos** ■ **D.Navarrette**
Sao Jose do Rio Preto 2007

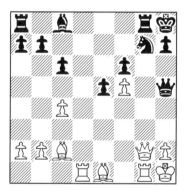

White to Play

575) ☐ **S.Farago** ■ **H.Grooten**
Sas van Gent 1988

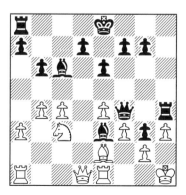

Black to Play

576) ☐ **K.Arakhamia Grant** ■ **C.Hanley**
Scarborough 2004

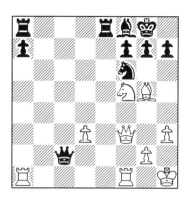

White to Play

577) ☐ **O.Sagalchik** ■ **I.Krush**
Seattle 2003

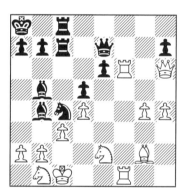

Black to Play

578) ☐ **V.Menchik** ■ **S.Graf**
Semmering 1937

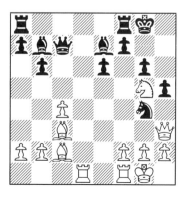

White to Play

579) □ **D.Cohen Gomez** ■ **G.Dizdar**
Seville 2007

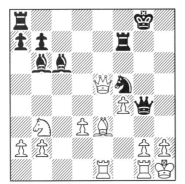

Black to Play

580) □ **M.Narciso Dublan** ■ **A.Lazaro Porta**
Seville 2007

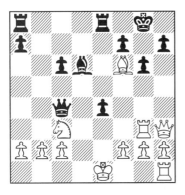

White to Play

581) □ **Wan Yunguo** ■ **Liang Chong**
Shandong 2007

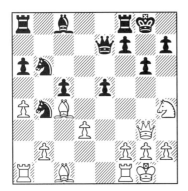

White to Play

582) □ **Xiu Deshun** ■ **Du Shan**
Shandong 2007

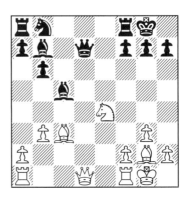

White to Play

583) □ **M.Allison** ■ **P.Hopwood**
Sheffield 1999

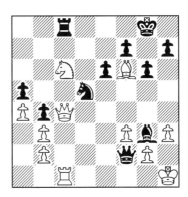

White to Play

584) □ **P.Hopwood** ■ **M.Newitt**
Sheffield 1997

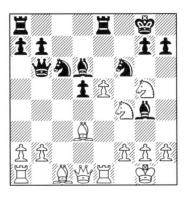

White to Play

585) ☐ **C.Garma** ■ **R.Shanmugam**
Singapore 2006

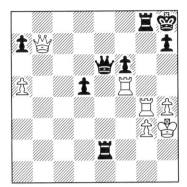

White to Play

586) ☐ **J.Tarjan** ■ **A.Karpov**
Skopje 1976

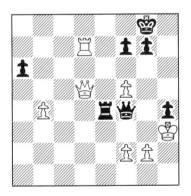

Black to Play

587) ☐ **E.Ovod** ■ **Hou Yifan**
Sochi 2007

Black to Play

588) ☐ **V.Gunina** ■ **Zhao Xue**
Sochi 2007

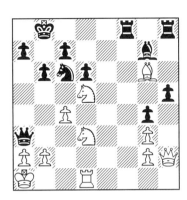

Black to Play

589) ☐ **V.Nebolsina** ■ **I.Gromova**
Sochi 2007

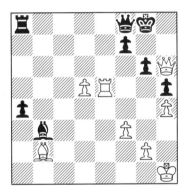

White to Play

590) ☐ **D.Alsina Leal** ■ **A.Mirzoev**
Soller 2007

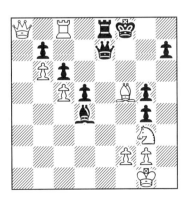

Black to Play

591) □ R.Fischer ■ L.Myagmarsuren
Sousse 1967

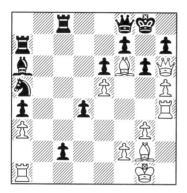

White to Play

592) □ E.Player ■ C.Fegan
Southend 2007

Black to Play

593) □ P.Plasgura ■ S.Feller
St Lorrain 2001

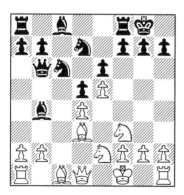

White to Play

594) □ A.Gantsevich ■ A.Smirnov
St Petersburg 2007

White to Play

595) □ A.Glazov ■ A.Stroganov
St Petersburg 2006

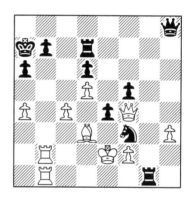

Black to Play

596) □ E.Kulikov ■ R.Gogin
St Petersburg 2007

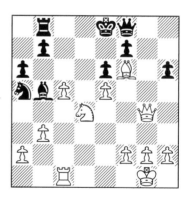

White to Play

597) □ **I.Malakhov** ■ **V.Nikiforov**
St Petersburg 2007

White to Play

598) □ **I.Popov** ■ **P.Ponkratov**
St Petersburg 2007

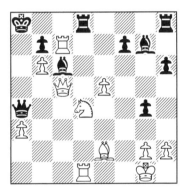

White to Play

599) □ **N.Chadaev** ■ **A.Lanin**
St Petersburg 2007

Black to Play

600) □ **P.Potemkin** ■ **A.Alekhine**
St Petersburg 1912

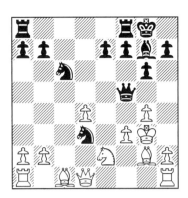

Black to Play

601) □ **T.Airapetian** ■ **A.Burtasova**
St Petersburg 2007

Black to Play

602) □ **V.Kurilov** ■ **E.Urjubdshzirov**
St Petersburg 2007

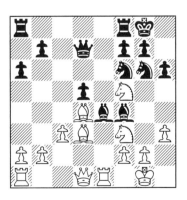

White to Play

603) □ **D.Andreikin** ■ **A.Lanin**
St. Petersburg 2007

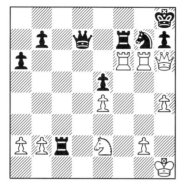

White to Play

604) □ **E.Sevillano** ■ **A.Stripunsky**
Stillwater 2007

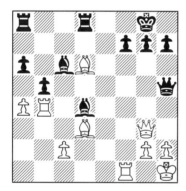

Black to Play

605) □ **G.Kaidanov** ■ **A.Ivanov**
Stillwater 2007

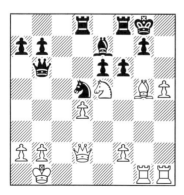

White to Play

606) □ **J.Ehlvest** ■ **D.Pruess**
Stillwater 2007

White to Play

607) □ **R.Anderson** ■ **A.Root**
Stillwater 2007

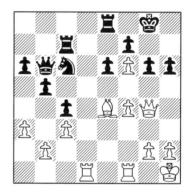

White to Play

608) □ **R.Plunkett** ■ **C.Latino**
Stillwater 2007

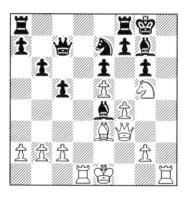

White to Play

609) ☐ **V.Akobian** ■ **E.Perelshteyn**
Stillwater 2007

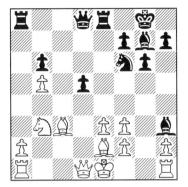

Black to Play

610) ☐ **Y.Shulman** ■ **I.Krush**
Stillwater 2007

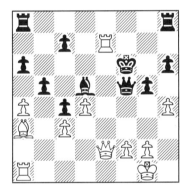

White to Play

611) ☐ **Z.Bayaraa** ■ **J.Veal**
Stillwater 2007

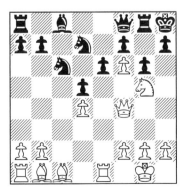

White to Play

612) ☐ **A.Pitson** ■ **S.Fraser**
Stirling 1998

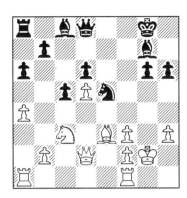

Black to Play

613) ☐ **J.Bellon Lopez** ■ **E.Berg**
Stockholm 2006

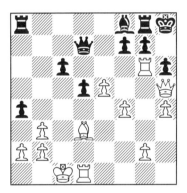

White to Play

614) ☐ **V.Gagarin** ■ **F.Andersson**
Stockholm 2007

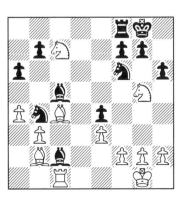

White to Play

615) □ R.Palliser ■ K.Cable
Streatham 1993

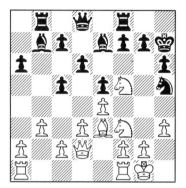

White to Play

616) □ S.Jasny ■ R.Palliser
Street 2004

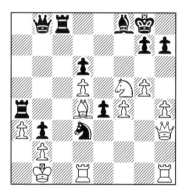

White to Play

617) □ J.Bernardino ■ D.Dragicevic
Sydney 2007

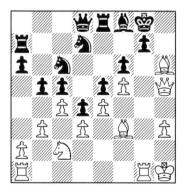

White to Play

618) □ Z.Borosova ■ K.Newrkla
Szeged 2007

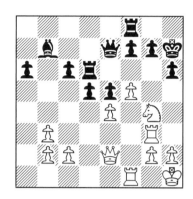

White to Play

619) □ N.Short ■ Ye Jiangchuan
Taiyuan 2004

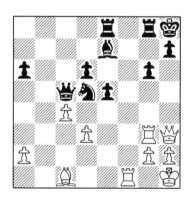

White to Play

620) □ E.Sild ■ L.Piarnpuu
Tallinn 2007

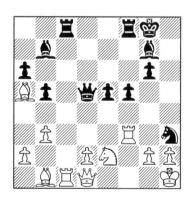

Black to Play

621) □ **I.Shvyrjov** ■ **V.Gansvind**
Tallinn 2007

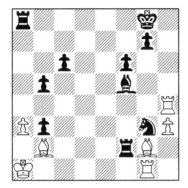

Black to Play

622) □ **N.Miezis** ■ **B.Lelumes**
Tallinn 2007

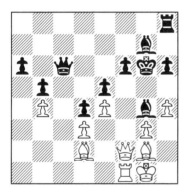

White to Play

623) □ **V.Mikenas** ■ **D.Bronstein**
Tallinn 1965

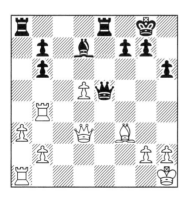

Black to Play

624) □ **T.Grabuzova** ■ **D.Batyte**
Tallinn (rapid) 2006

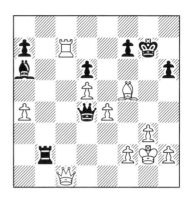

White to Play

625) □ **F.N.Stephenson** ■ **D.Humphries**
Teeside 1966

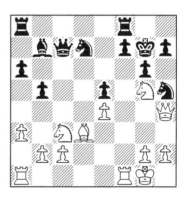

White to Play

626) □ **Y.Stisis** ■ **J.Lundvik**
Tel Aviv 2001

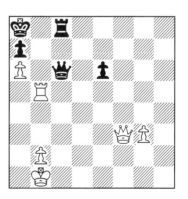

White to Play

627) □ J.Lener ■ J.Trapl
Teplice 2007

Black to Play

630) □ F.N.Stephenson ■ F.Rayner
Torquay 1998

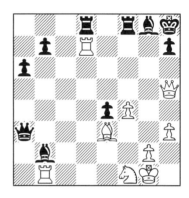

White to Play

628) □ R.Svarc ■ M.Vokac
Teplice 2007

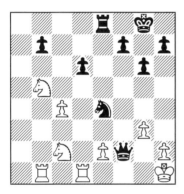

Black to Play

631) □ O.Foisor ■ M.Pavlovic
Triesen 2007

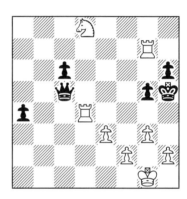

White to Play

629) □ E.Geller ■ K.Langeweg
The Hague 1962

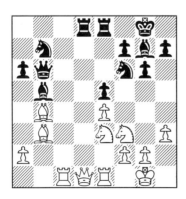

White to Play

632) □ A.Volokitin ■ M.Kravtsiv
Ukrainian Team Championship 2007

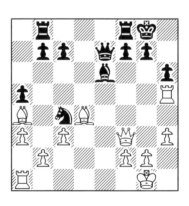

White to Play

633) ☐ **C.Schlechter** ■ **P.Meitner**
Vienna 1899

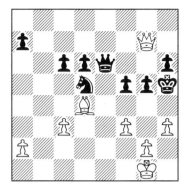

White to Play

634) ☐ **R.Spielmann** ■ **Hoenninger**
Vienna 1929

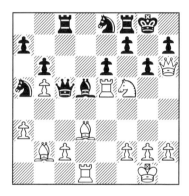

White to Play

635) ☐ **S.Azarov** ■ **Y.Zherebukh**
Voronezh 2007

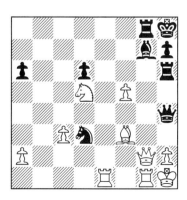

White to Play

636) ☐ **B.Tadic** ■ **D.Solak**
Vrsac 2007

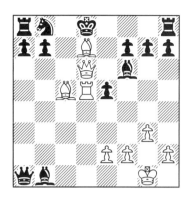

White to Play

637) ☐ **D.Solak** ■ **Z.Arsovic**
Vrsac 2007

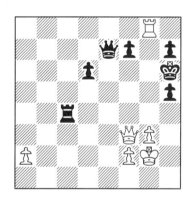

White to Play

638) ☐ **I.Ivanisevic** ■ **D.Pikula**
Vrsac 2007

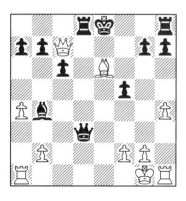

Black to Play

639) □ **Pham Minh** ■ **Tran Quoc Ding**
Vung Tau 2002

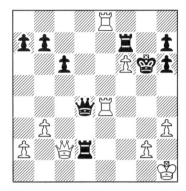

White to Play

640) □ **G.Spalding** ■ **S.Robertson**
Wantage 2006

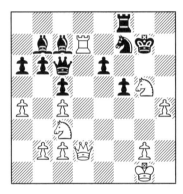

White to Play

641) □ **A.Naiditsch** ■ **L.Ftacnik**
Warsaw 2005

Black to Play

642) □ **M.Krasenkow** ■ **T.Markowski**
Warsaw 2004

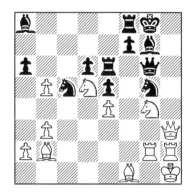

White to Play

643) □ **Z.Belsitzman** ■ **A.Rubinstein**
Warsaw 1926

Black to Play

644) □ **A.Leniart** ■ **J.Gdanski**
Warsaw (rapid) 2006

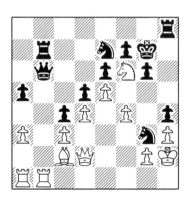

Black to Play

645) □ **G.Gajewski** ■ **A.Aleksandrov**
Warsaw (rapid) 2006

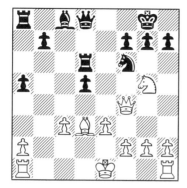

White to Play

646) □ **E.L'Ami** ■ **J.Smeets**
Wijk aan Zee 2007

White to Play

647) □ **H.Jonkman** ■ **E.Berg**
Wijk aan Zee 2007

White to Play

648) □ **J.Van der Wiel** ■ **Z.Peng**
Wijk aan Zee 2007

Black to Play

649) □ **L.Van Wely** ■ **S.Karjakin**
Wijk aan Zee 2007

Black to Play

650) □ **M.Adams** ■ **J.Piket**
Wijk aan Zee 1991

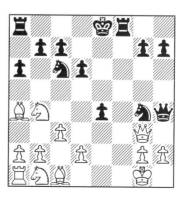

Black to Play

651) □ **M.Bosboom** ■ **T.Willemze**
Wijk aan Zee 2007

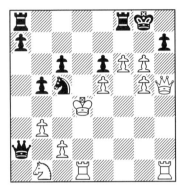

Black to Play

652) □ **M.Krasenkow** ■ **E.Van Haastert**
Wijk aan Zee 2007

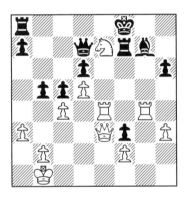

White to Play

653) □ **N.Kosintseva** ■ **E.Berg**
Wijk aan Zee 2007

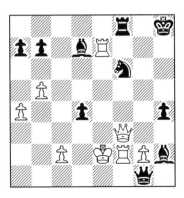

Black to Play

654) □ **W.Spoelman** ■ **E.Van Haastert**
Wijk aan Zee 2007

Black to Play

655) □ **K.Smallbone** ■ **D.Hackett**
Witney 2002

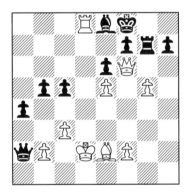

White to Play

656) □ **R.Palliser** ■ **T.Headlong**
Witney 2003

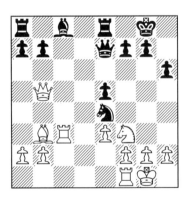

White to Play

657) □ J.Speelman ■ Peng Xiaomin
Yerevan 1996

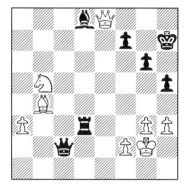

Black to Play

658) □ Y.Hambartsumian ■ A.Yegiazarian
Yerevan 2007

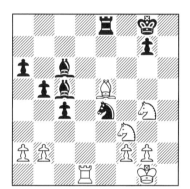

Black to Play

659) □ A.Moran ■ T.Turner
York 2000

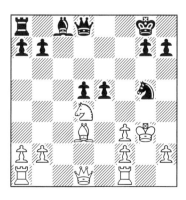

Black to Play

660) □ C.Costello ■ R.Palliser
York 2003

Black to Play

661) □ D.Adams ■ T.Braithwaite
York 2006

White to Play

662) □ J.Woolley ■ R.Tozer
York 2006

White to Play

663)   □ **M.Bridger** ■ **R.Palliser**
York 2006

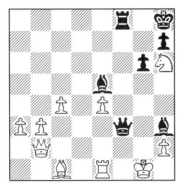

Black to Play

666)   □ **P.Hopwood** ■ **J.Bennett**
York 1998

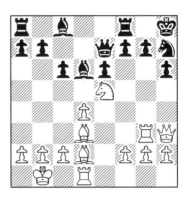

White to Play

664)   □ **P.Barber** ■ **B.Marshall**
York 2005

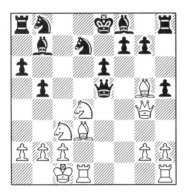

White to Play

667)   □ **P.Hopwood** ■ **P.Blacker**
York 1997

White to Play

665)   □ **P.Hopwood** ■ **E.Cameron**
York 2000

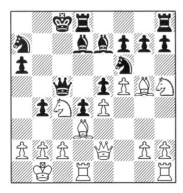

White to Play

668)   □ **R.Palliser** ■ **D.Baldwin**
York 1997

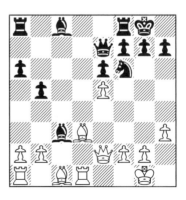

White to Play

669) ☐ **R.Palliser** ■ **J.Woolley**
York 2006

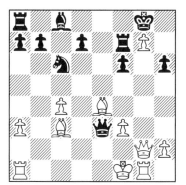

White to Play

670) ☐ **R.Palliser** ■ **M.Rogerson**
York 2005

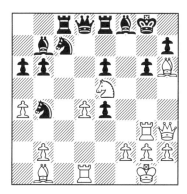

White to Play

671) ☐ **T.Turner** ■ **P.Hopwood**
York 2003

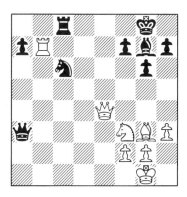

White to Play

672) ☐ **R.Palliser** ■ **R.Mitchinson**
York simul 2001

White to Play

673) ☐ **M.Franic** ■ **R.Zelcic**
Zadar 2006

Black to Play

674) ☐ **K.Sasikiran** ■ **R.Ponomariov**
Zafra (rapid) 2007

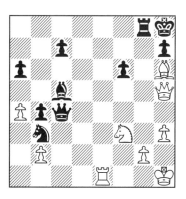

White to Play

675) □ J.Pavic ■ Z.Petrovic
Zagreb 2007

Black to Play

676) □ M.Mrdja ■ M.Vukusic
Zagreb 2007

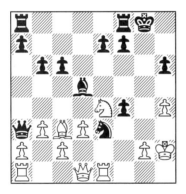

White to Play

677) □ S.Kosanski ■ L.Lasic
Zagreb 2007

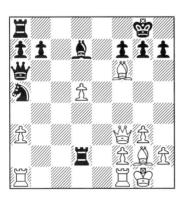

White to Play

678) □ Z.Takac ■ M.Vucic
Zagreb 2007

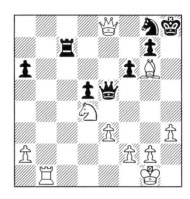

White to Play

679) □ R.Krajewski ■ D.Ziolkowski
Zakopane 2001

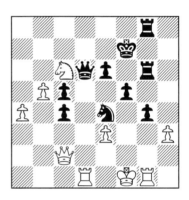

Black to Play

3: Opening Tricks and Traps

Tactics are a part of chess virtually right from the word go and we must all be careful even in the opening phase, especially when caught in an unfamiliar situation. Here I've included a number of the more common opening traps as well as a few favourites. This should help the reader to avoid falling for them ever again, as well as making you ready to pounce should your opponent slip up in the opening or very early middlegame phase.

680) □ **A.Genzling** ■ **J.Menendez Villar**
Aviles 2006

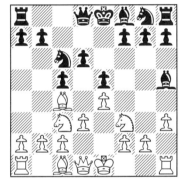

White to Play

682) □ **S.Ruzicic** ■ **P.Ljangov**
Belgrade 2006

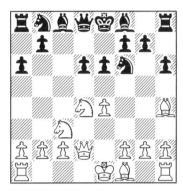

Black to Play

681) □ **D.Jeremic** ■ **N.Nestorovic**
Belgrade 2006

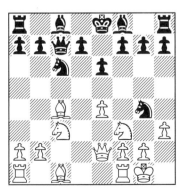

Black to Play

683) □ **B.Budimir** ■ **V.Jakovljevic**
Bosnian Team Championship 2007

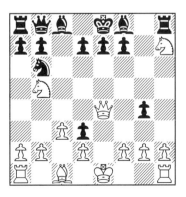

Black to Play

684) ☐ **A.A.Smith** ■ **H.Hunt**
British League 2004

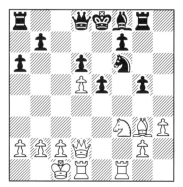

White to Play

685) ☐ **D.Cork** ■ **G.Morris**
British League 2006

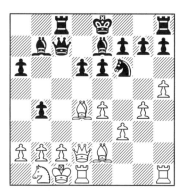

Black to Play

686) ☐ **J.Waterfield** ■ **C.Klein**
British League 2005

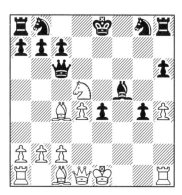

White to Play

687) ☐ **K.Williamson** ■ **J.Foster**
British League 2007

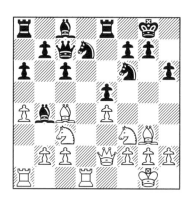

White to Play

688) ☐ **J.Boguszlavszkij** ■ **S.Cherednichenko**
Budapest 2007

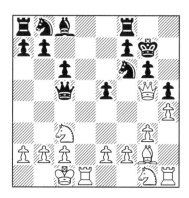

White to Play

689 ☐ **J.Mueller** ■ **S.Tidman**
Bunratty 2007

Black to Play

690) □ **R.Albrecht** ■ **A.Bering**
Copenhagen 2006

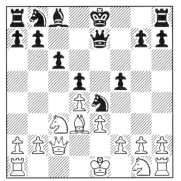

White to Play

693) □ **A.Harvey** ■ **R.Palliser**
Doncaster 2006

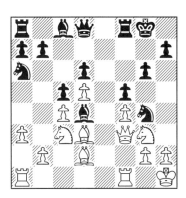

Black to Play

691) □ **M.Young** ■ **R.Palliser**
Cork 2005

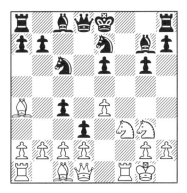

Black to Play

694) □ **I.Rajlich** ■ **P.Schuurman**
Dresden 2007

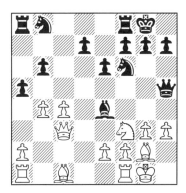

White to Play

692) □ **J.Soufflet** ■ **J.Bellay**
d'Angers 2007

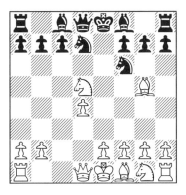

Black to Play

695) □ **J.Kregelin** ■ **J.Kleinert**
Dresden 2007

White to Play

696) □ P.Johansen ■ E.Peterson
Dresden 2007

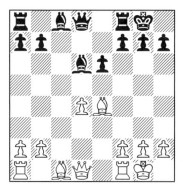

Black to Play

699) □ A.Santos ■ M.Ferro
Evora 2006

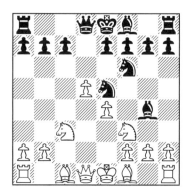

White to Play

697) □ P.Wells ■ A.Kharlov
Dresden 2007

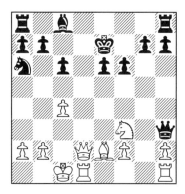

White to Play

700) □ F.Libiszewski ■ L.Roos
French League 2007

White to Play

698) □ T.Lopang ■ O.Sikorova
Ekaterinburg 2007

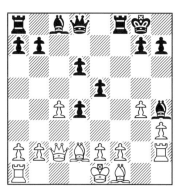

Black to Play

701) □ I.Khenkin ■ C.Vernay
Geneva 2007

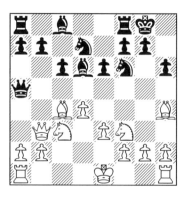

White to Play

702) □ **U.Von Herman** ■ **D.Hausrath**
German League 2007

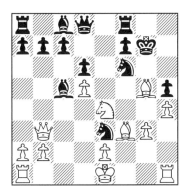

Black to Play

705) □ **R.Palliser** ■ **P.Taylor**
Golders Green (rapid) 2004

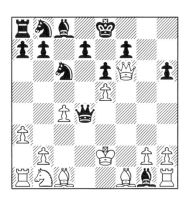

White to Play

703) □ **V.Schudro** ■ **W.Schmeing**
German League 2005

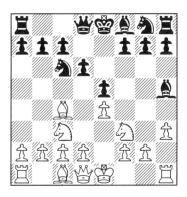

White to Play

706) □ **A.Wilson** ■ **G.Dickson**
Hastings 2007

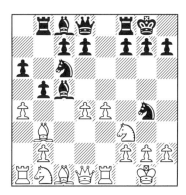

Black to Play

704) □ **D.Jameson** ■ **T.Nyland**
Gibraltar 2007

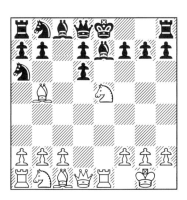

White to Play

707) □ **R.Mateo** ■ **C.Larduet Despaigne**
Havana 2007

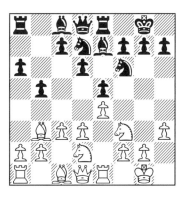

White to Play

708) □ **C.Hanley** ■ **J.Hickman**
Isle of Man 2005

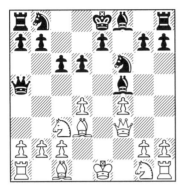

White to Play

709) □ **P.Adams** ■ **C.Vitoux**
Isle of Man 2005

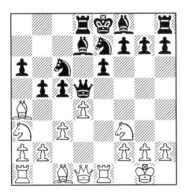

White to Play

710) □ **P.Schmidt** ■ **V.Rohmann**
Kiel 2003

White to Play

711) □ **R.Palliser** ■ **C.L.Lim**
Leeds (rapid) 1998

White to Play

712) □ **D.Terentiev** ■ **J.Gallagher**
Liechtenstein 1990

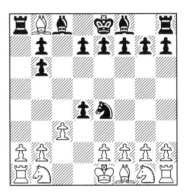

Black to Play

713) □ **O.Romanishin** ■ **A.Brenke**
Lippstadt 2004

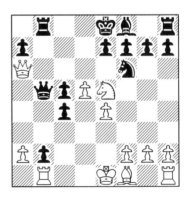

White to Play

714) ☐ **R.Palliser** ■ **K.Smallbone**
London 2002

White to Play

715) ☐ **H.Van Gool** ■ **P.Blijlevens**
Maastricht 2007

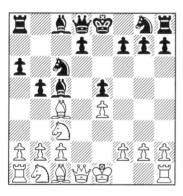

White to Play

716) ☐ **S.Tiviakov** ■ **R.Rivera Rodriguez**
Morelia 2007

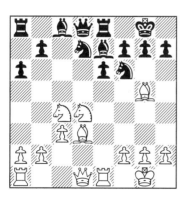

White to Play

717) ☐ **H.Lahlum** ■ **J.Ulrichsen**
Norwegian League 2007

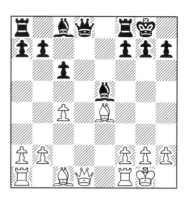

White to Play

718) ☐ **'Sofine'** ■ **R.Palliser**
online blitz 2007

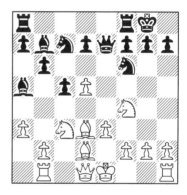

White to Play

719) ☐ **R.Palliser** ■ **S.Semkov**
online blitz 2007

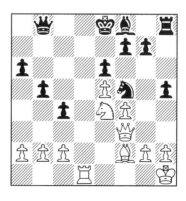

White to Play

720) ☐ **L.Bianchini** ■ **S.Vitri**
Palermo 2007

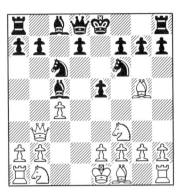

Black to Play

721) ☐ P.Morphy ■ **Duke Brunswick & Count Isouard**
Paris 1858

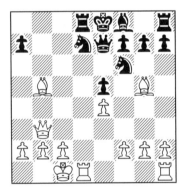

White to Play

722) ☐ **I.Danilov** ■ **T.Tanav**
Parnu 2002

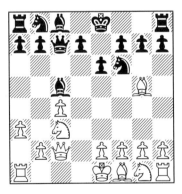

Black to Play

723) ☐ **J.Pau** ■ **N.Farber**
Parsippany 2007

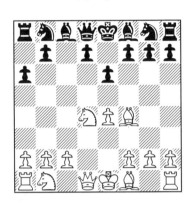

Black to Play

724) ☐ **H.Yasin** ■ **A.Istratescu**
Patras 2001

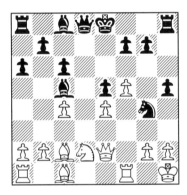

Black to Play

725) ☐ **L.Milov** ■ **A.Castro Acosta**
Sauzal (rapid) 2004

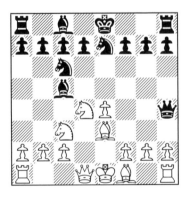

White to Play

726) □ **B.Willin** ■ **R.Auschkalnis**
Seefeld 2005

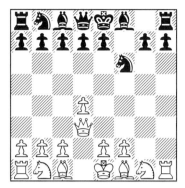

White to Play

727) □ **L.Shakarova** ■ **V.Zankovich**
Simferopol 1989

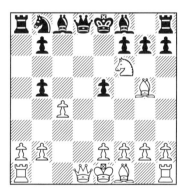

Black to Play

728) □ **R.Gibbons** ■ **T.Rej**
Sydney 2007

Black to Play

729) □ **A.Flitney** ■ **J.Escribano**
Tuggeranong 2007

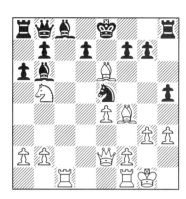

White to Play

730) □ **L.Aronian** ■ **D.Navara**
Turin 2006

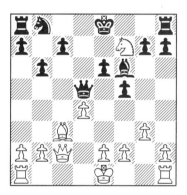

White to Play

731) □ **N.Ola** ■ **R.Tia**
USA 2005

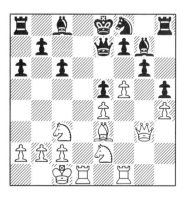

White to Play

732) □ **R.Reti** ■ **S.Tartakower**
Vienna 1910

White to Play

733) □ **D.Baramidze** ■ **L.Babuiian**
Yerevan 2006

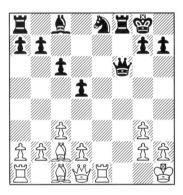

Black to Play

734) □ **Z.Kozul** ■ **M.Illescas Cordoba**
Yerevan 1996

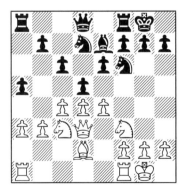

Black to Play

735) □ **A.Nezis** ■ **C.Duggan**
York 2007

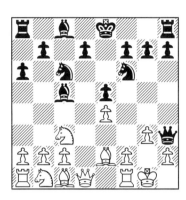

Black to Play

736) □ **E.Hurwitz** ■ **P.Hopwood**
York 2003

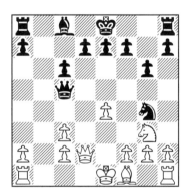

Black to Play

737) □ **L.Cornhill** ■ **P.Hopwood**
York 2006

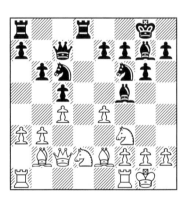

Black to Play

738) □ P.Anderson ■ R.Palliser
York 2007

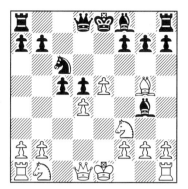

Black to Play

739) □ I.Armanda ■ I.Sitnik
Zagreb 2007

White to Play

4: Skill in the Endgame

Studying the endgame is one of the best ways to improve and, while this isn't an endgame guide, it would have been remiss not to have featured this most rich part of the game. Many endgames are extremely tactical, while others are decided by some fundamental piece of knowledge and, as such, this chapter will test your calculation, tactical eye and general endgame understanding.

740) □ **T.Walter** ■ **D.Hiermann**
Aschach an der Donau 2006

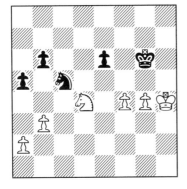

White to Play

741) □ **F.Yates** ■ **S.Tartakower**
Bad Homburg 1927

White to Play

742) □ **C.Balogh** ■ **L.Paichadze**
Baku 2007

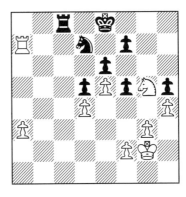

White to Play

743) □ **L.Van Wely** ■ **G.Guseinov**
Baku 2007

White to Play

744) □ **A.Shirov** ■ **V.Kramnik**
Belgrade 1999

White to Play

745) □ **C.McNab** ■ **A.Kunte**
Blackpool 2003

White to Play

746) □ **R.Westra** ■ **R.Palliser**
Bolton 1998

Black to Play

747) □ **F.Berkes** ■ **B.Tomic**
Bosnian Team Championship 2007

White to Play

748) □ **R.Palliser** ■ **M.Round**
Bradford 2000

Black to Play

749) □ **A.Collinson** ■ **D.King**
British League 2004

Black to Play

750) ☐ **A.Galliano** ■ **K.Smallbone**
British League 2007

Black to Play

753) ☐ **K.Ozeren** ■ **S.Clarke**
British League 2002

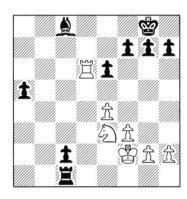

Black to Play

751) ☐ **B.Savage** ■ **S.Shikerov**
British League 2002

Black to Play

754) ☐ **S.Barrett** ■ **P.Taylor**
British League 2007

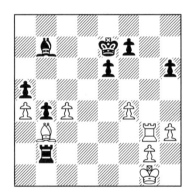

Black to Play

752) ☐ **C.Cobb** ■ **C.Duncan**
British League 2000

Black to Play

755) ☐ **S.Haslinger** ■ **R.Bates**
British League 2003

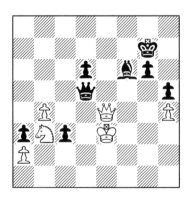

Black to Play

756) □ **R.Wade** ■ **V.Korchnoi**
Buenos Aires 1960

White to Play

759) □ **B.Jones** ■ **R.Dive**
Christchurch 2001

Black to Play

757) □ **Y.Vovk** ■ **P.Bobras**
Cappelle la Grande 2007

Black to Play

760) □ **P.Shaw** ■ **R.Palliser**
Doncaster 2005

Black to Play

758) □ **A.Safronov** ■ **I.Lysyj**
Cheboksary 2006

Black to Play

761) □ **A.Timofeev** ■ **G.Guseinov**
Dresden 2007

Black to Play

762) □ R.Zelcic ■ A.Riazantsev
Dresden 2007

Black to Play

763) □ T.Kotanijian ■ L.Pantsulaia
Dubai 2007

Black to Play

764) □ J.Gustafsson ■ N.V.Pedersen
Dutch League 2005

White to Play

765) □ M.Socko ■ K.Le Kieu Thien
Ekaterinburg 2007

Black to Play

766) □ A.Grischuk ■ S.Rublevsky
Elista 2007

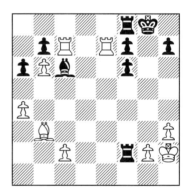

White to Play

767) □ W.Kreuscher ■ G.Sarthou
French League 2003

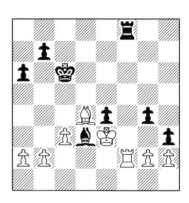

Black to Play

768) □ **M.Borriss** ■ **H.Steingrimsson**
Fuegen 2006

Black to Play

769) □ **I.Khenkin** ■ **A.Vuilleumier**
Geneva 2007

White to Play

770) □ **E.Bacrot** ■ **P.Tregubov**
German League 2007

White to Play

771) □ **I.Glek** ■ **M.Roos**
German League 2005

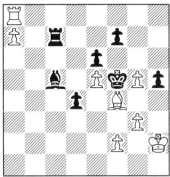

White to Play

772) □ **J.Timman** ■ **D.Baramidze**
German League 2007

White to Play

773) □ **G.Quillan** ■ **S.Ansell**
Gibraltar 2007

White to Play

774) □ **H.Nakamura** ■ **K.Arakhamia Grant**
Gibraltar 2007

Black to Play

775) □ **M.Adams** ■ **M.Al Modiahki**
Gibraltar 2007

Black to Play

776) □ **S.Citak** ■ **D.Dimitrijevic**
Gibraltar 2007

White to Play

777) □ **J.Trevelyan** ■ **F.Jenni**
Gothenburg 2005

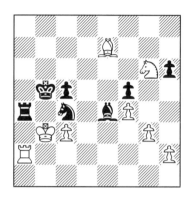

Black to Play

778) □ **K.Terrieux** ■ **Y.Kryvoruchko**
Guingamp 2007

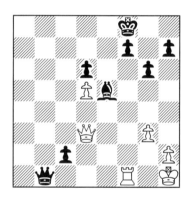

Black to Play

779) □ **K.Arkell** ■ **R.Palliser**
Halifax (rapid) 2004

White to Play

780) □ **R.Wade** ■ **R.Palliser**
Hampstead 1998

Black to Play

783) □ **S.Mannion** ■ **V.Sareen**
Isle of Man 2005

Black to Play

781) □ **H.Hunt** ■ **P.Hopwood**
Harrogate simul 1997

White to Play

784) □ **F.Yates** ■ **F.Marshall**
Karlsbad 1929

Black to Play

782) □ **O.L.Napoles** ■ **M.Gongora Reyes**
Havana 2007

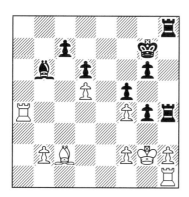

Black to Play

785) □ **R.Spielmann** ■ **O.Duras**
Karlsbad 1907

Black to Play

786) ☐ **A.Bannik** ■ **Y.Nikolaevsky**
Kiev 1958

White to Play

787) ☐ **N.Djukic** ■ **M.Pavlovic**
Kopaonik 2005

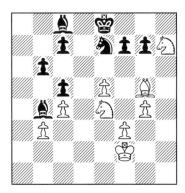

White to Play

788) ☐ **C.Davies** ■ **D.Morgan**
Leeds 2005

Black to Play

789) ☐ **I.Gourlay** ■ **R.Palliser**
Leeds 2002

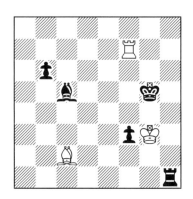

Black to Play

790) ☐ **R.Palliser** ■ **J.Hunt**
Leeds 2001

Black to Play

791) ☐ **R.Palliser** ■ **J.Hodgson**
Leeds (rapid) 2000

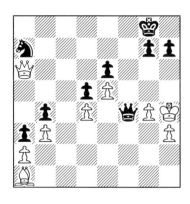

Black to Play

792) □ **P.Barata** ■ **J.Costa**
Lisbon 2001

Black to Play

795) □ **J.Capablanca** ■ **Ed.Lasker**
London 1914

White to Play

793) □ **A.Savickas** ■ **J.Garnelis**
Lithuanian Team Championship 2007

White to Play

796) □ **I.Bilek** ■ **W.Heidenfeld**
Lugano 1968

Black to Play

794) □ **P.Leko** ■ **V.Kramnik**
Monaco (blindfold) 2007

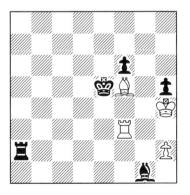

Black to Play

797) □ **K.Rasmussen** ■ **J.Nunn**
Lugano 1985

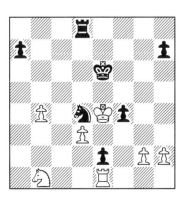

Black to Play

798) □ **V.Smyslov** ■ **H.Rossetto**
Mar del Plata 1962

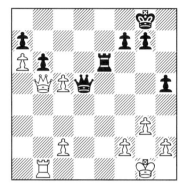

White to Play

799) □ **F.N.Stephenson** ■ **D.Spence**
Middlesbrough 1999

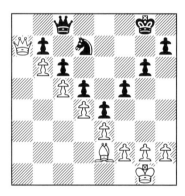

White to Play

800) □ **F.N.Stephenson** ■ **T.Wise**
Middlesbrough 1959

White to Play

801) □ **W.Banach** ■ **S.Birjukov**
Mielno 2007

Black to Play

802) □ **A.Volokitin** ■ **S.Ganguly**
Moscow 2007

White to Play

803) □ **D.Bronstein** ■ **M.Botvinnik**
Moscow 1944

White to Play

804) □ **G.Garcia Gonzales** ■ **M.Quinteros**
Moscow 1982

White to Play

807) □ **S.Novikov** ■ **D.Jakovenko**
Moscow 2007

White to Play

805) □ **S.Movsesian** ■ **Y.Kuzubov**
Moscow 2006

Black to Play

808) □ **J.Ehlvest** ■ **M.Bluvshtein**
New York 2003

White to Play

806) □ **S.Grigoriants** ■ **E.Shaposhnikov**
Moscow 2007

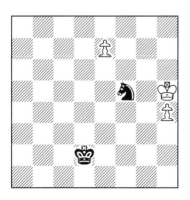

White to Play

809) □ **C.Schlechter** ■ **H.Wolf**
Nuremberg 1906

Black to Play

810) □ **B.Savchenko** ■ **R.Har Zvi**
online blitz 2007

Black to Play

811) □ **M.Chigorin** ■ **S.Tarrasch**
Ostende 1905

White to Play

812) □ **T.Michalczak** ■ **R.Schoene**
Osterburg 2006

Black to Play

813) □ **K.Smallbone** ■ **M.Brown**
Oxford 2000

White to Play

814) □ **R.Palliser** ■ **J.Lappage**
Oxford 2002

White to Play

815) □ **R.Palliser** ■ **J.Lappage**
Oxford 2003

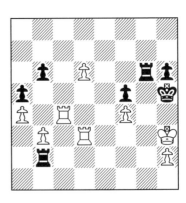

Black to Play

816) □ **D.Milovanovic** ■ **D.Jacobs**
Parsippany 2007

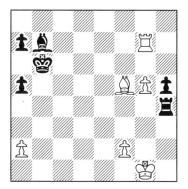

White to Play

819) □ **A.Berke** ■ **B.Franciskovic**
Rijeka 2007

White to Play

817) □ **D.Bronstein** ■ **O.Panno**
Petropolis 1973

White to Play

820) □ **D.Bocharov** ■ **M.Roiz**
Russian Team Championship 2007

White to Play

818) □ **P.Acs** ■ **V.Ivanchuk**
Rethymnon 2003

Black to Play

821) □ **A.Nimzowitsch** ■ **S.Tarrasch**
San Sebastian 1911

Black to Play

822) ☐ **E.Bystryakova** ■ **S.Airumian**
St Petersburg 2007

White to Play

823) ☐ **V.Gunina** ■ **O.Dolgova**
St Petersburg 2007

Black to Play

824) ☐ **A.Shabalov** ■ **G.Kaidanov**
Stillwater 2007

White to Play

825) ☐ **L.Karlsson** ■ **J.Furhoff**
Stockholm 2007

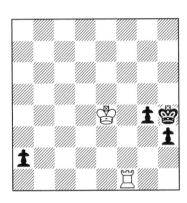

White to Play

826) ☐ **V.Onischuk** ■ **G.Timoshenko**
Tallinn 2007

Black to Play

827) ☐ **T.Petrosian** ■ **B.Ivkov**
Teslic 1979

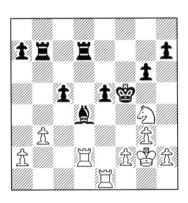

White to Play

828) □ **G.Wall** ■ **F.N.Stephenson**
Torquay 1998

Black to Play

829) □ **K.Arakhamia Grant** ■ **A.Baburin**
Triesen 2007

Black to Play

830) □ **A.Shirov** ■ **L.Aronian**
Wijk aan Zee 2007

White to Play

831) □ **L.Van Wely** ■ **L.Aronian**
Wijk aan Zee 2007

Black to Play

832) □ **L.Winants** ■ **L.B.Hansen**
Wijk aan Zee 1994

Black to Play

833) □ **T.Warakomski** ■ **D.Baramidze**
Yerevan 2006

White to Play

834)   □ **M.Carpenter** ■ **J.Wallace**
York 2006

White to Play

835)   □ **M.Round** ■ **R.Palliser**
York 2007

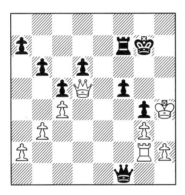

Black to Play

836)   □ **R.Palliser** ■ **P.Gayson**
York 2006

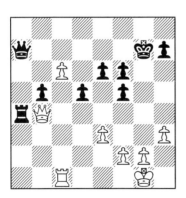

White to Play

837)   □ **V.Krutti** ■ **R.Palliser**
York 2000

Black to Play

838)   □ **I.Sokolov** ■ **K.Sasikiran**
Zafra 2007

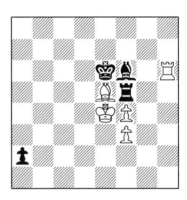

White to Play

5: Loose Pieces and Overloading

As several of the puzzles in the previous four chapters should have emphasized, whenever there's a loose piece on the board (remember LPDO!) make sure that there isn't a tactic available against that undefended piece. Solving the following puzzles should further emphasize that point, while also helping the reader to master how to give the enemy a loose piece: often by decoying a defender away or by overloading the defensive responsibilities of any covering piece.

839) □ J.Lacasa Diaz ■ J.Moreno Ruiz
Abierto 2007

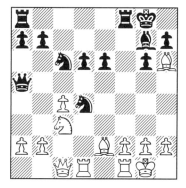

Black to Play

841) □ M.Tal ■ P.Benko
Amsterdam 1964

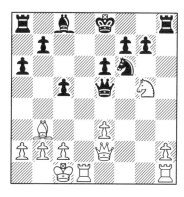

White to Play

840) □ R.Perez ■ J.Ramirez Garcia
Aguascalientes 2007

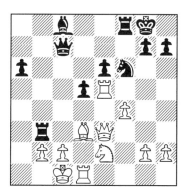

White to Play

842) □ E.Can ■ M.Erdogdu
Ankara 2007

White to Play

843) □ **F.Caruana** ■ **C.Majer**
Arvier 2007

White to Play

844) □ **V.Korchnoi** ■ **A.Karpov**
Baguio City 1978

White to Play

845) □ **M.Narciso Dublan** ■ **J.Timman**
Barcelona 2006

White to Play

846) □ **R.Lundberg** ■ **A.Czerownski**
Barlinek 2007

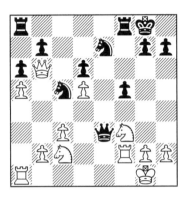

Black to Play

847) □ **K.Faranka** ■ **S.Al Aqrabi**
Beirut 2007

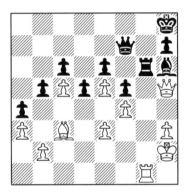

Black to Play

848) □ **R.Damaso** ■ **V.Malakhov**
Benidorm (rapid) 2006

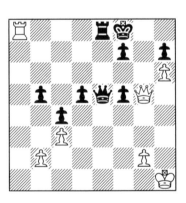

White to Play

849) □ **F.Parr** ■ **M.Collins**
Blackpool 1956

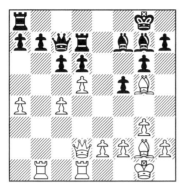

White to Play

852) □ **D.Rosen** ■ **P.Taylor**
British League 2007

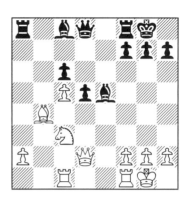

Black to Play

850) □ **W.Heidenfeld** ■ **M.Franklin**
Blackpool 1956

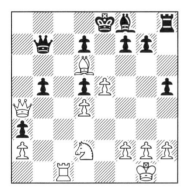

White to Play

853) □ **I.Thompson** ■ **B.Lund**
British League 2005

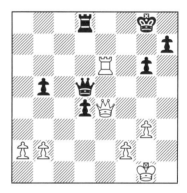

White to Play

851) □ **A.Kosten** ■ **M.Taylor**
British League 2004

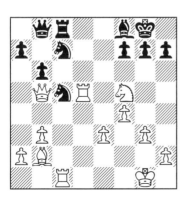

White to Play

854) □ **J.Parker** ■ **N.Pert**
British League 1999

Black to Play

855) ☐ **J.Plaskett** ■ **J.Gallagher**
British League 2001

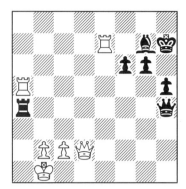

White to Play

856) ☐ **J.Shaw** ■ **L.Johannessen**
British League 2005

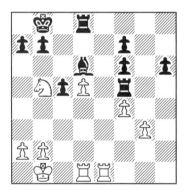

White to Play

857) ☐ **J.Shepley** ■ **D.Rosen**
British League 2006

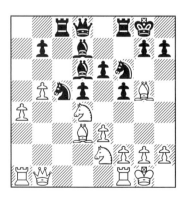

Black to Play

858) ☐ **K.Bhatia** ■ **E.Bentley**
British League 2007

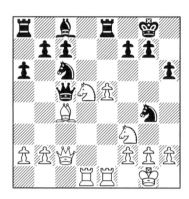

White to Play

859) ☐ **K.Richardson** ■ **K.Ozeren**
British League 2007

Black to Play

860) ☐ **L.Davis** ■ **C.Rice**
British League 2007

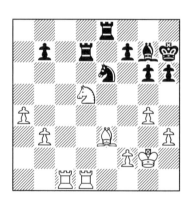

White to Play

861) □ **N.Alfred** ■ **K.Smallbone**
British League 2007

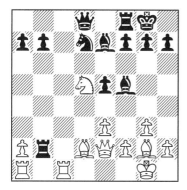

White to Play

862) □ **R.Palliser** ■ **A.Brameld**
British League 1998

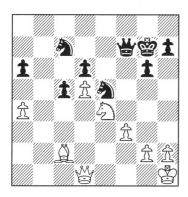

White to Play

863) □ **R.Palliser** ■ **J.Houska**
British League 2003

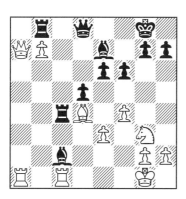

White to Play

864) □ **T.Hagesaether** ■ **D.Rabbitte**
British League 2005

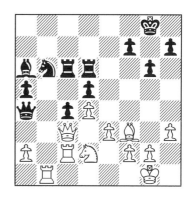

White to Play

865) □ **A.Salem** ■ **P.Doggers**
Budapest 2007

Black to Play

866) □ **W.Weiler** ■ **L.Toth**
Budapest 2007

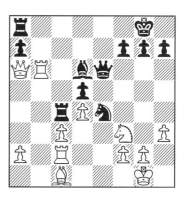

Black to Play

867) □ **L.Cooper** ■ **P.Walsh**
Bunratty 2007

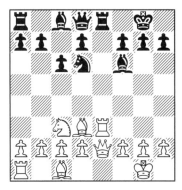

White to Play

870) □ **M.Carlsen** ■ **L.Fressinet**
Cap d'Agde (rapid) 2006

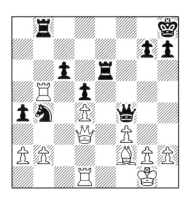

White to Play

868) □ **H.Pilaj** ■ **A.Naranjo Moreno**
Campillos 2007

White to Play

871) □ **Y.Drozdovskij** ■ **V.Georgiev**
Cappelle la Grande 2007

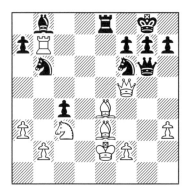

White to Play

869) □ **I.Rogers** ■ **A.Fitzpatrick**
Canberra 2007

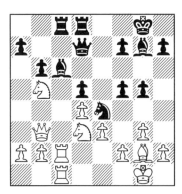

White to Play

872) □ **L.Mkrtchian** ■ **A.Riazantsev**
Chelyabinsk 2007

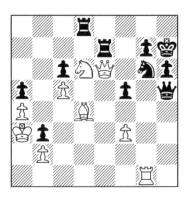

White to Play

873) □ **T.Rendle** ■ **V.Arjun**
Coulsdon 2007

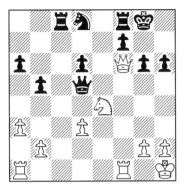

White to Play

874) □ **M.Ferro** ■ **A.Rotstein**
Cutro 2007

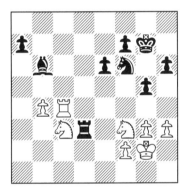

Black to Play

875) □ **S.Krivoshey** ■ **M.Ferro**
Cutro 2007

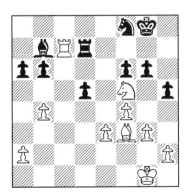

White to Play

876) □ **A.Aoustin** ■ **A.Perez**
d'Angers 2007

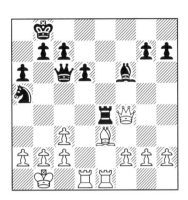

White to Play

877) □ **S.Reefat** ■ **I.Hakki**
Doha (rapid) 2006

White to Play

878) □ **R.Palliser** ■ **A.Khandelwal**
Doncaster 2005

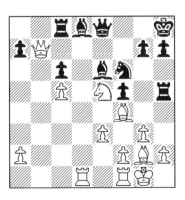

White to Play

879) □ R.Palliser ■ B.Hague
Doncaster 1998

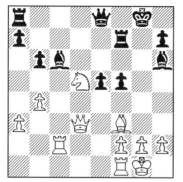

White to Play

880) □ A.Beliavsky ■ E.Van den Doel
Dresden 2007

White to Play

881) □ E.Zweschper ■ R.Glantz
Dresden 2007

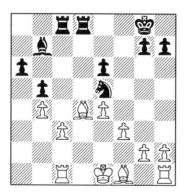

Black to Play

882) □ J.Jorczik ■ V.Gashimov
Dresden 2007

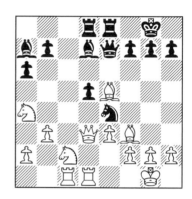

Black to Play

883) □ K.Georgiev ■ F.Holzke
Dresden 2007

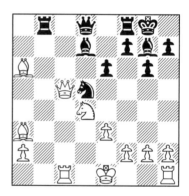

Black to Play

884) □ M.Womacka ■ L.Kritz
Dresden 2007

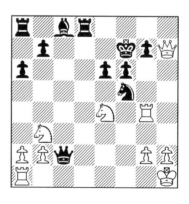

White to Play

885)   □ **N.Katte** ■ **R.Pert**
Dresden 2007

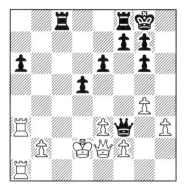

Black to Play

886)   □ **R.Ruck** ■ **A.Dreev**
Dresden 2007

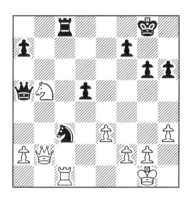

Black to Play

887)   □ **S.Zhigalko** ■ **V.Durarbayli**
Dresden 2007

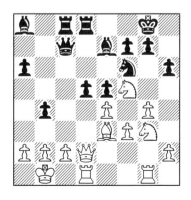

White to Play

888)   □ **A.Burnett** ■ **G.Bucher**
Edinburgh 2006

White to Play

889) □ **D.Eggleston** ■ **A.Ramaswamy**
Edinburgh 2003

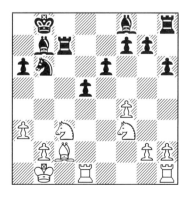

White to Play

890)   □ **R.Jones** ■ **K.Ruxton**
Edinburgh 2007

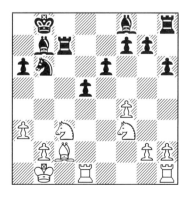

Black to Play

891) ☐ T.Kosintseva ■ J.Jackova
Ekaterinburg 2007

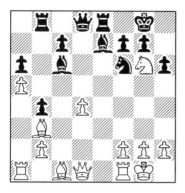

White to Play

892) ☐ D.Jakovenko ■ A.Shirov
Foros 2007

Black to Play

893) ☐ R.Hess ■ G.Kamsky
Foxwoods 2007

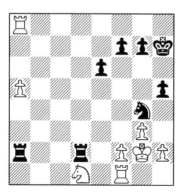

Black to Play

894) ☐ C.Wagner ■ G.Miralles
French League 2007

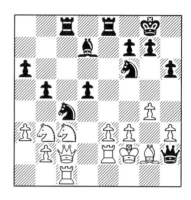

Black to Play

895) ☐ S.Tiviakov ■ D.Bunzmann
French League 2007

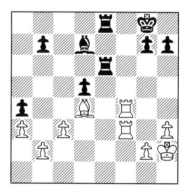

White to Play

896) ☐ B.Thorfinnsson ■ E.Najer
Fuegen 2006

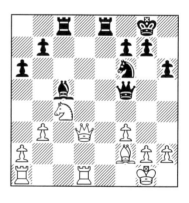

Black to Play

897)   □ **E.Porper** ■ **N.Mikkelsen**
Gausdal 2007

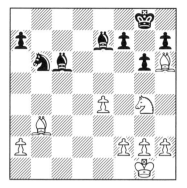

White to Play

898)   □ **G.Tallaksen** ■ **E.Lie**
Gausdal 2007

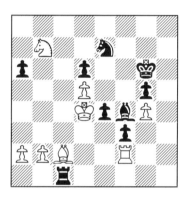

Black to Play

899)   □ **S.Reppen** ■ **V.Guddahl**
Gausdal 2007

Black to Play

900)   □ **A.Cherniaev** ■ **P.Pauchard**
Geneva 2007

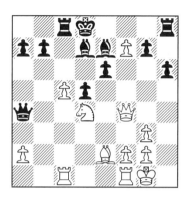

White to Play

901)   □ **A.Huss** ■ **I.Khenkin**
Geneva 2007

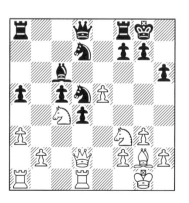

Black to Play

902)   □ **F.Handke** ■ **A.Reuss**
German League 2004

White to Play

903) ☐ **F.Langheinrich** ■ **Y.Pelletier**
German League 2006

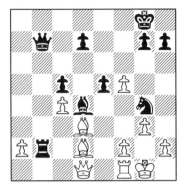

Black to Play

906) ☐ **S.Kindermann** ■ **I.Schneider**
German League 2007

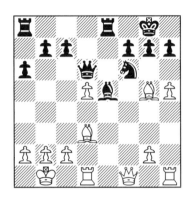

Black to Play

904) ☐ **G.Sargissian** ■ **L.Nisipeanu**
German League 2006

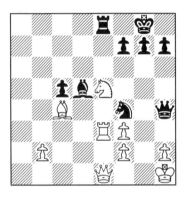

Black to Play

907) ☐ **T.Heinemann** ■ **T.Sarbok**
German League 2007

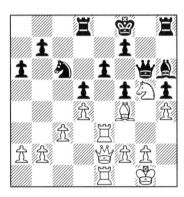

White to Play

905) ☐ **N.Firman** ■ **K.Sakaev**
German League 2007

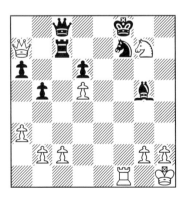

White to Play

908) ☐ **V.Ivanchuk** ■ **Z.Gyimesi**
German League 2006

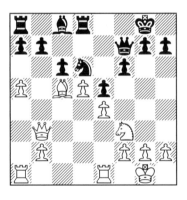

White to Play

909) □ **Z.Ribli** ■ **S.Kalinitschew**
German League 2007

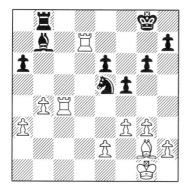

White to Play

910) □ **A.Butnorius** ■ **P.Cramling**
Gibraltar 2007

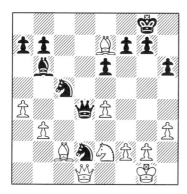

Black to Play

911) □ **I.Krush** ■ **K.Richardson**
Gibraltar 2007

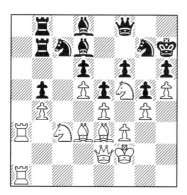

White to Play

912) □ **J.Rashleigh** ■ **M.Bucknell**
Gibraltar 2007

Black to Play

913) □ **J.Sarkar** ■ **F.Obers**
Gibraltar 2007

White to Play

914) □ **R.Ramesh** ■ **D.Werner**
Gibraltar 2007

White to Play

915) □ T.Abergel ■ P.Wallace
Gibraltar 2007

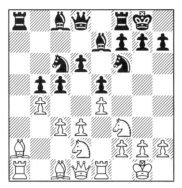

White to Play

916) □ P.Keres ■ B.Spassky
Gothenburg 1955

White to Play

917) □ J.Olivier ■ O.Adda
Grenoble 2007

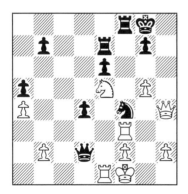

Black to Play

918) □ V.Smyslov ■ C.Kottnauer
Groningen 1946

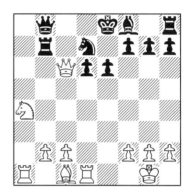

White to Play

919) □ A.Walton ■ R.Palliser
Halifax (rapid) 2006

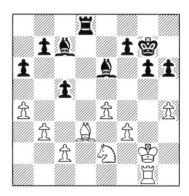

Black to Play

920) □ M.Breutigam ■ W.Pajeken
Hamburg 2006

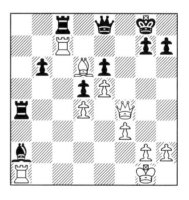

White to Play

921) □ **R.Palliser** ■ **C.Adrian**
Hampstead 1998

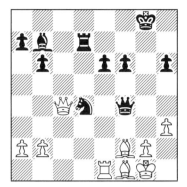

Black to Play

924) □ **J.Bowers** ■ **J.Stewart**
Hensol Park 2007

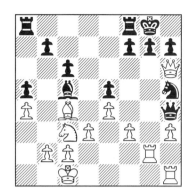

White to Play

922) □ **A.Greet** ■ **A.Grant**
Hastings 2006

White to Play

925) □ **D.Stellwagen** ■ **M.Bosboom**
Hilversum 2007

White to Play

923) □ **N.Donovan** ■ **R.Webster**
Hastings 2006

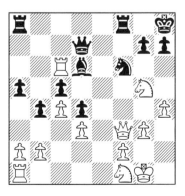

White to Play

926) □ **L.Kuznetsova** ■ **M.Bogorads**
Hockenheim 2007

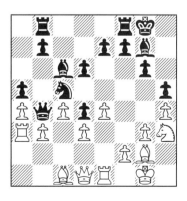

Black to Play

927) □ **A.Alekhine** ■ **M.Euwe**
Holland 1937

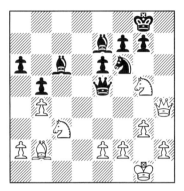

White to Play

930) □ **V.Ikonnikov** ■ **P.Negi**
Isle of Man 2005

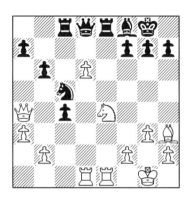

White to Play

928) □ **R.Palliser** ■ **A.Stalmans**
Hull 1996

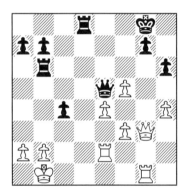

Black to Play

931) □ **V.Malakhatko** ■ **H.Groffen**
Isle of Man 2005

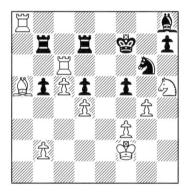

White to Play

929) □ **M.Georgiou** ■ **R.Palliser**
Hull (rapid) 1993

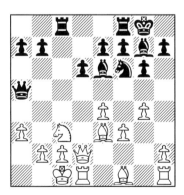

Black to Play

932) □ **D.Morris** ■ **M.Gilhespy**
Islington 1971

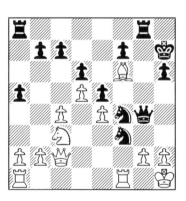

Black to Play

933) □ J.Gunnarsson ■ J.Iraheta
Istanbul 2000

White to Play

936) □ J.Morales ■ P.Heimbacher
La Laguna 2007

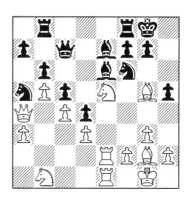

White to Play

934) □ S.Rublevsky ■ M.Gurevich
Khanty Mansiysk 2005

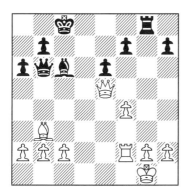

White to Play

937) □ T.Zapata ■ W.Moreno
Lima 2007

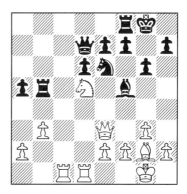

White to Play

935) □ G.Meins ■ D.Abel
Koenigshofen 2007

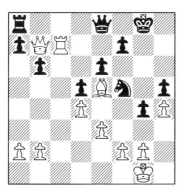

White to Play

938) □ M.Carlsen ■ V.Ivanchuk
Linares 2007

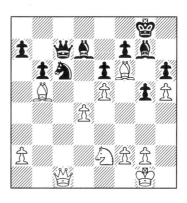

White to Play

939) □ E.Rayner ■ Z.Vranesic
London 1977

White to Play

942) □ P.Large ■ C.Baker
London 1977

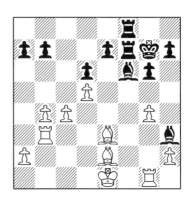

White to Play

940) □ G.James ■ P.Waters
London 1977

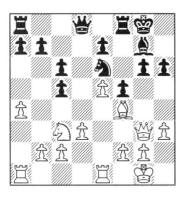

White to Play

943) □ T.Hebbes ■ R.Palliser
London 1993

Black to Play

941) □ J.Nunn ■ J.Plaskett
London 1986

White to Play

944) □ W.Hartston ■ M.Basman
London 1977

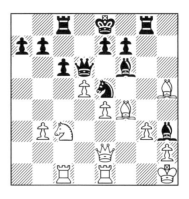

White to Play

945) ☐ **A.Tsirulnik** ■ **O.Kosyachenko**
Lviv 2007

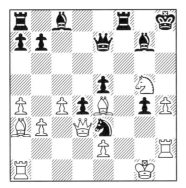

Black to Play

946) ☐ **D.Arutyunova** ■ **A.Maiko**
Lviv 2007

White to Play

947) ☐ **J.Blackburne** ■ **J.Owen**
Manchester 1890

White to Play

948) ☐ **L.Ausan** ■ **Chan Wei Yi**
Manila 2006

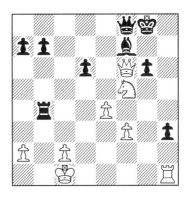

Black to Play

949) ☐ **M.Najdorf** ■ **H.Rossetto**
Mar del Plata 1956

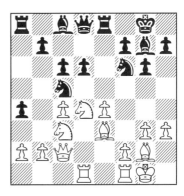

White to Play

950) ☐ **L.Klima** ■ **D.Boros**
Marianske Lazne 2007

White to Play

951) ☐ **J.Markiewicz** ■ **R.Sokolowski**
Mielno 2007

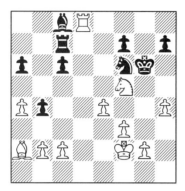

White to Play

952) ☐ **T.Warakomski** ■ **D.Orzech**
Mielno 2007

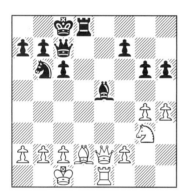

Black to Play

953) ☐ **L.Bergez** ■ **M.Vassallo Barroche**
Mislata 2001

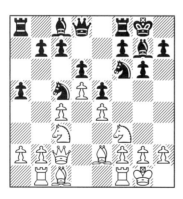

Black to Play

954) ☐ **E.Hodinott** ■ **R.Palliser**
Molescroft 1992

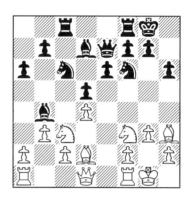

Black to Play

955) ☐ **V.Ivanchuk** ■ **V.Anand**
Monaco (blindfold) 2007

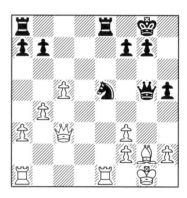

White to Play

956) ☐ **V.Kramnik** ■ **V.Ivanchuk**
Monaco (rapid) 2007

Black to Play

957) ☐ **M.Almada** ■ **B.Roselli Mailhe**
Montevideo 2007

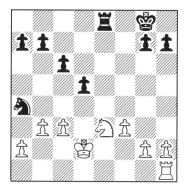

Black to Play

958) ☐ **V.Ivanchuk** ■ **V.Topalov**
Morelia 2007

White to Play

959) ☐ **V.Milov** ■ **V.Akobian**
Morelia 2007

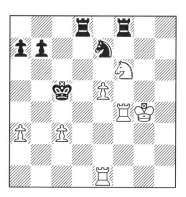

White to Play

960) ☐ **A.Chudinovskikh** ■ **A.Sitnikov**
Moscow 2007

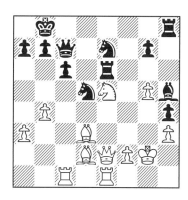

White to Play

961) ☐ **E.Vasiukov** ■ **R.Kholmov**
Moscow 1964

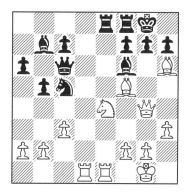

White to Play

962) ☐ **I.Kashdan** ■ **A.Kotov**
Moscow 1946

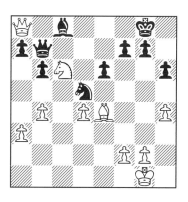

White to Play

963) □ **K.Ambartsumova** ■ **V.Gunina**
Moscow 2007

Black to Play

964) □ **T.L.Petrosian** ■ **K.Lahno**
Moscow 2007

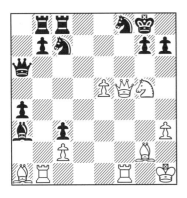

White to Play

965) □ **T.Petrosian** ■ **B.Spassky**
Moscow 1966

White to Play

966) □ **T.Petrosian** ■ **V.Simagin**
Moscow 1956

White to Play

967) □ **V.Burmakin** ■ **V.Burlov**
Moscow 2007

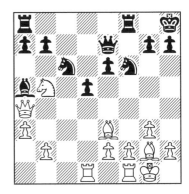

White to Play

968) □ **V.Malakhov** ■ **A.Areshchenko**
Moscow 2005

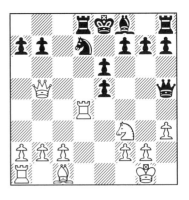

White to Play

969) □ **V.Ragozin** ■ **V.Panov**
Moscow 1940

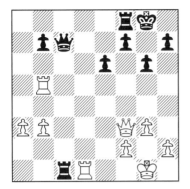

Black to Play

970) □ **C.Sandipan** ■ **M.Nezar**
Nancy 2007

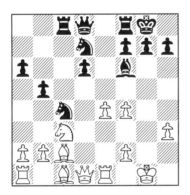

Black to Play

971) □ **A.Saidy** ■ **A.Santasiere**
New York 1955

White to Play

972) □ **J.Capablanca** ■ **M.Fonaroff**
New York 1918

White to Play

973) □ **J.Capablanca** ■ **W.Graham**
Newcastle upon Tyne 1919

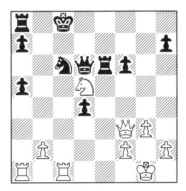

White to Play

974) □ **P.Maletin** ■ **E.Andreev**
Nizhnij Tagil 2007

White to Play

975) ☐ **R.Palliser** ■ **Ja.Gallagher**
Norwich 1994

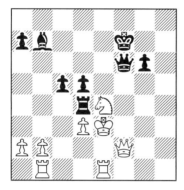

Black to Play

976) ☐ **M.Andrijevic** ■ **M.Grunberg**
Novi Becej 2007

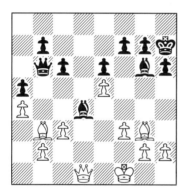

Black to Play

977) ☐ **J.Aagaard** ■ **R.Wiltshire**
Oban 2006

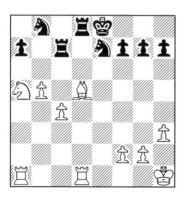

White to Play

978) ☐ **B.Rutkowski** ■ **S.Hilton**
Olsztyn 2005

White to Play

979) ☐ **'Erdnussbuddha'** ■ **R.Palliser**
online blitz 2007

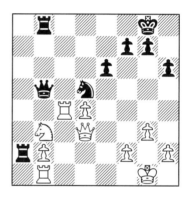

White to Play

980) ☐ **G.Kamsky** ■ **M.Sher**
online blitz 2007

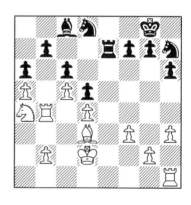

White to Play

981) ☐ **J.Lappage** ■ **K.Smallbone**
Oxford 2005

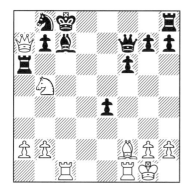

White to Play

982) ☐ **K.Smallbone** ■ **P.Lipman**
Oxford 2002

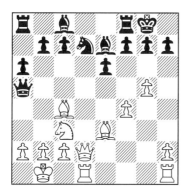

White to Play

983) ☐ **W.Burt** ■ **K.Smallbone**
Oxford 2003

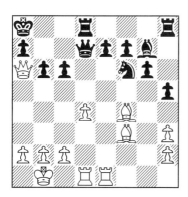

White to Play

984) ☐ **W.Burt** ■ **P.McIntosh**
Oxford 2002

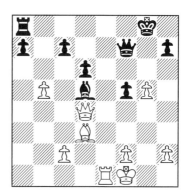

White to Play

985) ☐ **E.Dervishi** ■ **F.Vallejo Pons**
Palermo 2007

Black to Play

986) ☐ **W.Uhlmann** ■ **R.Fischer**
Palma de Mallorca 1970

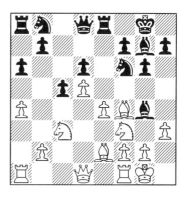

Black to Play

987) □ **An.Timofeev** ■ **D.Yevseev**
Peterhof 2007

Black to Play

988) □ **Nguyen Thien Viet** ■ **Pham Duc Thang**
Phu Quoc 2007

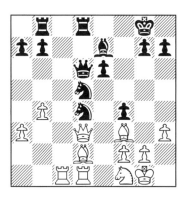

Black to Play

989) □ **F.Giani** ■ **S.Garofalo**
Porto Mannu 2007

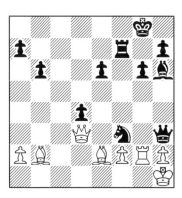

Black to Play

990) □ **P.Gnetti** ■ **A.Orlov**
Porto Mannu 2007

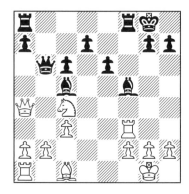

Black to Play

991) □ **A.Samuels** ■ **N.Miller**
Portsmouth 2003

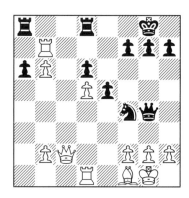

Black to Play

992) □ **F.Wegerer** ■ **A.Jankovic**
Pula 2007

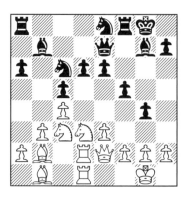

White to Play

993) □ U.Krstic ■ K.McPhillips
Pula 2007

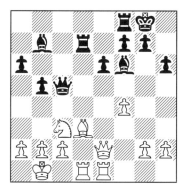

White to Play

994) □ K.Landa ■ F.Manca
Reggio Emilia 2007

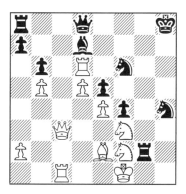

Black to Play

995) □ A.Huzman ■ G.Kasparov
Rethymnon 2003

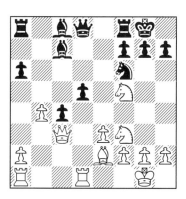

White to Play

996) □ H.Baldursson ■ T.Bjornsson
Reykjavik 2007

Black to Play

997) □ V.Doroshkievich ■ V.Tukmakov
Riga 1970

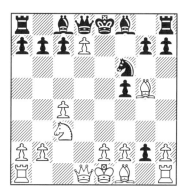

Black to Play

998) □ S.Solovjov ■ A.Belozerov
Russian Team Championship 2007

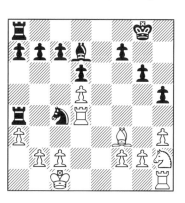

Black to Play

999) ☐ **R.Vera Gonzalez** ■ **F.Aguado Zabaleta**
San Sebastian 2007

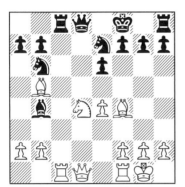

White to Play

1000) ☐ **P.Morales** ■ **R.Vera**
Santa Clara 2007

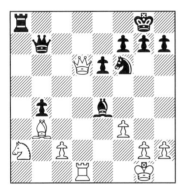

Black to Play

1001) ☐ **R.Palliser** ■ **A.Dyce**
Scunthorpe (rapid) 1998

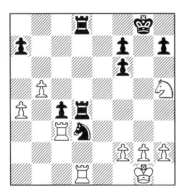

Black to Play

1002) ☐ **R.Palliser** ■ **M.Hankinson**
Sheffield 2007

White to Play

1003) ☐ **J.Sadorra** ■ **Dao Thien Hai**
Singapore 2006

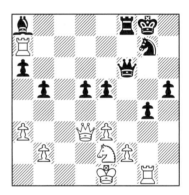

White to Play

1004) ☐ **V.Anand** ■ **V.Kramnik**
Sofia 2005

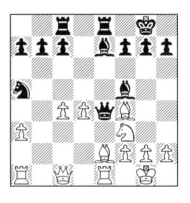

White to Play

1005) ☐ T.Vujcic ■ Z.Matas
Solin 2007

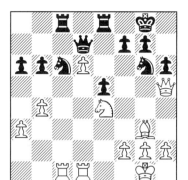

White to Play

1008) ☐ S.Kudrin ■ R.Robson
Stillwater 2007

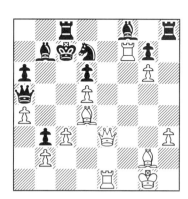

White to Play

1006) ☐ P.Obiamiwe ■ E.Player
Southend 2007

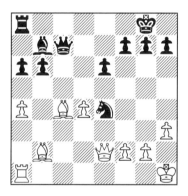

Black to Play

1009) ☐ C.Hanley ■ G.Jones
Street 2003

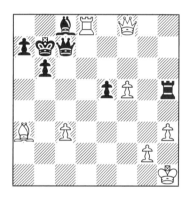

White to Play

1007) ☐ A.Yermolinsky ■ A.Stripunsky
Stillwater 2007

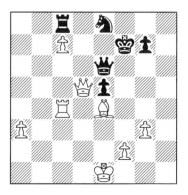

White to Play

1010) ☐ T.Gavriel ■ R.Palliser
Sutton 1997

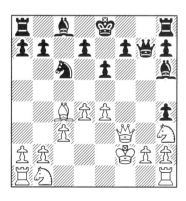

Black to Play

1011) ☐ B.Mandla ■ H.Cunanan
Sydney 2007

Black to Play

1012) ☐ I.Rogers ■ I.Ilic
Sydney 2007

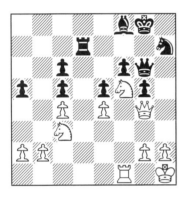

White to Play

1013) ☐ D.Benidze ■ D.Magalashvili
Tbilisi 2007

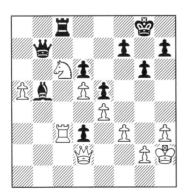

White to Play

1014) ☐ A.T.Martinez ■ P.Lezcano Jaen
Torrelavega 2007

White to Play

1015) ☐ E.Garcia ■ A.Ghobrial
Tuggeranong 2007

Black to Play

1016) ☐ A.Fedorov ■ A.Lastin
Voronezh 2007

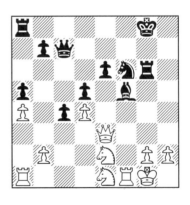

Black to Play

1017) ☐ **L.Van Wely** ■ **L.Aronian**
Wijk aan Zee 2007

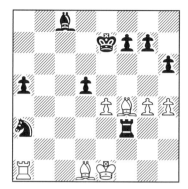

White to Play

1018) ☐ **V.Kramnik** ■ **A.Shirov**
Wijk aan Zee 2007

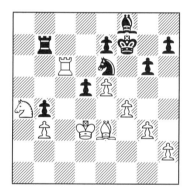

White to Play

1019) ☐ **R.Palliser** ■ **P.Tuplin**
Withernsea 1992

Black to Play

1020) ☐ **R.Palliser** ■ **S.Bekker Jensen**
Witley 1999

White to Play

1021) ☐ **A.Karpov** ■ **R.Bergmann**
Wolfsburg simul 2007

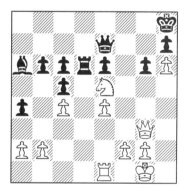

White to Play

1022) ☐ **A.Grigoryan** ■ **S.Jessel**
Yerevan 2006

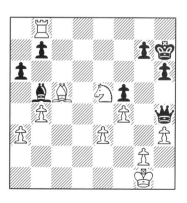

White to Play

1023) □ **V.Kramnik** ■ **L.Aronian**
Yerevan (rapid) 2007

White to Play

1024) □ **P.Hopwood** ■ **P.Barber**
York 2001

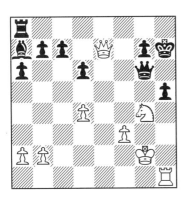

White to Play

1025) □ **P.Hopwood** ■ **T.Eggleston**
York 2001

Black to Play

1026) □ **S.Sriharan** ■ **P.Hopwood**
York 1995

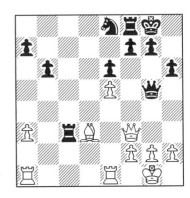

White to Play

1027) □ **S.Watson** ■ **H.Lockwood**
York 2003

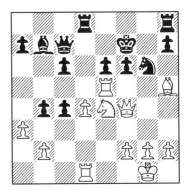

Black to Play

1028) □ **A.Ismail** ■ **R.Mitchinson**
York (rapid) 2007

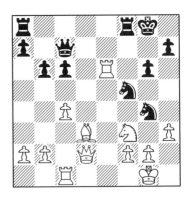

Black to Play

6: Fiendish Calculation

The main aim of this work has been to ensure that the reader is fully aware of the more important tactical motifs in all areas of the game. Working regularly through the previous five chapters should help to ensure that you rarely miss a common tactic ever again. However, it's also good to stretch ourselves from time to time and here are fifty puzzles to do just that: even the very strong club player should struggle with some of these!

1029) □ D.Sadvakasov ■ G.Baladjaev
Baku 2007

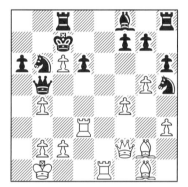

White to Play

1030) □ A.Trifunovic ■ S.Lalic
British League 1999

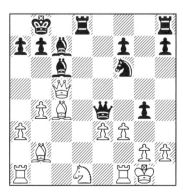

Black to Play

1031) □ D.Wheeler ■ J.Emms
British League 2005

Black to Play

1032) □ E.Sutovsky ■ I.Sokolov
British League 2005

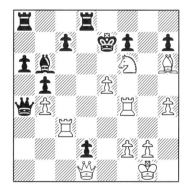

White to Play

1033) □ **M.Turner** ■ **D.Howell**
British League 2004

White to Play

1036) □ **T.Sakelsek** ■ **R.Rodriguez Lopez**
Campillos 2007

White to Play

1034) □ **P.Georghiou** ■ **C.Mogasha**
British League 1999

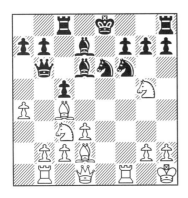

White to Play

1037) □ **A.Sokolov** ■ **A.Vovk**
Cappelle la Grande 2007

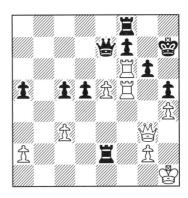

White to Play

1035) □ **W.Watson** ■ **R.Kuczynski**
Bundesliga 1995

Black to Play

1038) □ **P.Sott** ■ **P.Pokorny**
Czech League 2003

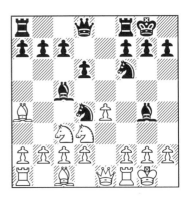

Black to Play

1039) □ **J.Plachetka** ■ **L.Zinn**
Decin 1974

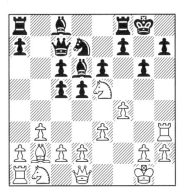

White to Play

1042) □ **C.McNab** ■ **S.Brunello**
Edinburgh (rapid) 2007

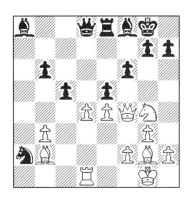

White to Play

1040) □ **R.Tozer** ■ **R.Palliser**
Doncaster 2005

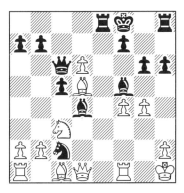

Black to Play

1043) □ **D.Trifunovic** ■ **H.Koch**
Feffernitz 2001

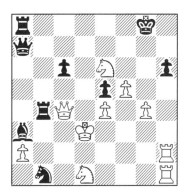

White to Play

1041) □ **D.Grassie** ■ **M.Duke**
Edinburgh 2006

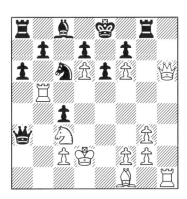

White to Play

1044) □ **S.Karjakin** ■ **L.Van Wely**
Foros 2007

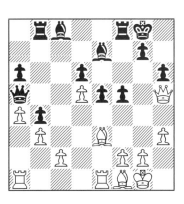

White to Play

1045) □ J.Horvath ■ A.Kosten
French League 2002

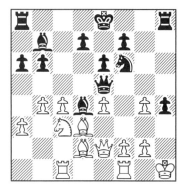

Black to Play

1046) □ L.Ftacnik ■ O.Cvitan
German League 1997

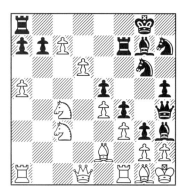

Black to Play

1047) □ M.Richter ■ G.Hertneck
German League 2007

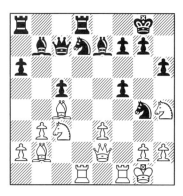

White to Play

1048) □ K.Spraggett ■ J.Speelman
Hastings 1989

White to Play

1049) □ S.Williams ■ V.Prosiriakov
Hastings 2007

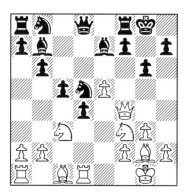

White to Play

1050) □ P.Johnson ■ R.Palliser
Hull 1997

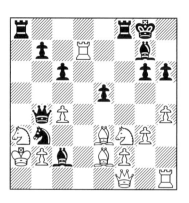

Black to Play

1051) □ B.Perenyi ■ A.Schneider
Hungary 1978

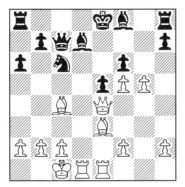

White to Play

1052) □ S.Fairbairn ■ P.Bobras
Isle of Man 2005

Black to Play

1053) □ B.Kantsler ■ I.Smirin
Jerusalem 2005

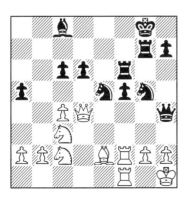

Black to Play

1054) □ A.Alekhine ■ A.Rubinstein
Karlsbad 1923

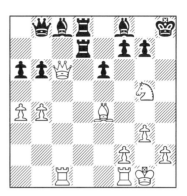

White to Play

1055) □ R.Palliser ■ R.Eames
Kenilworth 2001

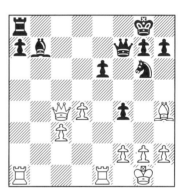

White to Play

1056) □ D.Marovic ■ T.Tsagan
Krakow 1964

White to Play

1057) ☐ **D.Mastrovasilis** ■ **B.Savic**
Litohoto 1999

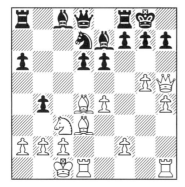

White to Play

1058) ☐ **D.King** ■ **J.Emms**
London 2003

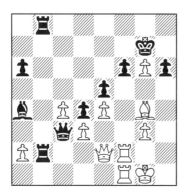

White to Play

1059) ☐ **Ed.Lasker** ■ **G.Thomas**
London 1912

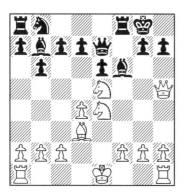

White to Play

1060) ☐ **F.N.Stephenson** ■ **M.Blaine**
London 1962

White to Play

1061) ☐ **NN** ■ **E.Mason**
London 1948

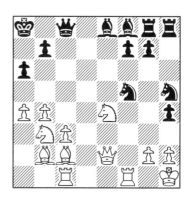

Black to Play

1062) ☐ **S.Williams** ■ **R.Palliser**
London 2000

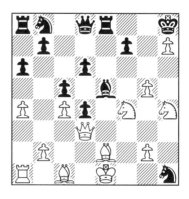

White to Play

1063) □ **Hsu Li Liang** ■ **J.Nunn**
Manila 1992

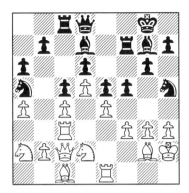

Black to Play

1064) □ **P.Leko** ■ **M.Carlsen**
Monaco (rapid) 2007

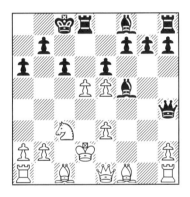

Black to Play

1065) □ **A.Morozevich** ■ **L.Aronian**
Morelia 2007

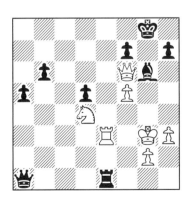

White to Play

1066) □ **S.Volkov** ■ **V.Zvjaginsev**
Moscow 2005

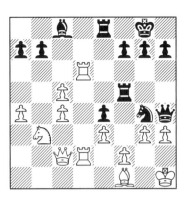

Black to Play

1067) □ **Zhou Jianchao** ■ **D.Bocharov**
Moscow 2007

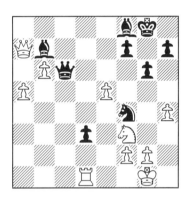

Black to Play

1068) □ **M.Sorokin** ■ **G.Nureev**
Russian Team Championship 2002

Black to Play

1069) □ **S.Karjakin** ■ **A.Rychagov**
Russian Team Championship 2007

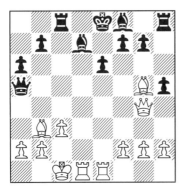

White to Play

1070) □ **B.Larsen** ■ **T.Petrosian**
Santa Monica 1966

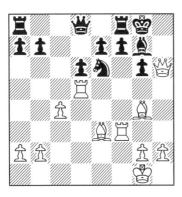

White to Play

1071) □ **A.Miles** ■ **M.Nedobora**
Seville 1994

White to Play

1072) □ **M.Ragger** ■ **A.Wirig**
Szeged 2007

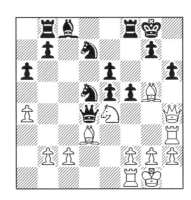

White to Play

1073) □ **L.Aroshideze** ■ **G.Nigalidze**
Tbilisi 2007

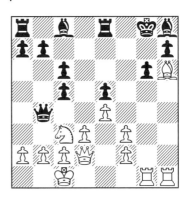

White to Play

1074) □ **E.Cordova** ■ **I.Smirin**
Turin 2006

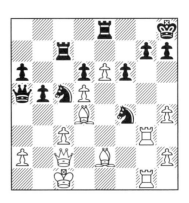

White to Play

1075) □ S.M.Gonzalez ■ M.Fernandez Juan
Valencia 1995

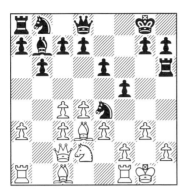

Black to Play

1076) □ V.Georgiev ■ D.Jakovenko
Wijk aan Zee 2007

Black to Play

1077) □ D.Karatorossian ■ T.Nalbandian
Yerevan 2007

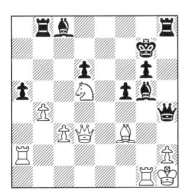

White to Play

1078) □ Li Chao ■ Wang Hao
Yerevan 2006

White to Play

1079) □ T.L.Petrosian ■ Ara.Minasian
Yerevan 2007

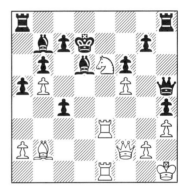

White to Play

1080) □ B.Marshall ■ P.Hopwood
York 2002

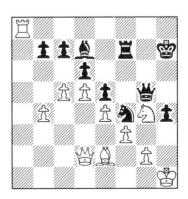

Black to Play

7: Ten tests

So has this work improved your tactical eye? I certainly believe that it should have done, but it's now time to check just how far you've advanced while reading (or rereading) this work. Ten tests now follow with points available for each position. Tot up your score as you work your way through each set of twelve puzzles and then compare your total with the table below.

20-22	Sure you're not a Grandmaster or International Master?
17-19	Strong club player.
14-16	Making progress towards the top end of your club.
11-13	Average club player.
8-10	Starting to grasp some of the essentials.
5-7	Beginning to progress after recently taking up the game.
0-4	Reread this book!

Test One

1081) □ **D.Rodriguez** ■ **S.Polgar**
Tunja 1989

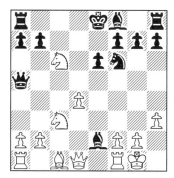

Black to Play

1082) □ **D.Bronstein** ■ **G.Ilivitzki**
Moscow 1948

White to Play

1083) □ **D.Adams** ■ **R.Palliser**
York 1999

Black to Play

1084) □ **A.Baburin** ■ **R.Palliser**
British League 2004

White to Play

1085) □ **R.Palliser** ■ **D.Hotham**
Hull 1994

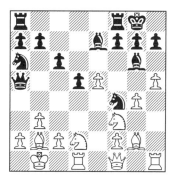

Black to Play

1086) □ **P.Gower** ■ **P.Hopwood**
York 2001

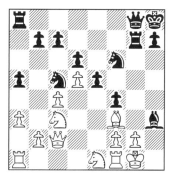

Black to Play

1087) □ **C.McNab** ■ **J.Sherwin**
British League 2003

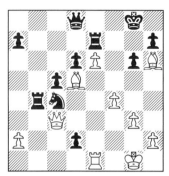

White to Play

1088) □ **R.Ziatdinov** ■ **V.Kotronias**
Cork 2005

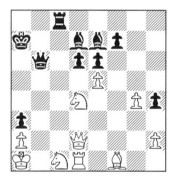

Black to Play

1089) □ **I.Berzina** ■ **D.Ciuksyte**
Tallinn (rapid) 2006

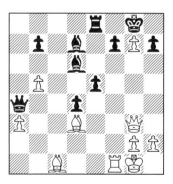

White to Play

1090) □ **S.Schulz** ■ **E.Kulovana**
Dresden 2007

Black to Play

1091) □ **I.Zakharevich** ■ **E.Ovod**
St Petersburg 2002

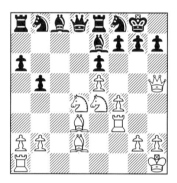

White to Play

1092) □ **J.Cox** ■ **L.Trent**
Southend 2007

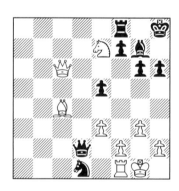

White to Play

Test Two

1093)   □ **L.Aronian** ■ **P.Svidler**
Moscow 2006

Black to Play

1094)   □ **P.Bielby** ■ **S.Smith**
correspondence 2000

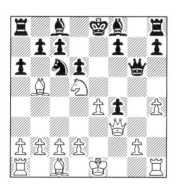

Black to Play

1095)   □ **J.Parkin** ■ **R.Palliser**
London 1993

Black to Play

1096)   □ **S.Levitsky** ■ **F.Marshall**
Breslau 1912

Black to Play

1097)   □ **A.Adorjan** ■ **Z.Ribli**
Budapest 1979

White to Play

1098)   □ **D.B.Lund** ■ **J.Rowson**
British League 1999

White to Play

1099) □ **T.Abergel** ■ **D.Tebb**
British League 2003

White to Play

1100) □ **C.Frostick** ■ **N.Miller**
British League 2004

Black to Play

1101) □ **A.Cullen** ■ **L.Varnam**
British League 2005

Black to Play

1102) □ **A.Slinger** ■ **P.Rooney**
Bradford 2006

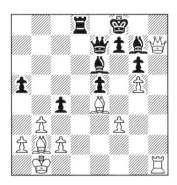

White to Play

1103) □ **Z.Zhao** ■ **J.Markos**
Athens 2001

White to Play

1104) □ **C.Cooley** ■ **N.Noden**
British League 2007

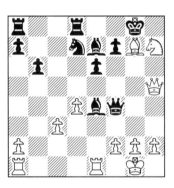

White to Play

Test Three

1105) ☐ **P.O'Neill** ■ **P.Hopwood**
York 2000

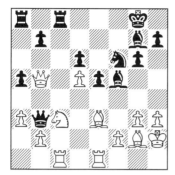

Black to Play

1106) ☐ **V.Balbashova** ■ **A.Sulejmanova**
Evpatoria 2007

Black to Play

1107) ☐ **R.Alonso** ■ **C.Claros Egea**
Lorca 2005

White to Play

1108) ☐ **Reiner** ■ **W.Steinitz**
Vienna 1860

Black to Play

1109) ☐ **D.Bronstein** ■ **C.Kottnauer**
Prague 1946

White to Play

1110) ☐ **A.Karpov** ■ **V.Malaniuk**
Moscow 1988

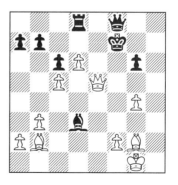

White to Play

1111) □ **M.Turner** ■ **J.Mestel**
British League 2000

Black to Play

1112) □ **P.Sowray** ■ **R.Palliser**
Oxford 2003

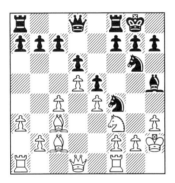

Black to Play

1113) □ **A.Potts** ■ **T.Rendle**
British League 2004

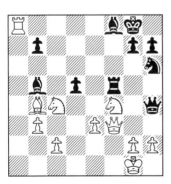

White to Play

1114) □ **A.Jones** ■ **J.Gallagher**
Lugano 2007

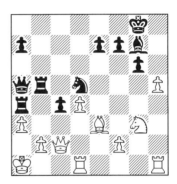

Black to Play

1115) □ **V.Anand** ■ **L.Van Wely**
Monaco (blindfold) 2007

White to Play

1116) □ **L.Aronian** ■ **G.Papp**
Athens 2001

White to Play

Test Four

1117) □ **E.Schon** ■ **W.Egan**
Tuggeranong 2006

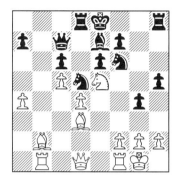

White to Play

1118) □ **P.Mahesh Chandran** ■ **P.Vavrak**
Dallas 2004

White to Play

1119) □ **Lin Zhigen** ■ **R.Hvistendahl**
Tuggeranong 2007

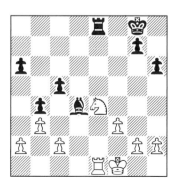

White to Play

1120) □ **Z.Izoria** ■ **A.Heimann**
Philadelphia 2006

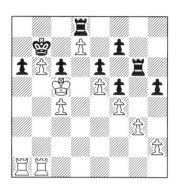

White to Play

1121) □ **A.Samedov** ■ **M.Kirikova**
Moscow 2007

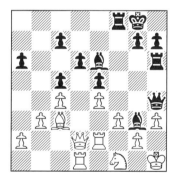

Black to Play

1122) □ **A.Kolev** ■ **J.Hernando Rodrigo**
La Laguna 2007

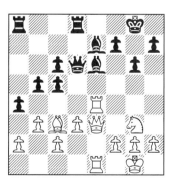

White to Play

1123) □ E.Grivas ■ A.Hrisostomidis
Halkidiki 2007

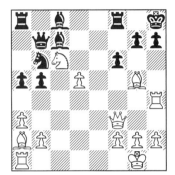

White to Play

1124) □ G.Pitl ■ B.Savchenko
Dresden 2007

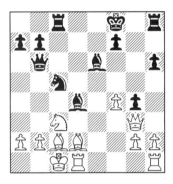

Black to Play

1125) □ I.Sokolov ■ I.Saric
Bosnian Team Championship 2007

White to Play

1126) □ S.Pucher ■ N.Gerard
Nancy 2007

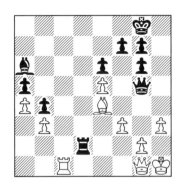

Black to Play

1127) □ R.Palliser ■ J.Burnett
Doncaster 2006

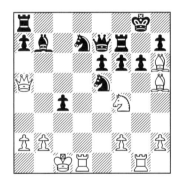

White to Play

1128) □ M.Euwe ■ R.Reti
Amsterdam 1920

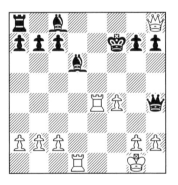

Black to Play

Test Five

1129) □ U.Von Herman ■ H.Tabatt
Koenigshofen 2007

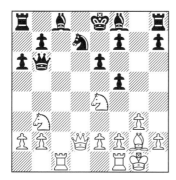

White to Play

1130) □ A.Pomar Salamanca ■ L.Liljedahl
Gothenburg 1971

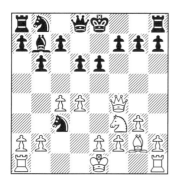

White to Play

1131) □ M.Ferguson ■ P.Wallace
British League 2005

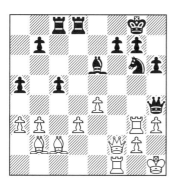

White to Play

1132) □ H.Stadt ■ K.Roehrl
Hockenheim 2007

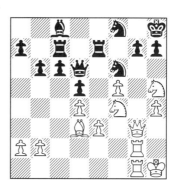

White to Play

1133) □ A.Alekhine ■ S.Reshevsky
Kemeri 1937

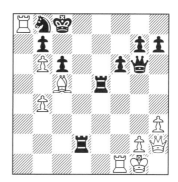

White to Play

1134) □ C.Morrison ■ M.Basman
Manchester 1981

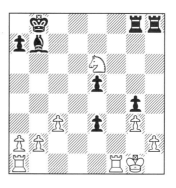

Black to Play

1135) □ **M.Cebalo** ■ **R.Aleksic**
Bizovac 2007

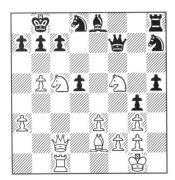

White to Play

1136) □ **K.Spraggett** ■ **M.Hernandez Garcia**
Seville 2007

White to Play

1137) □ **P.Svidler** ■ **S.Tiviakov**
Wijk aan Zee 2007

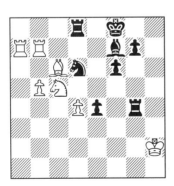

White to Play

1138) □ **W.Cnossen** ■ **G.Regniers**
Belgian League 2006

Black to Play

1139) □ **F.N.Stephenson** ■ **K.Neat**
Middlesbrough 1972

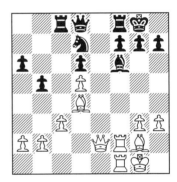

White to Play

1140) □ **A.Karpov** ■ **I.Csom**
Bad Lauterberg 1977

White to Play

Test Six

1141) □ **M.Vanderbeeken** ■ **C.Flear**
Cannes 2007

Black to Play

1142) □ **R.Palliser** ■ **R.Westra**
Doncaster 2006

White to Play

1143) □ **D.Dvirnyy** ■ **A.Pomaro**
Verona 2007

White to Play

1144) □ **G.Morris** ■ **R.Burton**
Guernsey 2002

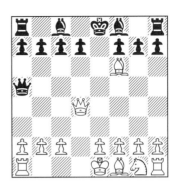

White to Play

1145) □ **C.Gibson** ■ **D.Cork**
British League 2006

White to Play

1146) □ **S.Narayanan** ■ **V.Ikonnikov**
Hastings 2006

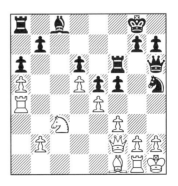

Black to Play

1147) □ **P.Szakolczai** ■ **A.Okara**
Budapest 2006

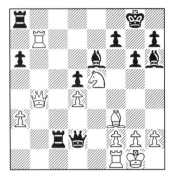

Black to Play

1150) □ **V.Sareen** ■ **R.Palliser**
Isle of Man 2005

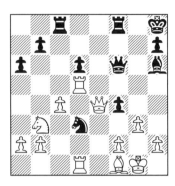

Black to Play

1148) □ **D.Bronstein** ■ **B.Ratner**
Moscow 1945

White to Play

1151) □ **V.Bologan** ■ **R.Vaganian**
Fuegen 2006

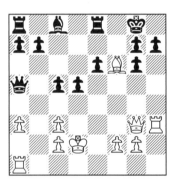

White to Play

1149) □ **C.McNab** ■ **P.Gayson**
British League 2002

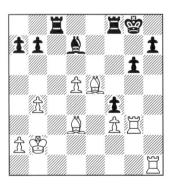

White to Play

1152) □ **P.Negi** ■ **E.Hermansson**
Malmo 2007

White to Play

Test Seven

1153) ☐ K.Berbatov ■ P.Suuronen
Campillos 2007

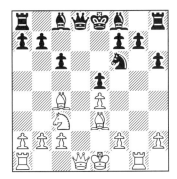

White to Play

1154) ☐ E.Repkova ■ P.Vlkovic
Triesen 2007

White to Play

1155) ☐ E.Akatova ■ V.Nebolsina
Sochi 2007

Black to Play

1156) ☐ A.Lukovnikov ■ S.Bezgodova
Voronezh 2007

Black to Play

1157) ☐ J.Ehlvest ■ M.Illescas Cordoba
Logrono 1991

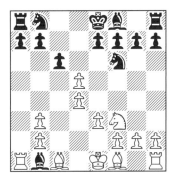

White to Play

1158) ☐ A.Brown ■ M.Hardman
British League 2007

White to Play

1159) □ **L.Debbage** ■ **R.Palliser**
Stoke on Trent 1994

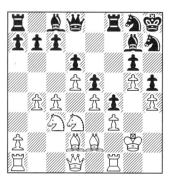

Black to Play

1160) □ **J.L.Weller** ■ **B.Clarke**
Halifax (rapid) 2006

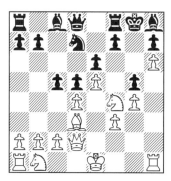

White to Play

1161) □ **V.Cmilyte** ■ **E.Atalik**
Dresden 2007

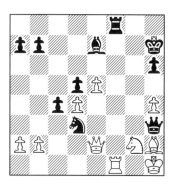

Black to Play

1162) □ **G.Rotlewi** ■ **A.Rubinstein**
Lodz 1907

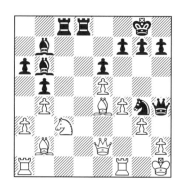

Black to Play

1163) □ **L.Evans** ■ **B.Larsen**
Dallas 1957

Black to Play

1164) □ **B.Spassky** ■ **M.Tal**
Montreal 1979

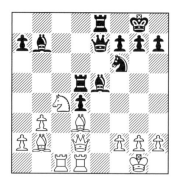

Black to Play

Test Eight

1165) □ **O.Hindle** ■ **A.Horton**
Birmingham 1961

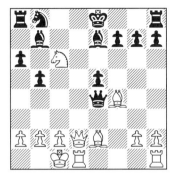

White to Play

1166) □ **R.Kynoch** ■ **S.Hogg**
Glenrothes 2005

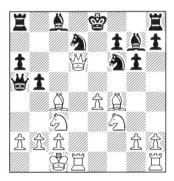

White to Play

1167) □ **G.Neave** ■ **D.Bryson**
Edinburgh 2006

Black to Play

1168) □ **G.Ballon** ■ **S.Meenakshi**
Triesen 2007

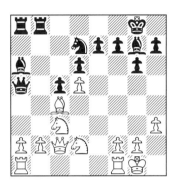

Black to Play

1169) □ **R.Irizanin** ■ **D.Sarenac**
Belgrade 2007

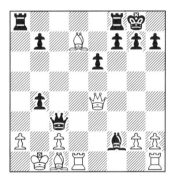

Black to Play

1170) □ **E.Rozentalis** ■ **D.Preuss**
Cappelle la Grande 2007

Black to Play

1171) □ **R.Palliser** ■ **D.Howell**
Cork 2005

Black to Play

1172) □ **J.Valmana Canto** ■ **T.Eggleston**
Swansea 2006

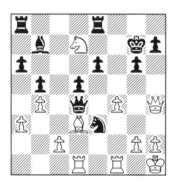

White to Play

1173) □ **V.Zheleznov** ■ **A.Vovk**
Ukrainian Team Championship 2007

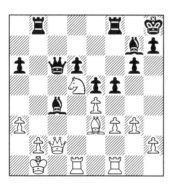

Black to Play

1174) □ **A.Hunt** ■ **D.Howell**
British League 2005

Black to Play

1175) □ **K.Spraggett** ■ **P.Llaneza Vega**
San Sebastian 2007

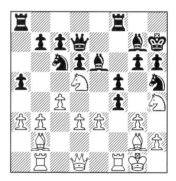

White to Play

1176) □ **J.Smeets** ■ **Bu Xiangzhi**
Wijk aan Zee 2007

Black to Play

Test Nine

1177) ☐ **O.Bernstein** ■ **J.Capablanca**
Moscow 1914

Black to Play

1180) ☐ **G.Cooper** ■ **J.Smith**
British League 2006

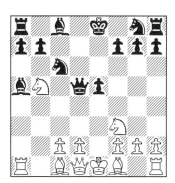

White to Play

1178) ☐ **K.Smallbone** ■ **J.Cliffe**
Wantage 2000

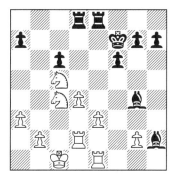

White to Play

1181) ☐ **V.Ivanchuk** ■ **L.Van Wely**
Monaco (rapid) 2007

White to Play

1179) ☐ **R.Donner** ■ **F.N.Stephenson**
Gisborough 2001

Black to Play

1182) ☐ **H.Lehtinen** ■ **K.Kaiju**
Finnish League 2007

White to Play

1183) □ **V.Kramnik** ■ **P.Svidler**
Dortmund 1998

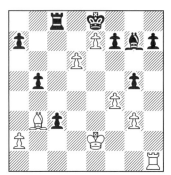

White to Play

1184) □ **V.Onischuk** ■ **M.Kravtsiv**
Lviv 2007

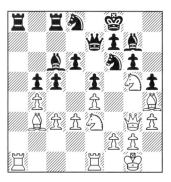

White to Play

1185) □ **M.Coleman** ■ **G.Simms**
Tulsa 2007

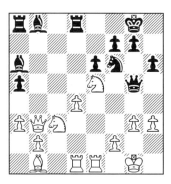

White to Play

1186) □ **T.Taylor** ■ **T.Mirabile**
Foxwoods 2007

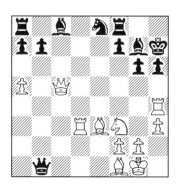

White to Play

1187) □ **G.Lisitsin** ■ **V.Ragozin**
Leningrad 1934

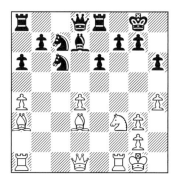

White to Play

1188) □ **A.Alekhine** ■ **M.Prat**
Paris simul 1913

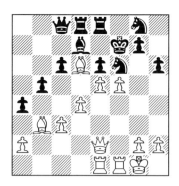

White to Play

Test Ten

1189) ☐ **R.Palliser** ■ **P.Davies**
Doncaster 1998

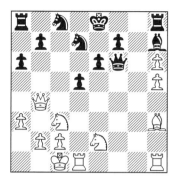

White to Play

1190) ☐ **J.Bonilla Guzman** ■ **R.Michelmann**
Bad Homburg 2005

Black to Play

1191) ☐ **W.Arluck** ■ **J.Benjamin**
Parsippany 2007

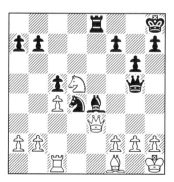

Black to Play

1192) ☐ **N.Katte** ■ **E.Zweschper**
Dresden 2007

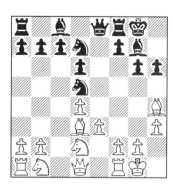

Black to Play

1193) ☐ **M.Granados Gomez** ■ **D.Larino Nieto**
Torrelavega 2007

White to Play

1194) ☐ **D.Navara** ■ **R.Ponomariov**
Wijk aan Zee 2007

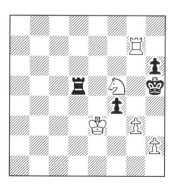

White to Play

1195) ☐ **L.Milman** ■ **J.Rukavina**
Pula 2007

White to Play

1196) ☐ **G.Meier** ■ **M.Saltaev**
German League 2007

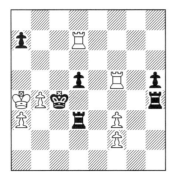

White to Play

1197) ☐ **A.Pashikian** ■ **A.Yegiazarian**
Yerevan 2007

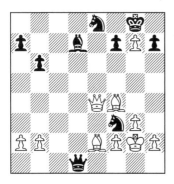

Black to Play

1198) ☐ **L.Portisch** ■ **B.Berger**
Amsterdam 1964

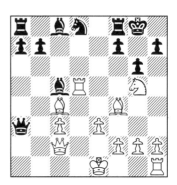

White to Play

1199) ☐ **T.Sammalvuo** ■ **J.Smeets**
Gausdal 2004

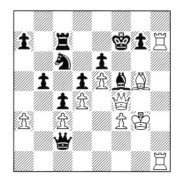

White to Play

1200) ☐ **R.Palliser** ■ **R.Dineley**
British League 2001

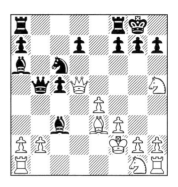

White to Play

8: Solutions

Chapter One

1) Andres Gonzalez-De la Villa Garcia
1 ♖a7! exploits the weakness of Black's back rank to pick up the a-pawn.

2) Yermolinsky-Kurosaki
1 ♘f7+! 1-0
Black's queen is lost after 1...♖xf7 2 ♕xc7.

3) Esen-Demirel
1 ♗xa6! exploits the pin down the c-file to win a pawn.

4) Mortola-Scanferla
1...♕xg1+! 0-1
It's mate after 2 ♖xg1 ♖e1+ 3 ♖xe1 ♖xe1#.

5) Fedorov-Mamedjarova
1 ♘g6+! 1-0
It's mate after 1...♖xg6 2 ♕xh7#.

6) Khudaverdieva-Miezis
1...♘h3+! 0-1
White's queen is lost.

7) Baudson-Gil
1 ♗xa7! netted a pawn in view of 1...♖xa7? 2 ♗xc6 after which Black must give up a piece on d7 since 2...♖xd8? fails to 3 ♖xd8#.

8) Damjanovic-Panic
1 ♘xg6! fxg6 2 ♖xe6 wins a pawn.

9) Mitrovic-Mihajlovic
1...♖xc2! sees Black win a piece in view of 2 ♔xc2 ♘xd4+ and 3...♘xf3.

10) Emms-Burgess
1 b4! 1-0
White wins a piece and gains a crushing attack after 1...♕xb4 2 ♘xe5.

11) Quinn-Lyell
Black wins a piece with **1...♖xc1! 2 ♖xc1 ♕xf4+ 3 ♔h3 ♕xc1 0-1**

12) Simons-Noyce
1 ♗c6! 1-0
White wins the queen in view of 1...♕xc6 2 ♕xf7#.

13) Soszynski-Stevenson
1...♗xf2+! 2 ♗xf2 ♖xd1 wins the exchange.

14) Ivanov-Sanduleac
1 ♖xh7+! 1-0
It's mate with 1...♔xh7 2 ♕h4+ ♕h6 3 ♘g5+ ♔h8 4 ♕xh6#.

15) Vadja-K.Haznedaroglu
1 ♖xe6! 1-0
Black must give up his queen to keep g7 defended.

16) Galyas-Wilke
1 ♕xh7+! 1-0
It's mate with 1...♘xh7 2 ♘g6#.

17) Farago-Gretarsson
1...♘xa3! wins a pawn in view of 2 bxa3 ♕xc3.

18) Drozdovskij-V.Georgiev
1 ♗xf7+! ♖xf7 2 ♖xb8+ wins a pawn.

19) Rrhioua-Debray
1...♘f3+! 0-1
Mate follows with 2 ♕xf3 ♕g1#.

20) Hylands-Uddin
1 ♗h6! 1-0
It's mate on g7 or on h7 after 1...gxh6 2 ♕xh7#.

21) Riazantsev-Galstian
1 ♗xg6! 1-0
Mate follows.

22) Abdul-Murshed
1 ♖xb7! wins either a rook or queen for rook: **1...♕xf2+** (or 1...♖xb7 2 ♕d8#, while 1...♕a4 fails to the mating 2 ♖b8+) **2 ♔h2 1-0**

23) Reefat-Abdul
1 ♘g6+! 1-0
It's mate after 1...hxg6 2 ♖h1#.

24) Graf-Gasthofer
1...♕h2+ 2 ♔f1 ♕h1+! 0-1
It's mate with 3 ♘xh1 ♖xh1#.

25) Hafenstein-Brunello
1...♗xh3! wins a key pawn since 2 gxh3 allows 2...♕g6+ 3 ♘g4 ♘xh3+ 4 ♔h2 ♕xg4.

26) Savickas-Hunt
1 ♖1a7+! ♕xa7 2 ♖xa7+ ♔xa7 3 ♕a5+ ♔b7 4 ♕xb5+ 1-0
White emerges queen for rook ahead.

27) Erdogdu-David
1...♕xh3+! 0-1
It's mate after 2 ♖xh3 ♖g1# and 2 ♔e1 ♕xh1+ 3 ♔d2 ♕xa1 only delays the inevitable.

28) Vaganian-Siebrecht
1 ♘xg6+! 1-0
It's mate after 1...hxg6 2 ♕h3+ ♗h6 3 ♕xh6#.

29) Durarbeyli-Damljanovic
1...♕xf3+! 0-1
Black wins a piece after 2 ♔xf3 ♘d4+ and 3...♘xc2.

30) Shalimov-Bagrationi
1 ♘c6! bxc6 2 ♕xb8 wins the exchange.

31) Gozzoli-Reinhart
1 ♘h6+! 1-0
Black's queen is lost.

32) Holland-Rough
1...♘xf2! 2 ♔xf2 (or 2 ♖xf2 ♖xg3) 2...♗c5+ 3 ♗e3 ♗xe3+ 4 ♔xe3 ♖xg3+ wins a pawn.

33) Garcia-Strand
1 ♗xf7+! 1-0
It's mate with 1...♔xf7 2 ♕h7+ ♔f8 3 ♖f6#.

34) Helin-Manetto
1 ♘c7+! wins a rook since 1...♕xc7? fails to 2 ♖be1+ ♔d8 3 ♕e7+ ♔c8 4 ♕xf8+.

35) Vea-Rasch
1 ♗xf7+! wins a pawn in view of 1...♖xf7? 2 ♘g5.

36) Wallace-Dekker
1 ♘f6+! ♗xf6 2 ♕xh7# 1-0

37) Westra-Palliser
1 ♖xf5! 1-0
White wins a rook after 1...♖xf5 2 ♕xg4+.

38) Wilman-Tate
1 ♕xc6! 1-0
White wins a piece in view of 1...♕xc6 2 ♘e7+ and 3 ♘xc6.

39) Salimbeni-Hutchinson
1...♗h2+! 2 ♔xh2 ♕xf1 wins the exchange.

40) Schut-Bensdorp
1...♖xd2+! 0-1
Black emerges a piece ahead after 2 ♔xd2 ♗b4+ and 3...♗xa5.

41) Bogorads-Jahr
1 ♖xf7+! 1-0
Black either loses his rook or emerges a piece down after 1...♖xf7 2 ♕xf7+ ♔xf7 3 ♘g5+ and 4 ♘xe4.

42) Gladyszev-Kidambi
1...♖h1+! 0-1
White cannot avoid losing his bishop and queen.

43) Siebrecht-Szieberth
1 ♘xd6! wins a clear pawn in view of the skewering 1...♕xd6? 2 ♗f4.

44) Zimmerman-Adams
1 ♕xd4+! 1-0
Mate follows with 1...♖xd4 2 ♖e8#.

45) May-Hecht
1...♘xa2! wins a pawn in view of 2 ♕xa2 ♕xc1+.

46) Nikolaeva-Vozovic
1...♖xh3+! 0-1
Mate follows with 2 gxh3 ♕g1#.

47) Vysochin-Sergeev
1 ♖xf7+! 1-0
White wins a piece after 1...♔xf7 2 ♘xg5+ ♔e7 3 ♘xh3.

48) Balanovskij-Kusnetsov
1...♘g3+! 0-1
White must give up his queen to avoid 2 hxg3 ♕h6#.

49) Kurajica-Schneider Sanchez
1 ♗xh7+! ♔h8? (better is 1...♔xh7, although after 2 ♕d3+ ♔g8 3 ♕xb5 White is the exchange ahead) **2 ♗d3 1-0**
Black cannot both save his rook and prevent mate.

50) Alonso Contreras-Trujillo Delgado
1 ♗xh6! wins a pawn in view of 1...♗xh6? 2 ♘f6+ and 3 ♘xd7.

51) Moreto Quintana-Koziak
1...♕h2+! 0-1
It's mate after 2 ♔xh2 g1♕#.

52) Hindle-Puig Puildo
1 ♕xg5! 1-0
White decisively threatens 2 ♕h4+ and 3 ♖xh7+ and, of course, 1...♕xg5 fails to 2 ♖xh7#.

53) Ficco-Godena
1...♖xa2! 0-1
Black picks up a second pawn and forks the white rooks after 2 ♖xa2 ♗xc4.

54) Martin del Campo-Alonso Arteaga
White wins the exchange: **1 ♘b6 1-0**

55) Kosten-Marchal
1 ♖d8+! 1-0
It's mate after 1...♕xd8 2 ♕xc6# or 1...♗xd8 2 ♕c8#.

56) Touret-Petkov
1...♘f3! 0-1
It's mate after 2 gxf3 (or 2 h3 ♗xh3! 3 g3 ♕h5) 2...♗xf3+ 3 ♔g1 ♕g4#.

57) Guliyev-Schweitzer
1 ♗xf7! ♕a5 (the main point is that 1...♘xf7 2 ♘de6+ ♗xe6 3 ♘xe6+ wins the black queen)
2 ♗d5 saw White pick up a key pawn and gain a large advantage.

58) Chudinovskih-Nikolenko
1 ♖h8+! ♔xh8 2 ♕h3+ ♔g8 3 ♕xe6+ 1-0
It's mate with 3...♔h7 4 ♖h2#.

59) Okara-Yuganova
1 ♕d8+! 1-0
It's mate after 1...♖xd8 2 ♖xd8+ ♔g7 3 h6#.

60) Venevtsev-Mozharov
1...♕xf3! 0-1
Black wins a rook since it's mate after 2 gxf3 ♖xh2#.

61) Bronstein-Koblencs
1 ♘e6! 1-0
Black must lose the exchange since 1...fxe6 2 ♕xf8+ mates.

62) Lasker-Steinitz
1 ♖g4! 1-0
White has an easy exchange-up win after 1...♖xh7 (or 1...♔d7 2 ♘f6+ ♔e6 3 ♖g8 ♗xf6 4 ♖xh8) 2 ♖g8+ ♔d7 3 ♘f6+ ♔d6 4 ♘xh7 ♗xh7 5 ♖d8+.

63) Aguilar-Leskovar
1...♖xh2+! 2 ♔xh2 ♕h6+ 3 ♔g1 ♕g5+ 0-1
It's mate on g2.

64) 'Andrei21'-Palliser
1 ♕b7! 1-0
Black can't prevent mate on g7 since 1...f5 2 ♖e5 is no help.

65) Palliser-'Perparim3'
1 ♕xc2! 1-0
White wins a rook in view of 1...♗xc2 2 ♖e8#.

66) Bruce-Palliser
1 ♖f8+! ♔xf8 2 a8♕+ ♔g7 and now the simplest win was 3 ♕b7+ ♔g6 4 ♕c6+ and 5 ♕xc4.

67) Smallbone-Terry
1 ♘f6+! 1-0
Black loses the exchange after 1...♗xf6 2 ♕d5+.

68) Chua-Izoria
1...♕xd4+! 0-1
Mate follows in view of 2 ♕xd4 ♖e1#.

69) Katz-Tomasko
1 ♖xh7+! ♔xh7 2 ♕h5+ ♔g7 3 ♕g6+ ♔h8 (or 3...♔f8 4 ♕f7#) **4 ♕h6# 1-0**

70) Hylapov-Lintchevski
1 ♗xh7+! ♔f8 (Black loses the exchange after 1...♘xh7 2 ♖xe8+) **2 ♖xe8+ ♘xe8 3 ♗f5** left
White a pawn up.

71) Nickel-Deruda
1 ♖h8+! 1-0
Black loses his queen.

72) Markus-Doric
1 ♗xb7! wins a pawn in view of Black's vulnerable back rank.

73) Hempson-Palliser
1...♘xd4! 0-1
Black wins a second pawn after 2 ♘xd4 ♗xc5 3 ♘f3 ♗xf2+.

74) Volokitin-Bareev
1 ♖h7+! 1-0
Mate follows with 1...♔xh7 2 ♕xf7+ ♔h6 3 ♖h1+ ♔g5 4 ♕f4#.

75) Tyomkin-Gaprindashvili
1 ♕xf5! 1-0
White wins the rook since 1...♘xf5? allows 2 ♖e8#.

76) Rodriguez-Needleman
1 ♖f7+! 1-0
It's mate with 1...♖xf7 2 ♘e8#.

77) Corrales-De la Paz
The pin down the e-file costs White his queen after **1...♘d3+! 0-1**

78) Morozevich-Movsesian
1...♘f1+! 2 ♔h1 ♘xh2 0-1
3...♘xf3+ is threatened and White can't avoid mate since 3 ♖xh2 fails to 3...♕xf3+.

79) Ward-Palliser
1 ♖xe8+! 1-0
White queens after 1...♔xe8 2 fxg7.

80) Palliser-Houska
1 ♗d8+! 1-0
Black loses her queen after 1...♔xd8 2 ♕xb6+.

81) Gavrilov-Perez Garcia
1 ♖xb7+! ♔c8 (and not 1...♔xb7? 2 ♘d6+ ♔b8 3 ♘xc4) **2 ♖b3** nets a key pawn.

82) Ambartsumova-Kochetkova
1 ♗xh6! wins a pawn in view of 1...gxh6 2 ♕xf6.

83) Bogdanov-Rodkin
1...♖xa7! 2 ♖xa7 ♗c5+ forks to win a piece.

84) Eliseev-Kurilov
1 ♖xh7+! 1-0
It's mate after 1...♔xh7 2 ♕xg6+ ♔h8 3 ♕h7#.

85) Guzenko-Klobukov
1 ♕a6+! bxa6 2 ♖a7# 1-0

86) Lomako-Airapetian
1...♗xg2+! 0-1
It's mate on the back rank, although also good and actually mating a move faster is 1...♕xg2+! 2 ♖xg2 ♖e1+.

87) Vunder-Zacurdajev
1...♘f3+! 2 gxf3 ♕g6+ 3 ♔h1 ♕h5 0-1
Mate follows down the h-file.

88) Palliser-Seymour
1 ♖xh5! and White won a piece in view of 1...gxh5? 2 ♕g5 and 3 ♕xg7#.

89) Zimmermann-Lener
1 ♖xe6! wins a piece in view of 1...♔xe6 2 ♘xc5+ and 3 ♘xb7.

90) Mordue-Dilleigh
1 ♗xh7+! ♔xh7 2 ♕d3+ ♔g8 3 ♕xd6 won a pawn.

91) Starostits-Bezler
1 ♗xc7! wins a pawn in view of Black's back-rank weakness.

92) San Segundo Carrillo-Wojtaszek
1...♖h1+! 0-1
It's mate after 2 ♔xh1 (or 2 ♔g3 ♕g4#) 2...♕f1+ 3 ♔h2 ♕xg2#.

93) Karpov-Stojanovic
1 ♕xh6+! gxh6 2 ♖g8# 1-0

94) Golovin-Ivanov
1 ♖xg7+! ♖xg7 2 ♘xf6+ 1-0
Black can only give up his queen to delay mate.

95) Walas-Gajewski
1...♗xd4 2 ♕xd4 ♘b3! wins the exchange on a1.

96) Rhodes-Hopwood
Black wins White's rook with a common and important tactic: **1...♖g1! 2 ♖xa2** (otherwise the pawn queens) **2...♖g2+ 3 ♔e3 ♖xa2**.

97) Rogerson-Palliser
1...♖xb4! 0-1
Black emerges a piece ahead after 2 ♖xb4 ♗a5 3 ♔e2 ♗xb4.

98) Cloudsdale-Hopwood
1...♖xc3! 0-1
Black wins a piece in view of 2 ♕xc3 ♕xe2.

99) Hopwood-Lockwood
1 ♖xd6! **♕b8** (capturing the rook costs Black material after 1...♕xd6 2 ♕xa8+ ♔e7 3 ♕xh8 and even the relatively best 1...0-0 2 ♖xd8 ♖fxd8 leaves White's extra queen and pawn somewhat superior to Black's rook and bishop) **2 ♕d7+ ♔f8 3 ♖dc6** and White won the black queen and shortly the game.

100) Pecnik-Galoic
1 ♕xh6+! 1-0
It's mate after 1...♔xh6 2 ♖h3+ ♔g7 3 ♖h7#.

Chapter Two

101) Pupols-Adamson
1...♘xh3+! 2 gxh3? (or 2 ♔f1 ♘xf2 3 ♕xf2 ♖c8 with an extra pawn and some advantage) **2...♕xh3 3 ♕e2 ♗h2+ 4 ♔h1 ♗f4+ 5 ♔g1 ♖d5** gave Black an overwhelming attack.

102) Yusupov-Reuss
1 ♘xg6+! ♗xg6 2 d6 ♔g8 3 d7 1-0
The d-pawn costs Black his queen.

103) Fontein-Euwe
It's mate on the back rank: **1...♖c1! 0-1**

104) Campbell-Beggi
1 ♘xf7! 1-0
The threat of discovered check is rather powerful after 1...♕c7 (it's mate after 1...♔xf7? 2 ♕e6+ ♔f8 3 ♘g5 ♘ce5 4 ♘xh7#) 2 ♕e6.

105) De Marco-Bashkite
1...♖xg2! 2 ♕xd2 (or 2 ♔xg2 ♘f4+ winning White's queen) **2...♕h2# 0-1**

106) Moiseenko-Ismagambetov
1...♗xg2! 0-1
White must lose his queen after 2 ♗xg2 ♘f3+ since 3 ♗xf3 fails to 3...gxf3+ and 4...♕g2#.

107) Zacarias-Valiente
1 ♗xa6! removes a key pawn, after which **1...♖b1+** (or 1...♕xa6 2 ♕xb2 with an overwhelming attack and an extra exchange) **2 ♔h2 ♕b2 3 ♗b7+!** gave White a crushing attack.

108) Skalkotas-Kotrotsos
1 ♖h8+! 1-0
It's mate on h8: 1...♘xh8 2 ♕xh8+ ♗xh8 3 ♖xh8#.

109) Ni Hua-Palliser
Black can prise open the a-file with decisive effect: **1...♖xa3! 2 bxa3 ♕xa3 3 ♖d4 cxd4 4 ♕b2 ♕a5! 0-1**
5...d3 follows.

110) Hoelzl-Knoll
Black is defenceless down the h-file: **1 ♗xh7+! ♔h8** (or 1...♔xh7 2 ♕h5+ ♔g8 3 ♖h3 and mates) **2 ♕h5 1-0**

111) Teske-Stangl
1 ♗xg6+! ♘xg6 (or 1...♔g8 2 ♘f7 ♕b6 3 ♕xb6 ♖xb6 4 ♘xd8 ♘xg6 5 ♖xd7 with an extra rook) **2 ♘xd7 ♖xd7 3 ♖xd7+ 1-0**
Black's queen is lost after 3...♕xd7 4 ♖c7.

112) Popovic-Pinter
1...♗xg2! 2 ♘xg2 ♘xh3+ 3 ♔f1 ♕h2 0-1
It's mate after 4 ♖xe7 ♕g1+ 5 ♔e2 ♕xf2#.

113) Narciso Dublan-Mecking
1 ♗xh7+! ♔xh7 (or 1...♔h8 2 ♕xd5 with two extra pawns) **2 ♕xd5 ♗d6** (Black loses his queen after both 2...♗e6 3 ♕e4+ and 2...♗c6 3 ♕f5+, while 2...♕b6 3 ♕xd7 leaves White two pawns ahead and still with a strong attack) **3 ♕xd6 ♖xe3 4 g6+ ♔h8 5 gxf7 ♕f8 6 ♕xd7** and White's extra pawns carried the day.

114) Korchnoi-Karpov
1...♘f3+! 0-1
It's mate after 2 gxf3 (or 2 ♔h1 ♘f2#) 2...♖g6+ 3 ♔h1 ♘f2#.

115) Mamedjarova-Naiditsch
1...♕xd1+! 2 ♗xd1 ♖e1+ 3 ♕g1 ♖xg1+ 4 ♔xg1 ♘xe4 left Black a pawn up in a highly favourable ending.

116) Horvath-Seres
1 ♕xh5+! ♔g8 (it's mate after 1...gxh5 2 ♖g7+ ♔h6 3 ♗c1#) **2 ♖xg6+! 1-0**
Mate follows after 2...fxg6 3 ♕xg6+ ♔f8 4 ♗a3+.

117) Berczes-Roussel Roozmon
1 ♗xh7+! ♔xh7 2 ♕b1+ ♔g8 3 ♕xb2 wins a pawn.

118) Molano Lafuente-Conde Chijeb
1 ♖xf7+! 1-0
It's mate after 1...♖xf7 (or 1...♔h8 2 ♖h7+!) 2 ♕xg6+ ♔h8 3 ♕g8#.

119) Colom Andres-Zohaib Hassan
1...♘f2+! 0-1
Mate follows after 2 ♘xf2 ♕f3+.

120) Alshoha-El Kawabia
1 ♗xf7+! ♚h8 (1...♚xf7 2 ♘eg5+ ♚g8 3 ♕c4+ leads to a smothered mate) **2 ♗xe8** won the exchange.

121) Leenhouts-Sielecki
1 ♖xf7+! ♚xf7 2 ♕h7+ 1-0
Mate follows after 2...♚f8 (or 2...♚e6 3 ♕f5#) 3 ♗h6+.

122) Motwani-Wiersma
1 ♘xe6! 1-0
White wins the exchange on f8 since 1...dxe6? 2 ♘f7+! ♖xf7 3 ♖d8+ forces mate.

123) Hautot-Saltaev
1...♘xc3! 2 ♕xb5 (worse is 2 bxc3 ♕xb4) **2...♘xb5 3 ♖d7 ♖c8 4 ♚b1 ♖c7** saw Black pick up a pawn.

124) Radulovic-Lajthajm
1...♘e2+! forces White to give up his queen since 2 ♘xe2 allows 2...♕xg2#.

125) Rajkovic-Tadic
1...♖xg2+! 0-1
White loses his queen after 2 ♚xg2 (2 ♚h1 ♖cc2 is terminal too) 2...♘e3+.

126) Martic-Irizanin
1 ♖a8+! 1-0
It's mate after 1...♗xa8 2 ♕b8#.

127) Vasic-Zivkovic
1...♖a1! overloads White's defence of g2: **2 ♕d4** (otherwise White loses his rook since 2 ♖xa1 allows 2...♕xg2#) **2...♕xe2 0-1**
Black wins a piece.

128) Ostojic-Conic
1 ♖xf7+! ♖xf7 (or 1...♚h8 2 ♖h7#) **2 ♘e6+ ♚h8 3 ♘xd8** wins Black's queen.

129) Blackburne-Schwarz
1 ♕xf4!! ♗xf4 2 ♖xh5! 1-0
Mate follows on h8.

130) Vadja-Ivkov
1 ♗xa7+! ♘xa7 2 ♖xe6 ♗xe6 gave White a near decisive advantage of queen and pawn against Black's extra rook and knight.

131) Marholev-Morelle
1 ♕xc7+! 1-0
It's mate after 1...♚xc7 (or 1...♚e6 2 ♖e8+ ♚f5 3 ♕d7+) 2 ♖1a7#.

132) Palliser-Callis
1 ♗g5! won the black queen since **1...hxg5 2 hxg5 ♕e7** failed to **3 ♗g8+ 1-0**
Mate follows on h7.

133) Matijasevic-Bender
1...♘g3+! 0-1
White can only prevent mate by giving up far too much material with 2 hxg3 hxg3+ 3 ♗h5 ♖xh5+ 4 ♕xh5 ♘xh5.

134) Prlac-Szakolczai
1...♗xg2+! 2 ♔g1 (White loses the exchange after 2 ♖xg2 h3) **2...♗f3** left Black with a strong attack and an extra pawn.

135) Rigg-Masters
1...♘d2! undermines White down the long diagonal: **2 ♘xd2** (Black gains a mating attack after 2 ♕xd2 ♖xg2+! 3 ♔xg2 ♕g5+ 4 ♔f1 ♗xf3, while 2 e4 ♘xf3+ 3 ♔xf3 ♗xe4 4 ♖xe4 fxe4 5 ♕xe4 sees White keep g2 covered but at the cost of the exchange) **2...♗xg2! 3 ♕c3** (trying to save the queen but now it's mate) **3...♗h3+ 4 ♔h1 ♕g5 5 ♖g1 ♗g2+ 6 ♖xg2 ♕xg2# 0-1**

136) Wheeler-Dore
1 ♖xg7+! ♔xg7 2 ♕g5+ ♔h8 3 ♕h6+ ♔g8 4 ♕g6+ ♔h8 5 ♘f3 1-0
Mate follows down the h-file.

137) Barden-Wood
1 ♕xf8+! 1-0
It's mate after 1...♔xf8 2 ♖h8# or 1...♔d7 2 ♖xf7+ ♔e6 3 ♕e7+ ♔f5 4 ♗h4+ ♔g6 5 ♕f6+ ♔h5 6 ♕g5#.

138) Haslinger-Gormally
White gains a crushing attack with **1 ♖xe7!! ♖xe7 2 ♕xg5 f6** (the only defence) **3 ♕xg6+**: **3...♔h8 4 ♗xe6! ♕c7 5 ♘d5! ♗xd5 6 exd5 ♖h7 7 ♖g1 1-0**
Mate is threatened and 7...♖e7 8 b3 ♕d8 9 ♕f5 ♖h7 10 ♖g6 leaves Black stuck in a horrible bind: White will advance his pawn to d7 and then look to break through with ♕g4 and ♖g8 or ♖g7.

139) Franco-Rodriguez
1 ♕xh7+! ♔xh7 2 ♖h3+ ♗h5 3 ♖xh5# 1-0

140) Burt-Dennis
1 ♗xa6+! ♖xa6 2 ♕c7# 1-0

141) Ibbotson-Hopwood
1...♖xf3! 2 gxf3 ♗xh3 gives Black a crushing attack: **3 f4** (not the best defence, but 3 ♖e1 ♕f6 4 ♘e2 ♕xf3 5 ♘e3 d4 is horrendous too for White and even 3 ♘e2 ♕f6 4 ♕d3 leaves Black with superb attacking chances after 4...♗f5 5 ♕e3 ♗h6) **3...exf4 4 ♕xf4 ♖c4! 5 ♕f3** (White is also destroyed after 5 ♕e3 ♕h4 6 ♘e2 ♖g4+! 7 ♘g3 ♗d4 8 ♕e6+ ♔h8) **5...♕g5+ 6 ♔h1 ♖h4 0-1**

142) Byron-Hosken
1 ♗xh7+! ♔h8 (or 1...♔xh7 2 ♕h5+ ♔g8 3 ♖h3 followed by mate down the h-file) **2 ♖h3!** (much stronger than the also rather good 2 ♕h5 ♘f6 3 ♘xf7+ ♖xf7 4 ♕xf7 ♘xh7 5 ♕xe7)

2...♘f6 3 ♗g5 left White with a decisive attack.

143) Hagesaether-Greet
1...♗xh3+!! 2 ♔xh3 ♕d7+ 3 ♔g2 (or 3 ♔h2 ♗f4+ 4 ♘g3 ♘g5 5 ♕f1 ♖e1! and wins) 3...♕g4+ 4 ♘g3 (the main point of Black's combination is revealed after 4 ♔h1 ♖e5 when White is powerless against the threat of doubling on the g-file; for example, 5 ♘h2 ♘xf2+! 6 ♘xf2 ♖e1+ 7 ♘f1 ♕f3+ 8 ♔g1 ♗e3 forces mate) 4...♘xg3 5 fxg3 ♖e2+ 6 ♘f2 ♗e3 7 ♕c8+ ♕xc8 0-1

144) Kosten-Hague
1 ♘d6+! exd6 2 exd6 ♕d7 (or 2...♕d8 3 d7+ ♔f8 4 ♖he1 with a crushing position) 3 ♘e5 1-0
Black can't move his queen in view of 4 d7+ and 3...♗xe5 4 ♕xe5+ costs him the other rook.

145) Law-Gallagher
1...♗xg2+! 0-1
It's mate after 2 ♗xg2 ♕h4+ 3 ♗h3 ♕xh3#.

146) Waters-Richmond
1 ♘xh6+! gxh6 2 ♕g4+ 1-0
White has a decisive attack after 2...♘g6 (or 2...♗g5 3 fxg5 h5 4 ♕xh5 ♖d7 5 d5! – always try to invite as many pieces as possible to the party!) 3 ♗xg6 since 3...fxg6? 4 ♕xg6+ forces mate next move.

147) Coleman-D'Costa
Black collapses on g7: 1 ♖xg7! ♖xg7 2 ♖g1 ♖c7 (relatively best is 2...♘f6, although White is winning easily enough after 3 ♗xg7+ ♔e8 4 ♕g6) 3 ♖xg7 ♕xg7 4 ♕h8+ 1-0

148) Ledger-Burnett
1 ♕f6+! 1-0
It's mate after 1...gxf6 2 gxf6+ ♔f8 3 ♖h8#.

149) Shaw-Low Ying Min
1 ♖xg7+! 1-0
Mate follows with 2 ♕xh6+ and 3 ♕h8#.

150) Wise-Blackburn
1 ♘d7! (with various nasty kingside threats, including 2 ♘xf8 ♖xf8 3 ♘xg7! and 2 ♘h6+ gxh6 3 ♘xf6+) 1...h5 (White is also left with a very strong attack after 1...♗c8 2 ♘xf6+! gxf6 3 h4) 2 ♘h6+! gxh6 3 ♕f5 ♖e6 (or 3...♗g7 4 ♘xf6+ and Black must give up his queen because 4...♔h8 5 h4 ♗c8 6 ♕g6 is completely crushing) 4 ♘xf6+ ♔f7? (relatively better is 4...♖xf6 5 ♗xf6 ♔e8 6 ♗xg5 when White is 'only' the exchange ahead while retaining attacking chances) 5 ♘h7+ ♔e8 6 ♘xg5 hxg5 7 ♕xe6+ ♕e7 8 ♗g6+ 1-0

151) James-Anderton
1...♖xg2+! 0-1
It's mate after 2 ♔xg2 ♕f2+ 3 ♔h3 ♕h2#.

152) Buckley-Mitchem
1 ♖xd7! ♔xd7 2 ♕f5+ ♔d8 3 ♕xc8+! (even stronger than 3 ♖b7) 3...♔xc8 4 ♗g4+ 1-0
The raking bishops force mate with 4...f5 5 ♗xf5+ ♔d8 6 ♖b8#.

153) Flear-Ansell

The forced **1 ♖xe5! ♖xe5 2 ♘f5 ♕f6 3 ♕xg7+ ♕xg7 4 ♖xg7** sees White win g7 while maintaining a decisive pin on the long diagonal: **4...♖be8 5 ♖c7 1-0**

Black will lose at least b7 before White regains the exchange, but actually even stronger was the fiendish 5 ♖g5! with the idea of 5...♘e4 6 ♘e7! ♘xg5 7 ♗xe5#.

154) Hoffmann-Munson

1 ♗xg6! wins a key pawn in view of 1...fxg6 2 ♖xc4 ♖xc4? 3 f7+.

155) Upton-Brown

1 ♖xb7! gives White a mating attack: **1...♚xb7 2 ♕e4+ 1-0**

Mate follows with 2...♚b6 3 ♖b1+ ♚a5 4 ♕b4#.

156) Bourne-Gregory

1...♘xf2! 0-1

There's no defence down the long diagonal since 2 ♚xf2 ♕c6 3 ♖g1 fails to 3...♕f6+.

157) Emms-Ledger

1 ♘xg7!! ♚xg7 (1...♕xg7 is a better try, but after 2 ♘f5 ♕f8 – 2...♘g4!? fails to 3 ♘xg7 ♗xf2+ 4 ♕xf2! ♘xf2 5 ♘xe6 ♘xh1 6 ♘xc7 with a substantial advantage – 3 ♗h6 Black is short of a good move; for example, 3...♕c5 4 ♕g3+ ♘g4 5 ♕xg4+ ♖g6 6 ♕f3 and White has by far the stronger attack or 3...♗xf2+ 4 ♚xf2 ♘xe4+ 5 ♕xe4 ♖xh6 6 a4 ♗d7 7 ♘xh6+ ♕xh6 8 ♖ad1 with an extra exchange and some advantage) **2 ♗h6+!** (now Black must either lose his queen or allow mate) **2...♚xh6 3 ♘f5+ ♚g6 4 ♕g3+ ♚h5 5 ♕g5# 1-0**

158) Foster-Parmar

1 ♘h6+ ♚h8 2 ♕g8+! 1-0

It's smothered mate with 2...♖xg8 3 ♘hf7# or 3 ♘gf7#.

159) Gilbert-Morris

1 ♘h5+! 1-0

Mate follows with 1...gxh5 (or 1...♚h7 2 ♘ef6+ ♚h8 3 ♕h6#) 2 ♕g5+ ♚h8 3 ♕h6+ ♚g8 4 ♘f6#.

160) Mestel-Hynes

1 ♖c8+! 1-0

Mate follows on d7.

161) Rudd-Arakhamia Grant

1...♘a3+! 2 bxa3 (2 ♚a1 ♘xd4 leads to disaster on c2 or down the b-file after 3 bxa3 bxa3) **2...bxa3+ 3 ♗b5 ♘xd4 4 c4 ♘xb5 5 ♕xb6 ♖xb6 6 cxb5 ♖xb5+ 7 ♚c2 ♗xg5** left Black three pawns ahead and still with the initiative.

162) Sherwin-Hague

1...♗xh2! 0-1

Mate is forced after 2 ♖g2 (or 2 ♖xh2 ♕xf3+) 2...♗f4+ 3 ♚g1 ♕h2+.

163) Smallbone-Gunter

1 ♖xh7+! 1-0

Mate follows on h4.

164) D'Costa-Wells
1...♖xh2+! 2 ♔xh2 ♕xg3+ 3 ♔h1 ♕h3+ 4 ♔g1 ♗c5+ 0-1
5 ♕f2 ♔h8! only delays the inevitable mate.

165) Trent-Tan
1 ♖xg7! (by far the most clinical, although 1 ♘g6+ ♔h7 2 ♕e6! should also do the business)
1...♔xg7 2 ♕g3+ ♔h8 3 ♘f7+ ♔h7 4 h5 ♖g8 5 e8♕! 1-0
Mate follows on g6, g8 or h8.

166) Adams-Hennigan
1 ♘xf7! 1-0
White wins a piece after 1...0-0 (or 1...♗xf7 2 ♕xe7+ ♕xe7 3 ♖xe7+ followed by capturing
on f7 or a8) 2 ♘d6.

167) Adams-Bates
1 ♖fxf7! 1-0
Mate follows after 1...♗xb2+ 2 ♕xb2! ♖xb2 3 ♖g7#.

168) Rich-Barrett
1 ♖xg6+! fxg6 2 ♕xg6+ ♔h8 3 ♕h5+ 1-0
3...♔g8 4 f7+ decides

169) Simons-Richards
1 ♖xh6+! ♔g8 (or 1...gxh6 2 ♗d4+ ♗f6 3 ♗xf6+ and Black must give up her queen to avoid
mate) **2 ♕e6+ 1-0**
Mate follows.

170) Povah-Sisask
1 ♖xh6!! gxh6 2 ♖f6 (threatening mate beginning with 3 ♕g4+ ♔f8 4 ♘f5) **2...♔f8** (or
2...♔g7 3 ♖xh6! – also rather effective is 3 ♕f3 ♖b7 4 ♖xh6! – 3...♖g8 4 ♕h5 ♔f8 5 ♖h7 ♖a7 6
♕h6+ ♔e8 7 ♕d6 and White wins back his rook while maintaining a decisive attack) **3 ♕h5**
♕d7 4 ♘f5 ♔e8 5 ♕xh6 ♔d8 6 ♖d6 ♘b7 7 ♕f8+ 1-0
Mate is forced, although 7 ♕f6+ ♔c7 8 ♖xd7+ ♔xd7 9 ♕e7+ ♔c8 10 d6 would have been
even more clinical.

171) Cooley-Moore
Black gains a large advantage by winning the white queen with **1...♖g1+! 2 ♖xg1 ♘f2+ 3**
♕xf2 (and not 3 ♔g2?? ♗h3#) **3...♕xf2**.

172) Helbig-Palliser
1 ♘fe6! fxe6 2 ♖xf6! ♗h6! (the only try since both 2...exf6 3 ♕h7+ ♔f8 4 ♘xe6+ and 2...♗xf6
3 ♕h7+ ♔f8 4 ♘xe6+ cost Black his queen) **3 ♖xg6+!** ♘xg6 **4 ♕xh6 ♘f8** and now **5 ♕h5**
(rather than the game's 5 ♘xe6? ♘xe6 6 ♕xe6+ ♔f8) **5...♕d8** (or 5...♕c8 6 ♕f7+ ♔h8 7 ♕xe7
♔g8 8 ♘f7 and White's deadly attacking team of queen and knight decides) **6 ♘f7 ♕a8** (or
6...♖xg2+ 7 ♔xg2 ♕a8 8 ♘h6+ ♔h8 9 ♔g3! when one possible mating finish is 9...♕a2 10
♘f5+ ♔g8 11 ♘xe7+ ♔g7 12 ♗h6+ ♔f6 13 ♘g8#) **7 ♘h6+ ♔h8 8 ♗f1!** would have left
Black's king helpless.

173) Valden-Smallbone
1...♕xe6! wins a rook in view of the back rank mate after 2 ♕xe6 ♖d1+.

174) Bates-Mason
1 ♕xf6! 1-0
White will emerge a rook ahead after 1...exf6 2 e7 ♕e8 3 ♘xd6.

175) De Coverly-Frost
1 ♗xd5! exd5?? (capitulation, although otherwise White retreats his bishop and plays a crushing d4-d5; for example, 1...♔c7 2 ♗g2 ♖a7 3 ♕f2! ♔b8 4 d5 exd5? 5 ♕b6+ ♖b7 6 ♖xc8+! ♔xc8 7 ♖g8+ forcing mate) **2 ♕xf5+ 1-0**
Mate follows on c8.

176) Eames-Simmons
1 ♖xc8! ♖xc8 2 ♕b7 wins a piece in view of the mate threat: **2...0-0 3 ♘e7+ ♔h8 4 ♘xc8** and White went on to win.

177) Edwards-Lalic
1...♗b5! 0-1
White must lose the exchange on f1 since 1...♗b5 2 ♕xb5?? ♖xg3+! forces mate and 2 c4 ♗xc4! is no help.

178) Granat-Bentley
1...♗h3+! 2 ♔xh3 (or 2 ♔f3 ♕d1+ 3 ♔e3 ♗c5+) **2...♕f1+ 3 ♔g4 ♕g2** traps the white king in a mating net: **4 h3 h5+ 5 ♔h4 g5+ 6 ♔xh5 ♕xh3+ 7 ♔g6 ♗e7 0-1**
8...♕h7# is unstoppable.

179) Palliser-Hunt
Rather than the game's 1 ♗d4, **1 ♗f7+!!** gives White a decisive material advantage after **1...♕xf7** (capturing with either knight allows mate, while 1...♔xf7 2 ♕xg7+ ♔e8 3 ♕xc7 wins the queen for even less material) **2 ♘h6+ ♔f8 3 ♘xf7 ♘dxf7**.

180) Palliser-Broomfield
1 ♖e7! (1 ♖e6 ♕d8 2 ♖e7! ♕xe7 3 d6+ actually comes to the same thing) **1...♕xe7** (or 1...♖f7 2 ♖xf7 ♔xf7 3 ♕xh7+ ♔e8 4 ♖e1+ with an overwhelming attack) **2 d6+ ♕f7 3 ♗xf7+ ♖xf7 4 ♖e1** and White went on to convert his decisive advantage.

181) Webb-Townsend
White simplified to a winning ending with **1 ♘g6+! ♖xg6** (1...hxg6? 2 ♖h3+ forces mate) **2 ♕e8+ ♗f8 3 fxg5 1-0**
3...♖g8 4 ♖xf8 ♕g7 is forced but hopeless.

182) Willis-Twitchell
1 ♗xg7! wins a key pawn since 1...♕xg7? 2 ♖g3 costs Black his queen.

183) Bibby-Johnston
1...♕xd4+! 0-1
It's back-rank mate after 2 ♖xd4 ♖e1#.

184) Macak-Rowson
1...♖xe4! (preventing mate and beginning a decisive counterattack) **2 ♗xe4** (or 2 ♖xe4 ♘xb2! 3 ♖d2 ♗xd5 4 ♖exd4 ♕c3 with a gigantic attack) **2...♘xb2! 3 ♖d2** (desperately trying to cover c2 rather than get mated by 3 ♔xb2? ♗a3+! 4 ♔xa3 ♕c3+ 5 ♔a4 ♖c4#) **3...♗a3 4 f6 ♘a4+ 0-1**

Mate follows on c3 or b2.

185) Cox-Dickson
1...♛xg3!! 2 hxg3 ♘f2+ 3 ♔h2 ♘eg4# 0-1

186) Bologan-Lautier
1 ♘xf5! 1-0
It's mate after 1...♛xf2 2 ♖d8+ ♖f8 3 ♘h6#.

187) Smallbone-Cupal
1 ♖xf8! ♛xg5 2 ♖1f7+ 1-0
It's mate after 2...♔h6 3 ♖h8#.

188) Milanovic-Grigore
1 ♖xd4! 1-0
It's mate after 1...cxd4 2 f6+ ♔g8 (or 2...♔g6 3 ♗d3+) 3 ♖c8+ ♔h7 4 ♗d3+ ♘e4 5 ♗xe4#.

189) Barnaure-Nanu
1 ♛g7+! 1-0
White wins a rook with 1...♖xg7 2 fxg7+ ♔xg7 3 ♗xd8.

190) Lengyel-To Nhat Minh
1 ♛xc6 ♖xc6 2 ♖d8+ ♛e8 3 ♖xe8+ wins a piece.

191) Bronstein-Keres
1 ♛h6! 1-0
After 1...♛xb1+ 2 ♔h2 ♖g8 White mates with 3 ♛xh7+! ♔xh7 4 ♖h4#.

192) Ignacz-Niemi
1...♖xf2+! 2 ♔xf2 ♛xh2+ 0-1
It's mate down the f-file after 3 ♔f1 ♖f8+.

193) Collins-Illner
1 ♖xf7! 1-0
White wins a rook after 1...♛xf7 (neither does 1...♛g8 2 ♖xg7! help Black) 2 ♖xc8+ ♗f8 3 ♛e5+ ♔g8 4 ♛xb2.

194) Szabo-Bisguier
1 ♗xh7+! ♔xh7 2 ♛h3+ ♔g8 3 ♖g4 1-0
It's mate on h8 after 3...f6 4 ♖h4 fxe5 5 g6.

195) Karpov-Hort
1 ♖xe6+!! 1-0
It's mate after 1...♛xe6 (or 1...♔f7 2 ♖f6+ ♔e7 3 ♖f7#) 2 ♛c7+ ♔f8 (more stubborn than 2...♛d7 3 ♗d6#) 3 ♗d6+ ♛e7 4 ♗xe7+ ♖xe7 5 ♛b8+! ♖e8 6 ♛f4+ ♔e7 7 ♛c7+ ♔f8 8 ♛f7#.

196) Mendelson-Quinn
1...♘xe3! 2 fxe3 (Black is two pawns up after 2 ♛h3 ♛xh3 3 ♖xh3 ♘xf5 4 ♗xc6 bxc6 5 ♖xc6 ♖d7) **2...♛xe3+ 3 ♔d1** (otherwise the rook on c1 falls) **3...♘xd4 4 ♗d5 ♘xf5** saw Black regain his material with interest in view of 5 ♖xe3 ♘xe3+ 6 ♔e2 ♘xg2 7 ♗xg2 c6 with five pawns and a rook for White's two extra minor pieces.

197) Peile-Miller

1 ♗xh7+!! ♔xh7 (White also has a winning attack after 1...♔h8 2 fxe7 bxa1♕ 3 exd8♕ ♖xd8 4 ♘g5 ♕f6 5 ♕h5 ♖d7 6 ♗b2!) **2 ♘g5+ ♔h6** (Black is mated after both 2...♔g8 3 ♕h5 ♗e4 4 f5! and 2...♔g6 3 ♕d3+) **3 ♕d3 ♖h8 4 ♘xf7+ ♔h5** and now White had a number of wins, including **5 f5! ♗xf6** (or 5...bxa1♕ 6 ♕h3#) **6 ♕d1+ ♗f3 7 ♕xf3+ ♔h4 8 ♕h3#**.

198) Sauvonnet-Ni Hua

1...♗xb3! 0-1

White is destroyed after 2 axb3 (or 2 ♔a1 ♘c3) 2...♖xb3+ 3 ♔c1 ♗a3+ 4 ♔d2 ♗b4+ 5 ♔c1 ♖c8+.

199) Kovalev-Stevic

1 ♕xg7+! 1-0

It's mate after 1...♗xg7 2 ♖xe8+ ♗f8 3 ♖xf8#.

200) Arlandi-Kveinys

1...♖xa3+! 0-1

It's mate after 2 ♔xa3 ♕a1# or 2 bxa3 ♕b1#.

201) Almasi-Winants

1...♕g4! 0-1

It's mate in the case of 2 ♖xe3 ♕d1#, while 2 ♘f3 costs White his rook after 2...♕c4+ 3 ♕xc4 dxc4+ 4 ♔xc4 ♖xe2.

202) Maz Machado-Fernandez Romero

1...♖xg2+! 2 ♔xg2 ♕d5+ 3 ♔f2 (or 3 ♔g3 ♕g5+ 4 ♔f2 ♖h2+ 5 ♔f3 ♕g2+ 6 ♔e3 ♖h3+ 7 ♔f4 ♕f2+ 8 ♔e5 ♖h5#) **3...♖h2+ 4 ♔e3 ♖h3+ 0-1**

It's mate after 5 ♔e2 (or 5 ♔f2 ♕f3+ 6 ♔g1 ♖h1#) 5...♕f3+ 6 ♔d2 ♕d3#.

203) Recuero Guerra-Valero Cano

1 ♗xg6! gives White a strong attack: **1...fxg6? 2 ♕xg6+ ♗g7 3 ♘g5 1-0**

It's mate after 3...♕e7 4 ♖h8+ ♔xh8 5 ♕h7#.

204) Tahirov-Shirov

1...♗c2+! 2 ♔e1 (or 2 ♔xc2 ♕xe2) **2...♖e8 3 ♕xe8+ ♘xe8 0-1**

White won't survive long after 4 ♘f3 ♗d3 5 ♗b2 ♕g4.

205) Guliyev-Mamedyarov

1...♘h3+! 2 gxh3 (or 2 ♔h1 ♗xd2 3 ♘xd2 ♕h4 4 g3 ♘xg3+ 5 hxg3 ♕xg3 6 ♘g2 ♘g5 with a rather powerful attack) **2...♗xd2** won the exchange in view of 3 ♘xd2 ♕g5+ 4 ♗g2 ♖xd2.

206) Gritsak-Bacrot

1 ♖xf7! 1-0

White is a piece up after 1...♕xb7 2 ♖xb7 and 1...♕xf7 fails to 2 ♗b3.

207) Smerdon-Cunanan

1 ♘xg6! hxg6 2 ♖xe6! ♘e4 (this fails to save Black, but 2...fxe6 3 ♕xg6+ ♔h8 4 ♗xf6+ would have led to mate) **3 ♘xe4 ♖xc1+** (White also wins a piece after 3...♗xg5 4 ♖xc8 ♕xc8 5 ♖xe8+ ♕xe8 6 ♘xg5) **4 ♗xc1 fxe6? 5 ♘d6! 1-0**

208) Saric-Gurevich
1 ♕c2! ♖e7 (not the best defence, but there was no way of saving the rook since 1...♖ac8 2 ♘xf7+! leads to mate and 1...♕d4 2 ♕g2 forces Black to part with his queen) **2 fxe7 ♕xe7 3 ♘xf7+! 1-0**
Mate follows down the long diagonal.

209) Libens-Fargere
1...♗xa3! 2 bxa3 (or 2 ♕b1 ♕d5 3 ♖e1 ♖xe5 with a decisive advantage) **2...♕xa3+ 3 ♔c2 ♕b3+ 4 ♔c1 ♕xc3+ 5 ♔b1 ♖xe5 0-1**
White cannot save all his loose pieces and his king.

210) Arsenault-Pepino
1 ♖e6! 1-0
White threatens 2 ♖xe6 and after 1...♖a1+ 2 ♔h2 ♖g8 3 ♖xe7 Black cannot both save his queen and prevent mate.

211) Van Hoolandt-El Gindy
1...♖xg3+! 2 ♔h2 (or 2 fxg3 ♕g2#) **2...♖xh3+! 0-1**
It's mate after 3 ♔xh3 ♕g4+ 4 ♔h2 ♕g2#.

212) Hrzica-Armas
1 ♖h8+! 1-0
It's mate after 1...♔xh8 2 ♕e8+ ♗f8 3 ♕xf8+ ♔h7 4 ♕g8#.

213) Collas-Lebel
1 ♘f6+! 1-0
Mate follows with 1...gxf6 (or 1...♔h8 2 ♕xh7#) 2 ♕g3+ ♔h8 3 ♗xf6#.

214) Zhao Xue-Karjakin
1 ♖xf8+! 1-0
Black loses his queen after 1...♔xf8 (or 1...♖xf8 2 ♕h7#) 2 ♕f2+ ♔e7 (it's mate after 2...♔g7 3 ♕f7+ ♔h6 4 ♕h7#) 3 ♕f7+ ♔d8 4 ♘e6+.

215) Arutinian-Danielian
1 ♕xh6+! ♔xh6 2 ♔f2 1-0
Mate follows after 2...♕e8 3 ♖h1+ ♕h5 4 ♖g6+ ♔h7 5 ♖xh5#.

216) Friedel-Cyborowski
1 ♖xf7+! ♔xf7 2 ♖c7+ ♕e7 3 ♖xe7+ ♔xe7 4 ♕g7+ 1-0
White emerges queen for rook ahead.

217) Keller-Slukova
1 ♕xh7+! ♔xh7 2 ♖h3+ 1-0
It's mate on h8.

218) White-Curnow
1...♖xc3! 2 ♕xc3 (and not 2 ♗xc3? ♕xa2+ 3 ♔c1 ♕a1#) **2...♕xa2+ 3 ♔c1 ♗xf6 4 ♕e3?** (4 ♕a3 was essential, although after 4...♗g5+ 5 ♖d2 ♕xa3 6 bxa3 ♖c8 Black will emerge a pawn ahead with a good position), and now **4...♕xb2+** (even better than the game's also rather powerful 4...♗xb2+ 5 ♔d2 ♕a5+ 6 ♔e2 ♖c8) **5 ♔d2 ♗d4** would have forced resignation in view of **6 ♕d3** (or 6 ♕e2 ♕b4+ 7 ♔c1 ♗b2+ and mates) **6...♕b4+ 7 ♔e2** (it's mate

after 7 ♔c1 ♗b2+ 8 ♔b1 ♗c3+ 9 ♔c1 ♕b2#) **7...♗c4** winning White's queen.

219) Romanov-Mkrtchian
1 ♘xh7! gives White a winning attack: **1...♗d7** (the knight is immune due to 1...♕xh7 2 ♕d8+ ♖f8 3 ♕xb6 winning the exchange) **2 ♖h3 1-0**

220) Almeida Saenz-Gagunashvili
1 ♘f5+!! **gxf5** (otherwise Black simply loses a piece on d6) **2 ♕xf5 ♖fd8** (or 2...♖h8 3 ♕f6+ ♔g8 4 g6 with a mating attack) **3 ♕xh7+** (also rather powerful is 3 g6) **3...♔f8 4 g6 ♖a7** (4...fxg6 allows mate: 5 ♗h6+ ♔e8 6 ♗xg6#) **5 g7+ ♔e7 6 ♗g5+ ♔d7 7 ♕f5+ ♔c6 8 ♗e4+ 1-0**

221) Bercys-Simutowe
1 ♖xf7! **♕xf7** (or 1...♔xf7 2 ♘xe5+ winning the queen) **2 ♘xe5 ♖g2+ 3 ♔e3** and White's double threat of 4 ♕c8# and 4 ♘xf7 was decisive.

222) Agustsson-Madland
1...♘xf3! 2 ♕g2 (wisely avoiding 2 ♘xf3? ♘xe4! with the point that 3 ♕d3 – or 3 ♘xe4 ♕xa2+ 4 ♔c1 ♗xb2# – 3...♘xc3+ 4 bxc3 ♗xc3 gives Black an overwhelming attack) **2...♘xd4** (quite possibly even stronger is 2...♘xe4!? 3 ♕xf3 ♘xc3+ 4 bxc3 ♕xa2+ 5 ♔c1 ♗d5) **3 ♗xd4 ♘xg4** saw Black net a couple of pawns, leaving him with some advantage.

223) Path-Rayner
1 ♘xf7!! **♔xf7** (Black is scarcely helped by 1...♕f6 2 ♘h6+ ♔h8 3 ♖c7) **2 ♖xh5!** **♔g8** (mate is forced after 2...gxh5 3 ♕xh5+ ♔f8 4 ♗c4 ♖e6 5 ♗h6+) **3 d7! ♘xd7** (White's last was a lovely interference tactic: the point being 3...♗xd7 4 ♗c4+ ♗e6 5 ♗xe6+ ♖xe6 6 ♕xd8+) **4 ♗c4+** (even more clinical is 4 ♕b3+ ♔g7 5 ♖xh7+! ♔xh7 6 ♕f7+ ♔h8 7 ♗xg6 ♘f8 8 ♗h6) **4...♔g7 5 ♖d5** (or 5 ♗h6+ ♔h8 6 ♗g5 when Black must give up his queen, just as he shortly has to in the game) **5...♕e7 6 ♖xd7! ♗xd7 7 ♕a1+ 1-0**

224) Bartel-Cicak
1 ♖xe6+! **♔f8** (trying to flee, rather than be crushed by 1...fxe6 2 ♕xe6+ ♔f8 3 ♘e5) **2 ♘e5! ♖g5** (or 2...♕xe2 3 ♘xg6+ fxg6 4 ♖xe2 with an easy win) **3 ♘d7+ ♔g8 4 ♖e8+ ♔h7 5 ♕d3+ 1-0**
A deadly check follows on f8.

225) Cafolla-Socko
1...♖h1+! 2 ♔xh1 ♕h7+ 3 ♗h5 ♕xh5+ 4 ♔g1 ♕h2+ 5 ♔f1 ♕xg2# 0-1

226) Almond-Rossi
1...♕xh2+! 2 ♔xh2 ♖h5+ 3 ♔g2 ♗h3+ 0-1
Mate follows with 4 ♔h1 ♗f1#.

227) T.Hickey-N.Ahern
1 ♗xg7+! **♔xg7 2 ♖g3+ ♔h8** (or 2...♔f6 3 ♘d2 ♔xe6 4 ♕g4+ ♔d5 5 ♖c3! with an overwhelming attack in view of 5...♕xc3 6 ♕xe4# and 2...♔h6 3 ♕e3+ also forces mate) **3 ♕g4 ♗g6 4 ♕d4+ 1-0**

228) Cmilyte-Benjamin
Instead of the game's 1 h3?, White could have forced mate: **1 ♖xg5+!** hxg5 2 ♕f6+ ♔h7 (or 2...♔g8 3 ♗f7+ ♔f8 4 ♗g6+ ♔g8 5 ♕f7+ ♔h8 6 ♕h7#) **3 ♗g6+ ♔h6 4 ♗f5+ ♔h5 5 ♕g6+ ♔h4 6 ♕h6#**.

229) Kotronias-Sarakauskas
1 ♖xh7+! 1-0
Mate follows with 1...♔xh7 2 ♖h1+ ♔g6 3 ♖h6#.

230) Kotronias-Benjamin
1...♖e1+! 0-1
It's mate on g2.

231) Gymesi-Fox
1 ♗xa6! fxe5 (or 1...bxa6 2 ♕xa6 ♖a7 3 ♘xc6+ ♖xc6 4 ♖b3+ ♔b7 5 ♖xc6 with a winning attack) **2 ♗d3 ♖c8 3 dxe5 ♖d7** (Black had to give up the rook, not that doing so would really have saved him) **4 ♕a7+ ♔c7 5 ♖xc6+! ♔d8 6 ♖xc8+ ♔xc8 7 ♖c3+ ♔c7 8 ♕a8+ 1-0**
Mate follows quickly after 8...♔d7 9 ♗b5+.

232) Rudd-Khantuev
1 ♖1h6+! 1-0
It's mate after 1...gxh6 2 ♖g8#.

233) Tavoularis-Snape
1...♗xb2! won a key pawn in view of **2 ♔xb2 ♖xc2+ 3 ♔b1 ♕c3 4 ♖d8+** (or 4 ♕d4 ♕xf3 regaining the piece) **4...♖xd8 5 ♕xc2 ♕xf3** with a winning ending.

234) Ivic-Pavasovic
1...♘xg2! removes a key pawn: **2 ♘d3** (White cannot avoid heavy material losses after 2 ♘xg2 ♕f3 3 ♔f1 ♕xg2+ 4 ♔e2 ♖e8+) **2...♘h4! 0-1**
White is undone down the long diagonal.

235) Ivic-Medic
1 ♕xh6! 1-0
White wins a piece in view of 1...♕xh6? 2 ♖e8+ ♖d8 3 ♗xf5+ ♔b8 4 ♖xd8#.

236) Zovko-Mohr
1...♗xh3! wins a pawn in view of 2 ♗xh3? ♘f3+ and 3...♘xd2.

237) Naumkin-Abatino
1 ♗xh7+! 1-0
White is a queen up with a mating attack after 1...♕xh7 (or 1...♔h8 2 ♖xf8+ ♕xf8 3 ♗e4+ ♔g7 4 ♕g6+ ♔h8 5 ♕h7#) 2 ♖xf8+ ♔xf8 3 ♕xh7.

238) Cheval-Gerfault
After **1...♘g3+!** White must give up his queen since it was mate following **2 hxg3 ♖h6# 0-1**

239) Cooper-Scott
1 ♕g5! leaves Black unable to satisfactorily save his light-squared bishop: **1...♗f5** (or 1...♖g7 2 ♕xg6! since 2...♖xg6 fails to 3 ♖xh7#; relatively best might be 1...♖g8, but after 2 ♘xg8 ♕xg8 3 ♖xd5 White is the exchange up with a crushing position) **2 ♕xf5!** (the main point) **2...exf5 3 ♖xe7 ♖xf6** (the rook is immune in view of 3...♗xe7 4 ♖xh7#) **4 ♖exh7+ 1-0**
White emerges a rook ahead after 4...♔g8 5 ♖h8+ ♔g7 6 ♖xc8.

240) Megaranto-Batchuluun
1 ♕xg8+! 1-0

It's mate on the back rank after 1...♔xg8 2 ♖d8+.

241) Catt-Lockwood
1...♘xe4+!! 2 fxe4 ♖f4 3 ♕h3 (now it's mate, although otherwise White loses his queen) **3...♖xg4+ 4 ♔f3 ♕f5+! 5 exf5 e4+ 6 ♔e3 ♗h6# 0-1**

242) Topalov-Naiditsch
1 ♕f6+! 1-0
Mate follows on the back rank after 1...♕xf6 2 ♖e8+.

243) Ardeleanu-Kachieshvili
1 ♖e8+! ♔c7 (it's mate after 1...♔xe8 2 ♕g8+ ♗f8 3 ♕xf8#) **2 ♖e7 ♘g3** (2...♕xe7 3 ♗xe7 threatens both 4 ♗d8# and the rook on a8) **3 ♖xd7+** (plenty good enough, but instead 3 ♗d6+ leads to mate) **1-0**

244) Naiditsch-Gustafsson
1...♖f4! 0-1
There's no defence to the threat of 2...♖h4 since 2 gxf4 ♗xf4 also leads to mate on h1 (or g2 after 3 ♘f1).

245) Naiditsch-Sowray
Instead of the game's 1...♗f2+? 2 ♔h1 ♖g2? 3 ♕f3 when White had gained the upper hand, **1...♗xh2+!** would have given Black a crushing attack: **2 ♔xh2** (or 2 ♔h1 ♖g2 3 ♕h5 ♗b8! 4 ♖ae1 – 4 ♕xh3 ♖ge2 prepares to exploit the open h-file after 5...♗e5 – 4...♗e5 5 ♖f5 ♖h2+ 6 ♔g1 ♗d4+ 7 ♔xh2 ♖xe1 8 ♕xg5 ♕d6+ 9 ♕f4 ♗e5 winning material) **2...♕d6+ 3 ♔h1 ♖g2 4 ♘f4 ♖ee2!** and White is done for in view of 5 ♕xe2 (or 5 ♘xg2 hxg2+ 6 ♔g1 ♕d4+) 5...♖xe2 6 ♘xe2 ♕c6+ 7 ♔g1 ♕g2#.

246) Korbut-Javakhishvili
1 ♖xg7+! ♔xg7 (or 1...♔h8 2 ♖xh7+! ♔xh7 3 ♕h6+ ♔g8 4 ♖g1+ ♔f7 5 ♕g7#) **2 ♘f5+! exf5 3 ♖g1+ ♔h8 4 ♕xc4** (White's extra queen and ongoing attack quickly decides) **4...♖f8 5 ♗h6 1-0**

247) Levushkina-Vogel
1...♕xh3 2 gxh3 ♘f3+ 3 ♔f1 ♘xd2+ 4 ♗xd2 saw Black pick up the exchange.

248) Najer-Neverov
1 ♗xg6! ♘xg6 (White's rooks outclass Black's minor pieces after 1...♖xg6 2 ♖xg6 ♔h7 3 ♖g2, while 1...♖f8 2 ♖d8 leaves Black pretty much in zugzwang) **2 ♖xg6! ♖xg6 3 ♖d8+ ♔h7 4 e7 1-0**
The pawns will cost Black all his pieces.

249) Zweschper-Hanemann
1 ♕xh6+! ♕xh6 2 ♖xh6+ 1-0
It's mate after 2...♔xh6 3 ♖h3# or 2...♔g8 3 ♖eh3 and ♖h8#.

250) Handke-Dinger
1 ♕xh7+! 1-0
It's mate after 1...♔xh7 2 ♖h6#.

251) Beckhuis-Jakubowski
1...♘e2+! 2 ♗xe2 (2 ♘xe2 ♕xg2+! is the same motif, while 2 ♔h1 fails to 2...♖xh2+! 3 ♔xh2 – or 3 ♖xh2 dxc4+ – 3...♕h5#) **2...♕xg2+! 3 ♔xg2 dxc4+ 4 ♔g3 cxb3** won the exchange.

252) Zakurdjaeva-Paehtz
1 ♕h6+! 1-0
It's mate after 1...♔xh6 2 ♖h8+ ♔g7 3 ♗f6#.

253) Geske-Ardeleanu
1...♗xa2+! 2 ♔xa2 ♕d5+ 3 ♔b1 a3 0-1
Black's queenside passers cannot be stopped.

254) Zawadzka-Stefanova
1...♖xh4+! 0-1
It's mate with 2 ♔xh4 ♕f2+ 3 ♔h3 ♕g3#.

255) Arakhamia Grant-Levushkina
1 ♕f7! d5 (mate follows after 1...♖xf7 2 ♖e8+, but there's no good defence in any case) **2 ♖e8 1-0**
The mate threat costs Black a huge amount of material after 2...♗e7 3 g5.

256) Roos-Stocek
1...♖xg2+! 2 ♔xg2 ♕g4+ 0-1
It's mate with 3 ♔h2 ♖e2+ 4 ♔h1 ♕h3+ 5 ♔g1 ♕h2#.

257) Schulz-Marville
1 ♖h7+! ♗xh7 2 ♕e7 1-0
Black cannot cover both g7 and h7.

258) Womacka-Kaphle
1 ♗xh7+! ♔xh7 (or 1...♔f8 2 ♕h5 f6 3 ♕g6 and f6 collapses) **2 ♕h5+ ♔g8 3 ♕xf7+ ♔h8 4 ♖e3 1-0**
It's mate down the h-file.

259) Pert-Aleksandrov
1 ♗f6+! ♘xf6 2 ♕xc7 ♖e7 3 ♕e5 1-0
Black has lost the exchange and remains horribly tied down.

260) Bobras-Can
1 ♖xg7+! ♔xg7 2 ♗xh6+ 1-0
Mate follows on g7 after 2...♔h7 3 ♗g5+ ♔g8 4 ♗f6 ♘g6 5 ♕h6.

261) Azarov-Sanikidze
1 ♗xh7+! ♔xh7 2 ♖h4+ (or 2 ♕d3+ ♔g8 3 ♖h4 transposing) **2...♔g8 1-0**
Mate follows down the h-file after 3 ♕d3.

262) Bakker-Gutman
1...♗f4+! 2 ♕xg4 (or 2 ♔f2 ♕g2+ 3 ♔e1 ♕xh1+ winning a large amount of material) **2...♗xe3# 0-1**

263) Neverov-Strohhaeker
1...♖xh6! 2 ♗xf6+ ♔xf6 0-1
Black recoups the queen leaving him a piece up after 3 ♕c3+ ♗e5 4 ♕c2 ♖xh2+ 5 ♕xh2 ♗xh2 6 ♔xh2.

264) Mamedjarova-Nemcova
1 ♘xh7! ♖f7 (or 1...♖xh7 2 ♕xg6+ winning one of the black rooks) **2 ♕xg6+ ♔h8 3 ♘f6 1-0**
White wins the exchange while retaining a strong attack.

265) Iljin-Sakaev
1 ♘g6+! fxg6 2 ♖e8+ ♔h7 3 ♗g8+ ♔h8 4 ♗f7+ ½-½
It's perpetual.

266) Georgiev-Socko
1 ♖h8+! ♔xh8 2 ♗xf7 1-0
3 ♖h1# follows.

267) Melkumyan-Petrosian
1...exd4! 2 cxd5 (White had to avoid 2 exd4? ♘f4 when he would have been unable to prevent mate, but there wasn't anything better than the text with both 2...♗e5 and 2...dxe3 threatened) **2...♗e5 3 f4 ♗xf4 4 ♘f3 ♕xf3 0-1**
Black threatens both 5...h3 and 5...♕h3, and emerges three pawns ahead after 5 ♕d1 ♕xd1 6 ♖fxd1 dxe3 7 ♗xh4 cxd5 8 ♖xd5 ♖ac8.

268) Mamedyarov-Al Modiahki
1 ♖xg6+! hxg6 2 h7+! 1-0
Mate follows with 2...♖xh7 (or 2...♔xh7 3 ♖h4+ ♔g8 4 ♖h8#) 3 ♕xg6+ ♔h8 4 ♕xe8+ ♔g7 5 ♕f8+ ♔g6 6 ♕f6+ ♔h5 7 ♖h4#.

269) Burnett-Palliser
1...♗xf3! 2 gxf3 ♘h4 3 ♕c3 (there's a nasty sting in the tail after this, but there wasn't a defence, partly because 3 ♔h1 fails to 3...♕f6) **3...♕d7! 0-1**
White can't cover g2 except with 4 ♔h1 ♕h3 5 ♖g1 which permits 5...♕xf3+ 6 ♖g2 ♕xg2#.

270) Stellwagen-Bosboom
1 ♕xf6+! 1-0
It's mate on the back rank after 1...♖xf6 2 ♖d8+.

271) Van Kerkhof-Piket
1 ♖xh7+! ♔xh7 2 ♖h1+ ♔g7 3 ♘h4 ♕c7 (or 3...♖g8 4 ♕xg6+ ♔f8 5 ♕f7#) **4 ♕xg6+ ♔h8 5 ♘f3+** (also rather good is 5 ♕g5) **5...♘h7 6 ♘g5 ♘gf6 7 ♗f7 1-0**
There's no good way to further defend h7.

272) Nijboer-Hoffmann
1 ♕xh7+! 1-0
It's mate after 1...♔xh7 2 g6+ ♔h8 (or 2...♔g8 3 ♗xf7+ ♔h8 4 ♖h4#) 3 ♖h4+ ♔g8 4 gxf7#.

273) Winants-Okkes
1 ♕xh6+! 1-0
Mate follows after 1...♔xh6 2 ♖h3# or 1...♔g8 2 ♖f8#.

274) Ferry-Ruxton
1...♖xh2+! 2 ♔xh2 (or 2 ♔f3 ♕f2+ 3 ♔g4 ♖h4#) **2...♕f2+ 3 ♔h3 ♖h8+ 4 ♔g4 ♖h4# 0-1**

275) Brechin-Aagaard
1 ♖xg7+! ♔h8 (or 1...♔xg7 2 ♖xe7+ ♔h8 3 ♕e5+ followed by mate) **2 ♖h7+** (2 ♕f7 also does the business) **2...♔xh7 3 ♖xe7+ ♔h8 4 ♕e5+ ♔g8 5 ♕g7# 1-0**

276) Mudongo-Andriasian
1...♖xh3+! 2 ♘h2 (or 2 gxh3 ♕g1#) **2...♖xh2+! 0-1**
It's mate after 3 ♔xh2 ♕h5#.

277) Sabure-Danielian
Black wins the exchange with **1...♘xg3!** since 2 hxg3?? is impossible on account of 2...♖h1+ 3 ♔f2 ♕h2#.

278) Korneev-Landenbergue
1 ♖xg7+! ♔xg7 2 ♕h6+ 1-0
It's mate after 2...♔h8 3 ♕f6+ ♔g8 4 ♖g1#.

279) Rozentalis-Adams
1...♕xe1+! 0-1
White loses the exchange after 2 ♖xe1 ♘xf5 since he can't both save his queen and cover his back rank.

280) Sudakova-Guseva
1 ♖dg1!! ♗xa2+ (or 1...♗xg5 2 ♕xg5 followed by mate on g7 or f6) **2 ♔xa2 f5?** (a much better attempt is 2...♕c4+, although after 3 ♔a1 ♗xg5 4 ♕xg5 ♕d4 5 f4! there's no defence to the threat of 6 e5) **3 ♕xh7+! 1-0**
It's mate with 3...♔xh7 4 ♖h5#.

281) Garcia Ilundain-Miles
1...♖xh3+! 2 ♔g1 (or 2 ♔xh3 ♕h5#) **2...♕e1+ 0-1**
White's queen is lost after 3 ♕f1 ♖xg3+.

282) Gritsayeva-Kolomiets
1 ♘xh7! (or 1 ♗f4 ♕b6 2 ♘xh7!) **1...♘xh7** (Black also emerges a pawn down after 1...♘xd2 2 ♘xf6+ ♗xf6 3 ♖xd2) **2 ♕d3 ♘f6 3 ♕xc4** wins a pawn.

283) Golubka-Bagrationi
1 ♗b7+! ♔b8 (or 1...♔xb7 2 ♖xd8+ ♔c7 3 ♖d7+ winning the black queen) **2 ♖xd8+ ♕xd8 3 ♗e5+ ♗d6 4 ♗a6 1-0**
There's no defence to mate on b7.

284) Galakhov-Olishevsky
1...♘xh3! 2 gxh3 (it's also mate after 2 ♕a7 ♘f4+ 3 ♔g1 ♘e2+ 4 ♔f2 ♗g3#) **2...♕xh3+ 3 ♔g1 ♗xf3! 0-1**
There's no good way to cover h1 in view of 4 ♕xf3 ♕h2#.

285) Hall-Brusey
1 ♕xh6+! 1-0
It's mate after 1...♔xh6 (or 1...♔g8 2 ♕g7#) 2 ♖h4#.

286) Mateuta-Iovan
1 ♘xh7! wins the exchange on f8 since it's mate after 1...♔xh7? 2 ♕h5+ ♗h6 3 ♕xh6#.

287) Ristic-Adam
1 ♖h8+! ♕xh8 2 ♖d7 ♕g8 3 ♕f6+ 1-0
It's mate after 3...♔e8 4 ♕e7#.

288) Marincas-Csilcser
1...♖h1+! 0-1
Mate follows with 2 ♔xh1 ♕h5+ 3 ♔g1 ♕h2#.

289) E.Hintikka-T.Paakkonen
1...♕xg2+! 0-1
It's mate after 2 ♕xg2 ♖xf1#.

290) Sammalvuo-Maki
1 ♘f6! 1-0
The threat is 2 ♖g8# and it's mate after 1...♗c5+ (or 1...♗xf6 2 ♕xf6+! ♖xf6 3 ♖d8+ ♖f8 4 ♖xf8#) 2 ♔h1 ♖f8 3 ♕xf8+! ♗xf8 4 ♖g8#.

291) Hindle-Van Oosterom
1 ♖h6! gxh6 (or 1...♗f5 2 ♖xh7+ ♗xh7 3 ♖h3 g6 4 ♗xe5+ and mate follows on h7) **2 ♕xe5+ 1-0**
The raking bishops force mate.

292) Taylor-Vavrak
1...♕g1+! 0-1
It's mate with 2 ♖xg1 ♘f2#.

293) Schukowski-Jacob
1...♕xh4! 0-1
It's mate after 2 gxh4 ♗h2#.

294) Wirig-Kazhgaleyev
1...♖xf2! 2 ♘e7+ (Black's queen is immune due to 2 ♖xb2 ♖xf1#, while 2 ♖xf2 fails to 2...♕c1+ and mate on the back rank) **2...♖xe7 0-1**
There's no way for White to prevent mate.

295) Nataf-Riff
1 g6! fxg6 2 ♖xg6! dxc3 3 ♗xc3 ♖f7 (the rook couldn't be touched in view of 3...hxg6 4 ♕h8+ ♔f7 5 ♕xe8+ ♔xe8 6 g8♕+, but Black might have tried 3...♗b6 4 ♖f6 ♖be7, although he is then very tied down and after 5 ♔b1 the threat of 6 ♖df1 is decisive) **4 ♖h6 ♗g5+** (a better defence was 4...♗g4 5 ♕xg4 ♖xg7, although after 6 ♕h5 ♗g5+ 7 ♔b1 ♕c8 8 ♖hd6 ♗f4 9 ♗a5 Black is becoming rather stretched) **5 ♕xg5 ♕xa2 6 ♖xh7! ♕a1+** (White mates after 6...♔xh7 7 g8♕+ ♖xg8 8 ♕h4+ ♔g7 9 ♖g1+) **7 ♔c2 ♕xd1+ 8 ♔xd1 ♔xh7 9 ♗xe5 1-0**
The threats created by the g7-pawn are crushing.

296) Apicella-Giffard
1 ♕xd8+! ♘xd8 2 ♖d7+ ♔b8 3 ♖xd8+ ♔c7 (or 3...♔a7 4 ♖a8#) **4 ♖d7+ ♔b8 5 ♖xb7# 1-0**

297) Pucher-Lautier
1...♘xf3! 0-1
Mate follows on g1 or h2 after 2 ♖ee1 ♖xh2#.

298) Pospisil-Mroziak
1 ♗xh7+! ♔f8 (or 1...♔xh7 2 ♕h5+ ♔g8 3 ♕xf7+ ♔h8 4 ♖e3 ♘f6 5 ♖h3+ ♘h7 6 ♘g6#) **2 ♕h5** leaves White a pawn up with an attack.

299) Motuz-Petran
1...♖xc2+! 2 ♔xc2 **♕b1+ 3 ♔d2 ♖b2+ 4 ♔e3 ♕e4+ 5 ♔f2 ♕xe2+** (even faster is 5...♕xf4+ 6 ♔e1 ♖b1+) **6 ♔g1 ♕e1+ 0-1**
It's mate after 7 ♔h2 ♕h4+ 8 ♔g1 ♖b1#.

300) Talla-Motuz
1...♖xb3+! 2 axb3 (or 2 ♔c1 ♖xa2 with an overwhelming attack) **2...♕xb3+ 3 ♘b2** (White is mated too after 3 ♔c1 ♕c3+ 4 ♔b1 ♗a2# or 4...♖a1#) **3...♖a1+! 0-1**
It's mate with 4 ♔xa1 ♕a2#.

301) Morozevich-Georgiev
White wins the exchange: **1 ♘d6+! cxd6** (similar is 1...♖xd6 2 ♕f8) **2 ♕f8 ♕e8** (otherwise it's mate on b8) **3 ♕xe8 1-0**

302) Naiditch-Mamedyarov
1...♖xh2+! 0-1
White loses his queen after 2 ♔xh2 (it's mate following 2 ♔g1? ♕h4) **2...♕h5+ 3 ♔g1** (or 3 ♔g3 ♘e2+) **3...♘e2+ 4 ♕xe2 ♕xe2**.

303) Greet-Pitl
1 ♖f8+! ♔xf8 2 ♕h8+ ♔f7 (or 2...♔e7 3 ♕d8+ ♔f7 4 ♗e8+ ♔e6 5 ♕d6+ ♔f5 6 ♕xe5#) **3 ♕e8+ ♔f6 4 ♗xe5+ ♔f5 5 g4# 1-0**

304) Jagstaidt-Zozulia
1...♖xh2+! 0-1
It's mate after 2 ♔xh2 ♖h8#.

305) Gehringer-Rausis
1...♘xf2! wins a key pawn in view of 2 ♔xf2? (or 2 ♕xf2? ♗xg3) **2...♗xg3+ 3 ♔f1** (Black's attack is extremely powerful in the case of 3 ♔g2 ♗xh4+ 4 ♔h3 ♖g3+ 5 ♔h2 ♘f6) **3...♕f6+** regaining the piece with some advantage.

306) Baramidze-Nielsen
1...♕xc4! 0-1
Black's attack decides after 2 bxc4 b3 3 ♔c1 ♗xg5+.

307) Navara-Rabiega
1...♘b4!! 2 ♘xb4 ♗h6+ 3 ♔b1 ♖e1+ 4 ♖xe1 ♕xe1+ 5 ♔c2 ♗f5 6 ♕xf5 ♕d2+ 0-1
Mate follows with 7 ♔b1 ♕d1+ 8 ♗c1 ♕xc1#.

308) Fischer-Beim
1...♖xg4+! 2 ♗xg4 (White also loses his queen after 2 ♕xg4 ♖g8) **2...♖g8 3 ♔f3 ♖xg4! 0-1**
4 ♕xg4 ♘e5+ is a decisive fork.

309) Nunn-Pritchett
1 ♕xh7+! 1-0
It's mate after 1...♔xh7 2 ♖h4+ ♔h5 3 ♖xh5#.

310) Werle-Mainka
1...h5! 2 ♘e5 (the queen is trapped in view of 2 ♕g3 ♘e2+ 3 ♘xe2 ♗xg3) **2...g5 0-1**
Black is simply a piece up after 3 ♕g3 fxe5.

311) Vogt-Teschke
1 ♕f5! 1-0
Black cannot prevent mate on both h7 and f8. He might try 1...♔g8 (White's main point is the back-ranker 1...♖xf5 2 ♖d8+), but after 2 ♕xh7+ ♔f7 3 ♕h5+ ♔g8 4 ♗h7+ mate follows in any case.

312) Zesch-Acs
1...♕xh4+! 0-1
Mate is forced: 2 gxh4 (or 2 ♔g1 ♖xg3+! 3 fxg3 ♕xg3+ 4 ♔f1 ♕g2#) 2...♖xh4+ 3 ♔g1 ♖g8+ 4 ♔f1 ♖h1#.

313) Borriss-Nisipeanu
1...♗xg2! 2 ♖xa3 (now Black's attack is decisive, but after 2 ♕xg2 ♖xa2 he wins the exchange) **2...♗e4+ 3 ♘g3 ♗xg3 4 ♕e2 ♗h2+! 0-1**
White loses his queen after 5 ♔xh2 ♕d6+ 6 ♔g1 ♕g3+ 7 ♔f1 ♗d3.

314) Hansen-Wintzer
1 ♗xe6! fxe6 (there isn't anything better, especially in view of the threatened 2 ♖xh7) **2 ♕xe6+ ♔h8 3 ♖xh7+! ♔xh7 4 ♖d3 ♘g8 5 ♖h3+ ♘h6 6 ♖xh6+! 1-0**
Mate follows with 6...gxh6 7 ♕f7+ ♗g7 8 ♕xg7#.

315) Ernst-Loeffler
1 ♖f4! (the cleanest finish; now Black cannot give up his queen for rook and bishop, unlike after 1 ♖h3, and 2 ♕xh6+ is threatened) **1...♕xf6 2 exf6 cxd3 3 ♗g5 d2 4 ♖h4! 1-0**
Even the new black queen is unable to prevent mate due to 4...d1♕+ 5 ♔h2 ♕h5 6 ♖xh5 gxh5 7 ♕g7#.

316) Luther-Sokolov
1...♘d3+! simplifies to a clearly better ending: **2 cxd3** (White is not helped by 2 ♔b1? ♘xb2!) **2...cxd3+ 3 ♗c3** (3 ♔b1? ♕c2+ 4 ♔xc2 dxc2+ wins the exchange) **3...♕xc3+! 4 bxc3 ♖xc3+ 5 ♔d2 ♖c2+ 6 ♔xd3 ♖xg2** and Black went on to convert.

317) Ribli-Muranyi
1 ♖xg7+! ♔xg7 2 ♖b7+ ♔g6 (now it's mate, but otherwise White simplifies and 2...♖d7 3 ♖xd7+ ♖xd7 4 ♕xd7+ should be winning easily enough) **3 ♕e8+ ♔f6 1-0**
It's mate next move, just as it is after 3...♔f5 4 ♖f7+ ♖f6 5 g4+! ♔xf4 6 ♖xf6+.

318) Caruana-Adams
1...♗xh3! obliterates White's defences. The game concluded **2 ♖e2** (the bishop was immune, of course, due to both 2 ♔xh3?? ♕h5# and 2 gxh3 ♖g8) **2...♖g8 3 ♖ae1? ♗xg2! 0-1**
Black wins the house after 4 ♖xg2 ♕h4+ 5 ♔g1 ♖xg2+ 6 ♕xg2 ♕xe1 and 7...♖g8.

319) Poggio-Livesey
1 ♖xa6! ♗xa6 2 ♕xe6+ ♔h8 3 ♘f7+ ♔g8 4 ♘xh6+ ♔h8 5 ♘f7+ gave White a crushing attack.

320) Rasch-Schiller
1 ♘xd6! ♘xd6 (Black's kingside is defenceless after 1...♖e7 2 ♖xe4) **2 ♕g5+ 1-0**
White's attack quickly leads to mate after 2...♔f8 3 ♕h6+! ♔g8 4 ♖xe8+ ♕xe8 (or 4...♘xe8 5 ♕f8#) 5 ♕g5+ ♔f8 6 ♗xd6+.

321) Krush-Ruxton
1 ♕xg7+! ♔xg7 2 ♖h7+ ♔g8 3 ♖h8+ ♔g7 4 ♖1h7# 1-0

322) Rogers-Ris
1...♕c6! 0-1
There's no satisfactory defence to the twin threats of 2...♕xc1+ and 2...♖xe1+ 3 ♖xe1 ♕xg2#.

323) Dworakowska-Cramling
1...♗xf2+! 2 ♔h1 (White's queen is lost after 2 ♔xf2 ♘g4+) **2...♘g4** gives Black a winning attack.

324) Hickman-Menon
1...♕a2+ 2 ♔c1 ♕a1+! 0-1
It's mate with 3 ♘xa1 ♖xa1#.

325) Lahno-Malmdin
1 ♕xh5! 1-0
White wins a piece after 1...gxh5 2 ♘xe6+ ♔h7 3 ♘xc7.

326) Arsenault-Ris
1...♖xh3+! 0-1
It's mate after 2 ♔xh3 (or 2 gxh3 ♕g1#) 2...♕h1#.

327) Wade-Horton
1 ♕xf6+! ♔xf6 2 ♘d7+ ♔e7 3 ♘xb6 ♖c6 4 ♖b1 wins a piece.

328) Kristjansson-Salgado Allaria
1...♖xh3! 2 gxh3 ♖xh3 3 f3 ♖g3+ 4 ♔f2 ♖xf3+ 0-1
Mate follows with 5 ♔g2 ♕g4+ 6 ♔h2 ♖h3#.

329) Korchnoi-Krush
Korchnoi actually resigned before Black could play **1...♕xe4!** winning a piece and the game in view of 2 ♘xe4? ♖d1+ 3 ♖f1 ♖xf1#.

330) Korchnoi-Krush
1 ♖f8+! ♔g7 (1...♖xf8 2 ♗d5 wins the queen) **2 ♖xd8 ♘xd8 3 ♕xc7+** picks up a clear pawn, but in the game Korchnoi actually blundered with 1 ♖f2?? (see the previous puzzle).

331) Popilski-Porat
1...♘f3+! 0-1
It's mate after 2 ♗xf3 ♕f2#.

332) Hopwood-Mackenzie
1 ♕xf7+! 1-0
It's mate with 1...♖xf7 2 ♖e8#.

333) Robertson-Stokes
1 ♘xb7! ♘xb7 (or 1...♔xb7 2 ♕a6+ ♔b8 3 ♕xc6) **2 ♕xc6** wins an important pawn.

334) Bodnaruk-Gunina
1 ♕g8+! 1-0
It's mate after 1...♘xg8 2 ♘h7#.

335) Seeman-Akesson
1 ♗xg6! fxg6 2 f7+ 1-0
Mate follows after 2...♔xf7 (or 2...♔g7 3 ♗f6+ ♔xf7 4 ♕h7+) 3 ♕h7+ ♗g7 4 ♖f1+.

336) Unzicker-Bronstein
1...♖xg2+! (just in time) **2 ♕xg2** (or 2 ♔xg2 ♖e2+ 3 ♔f3 ♕f2#) **2...♖e2 0-1**
The checks run out after 3 ♖g8+ ♔h7 4 ♖g7+ ♔h6.

337) McGowan-MacGregor
1 ♖xa6+! ♔xa6 (or 1...bxa6 2 ♕c7+ ♔a8 3 ♕c6+ ♔a7 4 ♖f7+ followed by mate) **2 ♕a3+ ♔b6 3 ♖b3+** (3 ♕b4+ is similar and a little faster) **3...♔c6 4 ♖c3+** (the computer points out that it was possible to mate by keeping checking: 4 ♕a4+ ♔d6 5 ♕d4+ ♔e6 6 ♖b6+ ♔f7 7 ♖xb7+ ♔e6 8 ♕c4+ ♔f6 9 ♖b6+ ♔e7 10 ♕c5+ ♔e8 11 ♖e6+ ♔f7 12 ♕e7+ ♔g8 13 ♖g6+ ♔h8 14 ♕g7#) **4...♔d7 5 ♖d3+ ♔e8 6 ♕a4+ ♔e7 7 ♕b4+ ♔e8 8 ♕b5+ ♔e7 9 ♕xb7+ ♔e8 10 ♕c6+ ♔e7 11 ♕c7+** and the black rook finally fell.

338) Adda-Janev
1...♖xd5 0-1
Black wins the bishop on d2 since 2 ♕xd5? allows 2...♕f1+ 3 ♖xf1 ♖xf1#.

339) Di Paolo-Olivier
1 ♖exf6! ♖xf6 2 ♖xf6 1-0
White wins a piece since 2...gxf6? 3 ♕xh6+ ♔g8 4 ♗c4+ forces Black to part with his queen.

340) Holt-Palliser
1 ♖xg5+! ♔f8 2 ♖g8+! 1-0
It's mate on g7 in any case after 2...♔xg8 3 ♕xh6.

341) Dorrington-Williams
1...♖xc2!! 2 ♘xa5 (or 2 ♔xc2 ♕xa2 3 ♗c1 ♖c8+ with a crushing attack and even 2 ♗d4 fails to save White in view of 2...♘c3+!) **2...♘d2+!** (now Black's raking bishops come into their own) **3 ♕xd2 ♖xb2+ 4 ♔c1 ♖b1# 0-1**

342) Slovineau-Rukminto
1 ♕b7+! ♖xb7 2 axb7+ 1-0
It's mate with 2...♔xb7 3 ♗c6+ ♔c8 4 ♖xa8#.

343) Rogerson-Palliser
1 ♕xh7+! 1-0
It's mate with 1...♔xh7 2 ♖h3+ ♗h4 3 ♖xh4#.

344) Smallbone-Brazier
1 ♖xf5! gxf5? (1...♖d6 prevents mate, but leaves Black a clear piece down after 2 ♕g5) **2 h6 1-0**

345) Taimanov-Persitz
1 ♖g8+! 1-0
It's mate with 1...♖xg8 2 ♘f7#.

346) Short-Biyiasis
1 ♕xe5+! 1-0
It's mate after 1...♕xe5 (or 1...♔g8 2 ♕xd4) 2 ♖xf8+ ♖xf8 3 ♖xf8#.

347) Mulligan-Foord
1...♕xh2+! 2 ♔xh2 ♖h6+ 3 ♔g3 ♗h4+ 0-1
It's mate after 4 ♔f4 (or 4 ♔h2 ♗xf2+ 5 ♗h3 ♖xh3#) 4...♖f6#.

348) Westerinen-Larsen
1...♘f3+! 0-1
Black wins a rook since it's mate after 2 gxf3 ♖d5+ 3 ♔c1 ♖xe1#.

349) Siebrecht-Diaz Diaz
1...♘h3+! 0-1
Black's attack becomes a mating one after 2 ♔h1 (or 2 gxh3 ♕g5+ 3 ♗g2 ♕xg2#) 2...♘xf2+ 3 ♔g1 ♘g4 4 g3 ♖c3! 5 ♖xc3 dxc3 6 ♕xc3 ♕e4.

350) Turner-Smallbone
1 ♗xg7! 1-0
Black loses his queen for insufficient compensation after 1...♔xg7 (or 1...♖fc8 when White has a pleasant choice between 2 ♕d2 and a strong attack after 2 ♗f6 ♔f8 3 ♕d2 ♔e8 4 ♖e1) 2 ♖g3+ ♔h6 3 ♕d2+ ♔h7 4 ♖h3.

351) Palliser-Horner
1...♖xe4! wins a piece since 2 fxe4 ♗b4+ 3 ♔f1 ♕h3+ 4 ♔g1 ♖d6 gives Black a crushing attack.

352) Otten-Bensdorp
1...♗xd4+! 2 ♕xd4 (it's mate down the e-file after 2 ♗xd4 ♕g5+ 3 ♔f2 ♕g2+ 4 ♔e1 ♖e8+) **2...♕g5+ 3 ♔f2 ♕g2+ 4 ♔e1 ♖e8+ 5 ♔d1 ♕xf1+** wins the exchange while retaining the initiative.

353) Grotenhuis-L'Ami
1...♖xc3! (or 1...♕h2+ 2 ♔f1 ♖xc3!) **2 ♖xf6** (Black has a winning attack after 2 ♗xc3 ♕h2+ 3 ♔f1 ♘e4; for example, 4 ♗d3 ♗b5! 5 ♗xb5 ♕h1+ 6 ♔e2 ♘xc3+ 7 ♔f2 ♕xa1 winning material) **2...♕h2+ 3 ♔f1 ♗g3 4 ♕xg3 ♕xg3 5 ♖f3 ♕c7 0-1**

354) Peng Zhaoqin-Van Nies
1 ♖xg7+! ♔xg7 2 f6+ ♔f8 (Black is defenceless too after both 2...♔h8 3 f7 and 2...♔h6 3 ♕g4) **3 ♕xh7 1-0**
White's queen and f-pawn force mate.

355) Schmoll-Giacomelli
1...♘h3+! 0-1
Black reaches a winning endgame after 2 gxh3 ♖g8 3 ♗h5+ ♔f8 4 ♕xg8+ ♔xg8.

356) Van Wely-Acs
1...♖e6! 2 ♘xe6 (there wasn't anything else to be done against the threat of 2...♖h6; even the computeristic 2 ♗g6 fails to save White after 2...♖xg6 3 ♘xg6 hxg6 4 ♘f4 ♕h6 followed by 5...g5) **2...♗f5+ 3 ♔g1 ♕h2+ 4 ♔f1 ♗g3 0-1**
It's mate on f2 or with 5 fxg3 ♗h3#.

357) Caveney-Tia
1...♘f3+! 2 ♔g2 (or 2 ♕xf3 ♕xe2+ 3 ♕g2 ♕xg2+ 4 ♔xg2 ♖e2+ 5 ♔f3 ♖xc2 with an extra rook) **2...♘xd4 3 ♗xg6+ ♕xg6 4 ♕xe8 ♘xe2 0-1**
Black emerges a piece ahead in the endgame.

358) Hunt-Palliser
1 ♖xg7+! ♔xg7 (or 1...♘xg7 2 ♕xh6+ ♔g8 3 ♕h7+ ♔f7 4 ♖f3+ ♔e8 5 ♕g6+ ♔d8 6 ♖xf8+ and Black is crushed) **2 ♕xh6+ ♔f7 3 ♖f3+ 1-0**
White recoups his material with an overwhelming advantage in the case of 3...♔e7 4 ♕xf8+ ♔d8 5 ♖f7.

359) Harper-Palliser
1...♘e3+! 0-1
Black wins the exchange while retaining the initiative after 2 fxe3 ♕xh1+.

360) Fomichenko-Anibar
1 ♘d7+! ♔e7 (or 1...♕xd7 2 ♕f6+ ♕f7 3 ♕xf7#) **2 ♕g7# 1-0**

361) Pruja-Muratet
1...♖xa2+! 0-1
It's mate down the a-file after 2 ♔xa2 ♖a8+.

362) Gerber-Bartel
1...♘xb2! 0-1
White loses the exchange since 2 ♔xb2? ♖xe2 is truly devastating.

363) Zapata-Welling
The immediate smothered mate fails as Black is covering f7 at the end, but White can prepare it with **1 ♖d8!! ♕c1+** (1...♖xd8 2 ♘f7+ ♔g8 3 ♘h6+ ♔h8 4 ♕g8+! and 5 ♘f7# is the main point of the combination; Black can try and check, but both in the game and after 1...♕b1+ 2 ♔g2 ♕e4+ 3 ♔h3 he quickly runs out of checks) **2 ♔g2 ♕g5+ 3 ♔f1 1-0**
After 3...♕c1+ 4 ♔e2 ♕c2+ 5 ♔f3 ♕c3+ 6 ♔g2 there's nothing to be done about White's back-rank threats.

364) Howell-Wells
1...♖xf2! 2 ♗b3+ (Black's main point is that 2 ♕xg3 ♖f1+ wins the queen after either 3 ♔g2 ♖g1+ or 3 ♔h2 ♗f4) **2...♔h7 3 ♕c7+ ♔h6 4 ♕xc8 ♖g1+! 0-1**
White's queen is lost.

365) Lutton-Palliser
1...♗xf2+! 0-1

Black wins the exchange while retaining a strong attack after 2 ♔xf2 ♕d4+ 3 ♖e3 (or 3 ♔e2 ♕d2#) 3...fxe3+.

366) Kritz-Kolbus
Black mistakenly forced a draw with 1...♖1c2+ 2 ♔b1 ♖c1+, missing **1...♖8c2+ 2 ♔a3 b4+!** which forces mate: 3 ♔a4 ♖xa2+ 4 ♔xb4 ♗a5# or 3 ♔xb4 ♗c5+ 4 ♔a4 ♖xa2#.

367) Devereaux-Lunn
1 ♖exh5! ♘xh5 (1...♖h8 also loses to 2 ♘f5+!, but Black could have put up some resistance with 1...♔g8 2 ♖h8! ♔f8!, if not 2...♖xh8? 3 ♘f5+!) **2 ♘f5+! ♔g8** (or 2...gxf5 3 ♕g5+ ♔f8 4 ♕h6+ ♔g8 5 ♖xh5 forcing mate) **3 ♖xh5 1-0**
Mate follows after 3...f6 (or 3...gxh5 4 ♕g5+ ♔h7 5 ♕g7#) 4 ♕h6 gxf5 5 ♕g6+ ♔f8 6 ♖h8#.

368) Ferguson-Eggleston
1 ♗f6!! ♘e7 (trying to shore up the kingside, rather than be mated after 1...gxf6 2 ♖g3+ ♔h8 3 ♕g4) **2 ♕h5** (threatening 3 ♖h3 h6 4 ♗xg7) **2...h6 3 ♖h3 ♘f5 4 g4! bxa4 5 gxf5 axb3 6 ♕xh6!** (not the only win, but by far the most aesthetic) **6...♖xa1+ 7 ♔g2 gxh6 8 ♖xh6 ♖g1+ 9 ♔xg1 b2 10 ♖h8# 1-0**

369) Korneev-Devereaux
Rather than the game's 1...♕g1 when White escaped with a draw, **1...g2!** would have decided proceedings since 2 ♕xg2 fails to 2...♗c3+ 3 ♔a4 ♕b1 when there's no good way to prevent mate on b4.

370) Palliser-Malakhatko
White levers open the black king's defences with **1 e6! ♕c5** (Black's king is ripped to shreds after 1...fxe6 2 ♕xd3 ♔h8 3 ♕xg6 ♖g8 4 ♕f6+ ♔h7 5 ♘d7!, while 1...♖xd6 loses to 2 ♕xf7+ ♔h8 3 e7) **2 ♕xf7+ ♔h8 3 ♕f6+ ♔h7 4 ♖xd3 ♕xb6** (or 4...♖g8 5 ♘d7 ♕c2 6 ♖f3 and wins) **5 ♕f7+ ♔h8 6 ♕xg6 ♕xf2 7 ♕xh6+ ♔g8 8 e7 ♖d7 1-0**

371) Van Kemenade-Dougherty
1 ♕xd5+! 1-0
1...♘xd5 2 ♖h8# is mate.

372) Ikonnikov-Palliser
1...♖e3! (the only move, but a good one) **2 ♕xe3** (White has nothing more than perpetual after 2 ♕h8 ♕xd5 3 ♕d8+ ♔f5!) **2...fxe3 3 ♖xf5+ ♔xf5 4 ♖e7** (there's no way for White to win; Black's passed e-pawn is fully the equal of the three extra white pawns: for example, 4 ♔g1 ♖c4! 5 ♖f7+ ♔e4 6 b6 ♔d3 forces White to take the draw with 7 b7 ♖c1+ 8 ♖f1 ♖xf1+ 9 ♔xf1 ♔d2 10 b8♕ e2+ 11 ♔f2 e1♕+ 12 ♔f3, because 7 ♖f1? loses to 7...e2 8 ♖e1 ♔d2 9 ♔f2 ♖f4+ 10 ♔g3 ♔xe1 11 ♔xf4 ♔f2 12 b7 e1♕ 13 b8♕ ♕e5+ 14 ♔g4 ♕f5+ 15 ♔h4 ♕h5#) **4...♖e4 5 g4+!** (prudent, whereas 5 ♖f7+? ♔e5 6 ♖f1 would have cost White the game after 6...e2 7 ♖e1 ♔f4) **5...♔f4 6 ♖xe4+ ♔xe4 7 ♔g2 ♔d3 8 b6 e2 9 b7 e1♕ 10 b8♕ ♕e2+ 11 ♔g3 ♕e3+ 12 ♔h4 ♕h6+ ½-½**
It's perpetual.

373) Sareen-Lohou
1 ♖xe3! ♕xe3 2 ♗xg7! gives White a winning attack: **2...♔xg7 3 ♕g6+ ♔h8 4 ♕h6+ ♔g8 5 ♕xe6+ ♔h7** (or 5...♔h8 6 ♘g6+ and 7 ♕xe3) **6 ♕xe7+** (even better is 6 ♗xf5+ forcing mate: 6...♖xf5 7 ♕xf5+ ♔h8 8 ♕h5+ ♔g8 9 ♕f7+ ♔h8 10 ♘g6#) **6...♔g8 7 ♗c4+ ♗d5 8 ♗xd5+ ♖xd5 9 ♕e6+ 1-0**

374) Kuzubov-Wademark
1 ♗xh7+! ♚xh7 2 ♖h3+ ♘h6 (desperately trying to plug the h-file; Black also would have faced a rather grim future after 2...♚g8 3 ♗e7 ♕xe7 4 ♕xg4 g6 5 e4) **3 ♕d3+ ♚g8 4 ♗xh6 f5** (not 4...gxh6? 5 ♖xh6 f5 6 exf6 when mate follows and neither would 4...♗h4 have saved Black in view of 5 g3 gxh6 6 ♖xh4 ♕g5 7 e4 ♗c6 8 exd5 exd5 9 ♖f1 with a huge attack) **5 exf6 ♗xf6** (5...♖xf6 6 ♗xg7! is rather strong too) **6 ♗xg7! ♚xg7? 7 ♕h7# 1-0**

375) Kuzubov-Palliser
1 ♖xf6! 1-0
1...♘xd3 2 ♘xd3 is crushing since the rook remains immune in view of 2...gxf6 3 ♕xf6+ ♚g8 4 ♗h6 and 5 ♕g7#.

376) Yakovich-Sarakauskas
1 ♘g5! fxg5 2 ♗e5+ f6 3 ♗xf6+ ♗xf6 4 ♕xf6+ ♚g8 (or 4...♕g7 5 ♕xd8+ ♕g8 6 ♕d6 with an extra exchange and the attack to boot) **5 ♗xe6+! ♕xe6 6 ♕xd8+ ♚f7 7 ♖c7+ ♚g6 8 ♖e7 ♕f6 9 ♕g8+ 1-0**

377) Dickson-Botterill
1...♘xc3! 2 bxc3 (White loses his queen after 2 ♗xc6 ♕xc6+) **2...♗xg2+ 3 ♚h2 ♖xd2 4 ♕xd2 ♘g4# 0-1**

378) Lambshire-Keely
1 ♖xf7+! ♖xf7 (or 1...♚h8 2 ♖h7+! ♚xh7 3 ♕xg6+ ♚h8 4 ♕h7#) **2 ♕xg6+ 1-0**
It's mate after 2...♚h8 (or 2...♚f8 3 ♕xf7#) 3 ♘xf7#.

379) Scott-Simonds
1 ♕f6! ♗xf2+ 2 ♚h1 1-0
White emerges a rook ahead after 2...♗d4 (2...gxf6 allows mate: 3 ♖g4+ ♚h8 4 ♗xf6#) 3 ♗xd4 ♖xd4 4 ♕xd4.

380) Webb-Bellin
1...♗h3! 0-1
Only a double sacrifice on e8 can avert mate since 2 ♕xh3 runs into 2...♖c1+.

381) Emms-Fressinet
Rather than the game's 1 h3, **1 ♗xg6+!** would have been all over since 1...♖xg6 2 ♕xh5+ forces mate after 2...♖h6 (or 2...♚g8 3 ♕xg6+ ♚f8 4 ♕g7+ ♚e8 5 f7+ ♚d7 6 f8♕+) 3 ♕f7+ ♚h8 4 ♕g7#.

382) Adams-Maki Uuro
1 ♗xh7+! ♚xh7 (or 1...♚g7 2 ♕g4+ ♚h8 3 ♖d3 with a crushing attack) **2 ♕h5+ 1-0**
A decisive rook-lift follows with 2...♚g7 3 ♕g4+! ♚h6 4 ♖d3.

383) Lucey-Miller
Rather than the game's 1...♘f4 2 ♕xf6+ when it was perpetual, **1...♖2g7!** would have won since **2 ♕d5** (or 2 ♕xh5+ ♖h7 and the exchange-up ending is an easy win) **2...♖h7** leaves White defenceless: for example, **3 ♘h2** (3 ♕c6 e4 is similar) **3...e4 4 ♕c6 e3** and White can't stop the e-pawn without losing his queen to the black knight.

384) James-Lobo
1 ♖xh7! ♖xb2+ 2 ♚c1 ♖b1+ (desperately trying to avoid 2...♚xh7 3 ♕xg6+ ♚h8 4 ♕xg7#) **3**

♔xb1 ♖b8+ 4 ♔a1 exf6 5 ♖xg7+ (plenty good enough, but slightly more accurate was 5 ♕xg6 forcing mate in view of the threatened 6 ♖h8+!) **5...♔xg7 6 ♕xg6+ ♔f8 7 ♕xf6+ ♕xf6 8 ♗xf6 ♔f7 9 ♗xc3 1-0**

385) Burt-Dams
1 ♘xe6!! ♘f6 (or 1...♔xe6 2 ♕f5+ ♔d6 3 ♗f4+ with a winning attack: for example, 3...♔c5 4 cxd4+ ♘xd4 5 ♖c1+ ♔b4 6 ♕e4! – by no means the only move, but by far the most attractive – 6...dxe4 7 ♗d2+ ♔b3 8 ♗c4+ ♔b2 9 ♖a2#) **2 ♕h3 ♕e7** (White emerges with an extra piece after 2...♔e8 3 ♘xd8 ♖xh3 4 ♘xc6) **3 ♗a3** (this wins the queen, but also rather good is 3 ♖e1) **3...♕xe6 4 ♗f5 1-0**

386) Spassky-Korchnoi
1 ♕h6+! 1-0
Mate follows after 1...♔xh6 (or 1...♔g8 2 ♖c8+) 2 ♖h1#.

387) Novik-Sakaev
1...♕xg2+! 2 ♔xg2 ♗xe4+ 3 ♔h2 (or 3 ♔g3 ♗d6+ 4 ♔g4 ♘d4! with an overwhelming attack in view of 5 ♕xd4 ♗f3#) **3...♖f2+ 0-1**
Black has far too many attacking pieces for the queen after 4 ♔g1 (or 4 ♔g3 ♖g2#) 4...♖xb2+ 5 ♔f1 ♖xb1+ 6 ♔e2 ♘d4+.

388) Darban-Paridar
1...♕xd6! wins a piece and gives Black a crushing attack: **2 ♕xd6 ♘e2# 0-1**

389) Schellmann-Kachiani
1...♖xb2+! 2 ♔xb2 (both 2 ♔c1 ♕b4 and 2 ♔a1 ♖d2! lead to mate) **2...♕b4+ 3 ♔c2 ♕xc4+ 0-1**
White loses his queen after 4 ♕c3 ♕a2+ 5 ♕b2 (or 5 ♔c1 ♗a3+) 5...♖e2+.

390) Henrichs-Prusikin
1...♘f3+! 2 gxf3 exf3 0-1
It's mate after 3 ♗e5 ♕xg4+ 4 ♗g3 ♖h1+ 5 ♔xh1 ♕h3+ 6 ♔g1 ♕g2#.

391) Malienko-Kruglyakov
1 ♖xe6+! ♔xe6 2 ♗b3+ ♔e7 3 ♖e1+ ♔d8 4 ♕a8+! 1-0
Black must give up a huge amount of material to delay mate after 4...♕c8 (or 4...♔c7 5 ♕xa7+ ♔c8 6 ♗e6) 5 ♕xa7.

392) Kovalenko-Chistiakov
1 ♗xh6! overloads Black's defence of g7: **1...♕g8** (or 1...♘xh6 2 ♕xe8+) **2 ♕f6+ 1-0**

393) Perez Celis-Mingorance Torres
1 ♘xh6+! gxh6 2 ♗h7+ ♔xh7 3 ♖xe5 ♖xe5 4 ♕xf4 left White with a near decisive material lead.

394) Damaso Tacoronte-Campos Vera
1 ♖xh6+! gxh6 2 ♕xh6+ ♖h7 3 ♕xf8# 1-0

395) Marrero Falcon-Vega Gutierrez
1 ♘xf7+! 1-0
Black's back-rank problems cost him far too much material after 1...♖xf7 2 ♖d8+.

396) Slaby-Mendoza
1 ♖xa7! ♖ae8 (and not 1...♖xa7? 2 ♖b8 followed by mate) **2 ♗xf8 ♖xf8 3 ♖c1** left White two pawns ahead.

397) Gimeno Higueras-Radulski
1...♗xb3+! 0-1
Following 2 ♕xb3 (or 2 ♔c1 ♗xc4 with an extra two pawns) 2...d3+ White must either give up his queen or lose his rook after 3 ♔b2 ♕xd2+.

398) Yermolinsky-Onyekwere
1 ♖a6+! ♔xa6 2 ♕xc6+ ♔a5 3 ♖b7 1-0
White's extra rook swiftly decides after 3...♔a4 4 ♕xb5+ ♔a3 5 dxe5.

399) Cottrell-Aigner
1...♕xh2+! 2 ♔xh2 ♖h4+ 3 ♔g2 ♗h3+ 0-1
It's mate with 4 ♔h1 ♗f1#.

400) Hopwood-Conroy
1 ♘f5+! ♔h8 (and not 1...gxf5? 2 ♕g5+ ♔h8 3 ♕xf6+ ♔g8 4 ♖g1#, while 1...♔g8 2 ♕h6 ♘e8 3 h4! gives White a rather powerful attack) and now, even stronger than the game's promising 2 ♘xd6, is **2 ♕h6! ♖g8 3 ♘xd6 ♕e7 4 dxe5 ♘bd7 5 ♖b7** leaving White two pawns up and with some advantage.

401) Palliser-Ansell
1 f6+! ♔xf7 2 ♕xh7+ ♔xf6 (and not 2...♔e6? 3 ♖e1+! when White wins) **3 ♕h8+** forces perpetual, although White must still be a little accurate: **3...♔f7 4 ♕h7+ ♔e6 5 ♕g8+ ♔d7 6 ♕g7+ ♔d8 7 ♕f6+ ♔c8 8 ♕h8+ ♔c7 9 ♕e5+** (preventing Black's king from hiding in the a8-corner) **9...♔c6 10 ♕f6+ ♔b5 11 ♕b6+ ♔c4 12 ♕e6+ ♔c5** (Black sensibly avoided 12...♔d3 on account of 13 ♕b3+ ♔e4 – and not 13...♔e2? 14 ♕f3# – 14 ♖e1+! ♕xe1 15 ♕e6+ ♔f4 16 ♕xe1 when White has at least a draw) **½-½**

402) Palliser-McNab
1...♖xe3! 2 ♖xd6 (2 fxe3 fails to 2...♘xg3#) **2...♕g5 0-1**
There's no defence on the kingside with 3...♕xg3 but one threat.

403) Van Wely-L'Ami
1...♘a2+! 0-1
It's mate after 2 ♕xa2 ♕c2#.

404) Palliser-Prole
Rather than the game's 1...♖xf3?, **1...♖xb3!** would have been fine for Black after **2 ♕c1** (or 2 axb3 ♕c3+ 3 ♔a2 ♗e6 when White must find 4 ♖b1! after which 4...♕a5+ 5 ♔b2 ♕xe5+ 6 ♔c1 ♕c3+ 7 ♔d1 ♕d3+ 8 ♔c1 ♕c3+ is perpetual) **2...♕xc1+ 3 ♖xc1 ♖xf3 4 ♖c7 ♗c6 5 hxg6 dxe5 6 ♖xe7 fxg6** with a likely draw.

405) Gordon-Hopwood
1...♗xa2+! 2 ♔a1 (the queen goes after 2 ♔xa2 b3+ 3 ♔b1 ♕xd2) **2...b3** (preventing possible defences with b3, although 2...a3 3 b3 ♗xb3 is also good enough for Black) **3 exf5?** (not the best, but 3 ♘c1 a3! 4 ♔b1 axb2 5 ♕xb2 ♗xd5! leaves Black with a powerful attack and two extra pawns to boot) **3...a3 4 ♔b1 ♗a2+!** (also crushing was 4...axb2 5 ♕xb2 e4, but the second bishop sacrifice on a2 is more aesthetic and decisively rips open further lines) **0-1**

406) Bailey-Palliser
1 ♗xh6! d5 (Black is mated after 1...gxh6 2 ♕xh6) **2 ♗xg7! ♗c5+ 3 ♔h1 ♘xg7 4 ♕h7+ ♔f8 5 ♕h8+ ♔e7 6 ♕xg7+ ♔d6 7 ♕xf6+** and White's extra pawns romped home.

407) Karpov-Taimanov
1...♘g3+!! 0-1
It's mate down the h-file after 2 hxg3 (or 2 ♕xg3 ♖xb1 3 ♕f3 e4 4 ♕e2 ♕d3 5 ♕xd3 exd3 and the d-pawn queens) 2...♖a8.

408) Bondarevsky-Botvinnik
1...♖xh3+! 0-1
There's no way to defend h3 after 2 gxh3 ♘df4.

409) Miralles-Thesing
1...♖xf2+! 2 ♕xf2 ♗h3+ 3 ♔f3 (or 3 ♔xh3 ♕xf2 with an extra queen and a winning attack) **3...♕e4# 0-1**

410) Garcia Castro-Arizmendi Martinez
1...♗g3!! 2 ♔xg3 (or 2 ♕xd1 ♕h2+ 3 ♔f1 ♕h1#) **2...♖h1 3 f5 ♕h3+ 4 ♔f4 ♕f3+ 5 ♔g5 ♖h5+! 6 gxh5 0-1**
It's mate after 6...♕g3#.

411) Neiksans-Stefansson
1...♕xh2+! 2 ♔xh2 ♔f7 0-1
Mate follows after 3...♖h8+.

412) Karpov-Salov
1 ♕xg6! 1-0
White is a piece up with a crushing attack since the queen is immune in view of 1...hxg6 2 ♖h4 and 3 ♖h8#.

413) Shirov-Kramnik
1...♘a3+! 2 ♔c1 (White must avoid 2 bxa3? ♖b8 when Black's queen outclasses his rooks, while 2 ♔a1 ♘c2+ 3 ♔b1 ♘a3+ repeats) **2...♗f4+! 3 gxf4 ♕xf4+ 4 ♖d2 ♖d8 5 ♖ed1 ♖xd2 6 ♖xd2 ½-½**
It's perpetual with 6...♕f1+ 7 ♖d1 ♕f4+.

414) Kulovana-Berescu
1 ♕h7+! 1-0
It's mate with 1...♔xh7 2 ♘xf6+ ♔h8 3 ♖xg8#.

415) Blecha-Berescu
1...♘a3+! 2 bxa3 (it's mate after 2 ♔a1 ♘dxc2#) **2...♕xc2+ 3 ♔a1 ♕c3+** (plenty good enough, but 3...b3! would actually have forced mate) **4 ♔b1 ♘c2 0-1**
White must give up his queen to prevent mate on a3.

416) Krupa-Giuriati
1 ♖xg7+! 1-0
It's mate down the h-file after 1...♔xg7 (or 1...♗xg7 2 ♕h7#) 2 ♘xf5+.

417) Addison-Palliser
1...♗xg2!! **2 ♖xd5** (White might try delaying this, but 2 ♔h2 ♕f3! 3 ♖xf3 ♗xf3 4 ♖xh5+ ♗xh5 5 ♕f4 ♗e2 is at least equal for Black, while 4 ♕f4 ♖g2+ 5 ♔h1 ♖g3+ forces perpetual) **2...♗xd5+ 3 ♔h2** (and not 3 ♔f1?? ♗c4+ 4 ♔e1 ♖g1+ when Black wins) **3...♖ef6!** (the point of the combination: White cannot avoid perpetual check) **4 ♖xf6** (4 ♖e2 also leads to a draw after either 4...♗f3 or 4...♖f1 5 e4 ♗xe4 6 ♖xe4 ♖f2+ 7 ♔h1 ♖f1+) **4...♖g2+ 5 ♔h1 ♖g6+ 6 ♔h2 ♖g2+ 7 ♔h1 ½-½**

418) Rubinstein-Hirschbein
1 ♖xd7! 1-0
Black must lose his queen after 1...♗xd7 2 ♘f6+ ♔f8 3 ♘d5! in view of the threat of 4 ♕h8#.

419) King-Crouch
1...♘f3+! 2 gxf3 ♘d4 3 ♕xd4 (otherwise 3...♘xf3+ leads to mate) **3...exd4 4 ♘cxe4 ♗e5 0-1**

420) Rowe-Boytsun
1 ♘xg6+! hxg6 2 ♕xg7 gave White an overwhelming attack.

421) Steinkuehler-Blackburne
1...♕g1+! 2 ♖xg1 ♘f2+ 3 ♔g2 ♗h3# 0-1

422) Leake-Emms
1...♖xc2! 2 ♕xc2? (White should restrict his losses to just a pawn with 2 ♖d2) **2...♖xg2+! 3 ♔h1?** (losing further material, but after 3 ♔xg2 ♘e3+ 4 ♔f2 ♘xc2 Black's queen is somewhat stronger than White's rooks, especially with White's king rather exposed) **3...♖xe2 4 ♕xe2 ♘g3+ 5 ♔g2 ♘xe2 6 ♔f2 ♘g3 0-1**

423) Mackinnen-Emms
1...♕xf3+! 0-1
It's back-rank mate after 2 ♖xf3 ♖e1+.

424) Spreeuw-Emms
1 g6+! fxg6 2 fxg6+ ♔h6 (now White's double threat wins a rook and the game, but 2...♔xg6 3 ♕f5+! ♕xf5 4 exf5+ ♔xf5 5 ♗xb7 would have left Black a piece in arrears) **3 ♕g8 ♔xg6 4 ♕xa2 ♕e7 5 ♗f2 1-0**

425) Adams-Hon
1 ♖xa5! ♕b7? (the rook was immune in view of 1...♕xa5? 2 ♘c6+, but even 1...♕e4 isn't much of an improvement since White has a winning attack after 2 ♖a7+ ♘d7 3 ♕h4+ ♔e8 4 ♘xe6!; for example, 4...♕b1+ 5 ♔g2 ♕e4+ 6 ♔h3 fxe6 7 ♕h7) **2 ♖a7! 1-0**
Black loses his queen after 2...♕xa7 3 ♘c6+ and 4 ♘xa7.

426) Cresswell-Wigbout
Rather than the game's 1 ♖h3 when 1...f5 would have been a good defence, **1 ♗xg7!** would have terminated proceedings in view of **1...♔xg7!** (or 1...f5 2 ♖xg6 with a crushing attack) **2 ♕f6+ ♔g8 3 ♖h3 ♗h7 4 ♖xh7! ♔xh7 5 ♖c3** and mate down the h-file.

427) Bellin-Hanreck
1 ♘xf6! 1-0
There's no defence against mate after 1...♗xf6 2 e5.

428) Kieran-Smallbone
1...♗xa3! 2 ♕e4 (it's also mate down the a-file after 2 bxa3 ♕xa3) **2...♗b4 0-1**

429) Schulder-Boden
1...d5! wins a piece: **2 ♗xd5? ♕xc3+! 3 bxc3 ♗a3# 0-1**

430) Menchik-Thomas
1 ♕xh7+! 1-0
Mate follows down the h-file.

431) Steinitz-Rosenthal
1...♖xg3+! 2 hxg3 f2+ 3 ♔xf2 (or 3 ♕xf2 ♕h1#) **3...♕g2+ 4 ♔e3 ♕f3# 0-1**

432) Andrenko-Kalinina
1...♘e2+ 2 ♔h1 ♕xh2+! 0-1
It's mate with 3 ♔xh2 ♖h6#.

433) Butkiewicz-Van der Veen
1...♘xh2! 2 ♔xh2 (otherwise 2...♕xg3+ occurs) **2...♕h5+ 3 ♔g1 ♕xe2** wins the exchange.

434) Saligo-Taverniers
1 ♗xh7+! ♔xh7 (or 1...♔h8 2 ♘g5 ♘cxe5 3 dxe5 ♘xe5 4 ♕h5 g6 5 ♗xg6+ ♔g7 6 ♖xe5! fxg6 – 6...♕xe5 7 ♗xf7 ♕f5 8 g4 is crushing – 7 ♕h7+ ♔f6 8 ♖ae1 with a rather powerful attack) **2 ♘g5+ ♔g8 3 ♘xd7 e5** (or 3...f6 4 ♘xf8 fxg5 5 ♘h7 ♕e7 6 ♕h5 and wins) **4 ♘xf8 ♔xf8 5 ♕h5** and White's attack and extra exchange shortly prevailed.

435) Martinez Martin-Hernandez Carmenates
1 ♕d4! (threatening 2 ♘g5+ and of course the knight is immune in view of 1...♕xe6 2 ♕h8#) **1...g5** (or 1...♔g8 2 ♕h8+ ♔f7 3 ♘d8+! ♔e7 4 ♘c6+ ♔f7 5 ♕h7+ ♔e6 6 ♕xh6 with an extra piece) **2 ♘xg5+ ♔g6 3 ♕d3+! ♔xg5 4 h4+ ♔f4** (or 4...♔g4 5 ♕h3+ ♔f4 6 ♕f3#) **5 ♕f3# 1-0**

436) Mateo-Hernandez Carmenates
1...♖h1+! 0-1
It's mate after 2 ♔xh1 ♕a1+ 3 ♔h2 ♕g1+ 4 ♔h3 ♕h1#.

437) Knox-Pytel
1 ♗xh7+! ♔xh7 (or 1...♔h8 2 ♘g5 g6 3 ♗xg6 fxg6 4 ♕g4 with a crushing attack) **2 ♘g5+ ♔g6** (neither 2...♔g8 3 ♕h5 ♖e8 4 ♕xf7+ ♔h8 5 ♘xe6 nor 2...♔h6 3 ♕g4 would have greatly helped Black) **3 ♕g4 f5 4 ♕g3** (rather strong too is 4 exf6 ♖xf6 5 ♘xc7) **4...♕d7?** (a blunder, although Black wouldn't have lasted long in the case of the slightly superior 4...♕c8 5 ♘xe6+ ♔f7 6 ♘bxc7) **5 ♘xe6+ ♔f7 6 ♕xg7+! ♔xe6 7 ♘d4# 1-0**

438) Konguvel-Del Valle Cirera
1 exf5! ♗xd5 2 f6 e4 (the inclusion of 2...h6 3 ♕f5 makes no real difference) **3 fxg7 ♔xg7 4 ♕xd5 exd3 5 ♕xc6** and White had won a piece.

439) Ripari-Cori
1 ♖xe6+! 1-0
It's mate after 1...♘xe6 2 ♖f7#.

440) Hungaski-Di Diego
1 ♗b5! ♘c6 (1...♕xe2 fails to, of course, 2 ♖a8#, but there was no defence in any case; for example, 1...♕b8 2 ♗f4 e5 3 ♕c4 is game over) **2 ♗xc6 1-0**
Black is crushed after 2...bxc6 3 ♕a6+ ♔d7 4 ♕b7+ ♔e8 5 ♕xc6+ ♔f8 (or 5...♖d7 6 ♖a8+ ♔e7 7 ♖xh8) 6 ♗h6+ ♔g8 7 ♖a8.

441) Frink-Horyna
1 ♗xg6! wins a pawn in view of 1...hxg6? 2 ♕xg6+ ♔h8 3 ♖xf6.

442) Stross-Benes
1 ♘h6+! ♔h8 (or 1...♕xh6 2 ♕a8+ ♗f8 3 ♖xf8#) **2 ♕f8+! 1-0**
Mate follows with 2...♗xf8 3 ♖xf8+ ♖g8 4 ♖xg8#.

443) Hruby-Baum
1...♗g3! wins White's queen: **2 ♕xg3 ♖xf3+ 0-1**

444) Milman-Fang
1 ♕g6+! fxg6 (the same finish occurs after 1...♘xg6 2 hxg6+ ♔xg7 3 ♖h7#) **2 hxg6+ ♔xg7 3 ♖h7# 1-0**

445) Zivkovic-Bodiroga
1...♖xf2+! 2 ♔e1 (or 2 ♘xf2 ♕e3+ 3 ♔f1 ♕xf2#) **2...♕e3+ 0-1**
White is defenceless after 3 ♘e2 ♖xg2 4 ♔f1 ♖h2.

446) Malakhatko-Hartmann
1 ♘xd6+! 1-0
White wins at least the exchange after 1...♕xd6 (or 1...♔f8 2 ♕xe5 with a crushing advantage) 2 ♗xe5 ♕e7 3 d6.

447) Leon Hoyes-Sanchez Enriquez
1 ♗xh6! removes a key pawn in view of 1...gxh6? 2 ♕xh6 ♘h7 3 ♖h3 with a crushing attack.

448) Stephenson-Rowntree
1 ♕xf8+! ♘xf8 2 ♖xf8+ ♕g8 3 ♖xg8# 1-0

449) Zakoscielna-Siembab
1...♖xb2+! 2 ♔xb2 ♕b7+ 0-1
It's mate after 3 ♔c1 (or 3 ♔c2 ♖a2+ 4 ♔d3 ♕b5+ 5 ♔d4 ♕c4#) 3...♖a1+ 4 ♔d2 ♖a2+ 5 ♔d1 ♕b3+ 6 ♔c1 ♕c2#.

450) Bobras-Kanarek
1...♖c1+! 0-1
It's mate after 2 ♕xc1 (or 2 ♔f2 ♖f1#) 2...♕g2#.

451) Stephenson-Greet
Rather than exchanging on g8 as in the game, **1 ♕d2!** would have forced resignation since White threatens to mate after taking on h6 and **1...gxh5** (or 1...♔g7 2 ♘xg8 gxh5 3 ♕xh6+!) fails to **2 ♕d3** followed by mate on h7.

452) Hellenschmidt-Sakayev
1 ♕f7! leaves no real defence to the threat of 2 ♖e8.

453) Maiorov-Aleksandrov
1...♗xg3! 2 ♔e2 (it's mate after 2 fxg3 ♕h1+ 3 ♔e2 ♖h2#) 2...♗xf2! 3 ♖h1 (3 ♔xf2 fails to 3...g3+! 4 ♔e1 – 4 ♔xg3 ♕h2+ 5 ♔g4 ♖h4+ 6 ♔g5 ♕g3# – 4...♕h1+ 5 ♘f1 g2) 3...♗h4 left Black two pawns ahead.

454) Botvinnik-Padevsky
1 ♕xh7+! 1-0
It's mate after 1...♔xh7 2 ♖h5+ ♔g8 3 ♖h8+ ♘xh8 4 gxh8♕#.

455) Svidler-Morozevich
1...♖xg2+! 0-1
White has nowhere near enough for the queen after 2 ♘xg2 exf4.

456) Perez-Vallejo Pons
1...♗xg2! 2 ♔xg2 (White might restrict his losses to just an exchange with 2 f4) 2...♕g4+ 3 ♔h1 ♕f3+ 0-1
The forthcoming rook lift is decisive after 4 ♔g1 ♖f6 5 ♖d1 ♕h3.

457) Handke-Kosten
1...♕xf1+! 2 ♕xf1 ♘f2+ 0-1
Black has far too much material for the queen after 3 ♔g1 ♘xd1+ 4 ♔h1 ♘f2+ 5 ♔g1 ♘h3+ 6 ♔h1 ♘xg5.

458) Roussel Roozmon-Moiseenko
1...♘f4+! 2 gxf4 (otherwise White loses his rook on e2) 2...gxf4+ 3 ♔h2 f3 0-1
There's no defence against the threat of 4...♖g2+ 5 ♔h3 ♖h1#.

459) Aronian-Carlsen
1...♗g6! (not fearing the exchange sacrifice; instead the game ended 1...♖d7? 2 e6! ♗xe6 3 ♖g8+ ♗f8 4 ♖xf8+ ♔xf8 5 ♕h6+ ♔e7 and 1/2-1/2 as it's perpetual) 2 ♖xg6 (the only real try) 2...hxg6 3 ♕xg6 ♕h3! and Black has a winning counterattack and one which prevents both 4 e6 (due to 4...♕f3+ and 5...♕xd1+) and 4 ♕xc6+ (in view of 4...♖d7 5 e6 ♕f3+ and again the white rook hangs).

460) Carlsen-Topalov
Topalov amazingly resigned here, presumably thinking his knight was lost, but Black can actually force a draw: 1...♕d5+ 2 ♔h2 (2 f3 e5 draws in similar fashion; the queen must cover g8) 2...e5 3 ♕h7+ ♔f8 4 ♕h8+ ♕g8 (the main point) 5 ♘h7+ ♔f7 6 ♘g5+ ♔f8 and White has nothing better than perpetual.

461) Capo Vidal-Magana
1 ♗xg6! hxg6 2 ♖xg6+ ♔f7 3 ♗h6 ♕e7 4 ♖g7+ ♗xg7 5 ♖xg7+ ♔e8 6 ♖xe7+ ♘xe7 7 ♗g5 saw White's queen comfortably outclass Black's rooks.

462) Gavrilov-Yuzhakov
1 ♘xe6! fxe6 (White wins the exchange after 1...♕xf6 2 ♘g5+ ♕f5 3 ♗xf5+ ♘xf5 4 ♘xh7) 2 ♕xe6+ ♔e8 (and not 2...♔c7? 3 ♕d6#) 3 ♕d7+ ♔f8 4 ♕xb7 picks up two pawns.

463) Karpov-Korchnoi
1 e5! (decisively cutting off the black queen) **1...♗xd5** (White's main idea is revealed by 1...dxe5 2 ♘xf6+ exf6 3 ♕h5! – there's no check on g5 and therefore mate is forced) **2 exf6 exf6 3 ♕xh7+ ♔f8 4 ♕h8+ 1-0**
4...♔e7 5 ♘xd5+ wins significant material in view of 5...♕xd5 6 ♖e1+.

464) Jobava-Ehlvest
1 ♖f7! 1-0
White's attack quickly assumes decisive proportions after 1...♔xf7 (or 1...♖g8 2 ♖xe7 with a crushing advantage) 2 ♕xh6 ♖g8 3 ♕h7+ ♔e8 4 ♕xg8+ ♔d7 5 ♖d1+.

465) Savchenko-Balogh
1...♘xh2! wins the exchange since the knight is immune in view of **2 ♔xh2?? ♕h4+** when White must give up his queen.

466) Torre Repetto-Sämisch
1 ♖xe6! ♘xe6 (it's mate after 1...fxe6 2 ♕g6+ ♔h8 3 ♕h7#, while 1...♖h8 2 ♘f5+ ♔f8 3 ♖xh6 gives White a crushing attack) **2 ♘f5+ ♔g8 3 ♘xh6+ 1-0**
White has a mating attack after 3...♔g7 4 ♘f5+ ♔g8 5 ♘xe7+ ♔g7 6 ♘f5+ ♔g8 7 ♘cxd6.

467) Bronstein-Kotov
1 ♗h6! 1-0
White mates with 1...♘xe5 2 ♗xg7+ ♔g8 3 ♗xe5+ ♗g5 4 ♖xg5#.

468) Bronstein-Geller
1 ♕g6! 1-0
1 ♖xf7 also wins, but Bronstein's choice is faster and more aesthetic: mate is threatened on g7 and occurs too after 1...fxg6 2 ♖xg7+ and 3 ♘xg6#.

469) Markosian-Bodnaruk
1...♕xh2+! 0-1
It's mate after 2 ♔xh2 ♗f4+ 3 ♔g1 ♗h2#.

470) Skurikhin-Samedov
1 ♖h4! ♕xe5 (or 1...♕c1+ 2 ♖e1 winning material) **2 ♘f5+ ♔g8 3 ♘e7# 1-0**

471) Alekseev-Novikov
1 ♕xh4+! ♗xh4 2 ♗d4+ (2 ♖h1 ♔g7 3 ♖xh4 is also more than good enough) **2...♗f6 3 ♗xf6+ exf6 4 ♖h1+ ♔g7 5 ♖h7+ ♔f8 6 g7+! 1-0**
White emerges the exchange ahead with an easy win after 6...♔xf7 7 g8♕+ ♔xg8 8 ♖xc7.

472) Kaidanov-Anand
1 ♕xf7+! 1-0
Mate follows with 1...♖xf7 2 ♘g6+ ♔g8 3 ♖h8#.

473) Khairullin-Vijayalakshmi
1 ♗xg6! ♔h8 (or 1...♕xg6 2 ♖g5 winning the black queen) **2 ♕xh7+! ♖xh7 3 ♖xh7+ ♔g8 4 ♘h6+ 1-0**
Mate follows down the f-file after 4...♔f8 5 ♖f1+.

474) Lysyj-Ehlvest
It's mate on the h-file: **1 ♘f6! 1-0**

475) Ulko-Zontakh
1 ♖xh7+! ♔xh7 (1...♔g8? 2 ♕h5 forces mate) **2 ♕h5+ ♔g8 3 ♗d5+ ♕f7** (or 3...♖f7 4 ♖c3 and the rook swings decisively into the attack) **4 ♗xf7+ ♖xf7 5 ♕g4** and White won shortly.

476) Kharmunova-Gavrilov
1...♖xg2! 2 ♔xg2 ♖g8+ **3** ♔f3 (or 3 ♔g3 ♕e3 and Black's attack is overwhelming) **3...♕g1 0-1**
Mate follows after 4 ♕c2 ♕f1+ 5 ♕f2 ♕d1+! 6 ♕e2 ♕h1+ 7 ♔f2 ♖g2+ 8 ♔f3 ♕xh3+.

477) Vaganian-Sargissian
1...♕h1+! 2 ♔f2 ♖xe5 **3 ♖xe5** (White is mated after 3 ♖ed4: 3...g1♕+! 4 ♖xg1 ♕h2+ 5 ♔f3 – or 5 ♖g2 ♖xf4+ 6 ♖xf4 ♕xf4+ 7 ♔g1 ♖e1# – 5...♕e2+ 6 ♔g3 ♖e3+ 7 ♔h4 ♕h2+ 8 ♔g4 ♕h3#)
3...g1♕+! (or 3...♖xf4+ 4 ♔e3 g1♕+ which transposes after 5 ♖xg1) **4 ♖xg1 ♖xf4+ 5** ♔e3 **♕f3+ 6** ♔d2 **♕c3+ 0-1**
Black emerges queen for rook ahead after 7 ♔d1 ♖d4+ 8 ♕xd4 ♕xd4+ 9 ♔c2 ♕xe5.

478) Ionov-Kremenietsky
1 ♗xh7+! ♔xh7 **2 ♖f7 ♖g8 3 ♕h3+** (3 ♖d4 is even more clinical) **3...♔g6 4 ♕xe6+ ♘f6 5 ♖xb7 ♖e8** (or 5...♕e8 6 ♖e7 ♕c8 7 ♕f7+ ♔h6 8 exf6 with a strong attack and an extra piece to boot) **6 ♕f7+ 1-0**

479) Botvinnik-Smyslov
Rather than the game's 1 ♗h3, **1 ♘d4!! ♘xd4** (it's mate after 1...cxd4 2 ♗d5+! ♖xd5 – or 2...♔h8 3 ♖e7! – 3 ♖e8, and 1...♕xa2 fails to 2 ♘e6 ♖f7 3 ♘xd8) **2 ♖e7 ♖f7** (or 2...♘e2+ 3 ♖1xe2 ♖f7 4 ♖xc2 ♖xe7 5 ♖d2 ♖e1+ 6 ♗f1 and White is queen for rook ahead) **3 ♗d5** would have been crushing, since 3...♖xd5 4 ♖e8+ forces mate.

480) Balashov-Ambartsumova
1 ♘f6! gxf6 (mate was threatened on h7 and 1...g6 2 hxg6 fxg6 3 ♕xg6 also leads to mate) **2 ♕g4 1-0**
Black's queen is lost due to the mate threat.

481) Yakovich-Naiditsch
1 b4!! 1-0
White has a mating attack after 1...♕xb4 2 ♕xg5+ ♘g6 3 ♗xg6 fxg6 4 ♖c7+ ♖f7 5 ♕e5+.

482) Kasparov-Anand
1 ♗d8! ♘e6 (Black must give up his queen after 1...♖xd8 2 ♘e7+, and the move 1...♕a7 is also insufficient due to 2 ♘e7+ ♖xe7 3 fxe7 ♕xe3+ 4 ♖f2 ♗g7 5 e8♕) **2 ♘e7+ ♖xe7 3 fxe7 ♕d7 4 ♖h3 1-0**
Mate follows.

483) Okhotnik-Marzolo
1 ♖d8+! 1-0
Black must either lose his queen after 1...♔c6 2 ♘d4+! or allow mate with 2...cxd4 3 ♕b5#.

484) Marciano-Prie
1 ♕xc6+! 1-0

It's mate after 1...♖xc6 2 ♖d8#.

485) Contin-Perdomo
1...♘xh2! wins the exchange: **2 ♘f4** (and not 2 ♗xh2?? ♘g4) **2...♕xf1 3 ♕xf1 ♘xf1 4 ♖xf1 ♗xe5** and Black won shortly.

486) Cubas-Shcherbine
1 ♘g6+! 1-0
It's mate after 1...hxg6 2 ♕h4+ ♔g8 3 ♘e7# or 3 ♘xf6#.

487) Barua-Dreev
1...♖xf2!! 2 ♔xf2 ♖xf4+ 3 ♔e2 (or 3 ♔g2 ♕xe3 with an overwhelming attack) **3...♗c4+ 4 ♔d2 ♕d4+ 5 ♔c2 ♖f2+ 0-1**
White is crushed after 6 ♖e2 (or 6 ♗e2 ♕xe3) 6...♗d3+ 7 ♔b3 ♕c4+ 8 ♔b2 ♖xe2+ 9 ♗xe2 ♕xb4+ 10 ♔a1 ♗xb1.

488) Shashikant-Hossain
1 ♗xg6! ♖g7 (or 1...hxg6 2 ♕h8#) **2 ♗xh7+ ♔f8 3 ♗g6 1-0**
There's no good defence to the threat of 4 ♕h8+ ♖g8 5 ♗h6#.

489) Marache-Morphy
1...♘g3! 0-1
White must lose his queen in view of the threat of 2...♘de2+ and of course it's mate after 2 ♕xg6 ♘de2#.

490) Evans-Bisguier
1 ♗c6! 1-0
There's no defence in view of 1...♕xa3 2 ♖xe8#.

491) Evans-Zuckerman
1 g5 ♘h5 2 ♗d3 creates the decisive threat of capturing on h5: **2...e4 3 ♖xh5! gxh5 4 ♘xe4!** (even stronger than 4 ♗xe4 ♕e5 5 ♗xh7+ ♔h8 6 ♗f5+ ♔g8 7 ♕h7+ ♔f8 8 ♗xe6 fxe6 9 g6 ♕g7 10 ♕xh5) **4...♕f4** (or 4...f5 5 gxf6 exf6 6 ♖g1+ with a crushing attack) **5 ♘f6+ exf6 6 ♗xh7+ ♔h8 7 ♗f5+ ♔g8 8 ♕h7+ ♔f8 9 ♕h8+ 1-0**
It's mate with 9...♔e7 10 gxf6#.

492) Kotronias-King
1 ♕h6! 1-0
It's mate after 1...gxh6 2 ♘xh6#.

493) *X3D Fritz*-Kasparov
1 ♖xe5!! dxe5 (it's far from easy to prevent the exchange-winning threat of 2 ♖e6; 1...♘d4 2 ♗xd4 dxe5 3 ♕xf8 exd4 transposes to the game) **2 ♕xf8 ♘d4** (White is somewhat better after 2...♖d7 3 ♕b8, but this was probably a better try) **3 ♗xd4 exd4 4 ♖e8 ♖g8 5 ♕e7+!** (neat) **5...♖g7 6 ♕d8 ♖g8 7 ♕d7+ 1-0**
The a-pawn will queen after 7...♖g7 8 ♕c8 ♖g8 9 ♖xg8 ♕xg8 10 ♕xb7+.

494) Palliser-Eggleston
1 ♖xf6! gxf6 2 ♕d7 ♔g8 3 ♕h7+ (even more effective is 3 ♕e6+ ♔g7 4 ♕e7+ ♔g8 5 ♗h7+! ♔h8 6 ♗g6) **3...♔f8 4 ♕h8+ ♔e7 5 ♕xb8 1-0**

495) Gordon-Palliser
1 ♘xg7! 1-0

White wins a key pawn in view of 1...♔xg7? 2 ♕xh7+ ♔f8 3 ♕h8+ ♔e7 4 ♗xf6+.

496) Tomashevsky-Popov
1 ♖xg6! 1-0

White's attack crashes through after 1...♖xg6 2 ♗xf5 since 2...♗xf5? 3 ♕xf5 ♖ag8 4 ♕xh5+ ♖h6 5 ♕f7+ leads to mate.

497) Skoberne-Hari
1...♘xg3+! 2 ♘xg3 ♖xh2+! 3 ♔xh2 ♖h8+ 4 ♘h5 ♖xh5+ 5 ♔g3 ♗f2+! 6 ♔xg4 (or 6 ♖xf2 ♕xe5+ 7 ♔xg4 ♕g5#) **6...♖h4+ 7 ♔g5 ♕e7# 0-1**

498) Kokol-Varini
1 ♘df7+! 1-0

It's mate after 1...♕xf7 (or 1...♗xf7 2 ♕xh7#) 2 ♘xf7+ ♗xf7 3 ♕f6+ ♖g7 4 ♕xg7#.

499) Jeric-Gombac
1...♗b2+! 2 ♔b1 (or 2 ♔xb2 ♘c4+ winning the white queen) **2...♘xb3 3 axb3** (the inclusion of 3 ♕e2 ♕b6 makes no real difference) **3...♕xb3** gave Black a mating attack.

500) Radosavljevic-Marholev
1 ♘xg6! 1-0

White has an overwhelming attack after 1...♔xg6 (or 1...♖g8 2 ♕h5+ ♔g7 3 ♘xe7 ♕xe6 4 ♘xf5+ ♔f8 5 ♘d4+ winning the queen) 2 ♕xf5+ ♔h6 3 ♕xe4 ♕xe6 4 ♖f5.

501) Mason-Gunsberg
1 ♕xg6+! ♔h8 (or 1...♔xg6 2 ♖g3#) **2 ♗xf5 1-0**

There's no defence to 3 ♕xh6+ followed by mate.

502) Blagidze-Stein
1...♖g4! 2 ♕d2 (or 2 hxg4 ♘xg4 and 3...♕xh2#) **2...♘f3+! 3 gxf3 ♕g3+ 4 ♗g2 ♗xf3 0-1**
Mate follows.

503) 'Aak'-Palliser
Black simplifies to a winning ending with **1...♖xe4! 2 ♖c3+** (or 2 ♕xe4? ♕xf2+ and 3...♕xg3) **2...♔b8 3 ♕xe4 ♕xf2+ 4 ♔c1 ♕f1+ 5 ♔d2 ♖xd5+! 6 ♖d3** (and not 6 ♕xd5 ♕e2+ 7 ♔c1 ♕e1+ 8 ♔d1 ♕xd1#) **6...♖xd3+ 7 cxd3** (Black escapes the checks after 7 ♕xd3 ♕xa1 8 ♕d6+ ♔c8, such as with 9 ♕c5+ ♔d7 10 ♕d4+ ♔e7 11 ♕b4+ ♔f6) **7...♕xa1 8 ♕xg4 ♕xb2+.**

504) 'La_Vie_en_rose'-Palliser
White wins the queen with **1 ♖c8! ♖xd5** (or 1...♖xc8 2 ♘e7+ ♔g7 3 ♘xc8) **2 ♖xd8+ ♖xd8 3 ♕a5** when his queenside majority should carry the day.

505) Gamzardia-Palliser
1...♗xg3! 2 ♖g2 (or 2 hxg3 ♖xg3+ 3 ♖g2 ♘f4 4 ♗xe6+ ♔h8 5 ♖xg3 ♕xg3+ 6 ♔f1 ♘xe2 7 ♘xe2 ♕xf3+ 8 ♔e1 e3 with an extra queen and a crushing attack) **2...♗xh2+ 3 ♔f1** (mate follows after 3 ♔h1 ♗f4+ 4 ♔g1 ♗e3+) **3...exf3 0-1**

506) Nakamura-Har Zvi
1 ♘xe6! fxe6 (White wins a piece after 1...♕c6 2 ♘xf8 ♔xf8 3 ♖d6) **2 ♗xb6 ♕xb6** (or 2...♕e7

3 ♕a4+ ♔f7 4 ♖d7 winning the queen) **3 ♕g6+ ♔e7 4 f5** (the huge threat of 5 f6+ is decisive) **4...♗d5 5 ♖xd5! 1-0**

507) Sammour Hasbun-Petrosian
1 ♕xh7+! ♔xh7 2 ♖h4+ ♔g7 3 ♖cg4# 1-0

508) Palliser-'Diliman12'
1 ♖xg7! ♔xg7 (now the rook-lift is decisive, but White also wins after 1...bxc3 2 ♖g4 ♕c7 3 ♘xc3!) **2 ♕g5+ ♔h8 3 ♕f6+ ♔g8 4 ♖f4 h5 5 ♕g5+ 1-0**

509) Palliser-'Maratonac'
1 ♖xf6! ♔xf6 (or 1...♕xf6 2 ♕h7#) **2 ♖e1** (2 ♖f1+ ♔e7 3 ♘xf7+ is more than sufficient too) **2...♖h8** and now I should have finished with 3 ♕f4+ ♔g7 4 ♕xf7+ ♔h6 5 ♘e6 (or even 5 ♘f5+! ♔xg5 6 ♖e6 ♖g8 7 h4+ leading to mate after 7...♔h5 8 g4+!).

510) Palliser-'NoMore'
1 ♗xa6! wins a pawn since 1...bxa6? 2 ♕xa6+ ♔d7 (or 2...♔b8 3 ♘b5 ♕d5 4 ♘e5! and wins) 3 ♘e5+ ♔e8 (3...♘xe5 4 dxe5 costs Black his queen) 4 ♘xc6 regains the piece with advantage.

511) Palliser-'Quike'
1 ♖xe7! ♖xe7? (losing a rook and getting mated in the bargain, although after 1...♕xe7 2 ♖xe7 ♖xe7 3 ♕xf6 ♔d7 4 ♕d4 White's queen and three extra pawns easily outclass the black rooks) **2 ♕f8+ 1-0**

512) Kochetkova-Lomako
1 ♕xh5+! 1-0
It's mate after 1...gxh5 2 ♖xh5#.

513) Reipsch-Zuse
1 ♘f4! sees the threat of 2 ♘xe6 fxe6 3 ♕g6# win material: **1...♗f7** (or 1...exf4 2 ♕g6#) **2 ♘xe5! 1-0**
It's mate after 2...fxe5 3 ♖xe5+ ♘xe5 4 ♕xd8#.

514) Henrichs-Namyslo
1 ♗xg5! hxg5 2 ♕xg5! ♗a5 (not the best defence, but White wins material after 2...♕xg5 3 ♘xg5+ ♔g6 4 ♘xf7 ♔xf7 5 ♖1e7+ ♔f6 6 ♖xc7 and even 2...♗d7 3 ♕h5+ ♔g7 4 ♕h8+ ♔g6 5 ♖xb8 ♗xb8 6 ♕xb8 leaves him with a crushing position) **3 ♕h5+ ♔g7 4 ♕h8+ ♔g6 5 ♘e5+ ♕xe5 6 ♖1xe5 ♔g7 7 ♖xc8 1-0**

515) Khantuev-Smallbone
1...♖xg2! 0-1
Disaster occurs on the long diagonal.

516) Timmins-Crouch
1 ♖h7+! ♔g8 (and not 1...♔xh7? when it's mate after 2 ♕b7+ ♔h6 3 ♕g7+ ♔h5 4 ♕h7+ ♔g4 5 ♕xg6+ ♔f4 – or 5...♔h4 6 ♕h6+ – 6 ♕h6+ ♔g4 7 ♕g5#) **2 ♖g7+ ½-½**
It's perpetual.

517) Bruce-Pafura
Instead of the game's 1...♕h1+? 2 ♔b2 ♘b5? 3 ♗e5 when Black had to resign, **1...♖xc4!! 2**

♕xc4 (and not 2 bxc4? when it's mate after 2...♕b1+ 3 ♔d2 ♕d1+ 4 ♔e3 ♗d4+ 5 ♔f4 ♕g4#)
2...♕h1+ 3 ♔b2 (3 ♔d2 fails to 3...♕d1+ 4 ♔e3 ♘d5+ when White must part with his queen)
3...♘b5+ 4 ♖c3 ♗xc3+ 5 ♔c2 ♘xd6 would have left Black a piece ahead in the endgame.

518) Smallbone-Marshall

1...♘f3+!! 2 ♔h1 (it's mate even faster after 2 gxf3 ♕g5+) **2...♕h4 3 gxf3** (now White is
mated on g2 or f3, but neither would 3 h3 have saved him in view of 3...♘xh3! 4 g3 ♕h5 5
♔g2 ♘f4+! 6 gxf4 ♕g4+ 7 ♔h1 ♕h3#) **3...♕h3 0-1**

519) Podgornei-Burt

1...♖xc4! (removing the key defender) **2 dxc4 ♖a1+! 3 ♔xa1 ♕a4+ 4 ♔b1 ♕a2+ 0-1**

520) Perryman-Brown

1...♖xa2! 2 d6 (White is mated after 2 ♔xa2 ♕c4+ 3 ♔xb2 – or 3 ♔b1 ♖a8 – 3...♕xb4+ 4 ♔c1
♖a8) **2...♕c4 3 ♕xb6 ♖da8 0-1**
It's mate down the a-file.

521) Palliser-Summerscale

White smashes open the black king position with **1 ♘xe6! fxe6?** (Black could have limped
on albeit in a somewhat worse position with 1...♕c6 2 ♘xf8 ♗xf8 3 ♖xf1 ♖d8) **2 ♕xe6+:**
2...♔h8 3 ♕xg6! (even stronger than the also decisive 3 ♕e7 ♕d8 4 e6+ ♘f6 5 ♕xd8 ♖axd8 6
e7) **3...♘f6 4 exf6 ♕xh2+ 5 ♔xf1 ♕h1+** (or 5...♕xg2+ 6 ♕xg2 ♗xg2+ 7 ♔xg2 and White's
bishops dominate proceedings – that's what I call a raking bishop-pair!) **6 ♔e2 ♖fe8+ 7
♔d2 ♖ad8+ 8 ♔c3 1-0**

522) Burt-King

1 ♗xd6! ♗xd6 (or 1...♖e8 2 ♕xf7 ♗xd6 3 ♘e6+ ♖xe6 4 ♗xe6 with an overwhelming attack)
2 ♕f6+ ♔c7 (White forces mate after 2...♗e7 with 3 ♘xc6+ ♔c7 4 ♕e5+ ♔b7 5 ♖xd7+) **3
♘b5+!** (the main point of the initial sacrifice) **3...cxb5 4 ♕xd6+ ♔b7 5 ♕xd7+ 1-0**
Black's king is finally trapped and then mated after 5...♖c7 6 ♗d5+ ♔b8 7 ♕xb5+ ♔c8 8
♕a6+ ♔d8 9 ♗f3+ ♔e8 10 ♕d6.

523) Bruce-Palliser

1 ♖xh6+! ♗xh6 2 ♕xh6+ ♔g8 (or 2...♕h7 3 ♕xf8+) **3 ♖c3 1-0**
Black loses his queen.

524) Yates-Rose

1 ♖h8+! ♗xh8 (or 1...♔xh8 2 ♕h1+ ♔g8 3 ♕h7#) **2 ♕h1 ♖e8 3 ♕h7+ ♔f8 4 ♕xf7# 1-0**

525) Riley-Burt

1...♕xa2+! 2 ♔xa2 ♖a4+ 3 ♔b1 ♖a1# 0-1

526) Speelman-Burt

1...b2! forces a draw: **2 ♖xd7 b1♕+ 3 ♔g2 ♕e4+ 4 ♔f1 ♖xf2+!** (it's perpetual) **5 ♔xf2 ♕f3+ 6
♔e1 ♕e3+ ½-½**

527) Palliser-Henbest

1 ♗d5! ♕xd5 (or 1...♖xe7 2 ♖xe7 winning the queen in view of the mating 2...♕xd5 3
♖xg7+) **2 ♕xe8 d3 3 ♕c8** and White's extra queen was sufficient for victory.

528) Palliser-Miller
1 ♘d7+! (by no means the only way to win, but by far the most clinical) **1...♖xd7 2 ♕e8+!** **♗xe8 3 ♖xe8# 1-0**

529) Lostuzzi-Spada
1...♖xh3+! 0-1
Black forces mate after 2 ♔xh3 ♕g4+ 3 ♔h2 ♕h5+.

530) Schulten-Kieseritzky
1...♕xh3+!! 2 ♔xh3 ♘e3+ 3 ♔h4 ♘f3+ (another attractive finish is 3...g5+ 4 ♔h5 ♗g4+ 5 ♔h6 ♗f8#) **4 ♔h5 ♗g4# 0-1**

531) Margiotta-Chen
1 ♗xh7+! ♔xh7 2 ♘g5+ ♗xg5 3 hxg5+ ♔g8 4 ♕xg4 left White a pawn ahead with a very strong attack.

532) Donskov-Prokuronov
1...♗xg2! 2 ♕e3 (White's king is eventually mated mid-board after 2 ♔xg2 ♖g8+ 3 ♔f3 ♖h3+ 4 ♔e4 – or 4 ♔f4 ♕xf5# – 4...d5+ 5 ♔e5 ♕c7+ 6 ♔d4 e5+ 7 ♔xd5 ♖d8+ 8 ♔e4 ♖d4#) **2...♗c6! 0-1**
Black has an overwhelming attack after 3 ♖g2 (or 3 ♕xc5 ♖h1#) 3...♕xf5.

533) Malofeev-Fedoseev
1 ♘xg7! removed a key pawn: **1...♔xg7 2 ♖b3 ♕a5 3 ♖g3 ♔h8 4 ♖xd8! ♕xd8 5 ♕e5 ♕d1+ 6 ♗f1 1-0**
Mate follows.

534) Mustaps-Somova
1 ♘e6+! fxe6 (otherwise the black queen is lost) **2 ♕xe6 1-0**
There's no defence to the mate threats on f7 and h6.

535) Fedoseev-Khamidulin
1...♕f2! 2 ♕c3+ (the queen is immune: 2 ♖xf2 ♖d1+ mates) **2...♔g8 3 ♖g1 ♖d1 0-1**
There's no defence along the first rank.

536) Strenzwilk-Thaler
1 ♕xh7+! ♔xh7 2 ♖h5# 1-0

537) Dimitrov-Janev
1...♗c2+! 2 ♔xc2 (or 2 ♔d5 ♘e3+ 3 ♔xd6 ♕xf4+ 4 ♔e7 ♘f5+ 5 ♔e8 ♗a4+ winning a monstrous amount of material) **2...♕e3+ 0-1**
It's mate after 3 ♔xf5 ♕e6#.

538) Sokolov-Bologan
1...♗xg2+! 0-1
Mate follows with 2 ♔xg2 ♕g3+ 3 ♔f1 (or 3 ♔h1 ♕xh3#) 3...♕g1#.

539) Bologan-Jakovenko
1...♖xg6! 2 ♘xg6 (or 2 ♖xg6 ♗xe5 trapping the rook) **2...♕b8! 0-1**
White cannot both prevent mate and save his rook.

540) Brugo-Grosse Honebrink
1...♘f3+! 2 ♖xf3 ♕xh2+ 3 ♔f1 ♗xg5 4 ♘xg5 (or 4 ♘2g3 ♕h4 5 ♔g1 f5 with an extra pawn and some initiative) **4...♕h1+ 5 ♘g1 ♖xe1+ 6 ♔xe1 ♕xg1+** picks up the exchange.

541) Erneker-Meijers
1...♗xb3+! 0-1
1...♕xb3+! comes to the same thing: Black is two pawns up in the ending after 1...♗xb3+ 2 ♕xb3+ ♕xb3+ 3 ♔xb3 ♖xd2.

542) Babula-Blatny
1 ♖h8+! ♔g7 (and not 1...♔xh8? 2 ♘f7+ ♔g7 3 ♘xg5) **2 ♖xb8** wins a piece.

543) Padurariu-Tutulan
1 ♕d8+! 1-0
Mate follows with 1...♘xd8 2 ♖xd8+ ♔f7 3 ♖f8#.

544) Palliser-Ellison
1 ♗xd5+! 1-0
More aesthetic would have been 1...cxd5 2 ♗xd5+ ♖e6 3 ♗xe6#, although it's mate in three in either case.

545) Bak-Palliser
1...♘g3+! 0-1
White must give up his queen and the exchange on d4 to avoid mate after 2 hxg3 ♕g5 in view of 3 g4 ♕h4#.

546) Rogic-Bulatovic
1 ♗f6+! wins the exchange on h8 in view of 1...♔xf6? 2 ♕d4#.

547) Plenca-Saric
1...♕d2! 0-1
Black wins a rook since it's mate after 2 ♕xd2 ♖xf1#.

548) Vaganian-Gallagher
1...♘xg3! 2 hxg3 ♕xg3+ 3 ♔h1 ♖d3! ½-½
Now that ♘h2 defences have been negated, it's perpetual after 4 ♕xd3 ♕h3+ 5 ♔g1 ♕g3+.

549) Sandipan-Nisipeanu
1...♕d4+! (forcing the white king to a worse square and thereby making the tactics work) **2 ♔f1** (or 2 ♔h1 ♕xc3! 3 ♗xc3 ♖xd1+ 4 ♗e1 ♖xe1#) **2...♗xb3! 3 ♕xb3** (White is also defenceless after 3 ♕b2 ♗c4+) **3...♕xd2 4 ♕xb6 ♖xc3 0-1**

550) Kasparov-Chuchelov
1 ♖xh7! ♔xh7 (or 1...♕g6 2 ♖dh1 ♘d4 – 2...♕xd6 3 ♕xe4 is crushing – 3 c5! and White wins since 3...♘xc2? 4 ♗c4+ forces mate) **2 ♗xf8 ♕xf8?** (now White finishes with a flurry, although otherwise he is a pawn ahead and still with good attacking chances) **3 ♕xe4+ ♔g8 4 ♕d5+ 1-0**
4...♕f7 5 ♕xf7+ ♔xf7 6 ♖xd7+ ♔g6 7 ♖xb7 regains the piece with a trivially winning endgame.

551) Parker-Rasmussen
1 ♖xg7! forces mate: **1...♔xg7 2 ♗xe8+ ♔g8 3 ♕xh7# 1-0**

552) Borriss-Palliser
1...♘xb2! 2 ♔xb2 ♕xa3+ 3 ♔c3 (or 3 ♔c2 ♕a2+ 4 ♔d3 ♕xb3+ 5 ♔e2 ♖a2+ 6 ♖d2 ♕xd5 and two pawns ahead, Black should be winning) **3...♖b8!** (the most precise; 3...♖c8+ 4 ♔d2 ♕b4+ 5 ♔e2 ♖c6 6 ♕d4 enables White to put up some resistance) **4 ♕d4?** (not the best defence; instead 4 ♖b1 ♖c8+ 5 ♔d3 ♕a6+ reveals the main point of Black's combination, leaving White's king devoid of a good square; however, perhaps White might have tried 4 ♖d3, although Black can at least reach a two-pawn up ending with 4...♖xb3+ 5 ♔d2 ♕a2+ 6 ♔e1 ♖b1+ 7 ♖d1 ♖xd1+ 8 ♔xd1 ♕xd5+) **4...♕xb3+ 5 ♔d2 ♖b4 6 ♕e3 ♕xd5+ 7 ♔e2 ♕g2+ 0-1**

553) Palliser-Zhigalko
1...♖xh3+! 2 gxh3 ♕e4+ 0-1
White both loses his queen and will be mated after 3 ♔g1 (or 3 ♔h2 ♖d2+ 4 ♔g3 ♖g2#) 3...♖g5+ 4 ♔h2 ♖g2+ 5 ♔h1 ♕xc6.

554) Miller-Murray-Smith
1 ♗xg7! ♗xg7? (Black is also crushed after 1...♗xh4? 2 ♕g4! h5 3 ♕xh4 ♔xg7 4 f6+, but he might have restricted his losses to that of an exchange with 1...♖e3 2 ♕xe3 ♗xg7) **2 f6 ♕xf6 3 ♖xf6 ♖e6 4 ♘f5 1-0**

555) Bronstein-Krogius
1 ♖xf6! (not the only way to win, but by far the simplest as Black now loses his queen) **1...♕xf6 2 ♘d7 1-0**

556) Voicu-Taras
1...♘xb2! 2 ♔xb2 ♗xc3+ removed a key defensive pawn.

557) Palliser-Surtees
Rather than the game's 1 ♕d1?, **1 ♗h4+! ♖xh4** (Black is mated after both 1...♔g6 2 ♕xe6+ ♔h7 3 ♕xf5+ ♔g8 4 ♕f7+ ♔h7 5 ♕xg7# and 1...g5 2 fxg5+ ♘xg5 3 ♕f7+ ♔e5 4 ♕e7+ ♘e6 5 ♗f6#) **2 ♕xa8** would have won the black queen with an overwhelming advantage.

558) Goloshchapov-Belov
1 ♖xe5! ♖xd2 (1...♕xe5 2 ♖xd8+ ♔g7 3 f6+ also leads to mate) **2 ♖e8+ ♔g7 3 f6+ ♔h6 4 g5+ 1-0**
It's mate with 4...♔h5 5 ♗f3#.

559) Bocharov-Babiy
1 ♖xf8+! ♕xf8 2 ♘g6+ 1-0
Black's queen is lost in view of 2...♖xg6 3 ♕xf8+.

560) Nepomniachtchi-Kurnosov
1 ♖xb2! ♕xb2 2 ♘g4 leaves Black unable to defend on the kingside: **2...♕c1+ 3 ♔h2 a3** (or 3...h5 4 ♘h6+ ♔h7 5 ♘xf7 ♖g8 6 ♘g5+ ♖xg5 7 hxg5 when the queen and pawns combine to force mate) **4 ♘h6+** (missing the even more precise 4 f4!) **4...♕xh6 5 ♕xh6 1-0**
White is winning easily after 5...f6 6 ♕e3 ♖a8 7 ♕b3+ ♔f8 8 ♕b7.

561) Rublevsky-Bologan
1...♖xf3! 2 ♕xf3 (White must give up his queen after 2 gxf3 ♗xf3+, while 2 ♖xf2 ♖xb3

leaves Black a clear piece ahead) **2...♛xd2! 3 ♛xg4** (Black again emerges a piece up after 3 ♖xd2 ♖c1+ 4 ♖d1 ♖xd1+ 5 ♛xd1 ♝xd1) **3...♖c1 0-1**
Serious material losses are unavoidable due to White's weak back rank.

562) Bologan-Van Haastert
1 ♛xh5+! gxh5 (or 1...♚g8 2 ♛xg6 with an overwhelming attack) **2 ♞f6+! ♝xf6 3 ♖xh5# 1-0**

563) Shabalov-Krush
1 ♞d4+! exd4 (now it's mate, but otherwise Black's queen is lost) **2 ♖g5+ ♚f4 3 ♛xd6+ ♚e3 4 ♛xd4# 1-0**

564) Colautti-Burijovich
1...♞e3+! 2 ♛xe3 ♛xe1 3 ♞f3 ♛h1 wins the exchange.

565) Garro Beraza-Estevez Pegenaute
1 ♝xg6! hxg6 (or 1...♚h8 2 ♝xe8 ♛xe8 3 ♝g7+ with an overwhelming attack) **2 ♛xg6+ ♚h8 3 ♝g7+ 1-0**
Now it's mate, but actually even faster is 3 ♝f8.

566) Garro Beraza-Kuende Gorostidi
1...♖h1+! 0-1
It's mate with 2 ♚xh1 ♛h4+ 3 ♚g1 ♛h2#.

567) Yrjola-Riesco Lekuona
1 ♖xe6+! 1-0
Mate follows with 1...♚xe6 (or 1...♚d8 2 ♛h8+ ♚c7 3 ♝a5+ ♚c6 4 ♝a4#) 2 ♖e1+ ♝e4 3 ♖xe4+ ♛xe4 4 ♛f6#.

568) Schrocker-Stahlberg
1...♛xh4! 0-1
It's mate after 2 gxh4 ♞h3#.

569) Dominguez-Iturrizaga
1...♖xh2+! 2 ♖xh2 ♛e1+ 0-1
Mate follows with 3 ♚g2 ♖xh2#.

570) Leon Hoyes-Dominguez
1 ♛h8+! ♚xh8 2 ♞xf7+ 1-0
It's mate with 2...♚g8 3 ♞h6#.

571) Rodrigues-Molina
1...♛xc2+! 2 ♚xc2 ♝f5+ 3 ♚c1 (or 3 ♚c3 ♖c4#) **3...♞d3+ 4 ♚b1 ♞xf2+** wins at least a piece.

572) Graf-Carlsen
1 ♝c6! 1-0
Black has no satisfactory defence to 2 ♖d8+ and cannot avoid losing a piece.

573) Reinaldo Castineira-Caselas Cabanas
1 ♖dd7! leaves Black defenceless: **1...♞xd7 2 ♛xa6+ 1-0**
It's mate with 2...bxa6 3 ♖a7#.

574) Santos-Navarrette
1 ♕xg7+! 1-0

Mate follows on the back rank after 1...♖xg7 2 ♖d8+.

575) Farago-Grooten
1...♖xh3+! 2 gxh3 g2+! 3 ♔xg2 ♕g5+ 0-1

It's mate after 4 ♔h2 (or 4 ♔h1 ♕g3) 4...♗f4+ 5 ♔h1 ♕g3 and ...♕h2#.

576) Arakhamia Grant-Hanley
1 ♘xg7! (those seeking something more flashy can be reassured that 1 ♘h6+! ♔h8 –
1...gxh6 2 ♗xf6 and mate down the g-file – 2 ♗xf6 gxf6 3 ♘xf7+ ♔g8 4 ♕d5 also does the
business) **1...♗xg7 2 ♗xf6 ♗xf6 3 ♕xf6 ♕xd3** (or 3...♕b3 4 ♖a5 and a rook-lift decides in
any case) **4 ♕xf7+ ♔h8 5 ♕f6+ ♔g8 6 ♖f5 1-0**

577) Sagalchik-Krush
1...♘xb2!! 2 ♖xe6 (an immediate 2 ♔xb2 loses to 2...♗xe2; for example, 3 ♖xe6 ♗xc3+ 4 ♔c2
♕b4 5 ♖xe2 ♗e1+ 6 ♔d3 ♖c3+ 7 ♘xc3 ♖xc3# or 3 ♕d2 ♗xf1 4 ♖xf1 ♗xc3+ 5 ♘xc3 ♖xc3 6
♕xc3 ♖xc3 7 ♔xc3 a5 with a winning ending) **2...♕d7 3 ♔xb2** (or 3 ♖f3 ♘a4 4 ♔d2 ♗xe2 5
♔xe2 ♘xc3+ 6 ♘xc3 ♗xc3 7 ♔f2 ♗xd4+ 8 ♔g3 ♗g7 with some advantage for Black)
3...♗xe2 4 ♖xe2 (this loses, but improvements are hard to suggest; for example, 4 ♖c1 ♗d3
and Black retains a rather strong attack) **4...♕b5 5 ♖c2** (now White loses her queen, but 5
cxb4 ♕xe2+ 6 ♔a1 ♕xg2 7 ♖f8 ♕xg4 also wins) **5...♗f8+ 0-1**

578) Menchik-Graf
1 ♖d7! 1-0

After 1...♕xd7, 2 ♕xh5! forces mate in view of 2...gxh5 3 ♗h7#.

579) Cohen Gomez-Dizdar
1...♘g3+! 0-1

It's mate after 2 hxg3 ♕h3#.

580) Narciso Dublan-Lazaro Porta
1 ♕xh7+! 1-0

It's mate with 1...♔xh7 2 ♖h3+ ♔g8 3 ♖h8#.

581) Wan Yunguo-Liang Chong
1 ♘xg6! hxg6 (or 1...♕f6 2 ♘xf8+ ♔xf8 with an extra exchange) **2 ♕xg6+ ♔h8 3 ♕h6+ ♔g8
4 ♗g5 1-0**

Black must lose his queen in view of 5 ♗f6.

582) Xiu Deshun-Du Shan
1 ♘f6+! gxf6 2 ♗xb7 1-0

White wins the exchange on a8 in view of 2...♕xb7? 3 ♕g4+ ♔h8 4 ♗xf6#.

583) Allison-Hopwood
1 ♘e7+! 1-0

It's mate after 1...♘xe7 2 ♕xc8+ ♘xc8 3 ♖xc8#.

584) Hopwood-Newitt
1 ♗xh7+! (full marks too for 1 exf6 which wins a piece since 1...♗xd1? is mated by 2 ♗xh7+
and 3 ♘g6#) **1...♘xh7** and now White neglected to play **2 ♕xd5+** when Black is crushed

after 2...♗e6 3 ♘gxe6 ♘b4 4 ♕b3.

585) Garma-Shanmugam
1 ♕xh7+! 1-0
It's mate with 1...♔xh7 2 ♖h5#.

586) Tarjan-Karpov
1...♖e3+! 0-1
It's mate after 2 fxe3 ♕g3#.

587) Ovod-Hou Yifan
1...♖8e3! 2 ♘xe3 ♖xe3 gives Black a winning attack: **3 ♖ce2 ♕xh3+ 4 ♔g1 ♖g3+ 5 ♔g2 ♘f3+ 6 ♔f1 ♕h1+ 7 ♔f2 ♕xg2+ 0-1**

588) Gunina-Zhao Xue
1...♖f2! overloads White's defence of b2: **2 ♖b1** (2 ♘xf2 fails to 2...♕xb2#) **2...♘a5 0-1**
The threat of 3...♘b3# is terminal (2...♘d4 comes to the same thing).

589) Nebolsina-Gromova
1 ♕h8+! 1-0
It's mate with 1...♔xh8 2 ♖xh5+ ♔g8 3 ♖h8#, although this solution is sadly cooked: 1 ♖e8! also does the business.

590) Alsina Leal-Mirzoev
1...♗xf2+! 2 ♔h2 (or 2 ♔xf2 ♕e1#) **2...♗xg3+ 3 ♔xg3 ♕e1+** (even faster is 3...♕e5+ 4 ♔xg4 ♕f4+ 5 ♔h5 ♕h4#) **4 ♔h2 g3+ 0-1**
Mate follows with 5 ♔h3 ♕h1+ 6 ♔xg3 ♕h4+ 7 ♔f3 ♕f4#.

591) Fischer-Myagmarsuren
1 ♕xh7+! 1-0
It's mate after 1...♔xh7 2 hxg6+ ♔xg6 (or 2...♔g8 3 ♖h8#) 3 ♗e4#.

592) Player-Fegan
1...♘f2+! 2 ♔g1 (or 2 ♖xf2 ♖e1+) **2...♘h3+ 3 ♔h1 ♕g1+! 4 ♖xg1 ♘f2# 0-1**

593) Plasgura-Feller
1 ♗xh7+! ♔xh7 2 ♘g5+ ♔g8 (the best defence since both 2...♔g6? 3 ♕d3+ f5 4 ♘f4+! ♔xg5 5 ♕g3+ and 2...♔h6 3 ♕d3! quickly culminate in mate) **3 ♕d3 g6?** (a much better defence is 3...♖e8, although 4 ♕h7+ ♔f8 5 ♕h5! ♘d8 – or 5...♘dxe5 6 dxe5 ♘xe5 7 ♗e3 ♕b5 8 ♕h8+ ♔e7 9 ♕xg7 with strong attacking chances – 6 ♕h8+ ♔e7 7 ♕xg7 ♖f8 8 a3 ♕a5 9 ♘h7 ♔e8 10 ♗g5 leaves White with the initiative and some advantage, not least due to his passed h-pawn) **4 ♕h3 1-0**
Mate follows on h7 (or f7 should the f8-rook move).

594) Gantsevich-Smirnov
1 ♘f7+! ♘xf7 (or 1...♖xf7 2 ♗xf7 ♖xh4 3 ♗xe8 with an extra exchange) **2 ♕xf6+ ♔g8** (White wins a piece after 2...♕g7 3 ♕xf7) **3 ♗h6! 1-0**
Black loses his queen in view of 3...♕xh6 4 ♗xf7+ ♔f8 5 ♗e6#.

595) Glazov-Stroganov
1...♕xb2+! 0-1

It's mate after 2 ♖xb2 ♖e1#.

596) Kulikov-Gogin
1 ♘xe6! 1-0
Black's queen is lost since White threatens mate on c7 and 1...fxe6 fails to 2 ♕xe6+ followed by mate.

597) Malakhov-Nikiforov
1 ♖xg7! 1-0
Mate follows after 1...♖xg7 2 ♕xh6+ ♖h7 3 ♕xf6+.

598) Popov-Ponkratov
1 ♖xc6! bxc6 2 b7+ ♔xb7 (or 2...♔b8 3 ♘xc6+ ♔xb7 4 ♖b1+ ♔a8 5 ♕b6 followed by mate) **3 ♖b1+ ♔a8** (neither is Black's cause helped by either 3...♔c7 4 ♘b5+ ♔b7 5 ♕e7+ ♔b6 6 ♘c3+ or 3...♔c8 4 ♗xg4+ ♔c7 5 ♕b6#) **4 ♖b4 1-0**
Black can no longer defend c6.

599) Chadaev-Lanin
1...♘c3+! 2 bxc3 ♖xd1 3 ♕xd1 ♕xc3 4 ♘e5 ♗xe5 forced White to give up the exchange with **5 ♖xe5 ♕xe5**.

600) Potemkin-Alekhine
1...♘xd4! 2 gxf5 (White only chance was to try 2 f4, although Black retains a large advantage after 2...♕d7 in view of 3 ♕xd3? ♘f5+; as he does too after 2 ♘xd4 ♕e5+ 3 f4 ♕xd4) **2...♘xf5+ 0-1**
Mate follows with 3 ♔g4 h5+ 4 ♔h3 ♘f2#.

601) Airapetian-Burtasova
1...♖g1+! 2 ♔xg1 ♕xf3 and the extra queen prevailed.

602) Kurilov-Urjubdshzirov
1 ♘xg7! wins a pawn in view of 1...♔xg7 (or 1...♗xd3 2 ♕xd3 ♔xg7 3 ♗xf6+ ♔xf6 4 ♕d4+ regaining the piece with some advantage in view of 4...♔f5? 5 g4#) 2 ♗xe4 dxe4? 3 ♗xf6+ ♔xf6 4 ♕xd7.

603) Andreikin-Lanin
1 ♕xg7+! ♖xg7 2 ♖f8+ 1-0
It's mate next move.

604) Sevillano-Stripunsky
1...♖xd6! 2 ♕xd6 ♗e5 3 ♖h4 (desperately trying to avert mate on h2 and there was nothing better) **3...♗xg2+! 0-1**
White loses the exchange after 4 ♔g1 ♕xh4 5 ♕xe5 ♗xf1 6 ♗xf1 or his queen following 4 ♔xg2 ♕g5+ and 5...♗xd6.

605) Kaidanov-Ivanov
1 h6! fxe5 2 ♗xe7 ♘xe7 (or 2...♕xd4 3 hxg7 ♘xe7 4 gxf8♕+ ♔xf8 5 ♕h6+ with an overwhelming attack) **3 ♖xg7+ ♔h8 4 ♕g5 1-0**
White threatens 5 ♖h7# and after 4...♖g8 5 ♕xe7 the mate threat on h7 continues to decide.

606) Ehlvest-Pruess
1 ♞c7! costs Black at least an exchange in view of 1...♞xc7 2 ♝c3 winning the queen.

607) Anderson-Root
1 ♝xg6! fxg6 2 ♛xg6+ ♔f8 3 ♛xh6+ ♔g8 4 ♖f3 (White has a mating attack) **4...♖h7 5 ♛g6+ 1-0**

608) Plunkett-Latino
1 ♖h8+! 1-0
It's mate after 1...♝xh8 2 ♛h3 ♖fd8 3 ♛h7+ ♔f8 4 ♛xf7#.

609) Akobian-Perelshteyn
1...♖xe3! 2 ♝d4 (White is crushed after 2 fxe3 ♞e4! since 3 fxe4 ♝xc3+ forces him to part with his queen as 4 ♔f2 allows mate: 4...♛h4+ 5 ♔g1 ♛g5+ 6 ♔f2 ♛g2#) **2...♖e8** and Black retained excellent attacking chances. The game concluding **3 ♖g1 ♞h5 4 ♛d2 ♖a4 5 0-0-0 ♛c8+ 6 ♔b1 ♝f5+ 7 ♔a1 ♛c2 0-1**

610) Shulman-Krush
1 g4! ♛f4 2 ♛e5+ ♛xe5 3 dxe5+ ♔g6 4 h5# 1-0

611) Bayaraa-Veal
1 ♞xh7! 1-0
It's mate after 1...♔xh7 (or 1...♛b4 2 ♝d2 ♛xd4 3 ♛h6 when mate follows) 2 ♛h4+ ♛h6 3 ♛xh6#.

612) Pitson-Fraser
1...♝xh3+! 2 ♔xh3 (or 2 ♔g3 ♛d7!? – simple and strong is 2...♝xf1 – 3 ♛e2 ♞xf3! 4 ♛xf3 ♝e5+ 5 ♝f4 ♖f8 6 ♞e2 g5 with a strong attack which should at least regain the material with interest) **2...♞xf3** (now White can only avoid mate by giving up his queen) **3 ♛e2 ♛h4+ 4 ♔g2 ♛g4+ 0-1**

613) Bellon Lopez-Berg
1 e6! ♛e7 (mate occurs after both 1...fxg6 2 ♛xg6 and 1...fxe6 2 ♛e5!) **2 exf7 axb3 3 ♛xh6+! gxh6 4 ♖xg8# 1-0**

614) Gagarin-Andersson
1 ♞xf7! ♖xf7 (1...♔h7 2 ♞e6 ♖xf7 3 ♞xc5 ♖c7 4 ♝a3 and White emerges ahead on material because of 4...a5? 5 ♝xb4 axb4 6 ♖xc2 ♖xc5 7 ♝g8+!) and now White missed the cleanest continuation of **2 ♝c3** (the game's 2 ♝xf6 gxf6 3 ♞d5 b5! 4 ♞xf6+ would not have been so bad at all for Black after 4...♔g7 5 ♞e8+ ♔f8 6 ♝xf7 ♔xf7 7 ♞c7 bxa4 8 bxa4 a5) **2...♝d3** (the only way to save the bishop) **3 ♝xf7+ ♔xf7 4 ♝xf6 ♝d6!? 5 ♝d4 ♞a2 6 ♖a1 ♞b4 7 ♞a8** with a clear extra exchange.

615) Palliser-Cable
1 ♝xh6! wins a pawn: 1...gxh6? 2 ♛xh6+ ♔g8 3 ♛xh5 regains the piece, leaving White two pawns ahead and still with good attacking chances.

616) Jasny-Palliser
1 ♞h6+! ♔h8 (or 1...gxh6 2 ♛e6#) **2 ♛e6 1-0**
Even 2...♝e7 doesn't save Black in view of the smothered mate: 3 ♛g8+! ♖xg8 4 ♞f7#.

617) Bernardino-Dragicevic
1 ♗xg7! ♗xg7 (otherwise 2 ♗xf6+ or 2 ♕h8+ ♔f7 3 ♕h7 decides) **2 ♖xg7+! ♔xg7 3 ♖g1+ ♔f8 4 ♕h7 1-0**
Mate follows on g8.

618) Borosova-Newrkla
1 f6! gxf6? (or 1...♕e6 2 fxg7 ♖g8 3 ♖h3 and h6 decisively falls) **2 ♘xh6! 1-0**
It's mate after 2...♔xh6 3 ♖f5 or 3 ♖h3+.

619) Short-Ye Jiangchuan
1 ♕xh7+! 1-0
It's mate after 1...♔xh7 2 ♖h3+ ♗h4 (or 2...♔g7 3 ♗h6+ ♔h8 4 ♗f8+ ♗h4 5 ♖xh4#) 3 ♖xh4+ ♔g7 4 ♗h6+ ♔h7 5 ♗f8#.

620) Sild-Piarnpuu
1...♕xf3! 0-1
It's mate after 2 gxf3 ♗xf3#.

621) Shvyrjov-Gansvind
1...♖xa3+! 0-1
Mate follows with 2 ♗xa3 ♖a2#.

622) Miezis-Lelumes
1 ♕f5+! 1-0
White wins a piece, either on g4 or after 1...♗xf5 2 exf5+ ♔f7 3 ♗xc6.

623) Mikenas-Bronstein
1...♖xa3! 0-1
White cannot both save his queen and prevent mate on the back rank.

624) Grabuzova-Batyte
1 ♖xf7+! ♔xf7 2 ♕c7+ 1-0
Mate is forced: 2...♔f6 (2...♔f8 3 ♕d8+ ♔f7 4 ♗e6+ transposes) 3 ♕d8+ ♔f7 4 ♗e6+ ♔g6 5 ♕e8+ ♔g5 6 ♕g8+ ♔f6 7 ♕f7+ ♔e5 8 ♕f5#.

625) Stephenson-Humphries
1 ♖xf7+! ♔g8 (Black loses his queen after 1...♔xf7 2 ♘e6+ and 3 ♘xc7) **2 ♖g7+!** (a nice touch) **2...♔h8** (2...♔xg7 3 ♘e6+ again wins the queen, while 2...♘xg7 fails to 3 ♕xh7#) **3 ♖xh7+ ♔g8 4 ♖g7+ ♔h8 5 ♖xg6 1-0**
White's attack is absolutely crushing after 5...♘df6 6 ♖f1.

626) Stisis-Lundvik
1 ♖c5! ♕xf3 2 ♖xc8# 1-0

627) Lener-Trapl
1...♖xc2+! 2 ♖xc2 (it's also mate after 2 ♔e1 ♘g2+ 3 ♔f1 – or 3 ♔d1 ♕xd3# – 3...♕xf2#) **2...♕xd3+ 3 ♔e1 ♘g2# 0-1**

628) Svarc-Vokac
1...♘xg3+! 0-1
Mate follows after 2 hxg3 ♖xe2.

629) Geller-Langeweg
1 ♗xf7+! 1-0
White wins an exchange either on e8 or with 1...♔xf7 2 ♕b3+ ♖e6 3 ♘g5+.

630) Stephenson-Rayner
1 ♖xb2! ♖xd7 (or 1...♕xb2 2 ♗d4+ ♕xd4+ 3 ♖xd4 ♖xd4 4 ♕e5+ ♖f6 5 ♕xf6#) **2 ♗d4+! ♖g7**
(the a1-h8 diagonal is also the deciding factor after 2...♖xd4 3 ♕e5+) **3 ♖xb7 ♗f7 4 ♖xf7 1-0**

631) Foisor-Pavlovic
1 ♖h4+! 1-0
It's mate after 1...gxh4 2 g4#.

632) Volokitin-Kravtsiv
1 ♗xg7! ♔xg7 (White has a winning attack after 1...♖fe8 2 ♗f6 and 1...f6 2 ♗xh6 ♖f7 3 ♗b3
is rather strong too) **2 ♕g3+ ♔h7 3 ♕f4 1-0**
It's mate after 3...f5 4 ♕xh6+ ♔g8 5 ♕h8+ ♔f7 6 ♖h7+ ♔g6 7 ♖h6+ ♔g5 (or 7...♔f7 8 ♕h7#) 8
h4+ ♔g4 9 ♗d1+ ♔f4 10 ♕d4#.

633) Schlechter-Meitner
1 g4+! fxg4 (or 1...♔h4 2 ♕xh6+! ♕xh6 3 ♔h2 fxg4 4 hxg4 transposing) **2 hxg4+ ♔h4 3
♕xh6+! ♕xh6** (otherwise Black loses his queen) **4 ♔h2! 1-0**
There's no good defence to 5 ♗f2#.

634) Spielmann-Hoenninger
1 ♘e7+! ♕xe7 2 ♕xh7+! ♔xh7 3 ♖h5+ ♔g8 4 ♖h8# 1-0

635) Azarov-Zherebukh
It's back-rank mate: **1 ♕xg7+! ♖xg7 2 ♖e8+ 1-0**

636) Tadic-Solak
1 ♗b6+! axb6 2 ♕xb6+ ♔e7 3 ♕c5+ ♔d8 4 ♗b5+ ♘d7 5 ♖xd7+ ♔e8 6 ♖d1# 1-0

637) Solak-Arsovic
1 ♖e8! 1-0
The rook is immune due to 1...♕xe8 2 ♕f6#, while 1...♕g5 2 ♕xf7 is crushing.

638) Ivanisevic-Pikula
1...♕d1+! 0-1
Black emerges the exchange ahead after 2 ♖xd1 ♖xd1+ 3 ♔h2 ♗d6+ 4 ♕xd6 ♖xd6.

639) Pham Minh-Tran Quoc Ding
1 ♖f4+! ♖xc2 2 ♖g8+ ♔h5 3 ♖f5+ 1-0
Mate follows after 3...♔h4 4 g3+ ♔xh3 5 ♖h5+.

640) Spalding-Robertson
1 ♖xc7! ♖d8 (with the point that Black loses his queen after 1...♕xc7 2 ♘xe6+), and now the
simplest win is **2 ♖xf7+ ♔g6 3 ♖f6+!**.

641) Naiditsch-Ftacnik
1...♖h1+! 0-1
White's queen is lost after 2 ♔xh1 ♕xf2.

642) Krasenkow-Markowski
1 ♘gf6+! ♗xf6 (it's immediate mate after 1...♖xf6 2 ♘e7#) **2 ♖xg5! 1-0**
Black loses his queen due to White's pressure down the h-file.

643) Belsitzman-Rubinstein
1...♕xh2+! 0-1
It's mate after 2 ♔xh2 hxg3+ 3 ♔g1 ♖h1#.

644) Leniart-Gdanski
1...♕xb1! 2 ♖xb1 ♖xb1 3 ♕f2 (now it's mate, but after 3 ♗xb1 ♘f1+ 4 ♔g1 ♘xd2 Black is a rook up) **3...♖h1# 0-1**

645) Gajewski-Aleksandrov
1 ♗xh7+! ♘xh7 (or 1...♔f8 2 ♗d3 with an extra pawn and a clear advantage) **2 ♕xf7+** (the choice of a human, although the machine points out that 2 ♘xf7!? ♕c7 3 ♘xd6 ♕xc3+ 4 ♔e2 ♕b2+ 5 ♔d3 might have been even stronger) **2...♔h8 3 ♕h5 ♖h6** (3...♕xg5 fails to 4 ♕e8+ ♘f8 5 ♕xf8+ ♔h7 6 ♕xd6) **4 ♘f7+ ♔g8 5 ♘xh6+ gxh6 6 ♕g6+ ♔h8 7 ♕xh6** left White better with a rook and three pawns for the two pieces.

646) L'Ami-Smeets
1 ♘xd5! ♘xd5 (or 1...♖xd5 2 ♖xd5 ♘xd5 3 ♕g6+ ♔d8 4 ♕f7 ♖e8 5 ♖xd5+! and wins as in the game) **2 ♕g6+ ♔d8 3 ♕f7 ♖e8** (Black also drops his queen after 3...♖h8 4 b4 ♖c1 – 4...♖b5 5 a4 – 5 b5 ♖xd1+ 6 ♖xd1 ♕xb5 7 ♖xd5+! ♕xd5 8 e7+) **4 ♖xd5+! 1-0**
Black loses heavy material after both 4...♖xd5 5 ♖xd5+ ♕xd5 6 e7+ ♖xe7 7 ♕xd5+ and 4...♔c8 5 ♖xc5 bxc5 6 ♕d7+.

647) Jonkman-Berg
1 ♘e5+ ♔h8 2 ♖xg7! 1-0
White forces mate in view of 2...♔xg7 (2...♕h4+ 3 ♔g1 changes little) 3 ♕g6+ ♔h8 (or 3...♔f8 4 ♕f7#) 4 ♘f7#.

648) Van der Wiel-Peng
1...♖c2+ 2 ♔g1 ♘xe3! would have forced resignation because of 3 ♕xa7 ♖xg2+ 4 ♔h1 ♘g3#.

649) Van Wely-Karjakin
1...♖xf2! forced perpetual: **2 ♔xf2 ♕h2+ 3 ♔f3 ♕xg3+ 4 ♔e2 ♕g2+ 5 ♔e1 ♕g1+ 6 ♔e2** (and not 6 ♔d2? ♕f2+ 7 ♔c1 ♕b2#) **½-½**

650) M.Adams-J.Piket
1...♖f1+! 2 ♔xf1 ♘xh2+ 3 ♕xh2 (the queen is lost too after 3 ♔f2 ♘g4+) **3...♕xh2 0-1**
Due to his exposed king and undeveloped queenside, White's three pieces are no match for Black's extra queen after 4 ♘xc6 b5.

651) Bosboom-Willemze
Rather than the game's 1...♘xb3+? 2 ♔e3 when Black had to resign, **1...♕b2+! 2 ♔e3** (White must avoid both 2 ♔xc5? ♕xe5+ 3 ♔b4 – or 3 ♔xc6 ♖ac8+ 4 ♔b7 ♕c7+ 5 ♔a6 ♕b6# – 3...a5+ 4 ♔a3 ♕a1# and 2 ♘c3? ♖fd8+ 3 ♔e3 ♕xc3+ 4 ♔f4 ♖d4+ 5 ♖xd4 ♕xd4+ 6 ♔g3 ♕xe5+ 7 ♔g2 ♕e4+ 8 ♔g3 ♕xg6) **2...♕xe5+ 3 ♔f3** (or 3 ♔d2 ♕f4+ 4 ♔c3 ♕e5+) **3...♕e4+ 4 ♔g3 ♕e3+ 5 ♔g2 ♕e4+** would have forced a repetition since 6 ♕f3? ♕xg6, while not fully clear, should favour Black.

652) Krasenkow-Van Haastert
1 ♖xg7! ♔xg7 (or 1...♖xg7 2 ♕xf3+ ♔e8 3 ♘c6+ winning serious material on e7) **2 ♖g4+ 1-0**
Black loses his queen after 2...♔h7 (or 2...♔h8 3 ♕xh6+ ♖h7 4 ♕f6+ followed by mate) 3 ♕e4+ ♔h8 4 ♘g6+ ♔g8 5 ♘e5+.

653) Kosintseva-Berg
1...♗g4! wins a further exchange and the game: **2 ♕xg4 ♕xf2+ 0-1**

654) Spoelman-Van Haastert
1...♗xc2+! **2 ♔c1** (2 ♔a1 ♖e5! 3 ♕g3 ♖xe1+ 4 ♕xe1 ♕f6 gives Black an easily winning endgame) and now Black missed **2...♗b3!** when he gets to consolidate all his extra pawns after **3 ♕f2** (3 axb3?? costs White his queen after 3...♖c5+) **3...♕c8+.**

655) Smallbone-Hackett
1 ♖xe8+! ♔xe8 2 ♗xb5+! 1-0
It's mate on d8.

656) Palliser-Headlong
1 ♖c7! 1-0
White enjoys a crushing attack after 1...♕xc7 2 ♕xe8+ ♔h7 3 ♗xf7.

657) Speelman-Peng Xiaomin
1...♖xg3+! 2 ♔xg3 ♕h4+! 3 ♔xh4 (or 3 ♔f4 ♕xf2+ 4 ♔e5 ♕e2+ winning White's queen) **3...♕xf2+ 4 ♔g5 f6# 0-1**

658) Hambartsumian-Yegiazarian
1...♘xf2! 2 ♘xf2 ♗xf3 3 gxf3 ♖xe5 wins a pawn.

659) Moran-Turner
1...♘e4+! 2 ♔g2 (or 2 fxe4 ♕g5+ 3 ♔f3 ♗g4+ 4 ♔g2 ♗xd1+ picking up the white queen) **2...♕g5+ 3 ♔h1 ♗h3 0-1**
It's mate after 4 ♖g1 ♘xf2#.

660) Costello-Palliser
1...♖xg3+! 2 fxg3 ♕xg3+ 3 ♔f1 ♗h3+ 4 ♖xh3 ♕xh3+ 5 ♔e1 ♗c3+ 6 ♔f2 ♕h2+ 7 ♔f1 ♖g8 8 ♘g4 ♕g2# 0-1

661) Adams-Braithwaite
1 ♗f8+! 1-0
It's mate after 1...♔xf8 2 ♕h8+ ♔e7 3 ♕e8#.

662) Woolley-Tozer
1 ♖xf7! ♖e8 (smothered mate occurs after 1...♔xf7 2 ♘g5+ ♔g8 3 ♕xe6+) **2 ♘g5 ♖xg3 3 ♖xe6 ♖xg2+ 4 ♔h1 ♖xe6 5 ♕xe6 1-0**
Mate follows.

663) Bridger-Palliser
1...♕f1+! 2 ♖xf1 ♖xf1# 0-1

664) Barber-Marshall
1 ♕xe6+! ♕xe6 (Black has to avoid 1...fxe6? 2 ♗g6#, but he might try 1...♔e7 when he is

only clearly worse after 2 ♕xe7+ ♕xe7 3 ♗xe7 ♔xe7 4 ♖he1+ ♔f8 5 ♗e4) **2 ♘xe6 ♗d6 3 ♘xg7+ ♔f8 4 ♘f5** and a pawn ahead and with the initiative, White went on to win.

665) Hopwood-Cameron
1 ♘xe5!! ♗b5? (Black had to avoid 1...♕xe5? 2 ♗f4 when he must give up his queen in view of 2...♕c5? 3 ♗xa6#; the text, though, fails to offer any resistance, although even 1...♘xh5 2 ♗xa6+ ♔b8 3 ♘d3 ♕d6 4 ♗xe7 ♕xe7 5 ♕xh5 leaves White two pawns up and doing rather well) **2 ♘xf7 ♘xh5 3 ♕xh5 ♗e8 4 ♗xa6+ ♔d7 5 ♖xd4+ 1-0**

666) Hopwood-Bennett
1 ♖xg7! ♗xe5 (1...♔xg7 is mated by 2 ♕xh6+ ♔g8 3 ♕xh7# and there's no defence) **2 ♖xh7+ 1-0**
The attack is crushing, just as it is too after 2 ♕xh6.

667) Hopwood-Blacker
1 ♘xd5! 1-0
Due to the pin on his c7-rook, Black has no defence and is crushed. Indeed it's mate after 1...exd5 2 ♖xd5+ ♕d7 3 ♖xd7+ ♔e8 4 ♖d8+! ♔xd8 5 ♕f6+ ♘e7 6 ♕d6+ ♖d7 7 ♕xd7#.

668) Palliser-Baldwin
1 exf6 ♗xf6 2 ♕e4 and the fork wins a rook.

669) Palliser-Woolley
1 ♗h7+! 1-0
It's mate with 1...♔xh7 2 g8♕#.

670) Palliser-Rogerson
1 ♘xg6! hxg6 (Black is destroyed too after 1...♔f7 2 ♘xf8 ♖xf8 3 ♖g7+) **2 ♖xg6+ ♔f7 3 ♕h5 ♗xh6** (or 3...♔e7 4 ♗xf8+ ♔d7 5 ♖g7+ winning serious material) **4 ♖xh6+ 1-0**
It's mate after 4...♔f8 5 ♖h8+ ♔e7 6 ♖h7+ ♔d6 7 ♕e5+ ♔c6 8 ♖c1+ ♘c2 9 ♖xc2#.

671) Turner-Hopwood
1 ♖xf7!! nets an important pawn, thereby giving White excellent attacking chances: **1...♕b3** (capturing the rook leads to mate: 1...♔xf7 2 ♘g5+ ♔f8 – or 2...♔f6 3 ♕f4+ ♔e7 4 ♕f7+ ♔d8 5 ♘e6# – 3 ♕f4+ ♔g8 4 ♕c4+ ♔h8 5 ♘f7+ ♔g8 6 ♘h6+ ♔h8 7 ♕g8+ ♖xg8 8 ♘f7#) **2 ♖d7** (2 ♘g5 is also rather powerful) **2...♗f6?** (dropping a piece, but in any case Black was hard pressed to meet White's ideas of 3 ♘g5 and 3 ♘d2) **3 ♖d6 1-0**

672) Palliser-Mitchinson
1 ♗f7+! ♔xf7 (or 1...♔f8 2 ♗h6+ ♔xf7 3 ♕h7+ ♔xf6 4 ♕g7+ ♔f5 5 ♕g5+ ♔e4 6 ♖d4#) **2 ♕h7+ ♔f8 3 ♕g7# 1-0**

673) Franic-Zelcic
1...♖h2+! 2 ♔xh2 (or 2 ♔g3 ♗e5+ 3 ♔xg4 ♕h4+ 4 ♔f3 ♕f4#) **2...♕h8+ 0-1**
Mate follows with 3 ♔g3 ♕h3+ 4 ♔f2 (or 4 ♔f4 g5#) 4...♗h4+ 5 ♖g3 ♕xg3#.

674) Sasikiran-Ponomariov
1 ♘e5! 1-0
Black must give up his queen since it's mate after 1...fxe5 2 ♕xe5+.

675) Pavic-Petrovic
1...♗xh3! 2 ♗e1 (or 2 gxh3 ♖e2+ 3 ♔h1 ♕xh3#) **2...♖xe1 3 g3 ♕h5 4 ♖xe1 ♗f1# 0-1**

676) Mrdja-Vukusic
1 ♖xe3! wins a piece: **1...fxe3? 2 ♕g4+ 1-0**
It's mate on h7.

677) Kosanski-Lasic
1 ♗xg7! ♔xg7 (or 1...♖d3 2 ♕f6 ♕xf6 3 ♗xf6 with an extra pawn and a rather useful passed d-pawn) **2 ♕c3+ ♕f6 3 ♕xd2 ♘b3 4 ♕a2 ♘xa1 5 ♕xa1** left White a pawn up in the ending.

678) Takac-Vucic
1 ♕xg8+! 1-0
It's back-rank mate after 1...♔xg8 2 ♖b8+.

679) Krajewski-Ziolkowski
1...gxh3! 2 ♖xg6 (Black forces mate after 2 ♖xd6 ♖xg1+ 3 ♔e2 ♖8g2+ 4 ♔f3 ♖f1+) **2...h2! 3 ♖h6** (or 3 ♖xd6 h1♕+ 4 ♔e2 ♖xg6 5 ♖d7+ ♔f6 with an overwhelming attack) **3...♖g1+ 4 ♔e2 ♘c3+! 0-1**
It's mate after 5 ♕xc3 (or 5 ♔f2 ♕g3#) 5...♕xd1+ 6 ♔f2 ♕f1#.

Chapter Three

680) Genzling-Menendez Villar
1 ♘xe5! ♘xe5 (and not 1...♗xd1? 2 ♗xf7+ ♔e7 3 ♘d5#) **2 ♕xh5** sees White win an important pawn.

681) Jeremic-Nestorovic
1...♘d4! and the Siberian trap costs White his queen for two pieces since he has to avoid 2 ♘xd4 ♕h2#.

682) Ruzicic-Ljangov
1...♘xe4! 2 ♕f4 (the main point is that White emerges a pawn down too after 2 ♗xd8 ♘xd2 3 ♗h4 ♘xf1 4 ♖xf1 ♘c6) **2...♘f6** saw Black net a most useful central pawn.

683) Budimir-Jakovljevic
1...♖xh7! 0-1
Black wins a piece since it's mate after 2 ♕xh7 ♕e5+ 3 ♔f1 (or 3 ♔d1 ♕e2#) 3...♕e2+ 4 ♔g1 ♕e1#.

684) Smith-Hunt
1 ♘xe5! dxe5 (neither does declining the piece help Black; for example, 1...♗e7 2 ♘g4 ♘xg4 3 hxg4 ♕d7 4 ♖de1 with strong pressure down the central files) **2 ♗xe5 ♘d7** (or 2...♖g6 3 ♖de1 ♔d7 4 ♕d4 ♗g7 5 ♖xf6 ♗xf6 6 ♕g4+ and wins, as does 2...♗e7 3 d6) **3 ♖de1 ♘xe5 4 ♖xe5+ 1-0**
White wins the queen in style with 4...♔d7 5 ♖xf7+ ♔c8 6 ♖e8! ♕xe8 7 ♕c3+.

685) Cork-Morris
1...♘xe4! wins material: **2 ♕d3** (or 2 fxe4 ♗g5 and White loses his queen) **2...♗g5+ 3 ♘d2 ♘g3 4 ♖he1 ♘xe2+ 5 ♖xe2 ♗xf3!** and White finally loses the exchange.

686) Waterfield-Klein
1 ♗b5! wins the queen in view of 1...♕xb5 2 ♘xc7+ and 3 ♘xb5.

687) Williamson-Foster
1 ♗xf7+! ♔xf7 **2 ♕c4+** ♔f8 **3 ♕xb4+** wins a pawn.

688) Boguszlavszkij-Cherednichenko
1 ♕xf6+! 1-0
Black loses a piece in view of 1...♔xf6 2 ♘e4+ and 3 ♘xc5.

689) Mueller-Tidman
Here Black resigned, missing **1...♗b4!** (1...♗e7 also averts defeat, but in a far less effective manner) **2 c3** (or 2 ♕xb4 ♕xg5 3 ♗xe4 ♕h4+ 4 ♔f1 ♕xe4 with a clear advantage) **2...♕d5! 3 ♘f3** (White loses the exchange after 3 cxb4? ♗xg2) **3...♗d6** which would have seen Black maintain her extra pawn.

690) Albrecht-Bering
1 ♘xd5! cxd5 (or 1...♕d8 2 ♗xe4 0-0 3 ♗f3 cxd5 4 ♘e2 with an extra pawn and a large positional advantage) **2 ♕xc8+** ♔f7 (White picks up even more pawns after 2...♕d8 3 ♕xb7 ♘d7 4 ♕xd5) **3 ♕xf5+!** and White is two clear pawns up.

691) Young-Palliser
1...b5! 0-1
White's bishop is lost in view of 2 ♗xb5 ♕b6+ 3 ♔h1 ♕xb5.

692) Soufflet-Bellay
The classic trap **1...♘xd5!** wins a piece in view of 2 ♗xd8 ♗b4+ 3 ♕d2 ♗xd2+ 4 ♔xd2 ♔xd8.

693) Harvey-Palliser
1...♘xh2! 0-1
White loses a ruinous amount of material after 2 ♕e2 (or 2 ♔xh2 ♕h4#) 2...♕h4.

694) Rajlich-Schuurman
White wins a piece: **1 g4! axb4** (Black's queen is trapped after 1...♕g6 2 ♘h4) **2 ♕xf6! 1-0**

695) Kregelin-Kleinert
1 ♘xf7! 1-0
White wins the rook on h8 in view of 1...♔xf7 2 ♕xe6+ ♔f8 3 ♕f7#.

696) Johansen-Peterson
Black wins a pawn: **1...♗xh2+! 2 ♔xh2 ♕h4+ 3 ♔g1 ♕xe4 0-1**

697) Wells-Kharlov
1 ♘g5! (threatening both the queen and mate with 2 ♕d6+ ♔e8 3 ♕d8#) **1...fxg5 2 ♕xg5+** ♔f7 **3 ♗g4 ♕xg4** (Black loses his queen too after 3...♕h6 4 ♗h5+) **4 ♕xg4** and White's extra queen was decisive.

698) Lopang-Sikorova
1...♗xf2+! 2 ♔d1? (or 2 ♖xf2 ♕h4 3 0-0-0 ♕xf2 with an extra exchange and pawn) **2...♗g1 0-1**

White must lose his rook.

699) Santos-Ferro
1 ♘xe5! ♗xd1 2 ♗b5+ c6 (or 2...♘d7 3 ♗xd7+ ♕xd7 4 ♘xd7 ♔xd7 5 ♔xd1 with an extra piece) **3 dxc6 ♗a4** (this fails to save Black, but there was no way to maintain the extra queen with 3...a6 insufficient too due to 4 c7+ axb5 5 cxd8♕+ ♖xd8 6 ♘xd1) **4 c7+ ♗xb5 5 cxd8♕+ ♖xd8 6 ♘xb5** and White went on to convert his extra piece.

700) Libiszewski-Roos
1 ♗xb7! wins a clear pawn in view of 1...♗xb7 2 ♕b5+ ♔d7 3 ♕xb7.

701) Khenkin-Vernay
1 ♗xe6! wins a pawn in view of 1...fxe6 (or 1...♘c5 2 ♗xf7+ ♖xf7 3 dxc5.) **2 ♕xe6+ ♔h8 3 ♕xd6**.

702) Von Herman-Hausrath
1...♘xe4! 2 ♗xd8 (otherwise Black is just a piece up after 2 ♗xe4 ♕e8) **2...♗b4+! 3 ♕xb4 ♘c2+ 0-1**
White remains a piece in arrears.

703) Schudro-Schmeing
White wins a pawn: **1 ♘xe5! ♘xe5** (and not, of course, 1...♗xd1? falling into Legall's mate: 2 ♗xf7+ ♔e7 3 ♘d5#) **2 ♕xh5 ♘f6** (or 2...♘xc4 3 ♕b5+ ♕d7 4 ♕xc4 regaining the piece) **3 ♕e2**.

704) Jameson-Nyland
1 ♘xf7! ♔xf7 2 ♗c4+ ♔f8 (now it's mate, but 2...♔e8 3 ♕d5 ♖f8 4 ♕h5+ g6 5 ♕xh7 also would have been rather strong) and now **3 ♕d5!** (rather than the game's 3 ♕f3+) **3...♕e8 4 ♕f5+** would have led to a beautiful mate after **4...♗f6 5 ♕xf6+! gxf6 6 ♗h6#**.

705) Palliser-Taylor
1 ♖xg1! ♕xg1 2 ♗e3 ♕xh2 (or 2...♕h1 3 ♕h8+ ♔e7 4 ♗xh6 with decisive threats along the eighth, while 2...♘d4+ 3 ♔d3 reveals why White needs his queen on f6 to cover f1) **3 ♕h8+ ♔e7 4 ♗g5+! 1-0**
Black loses his queen down the h-file.

706) Wilson-Dickson
1...♘xd4! either wins a clear pawn or gives Black an extremely strong attack: **2 ♘xd4 ♕h4 3 ♘f3??** (3 ♗e3 was essential, although 3...♕xh2+ 4 ♔f1 ♕h1+ 5 ♔e2 ♕xg2 is rather dangerous for White after something like 6 ♘c3 ♘xe3 7 ♔xe3 ♕h3+ 8 ♔e2 d5!) **3...♕xf2+ 4 ♔h1 ♕g1+! 0-1**
Smothered mate follows on f2.

707) Mateo-Larduet Despaigne
1 ♗xf7+! wins the exchange and a pawn in view of 1...♔xf7? 2 ♘g5+ ♔g8 3 ♘e6 trapping the black queen.

708) Hanley-Hickman
1 b4! wins a piece since Black's queen cannot remain covering his f5-bishop.

709) Adams-Vitoux

1 ♗xb5!! axb5 (probably Black should settle for 1...cxd4 2 ♗xa6 ♘f5 with only a clear disadvantage) **2 ♘xb5 ♖c8 3 c4 ♕h5 4 ♘d6+ ♔d8 5 ♘g5 ♕xd1 6 ♘gxf7+ ♔c7 7 ♖xd1 ♖g8 8 ♘xc8** gave White a large advantage with a rook and three useful pawns for the two pieces.

710) Schmidt-Rohmann

1 ♗xg6!! ♘xd1? (Black doesn't really have anything for the piece after 1...hxg6? 2 ♔xf2, but he might try 1...♗c5 when 2 ♕e2! – 2 ♘f3!? ♕f6 3 ♗xf7+ ♔f8 4 ♕xf6 gxf6 5 ♖f1 fxe5 6 ♗h5 ♔g7 7 ♖xf2 ♗xf2+ 8 ♔xf2 is promising too – 2...♕e7 – 2...0-0 fails to 3 ♗xf7+ ♖xf7 4 ♘xf7 ♔xf7 5 0-0 – 3 ♗xf7+ ♔d8 4 ♖f1 ♕xe5 5 ♖xf2 ♗xf2+ 6 ♔xf2 leaves White's two extra pieces far superior to Black's extra rook) **2 ♗xf7+ ♔e7 3 ♗g5+ ♔d6 4 ♘c4+ ♔c5 5 ♗xd8** (threatening mate with 5 ♘ba3 is a decent alternative) **5...♔xc4 6 ♔xd1** and White's extra piece prevailed.

711) Palliser-Lim

Rather than the game's 1 0-0, **1 ♗xf7+! ♔xf7** (or 1...♔f8 2 ♘g5 e6 3 ♘xe6+ ♖xe6 4 ♗xe6 with an extra exchange) **2 ♘g5+ ♔g8** (2...♔f6 fails to 3 e5+) **3 ♘e6** would have trapped the black queen.

712) Terentiev-Gallagher

1...dxc3! 2 ♗e5? (White misses Black's idea; he would have done better to restrict his losses to just a pawn with 2 ♘xc3 ♘xc3 3 bxc3 ♖xb8) **2...♖xa2! 3 ♘xc3** (White's problem is that he cannot stop Black's c-pawn queening after 3 ♖xa2? c2) **3...♖xa1+ 4 ♘d1 ♘xf2 5 ♔xf2 ♖xd1** left Black the exchange and three pawns ahead.

713) Romanishin-Brenke

1 ♖xb2! 1-0

Black's queen is lost since it's mate after 1...♕xa6 (or 1...♕xb2 2 ♕c6+ ♔d8 3 ♘xf7#) 2 ♖xb8+ ♕c8 3 ♖xc8#.

714) Palliser-Smallbone

1 ♕xg7!! ♗f6 2 ♕h6 ♘c2 (otherwise White is just a pawn up with a good position) **3 ♘c3 ♘xa1** (Black might wish to trade off his bishop before its trapped, but 3...♗xc3 4 bxc3 ♘xa1 fails to 5 ♕g7 ♖f8 6 ♗a3) **4 ♖d1 ♗d7** (or 4...♗d4 5 ♗g5 ♕d6 6 ♕xd6 cxd6 7 ♖xd4 ♘c2 8 ♖xd6 with two raking bishops and a crushing position) **5 ♘d5 1-0**

The bishop lacks a good square since both 5...♗e5 6 ♗g5 ♕c8 7 ♘f6+ ♗xf6 8 ♕xf6 and 5...♗e7 6 ♗g5! ♗xg5 7 ♕g7 ♖f8 8 ♕e5+ ♗e6 9 ♘xc7+ ♔e7 10 ♕xg5+ f6 11 ♕c5+ are crushing.

715) Van Gool-Blijlevens

1 ♗xf7+! ♔xf7 2 ♕d5+ ♔e8 3 ♕xc5 wins a pawn.

716) Tiviakov-Rivera Rodriguez

1 ♖xe6! wins a pawn since 1...fxe6? 2 ♘xe6 traps the black queen.

717) Lahlum-Ulrichsen

1 ♗xh7+! ♔xh7 2 ♕h5+ ♔g8 3 ♕xe5 saw White win a pawn.

718) 'Sofine'-R.Palliser

1 b4! cxb4 2 axb4 ♗xb4 3 ♖xb4! ♕xb4 4 ♘e4 ♕a3? (White wins back a piece after 4...♕e7? 5 d6 while retaining a large advantage, but Black should try 4...♕xe4! 5 ♗xe4 ♘xe4 changing White's task to one of a technical nature) **5 ♘xf6+ gxf6 6 ♕g4+ ♔h8 7 ♕f5 1-0**

719) Palliser-Semkov
1 ♘f6+! 1-0
It's mate after 1...gxf6 2 ♕c6+ ♔e7 3 ♕d7#.

720) Bianchini-Vitri
1...♗xf2+! wins a pawn in view of 2 ♔xf2 ♘e4+ and 3...♘xg5.

721) Morphy-Brunswick & Isouard
1 ♖xd7! ♖xd7 2 ♖d1 ♕e6 3 ♗xd7+ ♘xd7 (or 3...♔e7 4 ♕b4+ ♔d8 5 ♕b8+! ♔e7 6 ♕e8#) **4 ♕b8+! ♘xb8 5 ♖d8# 1-0**

722) Danilov-Tanav
1...♗xf2+! 2 ♔xf2 ♕c5+ wins a pawn since 3 ♗e3 fails to 3...♘g4+.

723) Pau-Farber
Black wins a piece with **1...e5!** in view of 2 ♗xe5 ♕a5+ 3 ♘c3 ♕xe5.

724) Yasin-Istratescu
1...♘xh2! forces White to give up the exchange, such as with 2 ♖d1 (and not 2 ♔xh2? ♕h4#) 2...♘g4 3 ♘f3 ♘f2+ 4 ♕xf2 ♕xd1+ 5 ♗xd1 ♗xf2.

725) Milov-Castro Acosta
1 ♘f3! ♕h5 2 g4! leaves Black unable to continue covering his c5-bishop.

726) Willin-Auschkalnis
1 ♖xh7! 1-0
Black must lose his rook in view of the threat of 2 ♕g6#.

727) Shakarova-Zankovich
1...♕xf6! wins a piece: **2 ♗xf6 ♗b4+ 3 ♕d2 ♗xd2+ 4 ♔xd2 gxf6 0-1**

728) Gibbons-Rej
1...♗xf2+! wins a pawn in view of 2 ♔xf2 ♘xe4+ and 3...♘xg5.

729) Flitney-Escribano
1 ♖xc8+! ♕xc8 2 ♘d6+ ♔e7 3 ♘xc8+ ♖axc8 4 ♗xe5 fxe6 5 ♕d2 1-0
White is a queen ahead and enjoys a powerful attack.

730) Aronian-Navara
White wins material on h8: **1 e4! fxe4 2 ♘xh8**.

731) Ola-Tia
1 f6! ♗xf6 2 ♖xf6 wins a piece in view of 2...♕xf6 3 ♗g5 ♕e6 4 ♖d8#.

732) Reti-Tartakower
1 ♕d8+!! ♔xd8 2 ♗g5+ ♔c7 (or 2...♔e8 3 ♖d8#) **3 ♗d8# 1-0**

733) Baramidze-Babuiian
1...♗g4! 0-1

White's queen is lost in view of 2 ♕xg4 (or 2 ♗xh7+ ♔h8 3 ♕c2 ♕f1+ 4 ♖xf1 ♖xf1#) 2...♕f1+ 3 ♖xf1 ♖xf1#.

734) Kozul-Illescas Cordoba
1...♘c5! 2 dxc5 (otherwise Black wins a pawn on e4) **2...dxe4 3 ♕xd8 ♖fxd8** and Black regains his piece with a large advantage, such as after 4 ♘g5 ♖xd2 5 ♘gxe4 ♘xe4 6 ♘xe4 ♖b2.

735) Nezis-Duggan
1...h5! 0-1
There's no defence to the threat of 2...♘g4 and 2 ♘d2 ♘g4 3 ♘f3 fails to the deflecting 3...♘d4.

736) Hurwitz-Hopwood
1...♘xf2! wins the exchange in view of 2 ♕xf2 ♕xc3+ 3 ♕d2 ♕xa1+ and 2 ♖g1 ♘d3+ 3 cxd3 ♕xg1.

737) Cornhill-Hopwood
1...♘xe4! wins a pawn after 2 ♘xe4 (even worse for White is 2 ♗xg7? ♘xd2 3 ♕b2 ♘xf1 4 ♖xf1 f6) 2...♗xe4 3 ♕xe4 ♗xb2.

738) Anderson-Palliser
1...♗xf3 0-1
Black wins a piece after 2 ♕xf3 (or 2 ♕d2 f6) 2...♕xg5.

739) Armanda-Sitnik
1 ♘xf7! ♗xf3 (or 1...♔xf7 2 ♘e5+ ♔g8 3 ♘xg4 with an extra pawn and excellent play on the light squares) **2 ♗g6!** threatens mate to win serious material.

Chapter Four

740) Walter-Hiermann
1 ♘xe6! wins a second pawn since 1...♘xe6 2 f5+ gives White a winning pawn endgame.

741) Yates-Tartakower
1 ♔b2 ♔c4 (or 1...♔d4 2 ♔xb3 ♔d3 when White draws by arranging to seize the opposition as soon as Black captures on b4, such as with 3 ♔a2 ♔c4 4 ♔b1 ♔xb4 5 ♔b2) **2 ♔a3! b2** (it's stalemate after 2...♔c3) **3 ♔a2! ½-½**
Following 3...♔c3 4 ♔b1 Black only has a choice between stalemate and giving White the opposition after 4...♔xb4 5 ♔xb2.

742) Balogh-Paichadze
1 ♘xf7! ♔xf7 2 ♖xd7+ wins a second pawn.

743) Van Wely-Guseinov
1 ♗xh7+! ♔xh7 (Black isn't helped either by 1...♔f8 2 g6 when the pawn queens) **2 g6+ ♔h6** (the f-pawn is unstoppable too after 2...♔g8 3 f7+ ♔g7 4 ♘d7) **3 f7** (missing the more attractive and faster 3 ♔h4 followed by 4 g5#) **3...♔g7 1-0**
4 ♘d7 is game over.

744) Shirov-Kramnik
1 b6! cxb6 (or 1...♔c6 2 ♖b8 and the a-pawn queens) **2 ♖h8 1-0**
Black either loses his rook on a8 or after 2...♖xa7 3 ♖h7+ and 4 ♖xa7.

745) McNab-Kunte
1 h8♕+! ♔xh8 2 ♔h6 1-0
Black cannot prevent the g-pawn from queening.

746) Westra-Palliser
1...h3! 2 gxh3 ♔h4 3 ♔b6 ♗xh3 0-1
Black queens first and wins after both 4 ♗xh3 ♔xh3 5 ♔xb7 c5 6 ♔c6 ♔g3 7 ♔xc5 h4 and 4 ♗e2 ♗g2 5 ♔xb7 ♔g5 6 ♔xc6 h4.

747) Berkes-Tomic
1 ♗g6+! ♔f8 (the d-pawn slips home after 1...♔xg6? 2 d7) **2 ♗xh5** won a pawn, leaving White's connected passed pawns to decide.

748) Palliser-Round
1...♕xf2+! ½-½
There's no way to escape Black's checks and it's stalemate after 2 ♔xf2.

749) Collinson-King
1...♘xb3! creates a decisive passed b-pawn: **2 ♔xb3 ♔xd3 3 ♗f1+** (or 3 a5 ♔e2 4 ♗h3 d3 5 ♗f5 d2 6 ♗g4+ ♔e1 7 ♔c2 transposing) **3...♔d2 4 a5 d3 5 ♔b2 ♔e3 6 ♔b3** (6 ♔c1 b3 forces one of the pawns home) **6...d2 7 ♔c2 ♔f2 8 ♗h3 ♔e1 9 ♗g4 b3+!** (le point) **10 ♔xb3 d1♕+ 11 ♗xd1 ♔xd1 12 ♔c3 ♔e2 0-1**
After 13 ♔c2 ♔e3 14 ♔c3 ♔e4 Black has the opposition and c4 will fall.

750) Galliano-Smallbone
1...♘d4! leaves White in zugzwang: **2 ♘xg6** (or 2 f4 ♘f3+ 3 ♘xf3 ♔xf3 4 ♔h3 ♔xf4 with a trivial win in the pawn ending) **2...hxg6! 3 h7 ♘f3# 0-1**

751) Savage-Shikerov
Black queens his g-pawn with the deflecting **1...♘c2+!**.

752) Cobb-Duncan
1...♖xe3+! 0-1
The a-pawn queens after 2 ♔xe3 b3 3 axb3 a3!.

753) Ozeren-Clarke
Rather than the game's 1...g6??, Black can simplify to a very promising ending with a neat intermezzo: **1...♖d1! 2 ♘xd1** (or 2 ♖xd1 cxd1♕ 3 ♘xd1 with an extra pawn and bishop against knight) **2...g5!** (other kingside pawn moves lead to the same outcome) and Black either queens on c1 or with 3 ♖d8+ ♔g7 4 ♖xc8 cxd1♕.

754) Barrett-Taylor
1...♗xg2! 2 ♖xg2 ♖xb3 won a key pawn.

755) Haslinger-Bates
Black wins a piece and the game with **1...♕xb3! 2 axb3 a2 3 ♕h1 c2**.

756) Wade-Korchnoi
1 b5! ♔h5 (or 1...♔f6 2 ♔g4 g5 3 ♔h5 with an easy win) **2 a5! 1-0**
The d-pawn queens after 2...bxa5 3 b6 cxb6 4 d6.

757) Vovk-Bobras
1...♗c5+! 0-1
White's king cannot reach the corner: 2 ♔e4 (or 2 ♔xc5 ♔xh5 3 ♔d4 ♔g4 4 ♔e3 ♔g3 and the h-pawn queens) 2...♗b6 (zugzwang) 3 ♔d3 ♔xh5 4 ♔e2 ♔g4 5 ♔f1 ♔f3 and the h-pawn runs home.

758) Safronov-Lysyj
1...♕c6+! 2 ♔a5 ♕b6+! 0-1
Black wins a rook with 3 ♕xb6 (or 3 ♖xb6 axb6+ 4 ♔xb6 ♖xd8) 3...axb6+ 4 ♔xb6 ♖xb8+.

759) Jones-Dive
1...gxh3!! 2 ♔xf3 g4+ **3** ♔f2 g3+ **4** ♔g1 (or 4 ♔f3 h2 5 ♔g2 f3+ and one of the pawns will queen) **4...h2+ 5** ♔h1 f3 **6** ♘e4 ♔f4 **7 b4** ♔g4 (or immediately 7...f2) **8 b5 f2 9** ♘d2 (Black has a choice of which pawn to queen after 9 ♘xf2+ gxf2 10 ♔g2) **9...**♔h3 **10 b6 g2# 0-1**

760) Shaw-Palliser
1...d3+ 2 ♔e3 (2 ♔f2 ♔b3 3 ♗xe5 d2 4 ♔e2 ♔c2 is similarly hopeless for White and otherwise he loses his f-pawn) **2...**♔c3! **3** ♗xe5+ ♔c2 **0-1**
The d-pawn cannot be stopped.

761) Timofeev-Guseinov
1...g5+! 2 ♔xg5 (or 2 hxg5 ♔g6 and the threat of 3...e5# is decisive) **2...**♖e5+ **3** ♔f4 ♖f5+ **4** ♔e3 d4+ **5** ♔xd4 ♖xb5 **0-1**

762) Zelcic-Riazantsev
1...g6! (but not 1...gxh6? 2 ♔xd4 f2 3 ♘xf2 ♗xf2+ with a draw since Black is left with the wrong coloured rook's pawn) **2 h7** (this doesn't come close to saving White, but the win is quite straightforward too after 2 ♔xd4 f2 3 ♘xf2 ♗xf2+ 4 ♔e4 ♗g3) **2...**♗e5 **3** ♘g5 ♗g7 **4** ♔e3 ♔e7 **5** ♘e4 ♗e5 **6** ♔f2 ♔f8 **7** ♔e3 ♔g7 **0-1**

763) Kotanijian-Pantsulaia
1...b3! 2 axb3 a3 3 ♗f3 (also hopeless for White is 3 b4 a2 4 ♖a3 a1♕+ 5 ♖xa1 ♖h1+ 6 ♔f2 ♖xa1, but perhaps he might have tried 3 ♔g1 a2 4 ♔xh2 a1♕ 5 ♗xh5 ♕b2+ 6 ♖e2 ♕d4 when Black still has some work to do) **3...**♖xh3 **4 b4 a2 5** ♖a3 and now I suspect that Black played **5...a1♕+** when 6 ♖xa1 ♖xf3+ is an easy win, rather than the gamescore's 5...♔e5? which allows White to mount a strong defence with 6 ♔g2 g4 7 ♖a5+ ♔f4 8 ♗d5.

764) Gustafsson-Pedersen
1 ♖f6! ♖a5 (White queens after 1...gxf6 2 g6+ ♔h6 3 g7, while the pure pawn ending is also an easy win with 1...♖xf6+ 2 gxf6 gxf6 3 ♔xf6 ♔g8 4 ♔e7) **2 ♖h6+! 1-0**
Mate follows.

765) Socko-Le Kieu Thien
1...♔e6! (and not 1...♔e5?? 2 ♔e7 ♔f5 3 ♔d6 ♔g4 4 ♔e5 ♔xh4 5 ♔f4 ♔h3 6 ♔f3 with a draw) **2** ♔e8 ♔f5 **0-1**
White's king has been shouldered away, allowing Black to win with 3 ♔e7 ♔g4 4 ♔f6 ♔xh4 5 ♔f5 ♔g3.

766) Grischuk-Rublevsky
1 ♖xc6! bxc6 2 ♖xf7 ♖f4 (the main point is that the b-pawn runs home after 2...♖xf7 3 b7) **3 c3!** (now there's no defence) **3...♖e4 4 ♖e7+ 1-0**

767) Kreuscher-Sarthou
1...g3! 2 hxg3 (Black queens too after 2 ♖xf8 gxh2) **2...♖xf2 3 ♔xf2** (now the h-pawn runs home, but otherwise White is simply a rook down) **3...h2 0-1**

768) Borriss-Steingrimsson
After White's hideous 1 bxa5, **1...b5!** ensured he was left with only a useless extra a-pawn: **2 a4 bxc4! 3 a6 ♔b6 4 a7 ½-½**

769) Khenkin-Vuilleumier
The Lucena position: **1 ♖d4! ♔c5** (or 1...♖g1 2 ♔e7 ♖e1+ 3 ♔f6 ♖f1+ 4 ♔e6 ♖e1+ 5 ♔f5 ♖f1+ 6 ♖f4 and White's 'bridge-building' technique triumphs) **2 ♖d7** (2 ♖f4 ♖a3 3 ♖g4 also wins) **2...♔c6 3 ♔e8 ♖f3 4 ♖e7! 1-0**

770) E.Bacrot-P.Tregubov
The Lucena position is always a common guest in tournament practice: **1 ♖d4! ♖g1 2 ♔e7 1-0**
White has built a bridge as shown by 2...♖e1+ 3 ♔f6 ♖f1+ 4 ♔e6 ♖e1+ 5 ♔f5 ♖f1+ 6 ♖f4 when the checks have run out.

771) Glek-Roos
1 g6! 1-0
White threatens to queen the g-pawn and after 1...fxg6 (or 1...♔xg6 2 ♖g8+ and the a-pawn queens) 2 ♖f8+! ♗xf8 3 a8♕ his extra queen is decisive.

772) Timman-Baramidze
1 f3! 1-0
Black's bishop is trapped after 1...♕xf3 2 ♕e1, while 1...♗xf3 loses to 2 ♖d8 f6 3 ♕xf6 ♕g7 4 ♕xf3.

773) Quillan-Ansell
1 ♖a3! Philidor's third-rank defence. White draws in view of 1...e3 2 ♖a8 followed by a barrage of checks from behind.

774) Nakamura-Arakhamia Grant
Black avoids the stalemate trick to win trivially: **1...♕g2! 0-1**

775) Adams-Al Modiahki
1...♖g1! 2 ♖f3 (2 ♖xg1 is an immediate stalemate) **2...♖f1! 3 ♖xf1 ½-½**

776) Citak-Dimitrijevic
1 ♖g7+ ♔f8 (or 1...♔h8 2 ♖h7+ ♔g8 3 f7+ ♔f8 4 ♖h8+) **2 ♖h7! 1-0**
There's no defence in view of 2...♔g8 3 f7+.

777) Trevelyan-Jenni
1...♗c2+! 2 ♖xc2 (now it's mate, although after 2 ♔xc2 ♖xa2+ 3 ♔c1 ♖xh2 Black's extra exchange is decisive) **2...♖a3# 0-1**

778) Terrieux-Kryvoruchko
1...♛xf1+! 0-1
2 ♕xf1 ♝b2 forces the c-pawn home, leaving Black a piece ahead.

779) Arkell-Palliser
1 ♖xa4! 1-0
The h-pawn queens after 1...♚xa4 2 ♚xd4.

780) Wade-Palliser
1...d1♕+! 2 ♚xd1 ♚d3 0-1
The e-pawn is unstoppable.

781) Hunt-Hopwood
1 f5+! gxf5 2 gxf5+ ♚d7 (2...♚xf5 3 ♚xd5 costs Black a piece) **3 ♚xd5 ♚xc7 4 ♚c5** (the pawn ending is a trivial win) **4...h6 5 ♚xb5 ♚d6 6 ♚xa4 ♚e5 7 b4 1-0**
White wins in straightforward manner after 7...♚xf5 8 b5 ♚e6 9 ♚a5 ♚d7 10 ♚a6 ♚c8 11 ♚a7.

782) Linares Napoles-Gongora Reyes
1...♝xf2! wins a key pawn in view of 2 ♚xf2 ♖xh2+ 3 ♖xh2 ♖xh2+ and 4...♖xc2.

783) Mannion-Sareen
1...g5!! (much clearer than 1...f4 2 gxf4 exf4 3 ♚xc5 g5 4 e5 gxh4 5 ♚d6 h3 6 e6 h2 7 e7 h1♕ 8 e8♕) **2 exf5** (Black also wins after both 2 hxg5 f4 and 2 ♚xc5 f4) **2...g4 3 fxg4 e4 4 gxh5 e3 5 ♚d3 c4+! 0-1**
Black queens by force in view of 6 bxc4 b3 7 axb3 a2 when White is helpless despite his four extra pawns.

784) Yates-Marshall
1...♚b2! 2 ♚xa4 ♚c3 ½-½
Black's king is in time to both halt and win the f-pawn.

785) Spielmann-Duras
1...♚g5! 0-1
Black decisively seizes the opposition after 2 ♖xf5+ ♚xf5.

786) Bannik-Nikolaevsky
1 ♝xb6! 1-0
One of the pawns will queen after 1...♝xb6 (or 1...♝c3 2 ♝a5!) 2 g6 ♝d4 3 b6.

787) Djukic-Pavlovic
White wins a pawn: **1 ♘ef6+! gxf6** (1...♚d8? 2 ♘d5 costs Black a piece) **2 ♘xf6+ ♚d8** (and not 2...♚f8? 3 ♝h6#) **3 ♘d5 ♝e6 4 ♝xe7+ ♚d7 5 ♝g5** and White went on to convert this clearly better ending.

788) Davies-Morgan
Rather than the game's 1...♚e7, the breakthrough **1...c3!** would have won: **2 b3 bxa3 3 g6 ♚f8 4 ♚h4 a2 5 ♚g5 a1♕ 6 ♚f6 ♕g1** and the extra black queen decisively halts White's passed pawns.

789) Gourlay-Palliser
1...♗d6+ 0-1
White loses a rook after 2 ♔xf3 ♖f1+ and a piece after 2 ♔f2 ♖h2+.

790) Palliser-Hunt
1...♔e8! (and not the game's 1...♔e6?? 2 ♔f8 ♔d6 3 ♔f7 and 1-0) **2 ♔h7 ♔d7!** maintains the opposition and draws.

791) Palliser-Hodgson
1...♔f7! 0-1
White's cause is hopeless in view of his horribly exposed king after 2 ♕e2 (or 2 ♕xa7+ ♔g6 and there's no defence against 3...♕f2#) 2...♘c6.

792) Barata-Costa
Black draws by bringing his king to c5 to prevent ♗c6: **1...♔d4!** (the game actually ended 1...♗c8? 2 ♗d7 ♗a6 3 ♗g4! ♗b5 4 ♗f3 and 1-0 in view of 5 ♗c6; Black faces the same outcome after 1...♗g4 2 ♗d7 ♗e2 3 ♗h3 ♗b5 4 ♗g2 – he needs his king to be playing a much greater role) **2 ♗d7 ♗c4** (both 2...♗b3 and even 2...♗f7 – in view of 3 ♗f5 ♗e8 4 ♗d8 ♔e5! – are also sufficient to draw) **3 ♗c8** (3 ♗h3 ♗b5 4 ♗g2 ♔c5 comes to the same thing) **3...♗b5 4 ♗b7 ♔c5** and with 5 ♗c6 ruled out, White cannot make progress; for example, 5 ♗c8 ♔d4 6 ♗d7 ♗c4 7 ♗e8 ♗e6 8 ♔d8 ♔e5 9 ♔e7 ♗g4 10 ♗d7 ♗d1 11 ♗e6 ♗a4 and Black continues to defend without too much difficulty.

793) Savickas-Garnelis
1 ♗b7+! 1-0
The ending is an easy win after 1...♔xb7 (and not 1...♖xb7 2 ♖d8#) 2 ♖xd7+ ♔c6 3 ♖xe7 ♔d6 4 ♖xg7 ♗d3+ 5 ♔f2 ♔xe6 6 ♔f3.

794) Leko-Kramnik
1...♖f2! 0-1
White loses his bishop.

795) Capablanca-Lasker
1 h6! 1-0
There's no defence to the threat of 2 g6 followed by queening.

796) Bilek-Heidenfeld
1...♕g3+! ½-½
It's stalemate after 2 ♕xg3.

797) Rasmussen-Nunn
1...f3! 0-1
After 2 gxf3 (otherwise 2...f2 follows and 2 ♔e3 fails to 2...♘c2+) 2...♘c2 White loses his rook in view of 3 ♖xe2 ♖d4#.

798) Smyslov-Rossetto
1 cxb6! ♖e1+ (or 1...♕xb5 2 ♖xb5 axb6 3 ♔g2 ♖e8 4 ♖xb6 with an easy win in the rook ending) **2 ♖xe1 ♕xb5 3 bxa7 ♕c6** (3...♕xa6 fails to 4 ♖e8+ ♔h7 5 a8♕) **4 ♖b1 ♔h7 5 ♖b8 1-0**
Black must give up his queen.

799) Stephenson-Spence
1 ♗a6! bxa6 2 ♕c7 ♕e8 (the only move, but now White's passed b- and c-pawns are decisive) **3 ♕xc6 ♔f8 4 ♕xd5 a5** (or 4...♘b8 5 ♕d6+ ♔f7 6 d5 ♕b5 7 h3 and White's pawn armada decides) **5 c6 ♘xb6 6 ♕c5+ ♔f7 7 ♕xb6 ♗e7 8 c7 ♕c8 9 ♕xa5** (the pawn ending is an easy win, but 9 d5 would have been even more clinical) **9...♔d7 10 ♕c5 1-0**

800) Stephenson-Wise
1 d3! (another move order is 1 e4 ♔c5 2 d3! – the key point in both cases is that White's rear d-pawn makes all the difference) **1...c3 2 e4 ♔c7 3 e5 ♔d7 4 d6 ♔e6 5 d4 ♔d7 6 d5 ♔e8 7 e6 ♔d8 8 d7 ♔e7 9 d6+ ♔d8 10 ♔b3** (having stalemated the black king, White now picks up the black pawns with a little care) **10...c2 11 ♔xc2 b3+ 12 ♔b1 b2 13 e7+ ♔xd7 14 ♔xb2 1-0**

801) Banach-Birjukov
1...♗a3! 2 ♘d1 (the b-pawn queens after 2 bxa3 b2) **2...♗xb2! 3 ♘xb2+ ♔a3 4 ♘d1 b2 5 ♘xb2 ♔xb2 6 ♔d2 ♘f4 0-1**
White is in zugzwang and c3 will decisively fall.

802) Volokitin-Ganguly
1 ♔f6! (and not the 1 ♘f3?? e5 2 ♔f5 e4 3 ♘g5 – crucially 3 ♘d2 e3 comes with tempo – 3...e3 4 ♔f4 e2 5 ♘f3 b3 and 0-1 of the game, although White can also begin with 1 ♔h5!) **1...b3** (1...e5 2 ♔f5 b3 3 ♘e4 b2 4 ♘d2 transposes) **2 ♘f3 e5 3 ♘d2 b2 4 ♔f5 ♔d4 5 ♘b1 e4 6 ♔f4 ♔d3 7 ♘a3 e3** (the only try; Black must keep both pawns) **8 ♔f3 e2 9 ♔f2** and Black cannot maintain his pawns in view of 9...♔d2 10 ♘c4+ ♔c1 11 ♘xb2.

803) Bronstein-Botvinnik
1 ♘e6! ♔f5 (after the continuation 1...♖h7 2 ♘g7 ♖h8 3 ♔c5, White wins due to his superior king) **2 ♘f8 1-0**
The h-pawn queens after 2...♖d8 3 ♗d6! ♖xd6 4 h7.

804) Garcia Gonzales-Quinteros
1 g6! f3 2 ♔g1 ♔f6 3 e5+! (forcing one of the pawns home) **3...dxe5 4 d6 e4 5 d7 1-0**
White queens first.

805) Movsesian-Kuzubov
1...♕d1+! 2 ♕e1 ♗g2+! 3 ♔f2 (now it's mate, but White loses his queen after 3 ♔xg2 ♕xe1) **3...♕f3+ 4 ♔g1 ♗h3 0-1**
Mate follows after 5 ♕f2 ♕d1+ or 5 ♕d2 ♕f1#.

806) Grigoriants-Shaposhnikov
1 e8♕! ♘g7+ 2 ♔g6 ♘xe8 3 h5 leaves the h-pawn unstoppable: **3...♘c7 4 ♔f7!** (and not 4 h6?? ♘e6 5 ♔f6 ♘f8 with a draw) **4...♘b5 5 h6 ♘d6+ 6 ♔g6 1-0**

807) Novikov-Jakovenko
White saves himself with a stalemate trick: **1 ♖f4+! ♖xf4 ½-½**

808) Ehlvest-Bluvshtein
1 ♗xg6! fxg5 (the pawn queens immediately in the case of 1...hxg6 2 h7) **2 ♖c1! 1-0**
The only way to halt White's h-pawn is 2...♖xc1 3 ♔xc1 ♔d6 4 ♗xh7 ♔e7 5 ♗e4 ♔f6, but after 6 ♗xd5 Black's cause is clearly completely hopeless.

809) Schlechter-Wolf
1...♖e1+! 2 ♖xe1 ½-½
It's stalemate.

810) Savchenko-Har Zvi
1...♗xh3! wins a pawn in view of 2 ♔xh3? ♖h1#.

811) Chigorin-Tarrasch
Rather than the game's 1 gxf6?, **1 ♔g4! ♔e4 2 g6 h6** (or 2...hxg6 3 fxg6 f5+ 4 ♔g5 f4 5 h5 f3 6 h6 and both sides queen with a draw) **3 ♔h5!** would have drawn since 3...♔xf5 is stalemate.

812) Michalczak-Schoene
As so often in opposite-coloured bishop endings, it is the number of passed pawns rather than the number of extra pawns which decides: **1...f4!** (creating a decisive second passed pawn) **2 gxf4** (or 2 ♗d2 ♗e4+ 3 ♔f2 fxg3+ 4 ♔xg3 ♔f5 5 ♗c3 h4+ 6 ♔h2 g4 7 hxg4+ ♔xg4 8 a4 ♗f5 9 ♗e5 a6 10 b5 axb5 11 axb5 ♗d7 12 ♗c7 ♗xb5 13 ♗xb6 ♗d7 14 ♗d4 ♔f3 15 ♔g1 ♔e2 and White will have to give up his bishop for the c-pawn) **2...g4 3 hxg4 hxg4 4 ♗d2 ♔f5 5 ♔g3 ♗c2** (now Black's king infiltrates with decisive effect) **6 ♗e3 ♗a4 7 ♗d4 ♗d7 8 ♗e5 ♔e4 0-1**
The black king and c-pawn decide.

813) Smallbone-Brown
1 a6+!! ♔a8 (now it's mate, but it also is after 1...♔xa6 2 ♗c8+ ♔b5 3 ♗xe3 ♖xe3 – or 3...h2 4 b7 h1♕ 5 b8♕+ ♔a5 6 ♗d2+ followed by mate on b4 – 4 b7 h2 5 b8♕+ ♔c5 6 ♕a7+: for example, 6...♔d6 7 ♕d7+ ♔c5 8 ♗b7 h1♕ 9 ♕xc6+ ♔b4 10 ♕b6+ ♔c4 11 ♗a6+ ♔d5 12 c4# or 6...♔b5 7 ♗a6+ ♔a4 8 ♗d3+ ♔b4 9 ♕a3#) **2 b7+ ♔b8 3 ♗d6+ 1-0**

814) Palliser-Lappage
1 b4! axb4 (or 1...h5 2 bxa5 bxa5 3 c5 ♔f6 4 ♔e4 with a trivial win) **2 c5 1-0**
White queens first and wins with 2...b3 3 ♔d3 ♔f6 (or 3...h5 4 ♔c3! when Black is in zugzwang and lost, such as after 4...e4 5 fxe4+ ♔e5 6 d6 cxd6 7 cxb6) 4 d6 b2 5 ♔c2 ♔e6 6 dxc7 ♔d7 7 cxb6 h5 8 a5 g4 (very similar is 8...e4 9 fxe4 g4 10 a6 gxh3 11 a7 h2 12 c8♕+) 9 fxg4 e4 10 a6 e3 11 a7 e2 12 c8♕+.

815) Palliser-Lappage
1...♖g4! 2 d7 ♖h4+ 3 ♔g3 ♖bxh2 0-1
Mate follows with 4 d8♕ ♖4h3#.

816) Milovanovic-Jacobs
1 ♖xb7+! creates an unstoppable g-pawn: **1...♔xb7 2 g6 ♖d4 3 g7 ♖d8 4 ♗e6 1-0**

817) Bronstein-Panno
1 ♔g5! (Black is powerless against the advance of the king – always improve your worst-placed piece!) **1...♗f5 2 ♔h6 ♖e7 3 ♕b3+ ♔e6 4 ♕b2 1-0**
The knight is lost since 4...♘f6 fails to 5 ♖xf8+! ♔xf8 6 ♕xf6+.

818) Acs-Ivanchuk
Black only has one way to draw: **1...h4!** (White wins easily after both 1...♔d5 2 ♔xf4 ♔e6 3 ♔g5 ♔f7 4 ♔xh5 ♔g7 5 ♔g5 and 1...♔d4 2 ♔xf4 h4 3 ♔g4 ♔e4 4 ♔xh4 ♔f4 5 g4) **2 ♔xf4** (or 2 ♔xh4 ♔d4 3 ♔g4 ♔e3 with a clear draw) **2...h3! 3 gxh3 ½-½**

The only way for White to prevent Black's king from reaching the corner is to allow his own king to become blocked in on the h-file.

819) Berke-Franciskovic

The game ended with the hideous 1 ♖b1 f3 2 ♖c1 ♖h2 0-1, but White should have held the draw with **1 ♖f7!**: 1...♔f3 (1...f3 2 ♖g7+ commences a barrage of checks and 1...♖a1+ 2 ♔e2 also sees Black failing to make progress) 2 ♔g1! (correctly heading for the short side) 2...♖a1+ 3 ♔h2 ♖f1 (or 3...♔e3 4 ♔g2 ♖a2+ 5 ♔f1 ♔f3 6 ♔g1 keeping Black at bay) 4 ♖a7 ♖e1 5 ♖f7 and Black can only go round in circles.

820) Bocharov-Roiz

Rather than the game's 1 ♖g8, **1 ♔g4! ♖xb3 2 ♖g8+ ♔f6 3 ♖g6+!** would have offered excellent chances to draw: for example, 3...♔e7 (and not 3...♔xg6? with stalemate) 4 ♖xg5 a4 5 ♖a5 a3 (or 5...♖b4+ 6 ♔f3 ♔d6 7 ♔e3 ♔c6 8 ♔d3 ♔b6 9 ♖a8 and the white king is again close enough to the a-pawn) 6 ♔f4 ♔d6 7 ♔e4 ♔c6 8 ♔d4 ♔b6 9 ♔c4 ♖h3 10 ♖a8 and White holds.

821) Nimzowitsch-Tarrasch

1...f5+! 0-1

It's an easy win after 2 ♔d4 (or 2 ♔xf5 a4 and the a-pawn queens) 2...f4! 3 ♔c5 ♔g6 4 ♔b5 ♔h5 5 ♔xa5 ♔xh4 6 ♔b4 ♔g3 7 ♔c3 ♔xg2.

822) Bystryakova-Airumian

1 ♗xb6! axb6 2 ♖xa6 wins a pawn.

823) Gunina-Dolgova

Black can queen the d-pawn: **1...♗b4+! 2 ♔xc1 d2+**.

824) Shabalov-Kaidanov

1 ♗c6+! ♔a5 2 b4+ ♔b6 3 bxc5+ 1-0

White's simplification leads to a winning pawn endgame after 3...♔xc6 4 ♘b4+ ♔b5 5 ♘xa6 ♔xa6 6 ♔d3.

825) Karlsson-Furhoff

1 ♖h1! ♔g3 (Black actually loses after 1...g3? 2 ♔f3 h2 – or 2...g2 3 ♖a1 – 3 ♔g2 ♔g4 4 ♖a1 when his pawns fall) **2 ♖g1+! ♔h2** (or 2...♔f2 3 ♖a1 h2 4 ♖xa2+ ♔g1 5 ♖a1+ ♔g2 6 ♖a2+ ♔h3 7 ♖a1 with a perpetual since 7...g3? forces Black to defend with knight against rook after 8 ♔f3 g2 9 ♖a8 g1♘+ 10 ♔f2 ♘f3!? 11 ♖a1 ♘g1 12 ♖a3+ ♔g4 13 ♔g2) **3 ♖a1 g3 4 ♔f3 g2 5 ♔f2 g1♕+ 6 ♖xg1 a1♕ 7 ♖xa1 ½-½**

It's stalemate.

826) Onischuk-Timoshenko

1...♘h6+! (the only defence but a good one) **2 ♔e7** (the best try; 2 ♔g6 ♘g4 3 h6 ♘xh6 4 ♔xh6 ♔d7 is a simple draw) **2...♔c6 3 e6 ♔d5** (Black's king is just in time to halt the h-pawn) **4 ♔d7** (or 4 ♔f6 ♘g4+ 5 ♔g5 ♔xe6 with a draw) **4...♘g8 5 e7 ♘f6+ 6 ♔d8 ♔e6 7 h6 ♔f7 8 h7 ♔g7 ½-½**

827) Petrosian-Ivkov

1 ♖xd4! 1-0

It's mate after any capture of the rook: e.g. 1...♖xd4 2 ♖xe5+ ♔xg4 3 f3#.

828) Wall-Stephenson
Instead of the game's 1...♔b2, **1...♔a4!** draws since 2 ♔g6 ♖xh7! 3 ♔xh7 is stalemate and 2 ♖f7 ♔xa3 3 ♔g6 ♔xb4 4 ♖f5 ♖xh7 5 ♔xh7 ♔c4 6 ♔g6 b4 leaves White's king too far from the front b-pawn.

829) Arakhamia Grant-Baburin
1...f2! 0-1
Black either has an easy win with queen versus rook (due to his passed f-pawn) or wins White's rook.

830) Shirov-Aronian
1 ♖xd4+! ♔xd4 2 ♘f5+ ♔xc5 3 ♔xe3 sees White solve his problems by simplifying. Aronian's last chance was **3...♘e5**, but after **4 g4! hxg4 5 h4** (a key move to have seen at the beginning of the combination) **5...♔c4** (White also draws after the long forcing line 5...♘c4+ 6 ♔f4 ♘xa3 7 h5 ♘c4 8 h6 f6 9 h7 ♘e5 10 ♘e3 a3 11 ♔f5 ♘f7 12 ♔xg4 a2 13 ♘c2 ♔c4 14 ♔f5 ♔c3 15 ♘a1 ♘h8 16 ♔xf6 ♔b2 17 ♔g7) **6 h5 ♔b3 7 ♔d4 ♘f3+ 8 ♔d3 ♔xa3 9 ♔c3** progress was impossible with Black's king incarcerated and his kingside pawns stymied. **½-½**

831) Van Wely-Aronian
1...♖xd1+! 2 ♔xd1 ♔f7 leaves White unable to save both rook and bishop: **3 ♖xh6** (or 3 ♔e1 ♔xg7 4 ♖h4 f5 5 gxf5 ♗xf5 again with rook against bishop and pawn, and a complete draw) **3...♗xg4+ ½-½**

832) Winants-Hansen
1...♔h3! 0-1
Black is too far ahead after 2 ♔e3 ♔g3 3 f4 ♔g4 4 ♔e2 ♔xf4 5 ♔f2 ♔e4.

833) Warakomski-Baramidze
1 f4! 1-0
White wins a piece with 1...gxf4 2 gxf4 ♖xd1 3 fxe5+ ♔xe5 4 ♗xd1.

834) Carpenter-Wallace
1 ♖xa1! forces the pawns home with shades of McDonnell-De Labourdonnais: **1...♖xa1 2 f7 ♖aa8 3 g6! 1-0**

835) Round-Palliser
1...♕xg2! won a rook in view of 2 ♕xg2 ♔g6 followed by mated on h7.

836) Palliser-Gayson
The c-pawn decides: **1 ♕xa4! 1-0**

837) Krutti-Palliser
1...h5! (White escapes after 1...♔f6? 2 ♖g8 h5 3 ♖f3+ ♔e7 4 ♔h4) **2 ♔h4** (or 2 g4 ♖h2+ 3 ♔g3 h4+ 4 ♔f3 ♖h3+ 5 ♔e4 ♖a4+ 6 c4 – 6 ♔d3 e4+ 7 ♔d2 ♖a2+ wins the rook on e3 – 6...♖xc4+ 7 ♔d3 ♖d4+ 8 ♔e2 ♖h2+ 9 ♔e1 – 9 ♔f3 ♖f4# – 9...♖b4 and White must finally lose his rook with 10 ♖e2 ♖b1+ 11 ♔d2 ♖b2+ 12 ♔c3 ♖bxe2 to avert mate) **2...♔f6 0-1**
The mate threat costs White a rook.

838) Sokolov-Sasikiran
1 ♗a1! 1-0
The bishop has to retreat to a1 so that White can win the a-pawn at the end with 1...♔f7 2

♔xf5 ♗xa1 3 ♖a6.

Chapter Five

839) Lacasa Diaz-Moreno Ruiz
1...♕xc3! 0-1
Black emerges a piece ahead after 2 ♕xc3 ♘xe2+ 3 ♔h1 ♘xc3 4 ♗xg7 ♘xd1 5 ♗xf8 ♔xf8 6 ♖xd1.

840) Perez-Ramirez Garcia
1 ♗xh7+! ♘xh7 2 ♕xb3 ♖xf4 3 ♘xf4 ♕xe5 4 ♕g3 left White a clear exchange ahead.

841) Tal-Benko
1 ♖d8+! won the exchange on h8 in view of 1...♔xd8? 2 ♘xf7+ and 3 ♘xe5.

842) Can-Erdogdu
1 ♗xg5! wins a pawn: **1...fxg5 2 ♘e5 ♕e6 3 ♘xc6+! ♕xc6 4 ♕xe7+ ♔c8 5 ♕xf7 ♕xc3 6 ♕d5** left White clearly better.

843) Caruana-Majer
1 ♘xg6! wins a pawn in view of 1...fxg6? 2 ♕xe6+ ♖f7 3 ♗xd6.

844) Korchnoi-Karpov
White must keep e5 defended: **1 ♘d3! ♖xd3+ 2 ♔c4 1-0**
The b-pawn costs Black his remaining pieces.

845) Narciso Dublan-Timman
1 ♗h5+! ♔h6 2 ♗f7 1-0
White wins the rook on c4 in view of the threat of 3 ♖h5#.

846) Lundberg-Czerownski
1...♕xf2+! 2 ♔xf2 ♘xd5 trapped White's queen and saw Black emerge the exchange ahead after **3 ♕xc5** (or 3 ♕xd6 ♘e4+ and 4...♘xd6) **3...dxc5**.

847) Faranka-Al Aqrabi
Black wins queen for rook: **1...♖g2+! 2 ♖xg2 ♕xh5 0-1**

848) Damaso-Malakhov
1 ♕g7+! 1-0
The h-pawn queens after 1...♕xg7 2 ♖xe8+ ♔xe8 3 hxg7.

849) Parr-Collins
1 ♖xb7! 1-0
White wins significant material after 1...♕xb7 (or 1...♕c8 2 dxc6 ♖c7 3 ♕xd6) 2 dxc6 ♕b6 3 cxd7.

850) Heidenfeld-Franklin
1 ♕a7! 1-0
Black loses his queen in view of 1...♕xa7 2 ♖c8#.

851) Kosten-Taylor
White simplifies with **1 ♖dxc5! ♗xc5** (or 1...bxc5 2 ♕xb8 ♖xb8 3 ♗e5 ♖b7 – 3...♖c8 4 ♗xg7! – 4 ♘d6 ♗xd6 5 ♗xd6 ♘a6 6 ♗xc5 with a trivially winning ending) **2 ♕c6** (with the rather awkward thread of 3 ♖xc5 bxc5 4 ♘e7+ ♔h8 5 ♘xc8 ♕xc8 6 ♗e5) **2...♘e6** (there wasn't anything better; for instance 2...♖e8 3 b4 and White wins a piece) **3 ♘e7+! 1-0**

852) Rosen-Taylor
1...♗xh2+ 2 ♔xh2 ♕h4+ 3 ♔g1 ♕xb4 left Black a clear pawn ahead.

853) I.Thompson-B.Lund
1 ♖e8+! 1-0
Black loses his queen in view of 1...♔f7 2 ♕e7#.

854) Parker-Pert
1...♖h1+! 0-1
White loses his queen after 2 ♔xh1 ♘xf2+ 3 ♖xf2 ♕xc3.

855) Plaskett-Gallagher
1 ♖xg7+! ♔xg7 2 ♕d7+ 1-0
White wins a rook after 3 ♖xa4.

856) Shaw-Johannessen
1 ♖e8! ♗c7 (White wins a piece after 1...♖xe8 2 ♘xd6) **2 d6 ♗a5 3 d7 1-0**
There's no stopping the decisive threat of 4 ♘d6 and 5 ♘xf7.

857) Shepley-Rosen
1...♗xh2+! 2 ♔xh2 (or 2 ♔h1 ♗d6) **2...♘g4+ 3 ♔g3? ♕xg5** and Black was a pawn up with a rather strong attack.

858) Bhatia-Bentley
1 ♘f6+! gxf6 (or 1...♔f8 2 ♕h7 with a winning attack) **2 ♗xf7+! ♔xf7 3 ♕xc5** wins the black queen.

859) Richardson-Ozeren
1...♖xe3! saw Black win a pawn before favourably simplifying with **2 ♖xe3 ♘g4+ 3 ♔f3 ♘xe3 4 ♖e1 ♘f5 5 ♖xe7 ♘xe7.**

860) Davis-Rice
1 ♘f6+! 1-0
White wins the exchange with 1...♗xf6 2 ♖xd7.

861) Alfred-Smallbone
Black loses his queen: **1 ♖c8! 1-0**

862) Palliser-Brameld
Rather than the game's 1 ♗b3, **1 ♘xd6! ♕d7** (the main point is that 1...♕xd5? 2 ♘e8+! and 3 ♘xc7 wins a piece) **2 ♘e4 ♕xd5 3 ♕xd5 ♘xd5 4 ♘xc5** wins a pawn.

863) Palliser-Houska
1 ♕xb8! ♕xb8 2 ♖a8 ♗d6 3 ♗a7 1-0
The b-pawn costs Black a piece.

864) Hagesaether-Rabbitte
1 ♖cb2! 1-0
White wins the b6-knight since Black must move his c6-rook in order to give his queen an escape square against the threatened 2 ♗d1.

865) Salem-Doggers
1...♗xf2+! wins a pawn in view of 2 ♗xf2? ♕xc7.

866) Weiler-Toth
1...♗h2+! 0-1
Black wins the exchange with 2 ♔xh2 ♕xb6.

867) Cooper-Walsh
White wins a pawn with **1 ♗xh7+! ♔xh7 2 ♕d3+** (and not 2 ♕h5+?? ♔g8 3 ♖h3 ♖e1#)
2...♔g8 3 ♕xd6.

868) Pilaj-Naranjo Moreno
1 ♘xg6! 1-0
White wins a second pawn in view of 1...♖xe4? 2 ♘xf8+ ♔g8 3 fxe4.

869) Rogers-Fitzpatrick
1 ♘xa7! ♕xa7 (or 1...♗a4 2 ♖xc8 ♗xb3 3 ♖xd8+ ♕xd8 4 ♖c8 – the key point: White regains the queen – 4...♕xc8 5 ♘xc8 ♗xa2 6 ♘xb6) **2 ♖xc6** wins a pawn.

870) Carlsen-Fressinet
1 ♕f5! 1-0
White wins a rook in view of 1...♕xf5 2 ♖xb8+ with mate on the back rank.

871) Drozdovskij-Georgiev
White missed the fork **1 ♖xb8! ♖xb8** (or 1...♕xf5 2 ♖xe8+ ♘xe8 3 ♗xf5) **2 ♕f4** winning a piece and the game.

872) Mkrtchian-Riazantsev
1 ♕xe7! (much better than 1 ♖xg6? ♖dd7!) **1...♖g8** (after 1...♘xe7 White picks up a piece with 2 ♖xg7+ ♔h8 3 ♖g5+ ♔h7 4 ♖xh5) **2 ♕f7 1-0**

873) Rendle-Arjun
1 ♕xd8! ♕xd3 (or 1...♖fxd8 2 ♘f6+ ♔g7 3 ♘xd5) **2 ♕e7** saw White win a piece.

874) Ferro-Rotstein
1...♗xf2! 2 ♔xf2 ♖xc3 3 ♖xc3 ♘e4+ 4 ♔e3 ♘xc3 left Black two pawns up in the endgame.

875) Krivoshey-Ferro
1 ♖xb7! ♖xb7 (or 1...gxf5 2 ♖xd7 ♘xd7 3 ♗xd5+ ♔g7 4 ♗e6 ♘b8 5 ♗xf5) **2 ♗xd5+ ♘e6 3 ♗xb7 gxf5 4 ♗xa6** forced a winning endgame.

876) Aoustin-Perez
1 ♕xe4! ♕xe4 2 ♗a7+ ♔xa7 3 ♖xe4 saw White pick up a second exchange.

877) Reefat-Hakki
1 ♕xh7+! 1-0

White is a piece up after 1...♔xh7 2 ♗xf5+ ♔g7 3 ♖xb2.

878) Palliser-Khandelwal
1 ♕xc8! 1-0
White wins a rook in view of 1...♗xc8 2 ♖xd8 ♕xd8 3 ♘f7+ ♔g8 4 ♘xd8.

879) Palliser-Hague
1 ♖xc6! 1-0
White wins a piece since 1...♕xc6? (or 1...e4 2 ♕c4 exf3? 3 ♘f6+) 2 ♘e7+ ♖xe7 3 ♗xc6 wins the black queen.

880) Beliavsky-Van den Doel
1 ♗a7+! ♔xa7 2 ♖xe6 wins the exchange.

881) Zweschper-Glantz
1...♖xd4 2 cxd4 ♘d3+! 0-1
Black is a piece ahead after 3 ♔d2 ♘xc1 or a rook ahead after 3 ♗xd3 ♖xc1+ 4 ♔f2 ♖xh1.

882) Jorczik-Gashimov
1...♗b5! traps the queen: **2 ♕xd5 ♖xd5 3 ♖xd5 ♗c6 4 ♖a5? ♕d8 0-1**

883) Georgiev-Holzke
1...♖e8! created the decisive threat of 2...♗f8, winning the b3-bishop or the queen, since 2 ♕c4 (or 2 ♕c2) runs into 2...♕a5+ and again White's dark-squared bishop is a goner.

884) Womacka-Kritz
1 ♖xg7+! 1-0
Black loses his queen after 1...♘xg7 2 ♘g5+ fxg5 3 ♕xc2.

885) Katte-Pert
Black wins queen for rook: **1...♖c2+! 0-1**

886) Ruck-Dreev
1...♘e2+! 2 ♕xe2 ♖xc1+ wins the exchange.

887) Zhigalko-Durarbayli
1 ♗b6! ♕xb6 (or 1...♕b7 2 ♗xd8) **2 ♘xe7+ ♔f8 3 ♘xc8** wins the exchange.

888) Burnett-Bucher
1 ♗xc7! wins a second pawn in view of 1...♔xc7 2 ♖xe7+.

889) Eggleston-Ramaswamy
1 ♖xe7+! 1-0
White wins a piece in view of 1...♔xe7 2 ♘d5+ and 3 ♘xb6.

890) Jones-Ruxton
1...♗xa3! 2 bxa3 ♖xc3 picks up a second pawn.

891) Kosintseva-Jackova
1 ♗xf7+! wins the exchange in view of 1...♔xf7 (or 1...♔h7 2 ♗xe8) 2 ♘e5+ ♔g8 3 ♘xc6 and 4 ♘xb8.

892) Jakovenko-Shirov
Black wins a pawn: **1...♕xc3+! 2 ♔xc3 ♗b4+ 3 ♔d4 ♖xf7** and Black's connected passed pawns carried the day.

893) Hess-Kamsky
1...♖xd1! 0-1
Black wins a piece in view of 2 ♖xd1 ♘e3+ 3 ♔g1 ♘xd1.

894) Wagner-Miralles
1...♖xe3! wins a pawn and leaves White in all sorts of trouble: **2 ♖xe3 ♕xg2+! 3 ♔xg2 ♘xe3+ 4 ♔f2 ♘xc2 5 ♖xc2** and now **5...b4!** (rather than the game's 5...g5) **6 axb4 ♗a4** would have won the exchange.

895) Tiviakov-Bunzmann
1 ♗xg7! netted a pawn in view of 1...♔xg7 2 ♖f7+ and 3 ♖xd7.

896) Thorfinnsson-Najer
1...♖e1+! 0-1
White's queen is lost in view of 2 ♖xe1 ♕xd3.

897) Porper-Mikkelsen
1 ♗xf7+! 1-0
White is two pawns up after 1...♔xf7 2 ♘e5+ and 3 ♘xc6.

898) Tallaksen-Lie
1...♖xc2 2 ♖xc2 e3 forces White to give up his rook to halt the pawns: **3 ♔d3 e2 4 ♖xe2 fxe2 5 ♔xe2 ♘xd5 0-1**

899) Reppen-Guddahl
1...♕xc3! 2 ♕xc3 d2 0-1
White can only stop the d-pawn by giving up his queen.

900) Cherniaev-Pauchard
1 ♘xe6+! 1-0
Black loses his queen after 1...♗xe6 2 ♕xa4.

901) Huss-Khenkin
1...♖xb2! (threatening mate on c2) **2 ♔xb2 d2 0-1**
White must give up his rook to stop the d-pawn.

902) Handke-Reuss
1 ♘xd4! 1-0
White emerges two pawns ahead after 1...cxd4 2 ♕xd4 ♕c7 (or 2...♘e7 3 ♗xc6 ♘xc6 4 ♕xd7) 3 ♗xd5 ♗xd5 4 ♕xd5.

903) Langheinrich-Pelletier
1...♗xf2+! 2 ♖xf2 ♕h1+! 0-1
Black emerges the exchange ahead after 3 ♔xh1 ♘xf2+ 4 ♔g1 ♘xd1.

904) Sargissian-Nisipeanu
1...♖xe5! 2 ♗xd5 (it's mate after 2 ♖xe5? ♗xf3+ 3 ♔g1 ♕g4+ 4 ♔f1 ♕g2#) **2...♕g5** (or

2...♕h3; the mate threat is decisive) **3 ♕g1 ♕xg1+ 0-1**
Black emerges a piece up after 4 ♔xg1 ♖xe3 5 fxe3 ♘xd5.

905) Firman-Sakaev
1 ♕xc7! 1-0
White emerges the exchange ahead after 1...♕xc7 2 ♘e6+ and 3 ♘xc7.

906) Kindermann-Schneider
1...♗xb2! 2 ♔xb2 ♕e5+ 3 ♔b1 ♕xg5 won a pawn.

907) Heinemann-Sarbok
1 ♘xe6+! fxe6 2 ♖xe6 1-0
Black cannot both cover e8 and defend his bishop on h6.

908) Ivanchuk-Gyimesi
1 ♗xa7! cxd5 (the main point is that 1...♖xa7? 2 ♕b6 forks Black's rooks) **2 ♗b6 ♖e8 3 exd5**
won a pawn.

909) Ribli-Kalinitschew
1 ♖xb7! ♖xb7 2 ♖c8+ ♔g7 3 f4 wins a piece.

910) Butnorius-Cramling
1...♕xf2+! 2 ♔h1 (the main point is that 2 ♔xf2? runs into 2...♘cxe4+ 3 ♔e1 ♗f2#) **2...♘cxe4**
picked up two important pawns.

911) Krush-Richardson
1 ♘xd6! wins either the exchange or Black's queen after 1...♕xd6 2 ♗c5.

912) Rashleigh-Bucknell
1...♖xc2+! 0-1
White loses his queen after 2 ♔xc2 ♕xa2+ and 3...♕xg2.

913) Sarkar-Obers
1 ♕xf7+! ♔xf7 2 ♘d8+ 1-0
White emerges a piece ahead after 3 ♘xc6.

914) Ramesh-Werner
1 ♘xc6! exploits Black's vulnerable back-rank and c8-rook to win a pawn.

915) Abergel-Wallace
1 ♗xf7+! ♖xf7 2 ♖xa8 won the exchange.

916) Keres-Spassky
1 ♕xg7+! 1-0
Black emerges a piece down with a hopeless position after 1...♔xg7 2 ♘xd7+ ♔g8 3 ♘f6+
♔f7 (even worse is 3...♔h8 4 ♘xe8+ ♔g8 5 ♘xc7) 4 ♘d5+ ♔g8 5 ♘xc7.

917) Olivier-Adda
1...♕xe1+! 2 ♔xe1 ♘g2+ 3 ♔f1 ♘xh4 wins a rook.

918) Smyslov-Kottnauer
1 ♘c5! dxc5 (or 1...♖c7 2 ♘xd7 ♖xc6 3 ♘xb8 with an extra piece) **2 ♗f4 ♗d6** (White's main point is that 2...♕xf4 fails to 3 ♕c8+ ♔e7 4 ♕xb7 and 5 ♖xd7+) **3 ♗xd6 ♖b6 4 ♕xd7+! 1-0** White wins a piece.

919) Walton-Palliser
Black wins a crucial pawn: **1...♗xb3! 2 ♖b1 c4** and White's position collapsed.

920) Breutigam-Pajeken
1 ♕f7+! 1-0
White wins a rook with 1...♕xf7 2 ♖xc8+ ♕e8 3 ♖xe8+.

921) Palliser-Adrian
1...♘f3+! 0-1
White loses his queen after 2 gxf3 (or 2 ♔h1 ♕h2#) 2...♖g7+ 3 ♗g2 ♕xc4.

922) Greet-Grant
1 ♕xf7+! ♔xf7 2 ♘e5+ ♔e6 3 ♘xd3 wins a pawn.

923) Donovan-Webster
1 ♖xd6! wins a piece in view of the simplifying trick 1...♕xd6 2 ♕xa8 ♖xa8 3 ♘f7+ ♔g8 4 ♘xd6.

924) Bowers-Stewart
White wins the black queen: **1 ♖xg7+! ♘xg7 2 ♕xh4**.

925) Stellwagen-Bosboom
1 ♗xa6! decisively won a second pawn in view of 1...♗xa6 (or 1...♘c6 2 ♖f4+) 2 ♖xe5.

926) Kuznetsova-Bogorads
1...♘xd3! wins a pawn in view of 2 ♕xd3? ♕xe1+.

927) Alekhine-Euwe
Rather than the game's 1 a3, **1 ♕h8+! ♔xh8 2 ♘xf7+ ♔h7 3 ♘xe5** would have simplified to a winning endgame.

928) Palliser-Stalmans
1...♖d1+! 0-1
White loses his queen after 2 ♖xd1 (2 ♔c2 is mated by 2...♖xb2+ 3 ♔xd1 ♕d4+ 4 ♔c1 ♕c3+ 5 ♔d1 ♖b1#) 2...♕xg3.

929) Georgiou-Palliser
1...♘xg4! wins a pawn in view of 2 fxg4?! ♗xc3 (2...♖xc3!? is pretty reasonable too) 3 bxc3? ♕xa3+ 4 ♔b1 ♕a2+ 5 ♔c1 ♕a1#.

930) Ikonnikov-Negi
White wins material with **1 ♕xe8: 1...♕xe8 2 ♘xc5 ♕c6 3 ♗xc8 1-0**
The d-pawn queens after 3...♕xc5 4 d7, while 3...♗xd6 fails to 4 ♖xd6!.

931) Malakhatko-Groffen
1 ♖xh8! 1-0

White wins a piece since 1...♘xh8 2 ♖f6+ ♔e8 3 c6 forks the black rooks.

932) Morris-Gilhespy
1...♘xh2! 2 ♖f2 (White's queen is lost after 2 ♔xh2 ♕h5+ 3 ♔g1 ♘h3+ 4 ♔h2 ♘f2+ 5 ♔g1 ♕h1+ 6 ♔xf2 ♕xg2+ 7 ♔e1 ♕xc2) **2...♕h5 0-1**
There's no good defence to the threats of 2...♘f3+ and 2...♘g4 since 3 ♔g1 ♘f3+ 4 ♖xf3 ♕xf3 leads to mate.

933) Gunnarsson-Iraheta
1 ♖xe6! ♗f5 (White mates after 1...♖xc3 2 ♖xe7 as, of course, he also does after 1...fxe6 2 ♕f8#) **2 ♕xd6! 1-0**
Black comes out a piece down in the ending after 2...♕xd6 3 ♖xd6 exd6 4 ♘xf5 gxf5 5 ♖xd6.

934) Rublevsky-Gurevich
1 ♗xe6+! 1-0
1...fxe6 2 ♕xe6+ costs Black the exchange and 1...♗d7 2 ♗xf7 is also crushing.

935) Meins-Abel
1 ♖xf7! ♕xf7 2 ♕xa8+ wins a pawn.

936) Morales-Heimbacher
1 ♘xf7! ♔xf7 (or 1...♗xf7 2 ♖xe7) **2 ♖xe6** wins a pawn.

937) Zapata-Moreno
1 ♘f6+! exf6 2 ♗c6 wins the exchange.

938) Carlsen-Ivanchuk
1 d5! exd5 2 ♘d4 wins a piece and the game.

939) Rayner-Vranesic
1 ♗xh7+! ♔xh7 2 ♕d3+ ♔g8 3 ♕xd5 wins a pawn.

940) James-Waters
1 ♗xh6! wins a pawn since 1...♗xh6? 2 ♕xg6+ forks Black's minor pieces.

941) Nunn-Plaskett
1 ♕f5! ♖e6 (the queen is immune due to 1...♕xf5? 2 ♖xe8# and 1...♕d8? fails to 2 ♖e7! followed by mate) **2 d5 ♘xd3 3 dxe6 fxe6 4 ♕xe6+** and White had won the exchange. **1-0**

942) Large-Baker
1 ♗h6+! ♔xh6 (or 1...♔g8 2 ♗xf8 ♗h4+ 3 ♔d2 ♗f2 4 ♖d1 with an extra rook) **2 g5+ ♗xg5 3 ♖xh3+ ♔g7 4 ♖xg5** and White's extra piece proved decisive.

943) Hebbes-Palliser
1...♖xc2+! 2 ♔xc2 ♕xe2+ 3 ♕d2 and now **3...♗c8+** would have won White's queen.

944) Hartston-Basman
1 ♗xf7+! ♔xf7 (otherwise Black loses the exchange on g8) **2 ♕h5+ ♖g6 3 ♕xh3** wins a pawn.

945) Tsirulnik-Kosyachenko
1...♕xa3! wins a piece in view of 2 ♖xa3? ♖f1#.

946) Arutyunova-Maiko
1 ♗xg6! hxg6 2 ♖xd7! won a key pawn and gained White a decisive initiative in view of 2...♕xd7 3 ♘f6+ ♔g7 4 ♘xd7.

947) Blackburne-Owen
1 ♕xf7+! ♕xf7 2 ♖ee7 1-0
Black's bishop is lost in view of 2...♖f8 3 ♖xb7.

948) Ausan-Chan Wei Yi
1...♖b1+! 2 ♔xb1 (or 2 ♔d2 ♖xh1 with an extra rook) **2...♗xa2+ 3 ♔xa2 ♕xf6 0-1**
Black's extra queen and passed h-pawn decide.

949) Najdorf-Rossetto
1 ♘xc6! wins a pawn in view of 1...bxc6 2 ♗xc5.

950) Klima-Boros
1 ♘xe6! fxe6 (or 1...♕d7 2 ♗xb6 ♘xc4 3 ♘c7 picking up the exchange) **2 ♗xb6 ♕c8 3 ♗xa5** wins two pawns.

951) Markiewicz-Sokolowski
1 ♖xc8! 1-0
White wins a piece after 1...♖xc8 2 ♘e7+ ♔g7 3 ♘xc8.

952) Warakomski-Orzech
1...♗xb2+! 2 ♔xb2 ♖xd2 wins a pawn and seizes the initiative in view of 3 ♕xd2? ♘c4+ and 4...♘xd2.

953) Bergez-Vassallo Barroche
1...♘fxe4! wins a pawn in view of the skewer 2 ♘xe4 ♘xe4 3 ♕xe4 ♗f5.

954) Hodinott-Palliser
1...♘xd4! 2 ♘xd4 ♗xc3 3 ♗xc3 ♖xc3 wins a pawn.

955) Ivanchuk-Anand
1 f4! ♕xf4 2 ♖e4 1-0
The knight is lost after 2...♕f5 3 ♖ae1 f6 4 f4.

956) Kramnik-Ivanchuk
1...♘ce7! wins a clear piece in view of the threat of 2...♗a4, and if 3 ♖b2, then 3...♘xc3. Kramnik tried **2 ♗xd5 ♘xd5 3 ♗b2,** but this failed to save the piece after **3...♗a4 4 ♖a3 ♖xb2 5 ♖xa4 ♘b6** (the crucial sting in the tail) **6 ♖a7 ♖xd2** when he might as well have resigned.

957) Almada-Roselli Mailhe
1...♘xc3! wins a pawn in view of 2 ♔xc3 ♖xe3+.

958) Ivanchuk-Topalov
1 ♕xc4! 1-0

White wins a piece in view of both 1...♖xc4 2 ♖xf7 and 1...♖xa7 2 ♖xa7 ♕xa7 3 ♕xc8.

959) Milov-Akobian
1 ♘d7+! ♖xd7 2 ♖xf8 wins the exchange.

960) Chudinovskikh-Sitnikov
1 ♘d7+! ♕xd7 2 ♕xe6 wins the exchange.

961) Vasiukov-Kholmov
1 ♘xc5! ♕xc5 (the inclusion of 1...♖xe1+ 2 ♖xe1 ♕xc5 makes little difference) **2 ♗xg7! 1-0**
Black loses his queen after 2...♗xg7 3 ♕h5 h6 4 ♗h7+ ♔xh7 5 ♕xc5.

962) Kashdan-Kotov
1 ♘e7+! 1-0
After 1...♕xe7 2 ♕xc8+ ♕f8 Black loses his queen to 3 ♗h7+!.

963) Ambartsumova-Gunina
Black wins a piece: **1...♖xf2! 2 ♔xf2 ♕f4+ 3 ♔g2 ♕xc1 0-1**

964) Petrosian-Lahno
White missed **1 ♕f7+ ♔h8 2 ♕a2** winning the bishop in view of the threatened smothered mate.

965) Petrosian-Spassky
1 ♕h8+! 1-0
White is a piece up in the endgame after 1...♔xh8 2 ♘xf7+ ♔g7 3 ♘xg5.

966) Petrosian-Simagin
1 ♕a8+ ♔g7 2 ♗xe5+! (far simpler than 2 ♘xf7 ♕d1+) **2...♕xe5 3 ♕h8+! ♔xh8 4 ♘xf7+ 1-0**
White will be a piece up in the ending.

967) Burmakin-Burlov
1 ♘xa7! wins a pawn in view of 1...♘xa7 2 ♕xa5.

968) Malakhov-Areshchenko
1 ♖xd7! ♖xd7 2 g4 1-0
White wins the rook after 2...♕xh3 3 ♘xe5 or a piece following 2...a6 3 ♕xd7+! ♔xd7 4 gxh5.

969) Ragozin-Panov
1...♕c6! 0-1
White must lose a rook in view of 2 ♕xc6 ♖xd1+ 3 ♔g2 bxc6.

970) Sandipan-Nezar
1...♘xb2! 2 ♗xb2 ♗xc3 wins a pawn.

971) Saidy-Santasiere
1 ♖xe6+! 1-0
Black loses his queen after 1...♖xe6 2 ♕xc6.

972) Capablanca-Fonaroff
1 ♕xe5! ♕xe5 2 ♘xf7+ 1-0
White emerges a piece ahead after 2...♔g8 (and not 2...♖xf7? 3 ♖d8+ with back-rank mate) 3 ♘xe5.

973) Capablanca-Graham
1 ♖xc6+! 1-0
Black's queen is lost after 1...♕xc6 2 ♘e7+ in view of 2...♖xe7 3 ♕xc6+.

974) Maletin-Andreev
1 ♗xg7! ♔xg7 2 ♕g4+ ♖g6 3 ♕xd7 wins a pawn.

975) Palliser-Gallagher
1...♖xe4+! 2 dxe4 d4+ wins the white queen and with check in view of 3 ♔d3 ♗a6+.

976) Andrijevic-Grunberg
1...♗xe5! 2 ♗xe5 ♕e3 (threatening the queen-winning 3...♗d3+) **3 ♗c2 ♕xe5** wins a pawn.

977) Aagaard-Wiltshire
1 ♗xf7+! ♔xf7 2 ♖xd8 wins the exchange.

978) Rutkowski-Hilton
1 ♕xb7 leaves Black unable to save both his rook and queen: **1...♖f8 2 ♘f6+! 1-0**
3 ♕xg2 follows.

979) 'Erdnussbuddha'-Palliser
Black resigned before White won his queen with **1 ♖c8+!**.

980) Kamsky-Sher
1 ♗xa6! decisively opened the queenside in view of 1...bxa6 2 ♖b8 ♖c7 3 ♘b6 regaining the piece along the eighth.

981) Lappage-Smallbone
1 ♕xa6! ♘xa6 2 ♘d6+ 1-0
2...♔b8 3 ♘xf7 ♖f8 4 ♘g5 (or 4 ♖xc7 ♔xc7 5 ♖c1+ ♔d7 6 ♖d1+ ♔e6 7 ♘d8+) 4...fxg5 5 ♗a7+ ♔xa7 6 ♖xf8 is pretty hopeless for Black.

982) Smallbone-Lipman
1 ♘d5! wins either Black's queen or a clear piece after 1...♕xd2 2 ♘xe7+.

983) Burt-Smallbone
1 ♖xe7! 1-0
Black must give up his queen since 1...♕xe7 2 ♗xc6+ forces mate.

984) Burt-McIntosh
Rather than the game's 1 c4, **1 g6! hxg6 2 ♖e7! ♕xe7** (the inclusion of 2...♗g2+ 3 ♔xg2 ♕xe7 4 ♕d5+ makes little difference, while the reason for White's first becomes clear after 2...c5 3 ♕h4) **3 ♕xd5+ ♔g7 4 ♕xa8** would have won a piece.

985) Dervishi-Vallejo Pons
1...♗xb3! exploits all the pins to win a key pawn in view of 2 ♖xb3 ♕xb3.

986) Uhlmann-Fischer
1...♞xe4! 2 ♞xe4 (Black also wins a pawn after 2 hxg4 ♝xc3 in view of 3 bxc3 ♞xc3 and 4...♞xe2+) **2...♜xe4 3 ♝g5 ♛e8 4 ♝d3 ♝xf3 5 ♛xf3 ♜b4** leaves Black a pawn up and somewhat better.

987) Timofeev-Yevseev
1...♜h1+! 2 ♚xh1 ♞gxf2+ 3 ♞xf2 ♞xf2+ 4 ♚g1 ♞xd3 leaves Black queen for rook ahead.

988) Nguyen Thien Viet-Pham Duc Thang
1...♞e3! 0-1
White must give up the exchange on d1 since 2 ♝xe3 (2 fxe3? drops the queen to 2...♞xf3+ 3 gxf3 ♛xd3) 2...♞xf3+ 3 gxf3 ♛xd3 4 ♜xd3 ♜xd3 loses it under even more unfavourable circumstances.

989) Giani-Garofalo
1...♛xg2+! 2 ♚xg2 ♞e1+ 3 ♚g3 ♞xd3 4 ♝xd3 ♝f4+ saw Black pick up the exchange.

990) Gnetti-Orlov
1...♝xf2+! wins a pawn: **2 ♜xf2?** (now Black wins the exchange) **2...♛xf2+ 3 ♚xf2 ♝c2+ 4 ♚e2 ♝xa4 0-1**

991) Samuels-Miller
Rather than the game's 1...♜dc8, **1...♞h3+ 2 ♚h1 ♛xd1!** would have forced resignation in view of 3 ♛xd1 ♞xf2+ 4 ♚g1 ♞xd1.

992) Wegerer-Jankovic
1 ♞xc5! wins a pawn in view of 1...dxc5 2 ♜d7 ♛h4 (or 2...♞d4 3 ♜xe7 ♞xe2+ 4 ♞xe2 ♝xb2 5 ♜xb7) 3 ♜xb7.

993) Krstic-McPhillips
1 ♝h7+! ♚xh7 2 ♜xd7 ♝xc3 3 ♛d3+ ♚g8 4 ♛xc3 ♛xc3 5 bxc3 gave White a clearly better endgame.

994) Landa-Manca
1...♜xf2+! 2 ♚xf2 (or 2 ♚e1 ♛g8 with an overwhelming attack) **2...♞xe4+** wins the queen and the game.

995) Huzman-Kasparov
White wins two pawns: **1 ♜xd5 ♛e8** (Black loses his queen after 1...♛xd5 2 ♞e7+ and the f6-knight is, of course, pinned against mate) **2 ♝xc4 1-0**

996) Baldursson-Bjornsson
1...♜xe3! 2 ♜xe3 ♝c5 3 ♚f2 g5 4 ♚f3 ♝xe3 5 ♚xe3 ♚g7 simplified to a winning pawn ending.

997) Doroshkievich-Tukmakov
1...♞xd7! 0-1
Black wins a piece after 2 ♝xg2 ♛xg5 or a rook after 2 ♝xd8 gxh1♛.

998) Solovjov-Belozerov
1...♞xb2! 2 ♜xa4 ♞xa4 wins a pawn.

999) Vera Gonzalez Quevedo-Aguado Zabaleta
1 ♗c7! 1-0
Black loses his queen after 1...♖xc7 2 ♘xe6+ fxe6 3 ♕xd8+.

1000) Morales-Vera
1...♗xc2! 2 ♖xc2 ♕a7+ 3 ♕d4 (White would have had better chances to defend after 3 ♔h1 ♕xa2 4 ♗e4 ♘d5 5 ♗xd5 exd5 6 ♕xb4) **3...♕xa2 4 ♗e4 ♘d5! 5 ♗xd5 ♕xd5 6 ♕xd5 exd5 7 ♖xd5 ♖b8** simplified to a winning rook ending.

1001) Palliser-Dyce
1...♘f4! 0-1
The mate threat on d1 costs White a piece.

1002) Palliser-Hankinson
1 ♕xh6+! ♔xh6 2 ♘g4+ fxg4 3 ♖xe6 g3 4 fxg3 ♗xg3 5 ♔c2 and the extra exchange proved sufficient.

1003) Sadorra-Dao Thien Hai
1 ♖xa8 ♕xf2+ 2 ♔d2 ♖xa8 3 ♕xd5+ ♔h7 4 ♕xa8 1-0
Black's pawns are no match for White's extra rook.

1004) Anand-Kramnik
1 ♗d1! ♕d3 (White forks Black's pieces immediately in the case of 1...♕c6 2 ♖e5) **2 ♖e3! ♕xc4 3 ♖e5 1-0**
Black loses a piece along the fifth.

1005) Vujcic-Matas
1 ♕xh6! wins an important pawn in view of 1...gxh6? 2 ♘f6+ and 3 ♘xd7.

1006) Obiamiwe-Player
1...♘xf2+! 2 ♕xf2 ♕xc4 wins a second pawn.

1007) Yermolinsky-Stripunsky
1 ♗g6+! 1-0
Black loses a piece after 1...♔e7 (or 1...♔xg6 2 ♕xe6+) 2 ♕xe6+ ♔xe6 3 ♗xe8 in view of 3...♖xe8? 4 c8♕+.

1008) Kudrin-Robson
1 ♗b6+! ♕xb6 2 ♖xd7+ 1-0
White is a queen up with an overwhelming attack after 2...♔xd7 3 ♕xb6.

1009) Hanley-Jones
White wins a piece: **1 ♖xc8! ♕xc8 2 ♕f7+ 1-0**

1010) Gavriel-Palliser
1...♘xd4! wrecks the white position: **2 cxd4? ♕xd4+ 3 ♔e1 ♕xb2! 4 ♕c3 ♗g7 0-1**

1011) Mandla-Cunanan
1...♖xh2+! 0-1
White loses his queen after 2 ♔xh2 ♘f3+ and 3...♘xf3.

1012) Rogers-Ilic
1 ♘h6+! ♗xh6 2 ♕xd7 wins the exchange.

1013) Benidze-Magalashvili
1 ♘e7+! ♕xe7 2 ♖xc8+ wins the exchange.

1014) Torrecillas Martinez-Lezcano Jaen
White wins the exchange and the game: **1 ♗xf7+! ♕xf7 2 ♕xd8+ ♔g7 3 ♖e1 1-0**

1015) Garcia-Ghobrial
1...♘xh3! 2 gxh3 ♖xf3 wins a key pawn.

1016) Fedorov-Lastin
1...♕xh2+! 2 ♔xh2 ♘g4+ 3 ♔g1 ♘xe3 wins a pawn.

1017) Van Wely-Aronian
The overloading **1 ♗c1!** wins a piece after which White should have won, but he later returned the favour in the scramble – see Puzzle 831.

1018) Kramnik-Shirov
Black resigned before White picked up a piece with **1 ♖xe6!** in view of 1...♔xe6 2 ♘c5+ ♔f5 3 ♘xb7.

1019) Palliser-Tuplin
1...♗xb6! removes a dangerous pawn in view of White's vulnerable back rank.

1020) Palliser-Bekker Jensen
1 ♖xe4+! ♔xe4 2 ♘xd6+ 1-0
White emerges a piece ahead after 3 ♘xc8.

1021) A.Karpov-R.Bergmann
1 ♘f7+! 1-0
White wins the exchange and gains a crushing initiative after 1...♕xf7 2 ♕xd6.

1022) Grigoryan-Jessel
1 ♖h8+! 1-0
Black's queen is lost after 1...♔xh8 2 ♘g6+ and 3 ♘xh4.

1023) Kramnik-Aronian
1 ♗xe6+! ♕xe6 2 ♕b3 leaves Black unable to save both pieces and after 2...♘f4+ 3 gxf4 ♕xb3 4 axb3 ♗xf4 5 ♖xa6 White had reached a highly favourable endgame.

1024) Hopwood-Barber
1 ♖xh5+! ♔g8 (White wins the queen after 1...♕xh5 with 2 ♘f6+ ♔g6 3 ♘xh5 ♔xh5 4 ♕xg7 leading to an easy win) 2 ♖g5 ♕c2+ 3 ♔g3 ♗xd4 4 ♕e6+ ♔f8 5 ♖f5+ and the attack was crushing.

1025) Hopwood-Eggleston
Rather than the game's 1...♗b5, **1...♘xb3! 2 axb3 ♕xb3** would have seen Black emerge a pawn ahead, such as after 3 ♗a3 ♖xc2 4 ♖b1 ♕a4 5 ♗xe7 ♘xe7 6 ♖xb7 ♖fc8.

1026) Sriharan-Hopwood
White wins the exchange: **1 ♗h7+! ♔xh7 2 ♕xc3**.

1027) Watson-Lockwood
1...♕xe5! 2 dxe5 (or 2 ♕g4 ♕f5 and wins, but not 2...♖xd4?? due to 3 ♖xd4 ♕xd4?? 4 ♘g5+!) **2...♖xd1+ 3 ♗xd1 ♘xf4** and Black's extra material and potential passed c-pawn shortly prevailed.

1028) Ismail-Mitchinson
Black wins the exchange with **1...♘d4! 2 hxg4** (and not 2 ♘xd4? ♕h2+ 3 ♔f1 ♕h1+ 4 ♔e2 ♖xf2#) **2...♘xe6**.

Chapter Six

1029) Sadvakasov-Baladjaev
1 ♖e5!! d5 (the rook is immune due to 1...dxe5 2 ♖d7+ ♔b8 – it's mate even faster after 2...♘xd7 3 ♕a7+ – 3 ♖b7+ ♔a8 4 c7 with a crushing attack and 1...♕xb4 2 ♖b3 is also terminal) **2 ♖exd5! ♘xd5 3 ♖xd5** (an immediate 3 ♕a7+ is also rather powerful) **3...♕xc6 4 ♕a7+ 1-0**

1030) Trifunovic-Lalic
1...gxf3!! 2 ♗xf6 (or 2 ♖xf3 ♖hg8 3 ♗e2 ♖xg2+! 4 ♔xg2 ♕g4+ 5 ♔f2 ♗xf3 6 ♗xf3 ♘e4+! and mates) **2...♖hg8 3 ♖f2** (there's nothing better: 3 g3 f2+ forces mate and 3 ♖a2 f2+! 4 ♖fxf2 ♖xd1+ 5 ♗f1 ♕b1 is crushing) **3...♖xg2+ 4 ♖xg2** (or 4 ♔f1 ♗xh2 5 ♔e1 ♖g1+ 6 ♗f1 ♕d3 with the decisive threat of 7...♖xf1+ 8 ♖xf1 ♕d2#) **4...f2+!** (the star move in the combination; mate is now forced) **5 ♔xf2 ♕xg2+ 6 ♔e1 ♕d2+ 7 ♔f1 ♗g2+ 8 ♔g1 ♗xh2+! 9 ♔xh2 ♗f3+ 10 ♗e2 ♕xe2+ 11 ♘f2 ♕xf2+ 0-1**

1031) Wheeler-Emms
1...♘xd3+!! 2 ♕xd3 ♖ee2 (with a decisive threat of 3...♕h6+) **3 ♔d1 ♕f6 4 ♕d5+?** (a better defence is 4 ♕d4 ♖d2+ 5 ♕xd2 ♕xa1+ 6 ♕c1 ♕xa2 – threatening both 7...♕e2# and 7...♕b3 – 7 ♘c3 ♕b3+ 8 ♔e1 ♖c2 9 ♕e3 ♕xc3+ 10 ♕xc3 ♖xc3 when Black is only a pawn up in a rook ending) **4...♔h8 5 ♖c1** (or 5 ♘c3 ♖e8 when White can't avoid losing his queen down the d-file) and now, rather than Emms' 5...♖xg2, **5...♖xa2! 6 ♖e1** (or 6 ♕d3 ♕g5 and the check on d2 forces mate) **6...♖f1** would have been decisive since White has no good way to meet the threat of 7...♖xe1+ 8 ♔xe1 ♕f2+ 9 ♔d1 ♕f1#.

1032) Sutovsky-Sokolov
1 ♘d5+!! ♖xd5 2 ♗xf7+! ♔d8 (Black is also mated in style after 2...♔xf7 3 ♕f3+ ♔e6 4 ♕f6+ ♔d7 5 ♕f5+ ♔d8 6 ♗g5+ ♔e8 7 ♕e6+ ♔f8 8 ♗h6#, while 2...♔e8 3 ♖f8+ ♔e7 4 ♗g5+! transposes to the game) **3 ♖f8+ ♔e7 4 ♗g5+! 1-0**
It's mate after 4...♔xf8 5 ♕f3+ ♔g8 6 ♕xd5+ ♔g7 7 ♗h6+! ♔xh6 8 ♕e6+ ♔g7 9 ♕f6+ ♔g8 10 ♖g3#.

1033) Turner-Howell
1 ♖d5! (threatening both mate and the black queen) **1...♗xd5 2 g5+ ♔xg5 3 ♕e5+ ♖f5 4 f4+ 1-0**
It's mate after 4...♔h6 5 ♘g4#.

1034) Georghiou-Mogasha
1 ♘xf7!! ♔xf7 2 ♘d5 ♕d8 (or 2...♕c6 3 ♕h5+ ♔f8 – 3...♔g8 4 ♘xf6+ gxf6 5 ♖xf6 forces mate

– 4 ♖xf6+! gxf6 5 ♗h6+ ♘g7 6 ♘xf6 and Black is helpless) **3 ♖xf6+!** (very aesthetic and even stronger than 3 ♕h5+ g6 4 ♕h3) **3...gxf6 4 ♕h5+ ♔f8** (this is not the most testing defence, but 4...♔g8 5 ♗c3 ♗e7 6 ♖f1 also gives White a decisive attack) **5 ♖f1 ♗e7 6 ♗h6+ ♔g8 7 ♖f3 1-0**

The rook lift decides.

1035) Watson-Kuczynski

1...♕xg1+!! (the only winning try; 1...fxg6? would have led to a draw after 2 ♕h6! ♕xg1+! 3 ♖xg1 bxa2 4 gxf8♕+ ♘xf8 5 ♖xg6+ ♘xg6 6 ♕xg6+) **2 ♖xg1 bxa2 3 gxf7+** (perhaps a better try was 3 ♕h6!?, although after 3...a1♕+ 4 ♔d2 fxg6 5 ♕h8+ ♔f7 6 ♕h7 ♔e8 7 ♖xa1 ♖xa1 8 ♕xg6+ ♔d8 9 gxf8♕+ ♗xf8 Black again has more than enough for the queen) **3...♔xf7 4 ♕g2 a1♕+ 5 ♔d2 ♕xg1!** (very aesthetic; a second queen is sacrificed on g1) **6 gxf8♕+ ♘xf8 7 ♕xg1 ♖a5** and Black's rook and two minor pieces outpowered White's queen.

1036) Sakelsek-Rodriguez Lopez

1 ♘xe6!! fxe6 2 ♕xe6+ ♗f7 (White also emerges with sufficient extra pawns after 2...♔f8 3 ♗d5 ♗f7 4 ♕xf7+! ♘xf7 5 ♗xc7; probably the best defence was 2...♔h8!?, although 3 ♘d5 – 3 ♖he1!? is also possible – 3...♕c8 4 ♕xc8 ♘xc8 5 ♘c7 ♘b6 6 ♘xa8 ♖xa8 7 ♖he1 leaves White with somewhat the better ending) **3 ♘d5 ♗xe6** (White gains a decisive lead too after 3...♕d7 4 ♘xe7+ ♘xe7 5 ♕xd6) **4 ♘xc7 ♗g4 5 ♘xa8 ♗xd1 6 ♖xd1** and White's two extra pawns were decisive.

1037) Sokolov-Vovk

The former candidate missed **1 ♖xh5+!! gxh5** (or 1...♔g7 2 ♖g5 ♕e8 3 ♖gf5! ♔h7 4 ♕f4 and h5 will follow with decisive effect) **2 ♖f5 ♔h6 3 ♕f4+ ♔g7 4 ♖g5+ ♔h6 5 ♕f3 ♖e1+ 6 ♔h2** when Black must give up his queen to avert mate, but **6...♕xg5 7 hxg5+ ♔g7 8 ♕f6+ ♔g8 9 g6 fxg6 10 ♕xg6+ ♔h8 11 ♕xh5+ ♔g7 12 ♕g4+ ♔f7 13 ♕f3+ ♔e8 14 ♕xd5** sees White's queen triumph over the black rooks.

1038) Sott-Pokorny

1...♘f3+!! 2 gxf3 ♗xf3 leaves White unable to prevent Black's queen from decisively infiltrating his kingside: **3 ♘xc5** (a better defence is 3 h3, but Black is still winning after 3...♘g4! 4 ♘f4 ♕h4 5 ♘ce2 g5; for example, 6 ♗d7 gxf4 7 ♗xg4 ♗xg4 8 hxg4 f3 9 ♘f4 ♖fe8 10 d4 ♕xg4+ 11 ♔h1 ♖e6! and mate follows) **3...♘g4! 4 d4** (as 4 h3 is also mated by 4...♕h4, the only defence is 4 ♕e3, not that that really helps White after 4...♘xe3 5 fxe3 ♕g5+ 6 ♔f2 ♕g2+ 7 ♔e1 dxc5 when Black is winning quite straightforwardly) **4...♕h4** (now it's mate on h2 or g2) **5 ♗f4 ♕h3 0-1**

1039) Plachetka-Zinn

1 ♕h5! ♘f6 (the only try: 1...gxh5? is mated by 2 ♖g3+ ♔h8 3 ♘xf7#) **2 ♘g4!!** (the main point of White's play) **2...gxh5** (and not 2...♘xh5? 3 ♘h6#) **3 ♘xf6+ ♔h8** (again it's mate in the case of 3...♔g7 4 ♘e8+ ♔h6 5 ♗g7+! ♔g6 6 ♖g3+ ♔f5 7 ♖g5+ ♔e4 8 ♘f6# or 8 ♘c3#) **4 ♖xh5 h6 5 ♘xd5+ 1-0**

White is no less than three pawns up after 5...♔h7 6 ♘xc7 ♗xc7 7 ♖xc5.

1040) Tozer-Palliser

1...♕xd5+!! 2 ♘xd5 ♗e4+ 3 ♖f3 ♗xd5 (3...♘e1 is also pretty effective) **4 ♔g2** (the inclusion of 4 d7 ♖e1+ 5 ♔g2 – 5 ♕xe1 ♗xf3# – 5...♔g7 changes little) **4...♖e1 0-1**

White must give up his queen as 5 ♕xc2 ♖g1+ 6 ♔h3 ♗xf3 leads to mate.

1041) Grassie-Duke

Rather than the game's 1 ♖g5, **1 ♖d5!!** (preventing ...♕xd6+) would have left Black without a defence to the threat of 2 ♕g7; for example, **1...exd5 2 ♕g7 ♘e7** (or 2...♕xd6 3 ♕xg8+ ♕f8 4 ♕xf8+ ♔xf8 5 ♖h8#) **3 dxe7** and Black can resign.

1042) McNab-Brunello

1 ♘h6+!! gxh6 (or 1...♔h8 2 ♕g4 ♕c8 – 2...♕e7 3 dxe5 fxe5 4 ♗xe5 wins – 3 dxe5 ♕xg4 4 ♘xg4 fxe5 5 ♘xe5 with an extra pawn and the initiative) **2 ♕g4+ ♔h8** (White gains a crushing attack after 2...♗g7 3 dxe5 ♕c8 4 ♕xc8 ♖xc8 5 exf6 ♗h8 6 ♗h3 ♖e8 7 ♗d7) **3 dxe5 ♕c8 4 exf6!** (4 ♖d7 is also easily sufficient) **4...♕xg4 5 f7+ ♖e5 6 ♗xe5+ ♕g7 7 ♗xg7+ ♔xg7 8 ♖a1** and White emerges the exchange ahead.

1043) Trifunovic-Koch

1 ♖xh6! ♕d7+ (it's mate after 1...♖xc4 2 ♖h8+ ♔f7 3 ♖1h7+ ♔f6 4 g5#) **2 ♕d5! ♖d4+** (White retains a crushing advantage after 2...♕xd5+ 3 exd5 ♖xg4 4 ♖h8+ ♔f7 5 ♖xa8) **3 ♕xd4! exd4 4 ♖g6+ ♔f7 5 ♖h7+ 1-0**
Mate follows on the back rank.

1044) Karjakin-Van Wely

1 ♗xh6!! wins a pawn: **1...gxh6? 2 ♕g6+ ♔h8 3 ♕xh6+ ♔g8 4 ♕g6+ ♔h8 5 ♖e3** (threatening 6 ♖g3 followed by mate) **5...f4 6 ♖xe5! dxe5 7 ♕h6+ ♔g8 8 d6 ♖f7** (Black is defenceless: another winning line being 8...♕d8 9 ♗c4+ ♖f7 10 dxe7 ♕xe7 11 ♕g6+ ♔f8 12 ♗xf7 ♕xf7 13 ♕d6+ ♔g7 14 ♕xb8) **9 ♗c4 ♗f5 10 dxe7 1-0**
White has a crushing attack after 10...♖e8 11 ♕g5+ ♔h8 12 ♗xf7.

1045) Horvath-Kosten

1...♕g3! 2 ♗e3 (White had to of course avoid 2 fxg3? hxg3+, while he also loses the exchange in the case of 2 ♕f3 ♘xg4 3 ♗f4 ♘xf2+ 4 ♖xf2 ♕xf2) **2...♘xg4!** (le point) **3 fxg3 hxg3+ 4 ♔g1 ♘xe3! 5 ♖f2 ♘f5 6 exf5 gxf2+ 7 ♕xf2 ♗xf2+ 8 ♔xf2 ♔e7** and Black's extra exchange prevailed.

1046) Ftacnik-Cvitan

1...♗xg2+! 2 ♔xg2 ♕h3+! 3 ♔xh3 ♘g5+ 4 ♔g2 ♘h4+ 0-1
Mate follows with 5 ♔h1 g2#.

1047) Richter-Hertneck

1 ♕xg4!! fxg4 2 ♖xf7 gives White a decisive attack due to his raking bishops: **2...♕c6** (neither 2...♔h8 3 ♘d5, with the idea of 3...♗xd5 4 ♘g6+ ♔h7 5 ♖xg7#, nor 2...♔h7 3 ♖xe7 ♖g8 – desperately trying to cover g7 – 4 ♗d3+ ♔h8 5 ♘g6+ ♔h7 6 ♘e5+ ♔h8 7 ♘f7# helps Black) **3 ♖xe7+ ♔h8** and now **4 ♘e4! ♖g8** (Black is also crushed after both 4...♕xe4 5 ♗xg7+ ♔h7 6 ♗e5# and 4...♘e5 5 ♖xd8+ ♖xd8 6 ♗xe5 ♖d1+ 7 ♔f2) **5 ♘d6** would have been even stronger than the game's 4 ♘d5.

1048) Spraggett-Speelman

Instead of the game's 1 ♘xg3, **1 ♘g5!,** threatening to capture on h7 would have forced mate in view of 1...♗xh2 2 ♖xh7+! ♕xh7 3 ♘xf7#.

1049) Williams-Prosiriakov

1 ♕h6!! f5 (White's main point is that 1...dxc3 2 ♘g5 ♗xg5 3 ♗xg5 cxb2 4 ♖ab1 f6 5 ♗xf6 ♕c7 6 ♖xd5! is rather powerful, especially since 6...♘c6? fails to 7 ♖d7! ♕xd7 8 ♗d5+ followed by mate) **2 ♘g5 ♗xg5 3 ♗xg5 ♕d7 4 e6!** ♕d6 (or 4...♕xe6 5 ♖e1 ♕f7 6 ♘xd5 ♗xd5 7

♖e7 winning material) **5 ♘xd5 ♗xd5 6 ♗f4** (6 e7 also does the trick) **6...♕xe6 7 ♖e1 ♗e4** (again 7...♕f7 is met by the decisive 8 ♖e7!) **8 f3** and White won a piece.

1050) Johnson-Palliser

1...♖xf3! 2 ♖xg7+ (White doesn't have to interpolate this, but he is mated in the same manner as in the game after 2 ♗xf3 ♘d2) **2...♔xg7 3 ♗xf3 ♘d2! 4 ♕c1** (Black's main point is revealed after 4 ♗xd2 ♕b3+ 5 ♔a1 ♖xa3+ 6 bxa3 ♕xa3#) **4...♕xc4+ 5 ♔a1 ♘b3+ 0-1**
It's mate after 6 ♔a2 ♘xc1+ 7 ♔a1 ♕a2#.

1051) Perenyi-Schneider

1 ♖xd7! **♕xd7** (or 1...♔xd7 2 ♗e6+ ♔e8 3 gxf6 ♘d8 4 ♕d5 ♗d6 5 ♖g1 with a ruinous attack) **2 gxf6** gives White a winning attack: **2...♗d6** (2...♕c7 3 ♖d1 ♗d6 4 f7+ ♔d8 5 ♗e6 leaves Black defenceless against the threat of 6 ♗c5 since it's mate after 5...♗e7 6 ♕h4+ ♔f8 7 ♗h6#) **3 ♗e6 ♕c7 4 f7+ ♔d8 5 ♖d1** (the simpler 5 ♗g5+ and if 5...♗e7, then 6 ♕d5+, is also crushing) **5...♗c8 6 ♕xe5!? 1-0**
White's f-pawn decides after 6...♘xe5 7 ♗g5+ ♕e7 8 ♖xd6+ ♔c7 9 ♗xe7 ♖a8 10 ♖d5, but no less stylish and even stronger is 6 ♗g5+ ♘e7 7 ♖xd6+! ♕xd6 8 ♕xb7.

1052) Fairbairn-Bobras

1...♖c2!! is a beautiful silent sacrifice which allows Black to force favourable simplification: **2 ♕xc2** (or 2 ♗c1 ♕c7 with serious pressure and after, for example, 3 ♗g4 ♘g5 4 ♘e4 ♘xe4 5 dxe4 ♕c6 6 ♗g5 ♘e3+! 7 ♗xe3 ♗xg4 Black is somewhat better) **2...♗xf2+! 3 ♖xf2** (3 ♔h1 ♘e3 4 ♖xf2 ♘xf2+ transposes) **3...♘e3+ 4 ♔h1 ♘xf2+ 5 ♔g1 ♘h3+ 6 ♔h1 ♘xc2** and Black went on to convert his extra pawn.

1053) Kantsler-Smirin

1...♕xh2+!! 2 ♔xh2 ♖h6+ 3 ♔g3 (it's mate after 3 ♔g1 ♘h3+ 4 ♔h1 ♘xf2+ 5 ♔g1 ♘h3+ 6 ♔h2 ♘f4+ 7 ♔g1 ♖xg2#) **3...♘e6+ 4 ♕g4** (Black wins material after 4 ♔g4? ♘xd4 since 5 ♘xd4 allows 5...♖xg4#) **4...♘xg4 5 ♗xg4 ♖xg4+ 6 ♔f3 ♖xc4** left Black two pawns up.

1054) Alekhine-Rubinstein

1 ♗g6!! ♕e5 (White threatens 2 ♕e4 and 1...fxg6 is mated by 2 ♕g2 ♔g8 3 ♕h3 ♗xb4 4 ♕h7+ ♔f8 5 ♕h8+ ♔e7 6 ♕xg7+ ♔e8 – or 6...♔d6 7 ♖fd1+ – 7 ♕g8+ ♗f8 8 ♕xe6+ ♖e7 9 ♕xg6+ ♖f7 10 ♕xf7#, while 1...♗b7 loses to 2 ♘xf7+! ♖xf7 3 ♕xe6 threatening both 4 ♕h3+ and the f7-rook) **2 ♘xf7+ ♖xf7 3 ♗xf7** and White's extra exchange soon proved decisive.

1055) Palliser-Eames

1 ♖xe6!! ♘xh4 (White's connected passed pawns will carry the day after 1...♖c8 2 ♕b3 ♘f8 3 ♖xa7! ♕xe6 4 ♖xb7 ♕xb3 5 ♖xb3, but Black might have tried 1...♘f8, although those central pawns should again eventually prove decisive after 2 ♖c6 ♗xc6 3 ♕xc6 ♖e8 4 f3) **2 ♖xa7! ♖c8** (White's main point is that it's mate after 2...♖xa7 3 ♖e8#) **3 ♕b3 1-0**
There's no defence along the seventh and 3...♘f5 4 ♖xb7 ♘xd4 fails to 5 ♖e8+! which forces mate.

1056) Marovic-Tsagan

1 ♕xg6! hxg6 2 ♗xf7+ ♖xf7 3 ♖h8+! ♔xh8 4 ♘xf7+ ♔h7 5 ♘xd6 ♖d8 6 ♖e6 and White went on to convert his extra pawn.

1057) Mastrovasilis-Savic

1 ♗xg7!! ♔xg7 (Black is crushed too after 1...bxc3 2 e5 and even 1...♘c5!? fails to save him after Movsesian's 2 ♕h6! ♖e8 3 ♘e2!) **2 ♕h6+ ♔g8?** (a tougher defence is 2...♔h8, although

3 e5 f5 4 g6! should be decisive, such as after 4...♖f7 5 gxf7 ♕f8 6 ♕xf8+ ♗xf8 7 ♖hg1 ♗h6+ 8 ♔b1 ♗b7 9 ♗c4! ♘xe5 10 ♗xe6 ♘xf7 11 ♗xf7 bxc3 12 ♖xd6 with an extra exchange in the ending) **3 e5 f5 4 gxf6 ♘xf6 5 ♖hg1+ 1-0**
Mate is forced after 5...♔f7 6 ♗g6+!.

1058) King-Emms

Rather than the game's 1 ♕f3, **1 ♖xf6!! ♖xe2 2 ♖f7+ ♔g8** (or 2...♔xg6 3 ♖1f6+ ♔g5 4 ♖f5+ and it's mate with either 4...♔xg4 5 ♖g7+ ♔h3 6 ♖h5+ or 4...♔g6 5 ♗h5#; it's also mate after 2...♔h8 3 ♖h7+ ♔g8 4 ♗e6#) **3 ♗e6** is crushing: 4 ♖h7# is the threat and **3...♖g2+** (the bishop cannot be dislodged by Black's rook in view of both 3...♖e8 4 ♖e7+ ♔h8 5 ♖h7# and 3...♖b6 4 ♖f8+ ♔g7 5 ♖g8#) **4 ♔xg2 ♕b2+ 5 ♔h3 ♕b6** fails to defend in view of **6 ♖f8+! ♔g7 7 ♖1f7+ ♔xg6 8 ♗f5+ ♔h5 9 ♖g7 ♗d1 10 g4+ ♗xg4+ 11 ♗xg4#.**

1059) Lasker-Thomas

1 ♕xh7+!! ♔xh7 2 ♘xf6+ ♔h6 (it's also mate after 2...♔h8 3 ♘g6#) **3 ♘eg4+ ♔g5 4 h4+ ♔f4 5 g3+ ♔f3 6 ♗e2+** (even quicker is 6 ♔f1 followed by 7 ♘h2#) **6...♔g2 7 ♖h2+ ♔g1 8 ♔d2# 1-0**

A classic king-hunt.

1060) Stephenson-Blaine

1 ♖d8+!! ♕xd8 2 ♕xe5 ♕d7 (the only way to cover g7, but White can't be prevented from forcing a neat mate in any case) **3 ♕h8+! ♔xh8 4 ♖f8# 1-0**

1061) NN-Mason

1...♗b5!! 2 axb5 (both 2 ♗d3 ♘hg3+ and 2 c4 ♗xc4 3 ♗d3 ♘hg3+ make no difference to Black's beautiful idea) **2...♘hg3+! 3 ♘xg3** (or 3 hxg3 hxg3+ 4 ♔g1 ♗c5+ winning the queen or mating after 5 ♘f2? gxf2+ 6 ♖xf2 ♘g3) **3...♘xg3+ 4 hxg3** (essential to avoid losing the white queen, but now it's mate) **4...hxg3+ 5 ♔g1 ♖h1+!** (even more accurate is 5...♗c5+! 6 ♘xc5 ♖h1+, avoiding any ♖f2 defences) **6 ♔xh1 ♖h8+ 7 ♔g1 ♗c5+! 8 ♘xc5** (White is also unable to avoid mate after 8 ♖f2 gxf2+ 9 ♕xf2 ♖h1+ 10 ♔xh1 ♗xf2) **8...♖h1+!** (completing the back-rank clearance) **9 ♔xh1 ♕h8+ 10 ♔g1 ♕h2# 0-1**

1062) Williams-Palliser

1 ♘hg6+!! fxg6 (1...♔g7 2 ♘h5+ ♔xh7 3 ♘e7+! ♔h8 4 ♘f6 doesn't help matters) **2 ♘xg6+ ♔g7 3 ♕h3 ♗g3+** (there wasn't anything better: 3...♔xg6 4 ♕h6+ ♔f7 5 g6+ ♔e7 6 ♗g5+ is hopeless, as is 3...♕a5+ 4 ♗d2 ♗g3+ 5 ♔f1 ♕xd2 6 h8♕+ ♖xh8 7 ♕xh8+ ♔xg6 8 ♕f6+ ♔h7 9 g6+ ♔h6 10 g7+ ♔h7 11 ♕f8 ♕f4+ 12 ♗f3) **4 ♔f1 ♔xg6** (now it's mate, but 4...♔h4 5 ♘xh4 ♕d7 6 ♗g4 ♕f7+ 7 ♗f5 is crushing) **5 ♕h6+ ♔f5 6 ♗g4+ ♔e5 7 ♕g7+ ♔e4 8 ♕g6+ ♔e5 9 ♕f5# 1-0**

1063) Hsu Li Liang-Nunn

1...♘xg3! 2 ♔xg3 (otherwise White just loses a key kingside pawn) **2...♕h4+! 3 ♔h2** (Black's main point is revealed by 3 ♔xh4 f4 4 ♔g5 ♖ff8 followed by 5...h6+ 6 ♔h4 ♗f6# or 6 ♔xg6 ♗e8#) **3...♕xe1** and Black's extra exchange shortly made its presence felt.

1064) Leko-Carlsen

1...♖xd5+!! 2 ♘xd5 ♕d8!! (much stronger than Carlsen's 2...♕e4 when 3 ♔e2 would have led to an immediate perpetual or to one after 3...♕xh1 4 ♘b6+ ♔c7 5 ♕a5 since 3...exd5 4 ♕g3 doesn't give Black enough for the sacrificed rook) **3 ♕g3** (there's no good way to avoid the threats of 3...♗b4+ and 3...♕xd5+ followed by 4...♕xh1; White might try 3 ♔e2, but he loses his queen after 3...♗g4+ 4 ♔f2 ♕h4+ 5 ♔g1 ♕xe1) **3...♕xd5+ 4 ♔e2 ♕xh1 5**

♗g2 ♕g1 sees Black decisively emerge two pawns ahead.

1065) Morozevich-Aronian

1 ♕d8+! (White can also begin with 1 ♔h4!, but in the game he failed to find the correct idea: 1 ♖f3? ♖f1? 2 fxg6? – 2 ♕d8+ ♔g7 3 f6+ ♔h6 4 ♔h4 was still on – 2...♖xf3+ 3 ♕xf3 ♕e1+ 4 ♔f4 hxg6 5 ♕xd5 ♕f2+ 6 ♘f3 1/2-1/2) **1...♔g7 2 f6+ ♔h6 3 ♔h4!!** and the white king plays a decisive attacking role: **3...♕xd4+ 4 g4 ♕b4** (trying to prevent the mate on f8, but...) **5 ♕f8+! ♕xf8 6 g5#.**

1066) Volkov-Zvjaginsev

1...♕xg3!! 2 hxg4 (Black's extra e-pawn is decisive after 2 fxg3 ♖xf1+ 3 ♔g2 ♘xe3+ 4 ♔h2 ♘xc2 5 ♖xc2 ♖e1) **2...♕h4+ 3 ♔g1 ♕xg4+ 4 ♗g2 ♖g5 5 f4 exf3 6 ♖d8 f2+! 0-1** Black is the exchange up and still attacking after 7 ♖xf2 (or 7 ♔xf2 ♕xg2+ 8 ♔e1 ♕g1+ 9 ♔e2 ♕xe3+ 10 ♔d1 ♖g1#) 7...♖xd8.

1067) Zhou Jianchao-Bocharov

1...♘xg2! 2 a6 (it's mate after 2 ♔xg2 ♕xf3+) **2...♕xf3 3 ♖xd3** (or 3 ♕xb7 ♕xd1+ 4 ♔xg2 ♕g4+ 5 ♔h2 d2 6 a7 d1♕ and again Black forces mate) **3...♕xd3 4 axb7 ♘f4 5 b8♕ ♕h3 0-1** The double mate threat decides and 5...♕f3 would have also done the job.

1068) Sorokin-Nureev

1...♖xg2+!! 2 ♔xg2 ♖g8+ 3 ♔h3 (Black's attack is overwhelming after 3 ♔h1 ♘xf3 4 ♖xf3 ♕h4 followed by 5...♕h3 or 5...♕g4; likewise 3 ♔f2 ♗xf3 doesn't assist White's cause) **3...♕f6 4 ♘g5** (or 4 ♖g1 ♕f5+ 5 ♔h4 ♘xf3+ 6 ♕xf3 ♖xg1 7 ♕xb7+ ♔xb7 8 ♖xg1 ♕xd3 and Black's queen is far too powerful) **4...hxg5 5 fxg5 ♖h8+** (also rather effective is 5...♕h8+ 6 ♔g4 ♕xh2) **6 ♔g4 ♕g6 7 ♔f4 ♕f5+ 0-1** It's mate with 8 ♔g3 ♖h3#.

1069) Karjakin-Rychagov

1 ♗xe6!! ♗a3 (White's pieces are immune in view of 1...hxg4 2 ♗xd7# and 1...fxe6 2 ♖xe6+ ♔f7 3 ♖xd7+ ♔g8 4 ♕f4 ♖h7 5 ♕f7+ ♔h8 6 ♗e7) **2 ♗xd7+ ♔f8 3 ♕g3** (3 ♕c4 ♕xg5+ 4 f4 also does the trick) **3...h4** (unfortunately for Black 3...♖xc3+ 4 ♔b1 ♖xg3 fails to mate in one with 5 ♖e8) **4 ♕e5 1-0**

1070) Larsen-Petrosian

1 ♕xg6!! ♘f4 (1...fxg6 fails to 2 ♗xe6+ ♔h7 3 ♖h3+ ♗h6 4 ♗xh6 with an overwhelming attack due to 4...♖f5 5 ♖xf5 gxf5 6 ♗f7!) **2 ♖xf4 fxg6 3 ♗e6+ ♔f7** (or 3...♔h7 4 ♖h4+ ♗h6 5 ♗xh6 ♕b6+ 6 c5 leaving Black defenceless) **4 ♖xf7 ♔h8** (4...♗e5 can be met by the cute 5 ♖d4! – 5 ♖f5+ ♔g7 6 ♖fxe5 dxe5 7 ♖xd8 ♖xd8 8 ♔f2 is simpler and also rather good – with the point that 5...♕b6 – or 5...♕e8 6 ♖f8+ ♔xf8 7 ♗h6+ ♗g7 8 ♖f4+ winning a piece – 6 ♖f3+ ♔g7 7 ♖g4 gives White a winning attack: for example, 7...♕xb2 8 ♖f7+ ♔g8 9 ♖f6+ ♔h7 10 ♖h4+ ♔g7 11 ♖f7+ ♔g8 12 ♖f2+ ♔g7 13 ♗h6+ ♔h7 14 ♗f8#) **5 ♖g5 b5 6 ♖g3 1-0** There's no good defence to the threat of 7 ♖h3+.

1071) Miles-Nedobora

1 ♖f8+! ♖xf8 2 ♖xf8+ ♔xf8 3 ♕f7+! (3 ♕e8+! also forces stalemate) **3...♔xf7 ½-½**

1072) Ragger-Wirig

1 ♗xh6! fxe4 (Black is crushed after 1...gxh6? 2 ♖g3+ ♔h7 3 ♘g5+ ♔g6 4 ♘xe6+) **2 ♗xg7! ♘5f6** (another possible defence is 2...♔f7, but after 3 ♗e2 ♘7f6 4 ♕g5 ♖g8 5 ♖h7! White has a decisive attack in view of 5...♘xh7? 6 ♗h5#) **3 ♕h8+** (rather strong too is 3 ♕g5 ♔f7 4

♜h6) **3...♔f7 4 ♗xf8 ♘xf8 5 ♗e2 ♛d2** (Black is also defenceless following 5...♘g6 6 ♜h7+! ♘xh7 7 ♛xh7+ ♔f6 8 ♗h5 when one neat finish occurs after 8...♘f4 9 ♛f7+ ♔g5 10 h4+! ♔h6 11 g4) **6 ♜g3! ♛f4** (or 6...♛xe2 7 ♛g7+ ♔e8 8 ♛xf6 with a winning attack) **7 ♗h5+! ♘xh5 8 ♛xh5+ ♔e7 9 ♜g7+ 1-0**

White's final piece joins in the attack after 9...♔d8 10 ♜d1+ when 10...♗d7 11 ♜gxd7+! ♘xd7 12 ♛h7 is decisive.

1073) Aroshideze-Nigalidze

1 ♗f8!! ♜xf8 (White also wins after both 1...♔xf8 2 ♜xh7 ♗g7 3 ♜xg6 ♜e7 4 ♜gxg7! ♜xg7 5 ♛h6 and 1...♔f6 2 ♛h6 ♗e6 3 ♜xg6+! hxg6 4 ♛xg6+ ♔xf8 5 ♛xf6+ ♗f7 6 ♜h8#) **2 ♛h6 ♜f7** (or 2...♔f7 3 ♛xh7+ ♔e8 4 ♛xg6+ ♔d8 5 ♛d6+ ♔e8 6 ♜xh8! ♜xh8 7 ♜g7 and mate follows) **3 ♜xg6+!** (the killer follow-up, exploiting the fact that Black cannot capture due to mate on h8) **3...♗g7 4 ♛xh7+ ♔f8 5 ♜hg1** wins the bishop with a crushing attack.

1074) Cordova-Smirin

1 ♜xg7!! ♘xe2+ (White's main point is seen after 1...♜xg7 2 ♗xf6 ♜eg8? – 2...♘fxe6 3 dxe6 ♘xe6 is a better defence, although after 4 ♛e4! ♛a4 5 c4! White's initiative is too strong; for example, 5...bxc4 6 ♗xc4 ♜c8 7 ♛g4 (now everything amazingly holds together) 7...d5 8 ♛xd5 ♛a3+ 9 ♔d2 ♛b4+ 10 ♔e2 ♜e8 11 ♜e4 and Black is out of good moves – 3 ♜xg7 ♜xg7 4 e7 when his e-pawn decides) **2 ♛xe2 ♘b3+ 3 ♔b1! 1-0**

Mate follows after 3...♘xd4 4 ♛h5.

1075) Morell Gonzalez-Fernandez Juan

1...♛h4! 2 ♘f3 (the only try since 2 gxh4 is mated by 2...♜g6+ 3 ♔h1 ♘xf2#) **2...♘g5! 3 gxh4 ♘xf3+ 4 ♔g2?** (now it's mate, but even 4 ♔h1 ♜xh4 5 h3 would have left White two pawns down after 5...♘xd4+ 6 ♔h2 ♘xc2 7 ♗xc2 ♜xc4) **4...♘e1+ 5 ♔g3 ♜g6+ 0-1**

It's mate after 6 ♔f4 ♜g4+ 7 ♔e5 ♘f3# or 7...♘c6#.

1076) Georgiev-Jakovenko

1...f5+! 2 gxf6+ ♔h6 (with a deadly threat of 3...♜hh3 and...♜ag3#) **3 ♜c1?** (White is helpless after 3 ♜a8? ♜g2+ 4 ♔h4 ♜e3! because 5 ♜a1 ♜gg3 6 ♔h1 g5+ 7 fxg5+ ♜xg5 8 ♜f1 ♜xe4+ 9 ♔h3 ♔h5 forces mate on h4; a better defence was 3 ♜h8! ♜hh3 4 f5, but then 4...exf5+ – and not 4...g5? 5 ♜xh7+! ♔xh7 6 ♔xg5 with serious counterplay – 5 ♔f4 (now 5 exf5? g5 6 ♜xh7+ ♔xh7 7 ♔xg5 fails to 7...♜hg3+ 8 ♔f4 ♜gc3 9 ♜d8 ♜c4+ 10 ♔g5 ♜g3+ 11 ♔h5 ♜c1) 5...♜h4+ 6 ♔e5 ♜xe4+ 7 ♔d5 ♜d3+! 8 ♔c5 ♜d7 9 ♜hf8 f4 should still be winning for Black) **3...♜g2+ 4 ♔h4 e5! 5 f7** (not 5 fxe5 g5#, but White had to try 5 ♜g8 ♜f2 6 ♜g1, although after 6...♜xf4+ 7 ♜g4 ♜xf6 Black has an easy win) **5...♜f2! 0-1**

White cannot prevent mate on f4.

1077) Karatorossian-Nalbandian

1 ♜xg5! ♛xg5 2 ♛d4+ ♔g8 (or 2...♔h7 3 ♘f6+ – another crushing option is 3 ♜g2 ♛d8 4 ♗h5! – 3...♔h6 4 ♜g2 and White either wins the queen or mates with 4...♛c1+ 5 ♜g1 ♛c2 6 ♛h4+ ♔g7 7 ♘h5+! ♜xh5 8 ♛e7+ ♔h6 9 ♛f8+ ♔h7 10 ♛f7+ ♔h8 11 ♛f6+ ♔h7 12 ♛xg6+ ♔h8 13 ♛g7#) **3 ♜g2 ♜h4** (3...♛c1+ 4 ♜g1 ♛h6 5 ♜xg6+! wins the black queen) **4 ♘f6+ ♔f7 5 ♗d5+ ♔e7** and now White sadly missed the only, if straightforward, path to victory: **6 ♜e2+ ♔d8 7 ♜e8+ ♔c7 8 ♛a7+ ♜b7** (or 8...♗b7 9 ♛xa5#) **9 ♜xc8+! ♔xc8 10 ♛xb7+ ♔d8 11 ♛d7#**.

1078) Li Chao-Wang Hao

1 ♜d8+! ♔h7 (Black loses his queen after 1...♜xd8 2 ♛xe2) **2 ♜g7+! ♔xg7** (or 2...♔h6 3 ♛f4+ ♔xg7 4 ♛g5+ ♔h7 5 ♛g8+ transposing) **3 ♛g2+ ♔h7 4 ♛g8+ ♔h6 5 ♛h8+ ♔g6 6 ♛f6+ ♔h5 7 ♛g5# 1-0**

1079) Petrosian-Minasian

1 ♘xc7!! ♕f7 (Not the best defence. The main point of White's combination can be seen after 1...♘xc7 2 ♖e7+! ♗xe7 3 ♖xe7+ when Black is undone on the dark squares: 3...♔d8 – or 3...♔b8 4 ♕xb6 ♕d1+ 5 ♔h2 ♕d5 6 ♕c7+ ♔a7 7 ♗d4+! forcing mate – 4 ♕xb6+! ♔xe7 5 ♗a3+ ♔d7 6 ♕e6+ ♔c7 7 b6+ ♔d8 8 ♕e7+ ♔c8 9 ♕c7#. Very similar is 1...♗xc7 2 ♖e7+ ♔c8 3 ♖xc7+!, while 1...♖ac8 fails to 2 ♕d2. However, perhaps Black might have tried 1...♖ag8!?, not that this would have saved him in the event of 2 ♖e7+!! – 2 ♘e6 ♗d5 with the idea of ...g6 isn't so clear – 2...♗xe7 – or 2...♔c8 3 ♘d5 and wins after both 3...♗xd5 4 ♕xb6 and 3...♗xe7 4 ♘xe7+ ♔b8 5 ♕xb6 – 3 ♕xb6 with a crushing attack; for starters both 4 ♖xe7+ and 4 ♕xb7 are threatened.) 2 ♘e6!? (there was nothing wrong with 2 ♘xa8 ♖xa8 3 ♖e6, but the young Armenian prefers to play for the attack) 2...♔c8 3 ♖c3 ♗d5? 4 ♕xb6 ♗b4! 5 ♖xc4+ ♗xc4 6 ♖c1 and the attack was decisive.

1080) Marshall-Hopwood

Rather than the game's 1...♖g7, 1...♗xg4 2 fxg4 h3! gives Black a winning attack: 3 g3 (3 gxh3 ♕h4 also leaves White defenceless; for example, 4 ♗f3 ♘xh3 5 ♖a3 ♖xf3! 6 ♖xf3 ♘g5+ 7 ♔g2 ♕xg4+ 8 ♔g3 ♕xg3+! 9 ♔xg3 ♘xe4+ 10 ♔g4 ♘xd2 with an extra piece in the endgame) 3...♘xe2!! is the main point when it's a picturesque mate after 4 ♕xg5 (or 4 ♕xe2 ♕c1+ 5 ♔h2 ♖f1, winning White's queen) 4...♖f1+ 5 ♔h2 ♖f2+ 6 ♔xh3 (or 6 ♔h1 ♘xg3+ 7 ♔g1 ♖g2#) 6...♘g1+ 7 ♔h4 ♖h2#.

Chapter Seven

Test One

1081) Rodriguez-Polgar

The desperado 1...♕xc3! 2 ♕xe2 (or 2 bxc3 ♗xd1 3 ♖xd1 bxc6) 2...♕xc6 left Black a clear piece ahead. (*1 point*)

1082) Bronstein-Ilivitzki

1 ♖cxd8! (*1 point*) 1...♕e1+ (after 1...♖bxd8 or 1...♖exd8, with 2 ♘h6+ White either wins the black queen with 2...♔h8 3 ♘xf7+ or mates with 2...gxh6 3 ♕xf7+ ♔h8 4 ♕xh7#) 2 ♔g2 1-0 White emerges a piece ahead after 2...♖bxd8 3 ♘h6+ ♔h8 4 ♘xf7+ ♔g8 5 ♖xd8 (*take a second point for seeing this far*).

1083) Adams-Palliser

1...♗xa3! 2 bxa3 ♖xc3 wins a pawn. (*1 point*)

1084) Baburin-Palliser

1 ♖e8+! (*1 point*) 1...♖xe8 2 dxe8♕+ ♔xe8 3 f4 leads to an easily winning pawn ending due to White's outside passed pawn: 3...a6 (or 3...gxf3 4 ♔f2 c4 5 ♔xf3 ♔d7 6 g4 a6 – 6...♔e6 7 ♔e4 ♔f6 8 ♔d5 ♔g5 9 ♔c6! sees the a-pawn queen shortly – 7 ♔e4 b5 8 axb5 axb5 9 ♔d4 and White's soon to be passed c-pawn decides) 4 c4! (*take a second point for seeing this useful follow-up*) 4...♔d7 5 ♔e2 ♔c6 6 ♔d3 b5 (Black cannot maintain the opposition in view of 6...♔d7 7 ♔e4 ♔e6 8 f5+ ♔d6 9 ♔f4 b5 10 axb5 axb5 11 cxb5 c4 12 f6 when White queens first) 7 cxb5+ axb5 8 a5 1-0

1085) Palliser-Hotham

1...♗xc2+! (*1 point*) 2 ♔xc2 ♘b4+ 3 ♔c3 (or 3 ♔c1 ♘fd3+ when White must give up his queen to avoid 4 ♔b1 ♕xa2#) 3...♘xa2+ 4 ♔c2 ♘b4+ 5 ♔c3 ♕c5+ and Black regained his piece with a huge advantage (also rather effective would have been 5...♘bd3+ 6 ♔c2 ♕a2).

1086) Gower-Hopwood
1...♗xg2! 2 ♘xg2 (or 2 ♔xg2 ♖xg2+ 3 ♔h1 ♕g4 4 ♘xg2 f3 followed by mate) **2...♖xg2+ 3 ♔h1** (3 ♗xg2 f3 and mate on g2 is the main point of the combination) **3...♖g6 0-1** (*2 points*)

1087) McNab-Sherwin
1 ♕g7+! 1-0
White forces mate with 1...♖xg7 2 e7+. (*1 point*)

1088) Ziatdinov-Kotronias
1...♗g5! 2 ♘b5+ (the only real try with White's queen being tied to the defence of both b2 and d4) **2...♗xb5 3 ♕xg5 ♗e2** (the main point: White can't both prevent mate and save his rook) **4 ♕e7+ ♔b8 0-1**
Take 1 point for finding 1...♗g5 and a second if you saw 3...♗e2.

1089) Berzina-Ciuksyte
1 ♗xh7+! ♔xh7 1-0
Mate follows with 2 g8♕+! ♖xg8 3 ♖xf7+ ♔h8 4 ♕h4#. (*2 points*)

1090) Schulz-Kulovana
1...♗xg2! 2 ♔xg2 ♕g5+ 3 ♔h2 ♕xd2 won a pawn. (*1 point*)

1091) Zakharevich-Ovod
1 ♘f6+!! ♗xf6 (or 1...gxf6 2 ♗xh7+! ♘xh7 3 ♖g3+ ♘g5 4 fxg5 fxg5 5 ♖h3 ♗f6 6 ♗b4 followed by mate) **2 ♗xh7+! ♘xh7 3 ♖h3 ♕xd4** (Black also can't escape from the white attack after 3...a5 4 ♕xh7+ ♔f8 5 ♗e3 ♗e7 6 ♖d1) **4 ♕xh7+ ♔f8 5 exf6 gxf6 6 ♗c3 ♕xf4 7 ♖f3 ♕xf3** (White mates too after 7...♕c4 8 ♗xf6 ♕g4 9 ♕h8+ ♕g8 10 ♕h6+) **8 ♗b4+ 1-0**
It's mate with 8...♖e7 9 ♕h8#.
Take two points for finding 1 ♘f6+ and a further two for seeing as far as 7 ♖f3.

1092) Cox-Trent
1 ♗xf7! wins a key pawn: **1...♖xf7 2 ♕e8+ ♖f8 3 ♘xg6+ ♔g8 4 ♘xf8 ♗xf8 5 ♕e6+ ♔h7** (or 5...♔h8 6 ♕xe5+ ♔g8 7 ♕e6+ ♔h8 8 ♕c8! ♕d6 9 ♕c2 trapping the black knight) **6 ♕f5+ 1-0**
Black loses his knight after 6...♔g8 7 ♕g4+.
Take one point for 1 ♗xf7 and a further two if you realised that the knight on d1 was trapped.

Test Two

1093) Aronian-Svidler
1...♖e1+! 0-1
White loses his queen after 2 ♖xe1 ♕xd3. (*1 point*)

1094) Bielby-Smith
1...axb5! 2 ♘xc7+ ♔e7 0-1
Black is a piece up for insufficient compensation after both 2...♔e7 3 ♘xa8 ♘d4 4 ♕xf4 ♗h6 5 ♕f2 ♘xc2+ 6 ♔f1 ♘xa1 and 3 ♘d5+ ♔d8 4 d3 ♕g3+.
Take 1 point for 1...axb5 and a further one if you saw as far as 4...♗h6.

1095) Parkin-Palliser
Black increases his advantage to an extra rook: **1...♖xd3 2 ♕xd3 ♕xa1** (*1 point*)

1096) Levitsky-Marshall
1...♕g3!! 0-1
Black emerges a piece ahead after 2 ♕xg3 (it's mate after both 2 hxg3 ♘e2# and 2 fxg3 ♘e2+ 3 ♔h1 ♖xf1#) 2...♘e2+ 3 ♔h1 ♘xg3+ 4 ♔g1 ♘e2+.
Only 2 points I'm afraid as there were less attractive ways to win and because this position is rather well known.

1097) Adorjan-Ribli
1 ♗xg7! ♗xg7 **2 h6** ♗f6 (it's also mate down the g-file after 2...♗f8 3 ♕g5 f6 4 ♕g6+ ♔h8 5 h7, while 2...♗h8 fails to either 3 ♕g5 or 3 ♖g7+) **3 ♕g2 1-0**
There's no defence to the threat of 4 ♕g7+!. (*2 points*)

1098) Lund-Rowson
White solves his back-rank difficulties in style by simplifying with **1 ♖xc5+!** ♔b8 (or 1...bxc5 2 ♕b7#) **2 ♖c8+! 1-0** (*2 points*)

1099) Abergel-Tebb
1 ♗xf7+! ♔xf7 **2 ♘d6+ 1-0**
Black must give up his queen since 2...♔g8 3 ♕b3+ mates. (*1 point*)

1100) Frostick-Miller
1...♖xg2+! (*1 point*) forces perpetual: **2 ♔xg2 ♕g6+ 3 ♔h2** (or 3 ♔f2 ♕f5+ 4 ♔e1 ♕b1+ 5 ♔d2 ♕b2+ and the white king cannot escape) **3...♕c2+ 4 ♔g1 ♕g6+ 5 ♔h2 ½-½**

1101) Cullen-Varnam
1...♗xf2+! 0-1
It's mate on the back rank after 2 ♖xf2 ♕a1+. (*1 point*)

1102) Slinger-Rooney
1 ♕h8+! ♗xh8 **2 ♖xh8+ ♔g7 3 ♗xe5+ f6 4 gxf6+ 1-0**
White emerges a rook up. (*2 points*)

1103) Zhao-Markos
1 ♘xh5!! ♖d8 (giving the king an escape square, while preventing the other threat of 2 ♘f6+; White's queen was immune in view of 1...♘xd3? 2 ♖g7+ ♔f8 3 ♘h7# or 2...♔h8 3 ♘f7#) **2 ♕xd5! gxh5** (or 2...♕xd5 3 ♘f6+ ♔h8 4 ♖h7#) **3 ♖f8+! 1-0**
Mate follows with 3...♔g7 4 ♕g8+ ♔h6 5 ♘f7#.
2 points for 1 ♘xh5 and a further two if you found 2 ♕xd5.

1104) Cooley-Noden
1 ♖xe4! (*1 point*) **1...♕f5** (after 1...♖xe4, 2 ♘g5 wins Black's queen in view of the mate threat on h8) **2 ♘f6+!** (*a further 2 points are available for this*) **2...♔xg7 3 ♖g4+ ♕g6?** (now it's mate, although after 3...♕xg4 4 ♕xg4+ ♔xf6 5 ♕h4+ ♔g6 6 ♕xe7 White's extra queen and pawns should decide) **4 ♕h7+ ♔xf6 5 ♖f4+ ♕f5** (or 5...♔g5 6 ♕h4#) **6 ♕h6# 1-0**

Test Three

1105) O'Neill-Hopwood
1...♖xc3! removes the white queen's defender to net a piece. (*1 point*)

1106) Balbashova-Sulejmanova
1...♕xa5! wins a piece in view of White's vulnerable back rank. (*1 point*)

1107) Alonso-Claros Egea
1 ♘xf7! ♔xf7 (a much better defence is 1...♕xf6 2 ♘xh8 ♕xh8, although White is the exchange ahead and doing rather well after 3 ♕h5+) **2 ♕h5+ ♔xf6** (now Black loses his queen, but 2...♔g8 was impossible on account of 3 ♕g6+ ♗g7 4 ♕xg7#) **3 ♕xh4+ 1-0**
1 point for 1 ♘xf7 and a bonus point if you spotted then 3 ♕xh4+.

1108) Reiner-Steinitz
1...♕h4! (*1 point*) **2 ♖g2** (or 2 ♖xh4 ♖g1#) **2...♕xh2+!** (*and a second point for this*) **3 ♖xh2 ♖g1#**
0-1

1109) Bronstein-Kottnauer
1 ♘e8! 1-0
The most elegant way of preventing Black's idea of ...♕b6-g1+ with perpetual, although 1 ♘g6+ ♔g8 2 ♕a4 is also more than good enough. After 1 ♘e8, if 1...♕b6 then White has the pretty 2 ♕h7+! ♔xh7 3 ♖xg7+ ♔h8 4 ♘g6#.
1 point for 1 ♘g6+ or two if you found both 1 ♘e8 and the queen sacrifice.

1110) Karpov-Malaniuk
1 ♗d5+! 1-0
Mate follows after 1...cxd5 2 ♕xd5+ ♔e8 3 ♕e6+. (*1 point*)

1111) Turner-Mestel
1...♘xe4!! **2 ♗xe4** (or 2 ♘xe4 ♗xa1 3 ♗e3 ♕a5+ and Black is the exchange up) **2...d5 3 cxd5 cxd5 4 ♗f3** (neither does 4 ♗xg6 fxg6 5 ♗b2 ♖ae8 6 0-0-0 save White in view of 6...♖c8 followed by 7...d4) **4...♗f5** gives Black a winning attack: **5 ♕d2 ♖fe8+ 6 ♔d1** (or 6 ♗e2 ♗xc3 7 ♕xc3 ♗g4 when White must resign) **6...♗xc3 7 ♕xc3 ♖ac8 0-1**
8 ♕d2 ♗c2+ 9 ♕xc2 ♖xc2 10 ♔xc2 ♕f2+ is absolutely crushing.
2 points for 1...♘xe4 and a further one if you realised that the attack was immensely powerful.

1112) Sowray-Palliser
1...♘xg2! (*1 point*) **2 ♔xg2 ♕f6!?** (also rather good is 2...♘h4+, pretty much forcing 3 ♘xh4 ♗xd1 4 ♖axd1 ♕xh4) **3 ♔h2 ♕f4+ 4 ♔g1 ♗xf3 5 ♕d2 ♕h4 6 ♗d1 ♕xh3 7 ♗xf3 ♕xf3 8 ♕e3 ♕g4+ 9 ♕g3 ♕xe4** and Black's extra pawns carried the day.

1113) Potts-Rendle
1 ♕xd5+! 1-0
White forces mate after 1...♔h8 (or 1...♖xd5 2 ♖xf8#) 2 ♕xf5!.
1 point for each queen sacrifice.

1114) Jones-Gallagher
1...♖xa3+! 2 bxa3 ♕xa3+ 0-1
Mate follows after 3 ♕a2 ♕c3+. (*1 point*)

1115) Anand-Van Wely
1 ♖xg7!! (*3 points*) **1...♔xg7** (the queen is immune in view of 1...♘xd5? 2 ♖xh7#) **2 ♖g1+ ♔h8 3 ♗h6 ♘g4** (setting a cheapo and there was no good way to cover g7, especially since 3...♘h5 fails to 4 ♗xf8 ♖xf8 5 ♖g8+ ♖xg8 6 fxg8♕#) **4 ♖xg4 ♖xf7 5 ♕xa8+! 1-0**

1116) Aronian-Papp

1 ♖xf7!! ♔xf7 (now the attack is too strong, but neither was there a good way to decline the rook: for example, 1...b5 2 ♖c7 ♕a8 3 ♗xe6+ ♖xe6 4 ♕b3 and the e6-rook falls) **2 ♕h7 ♖xd6** (desperation in the face of 3 ♖f1#; mate would also have occurred after both 2...♖f8 3 ♖f1+ ♔e8 4 ♕g6+ ♔d7 5 ♗xe6# and 2...♔f6 3 ♖f1+ ♔e5 4 ♕f5+ ♔d4 5 ♕d3+ ♔e5 6 ♖f5#) **3 cxd6 ♔f6 4 ♖f1+ ♔e5 5 d7** (5 ♕d3 was even stronger, but we're rather splitting hairs) **5...♕xd7 6 ♕f5+ 1-0**

Black will lose his queen.

3 points for finding both the rook sacrifice and the all-important follow-up, 2 ♕h7.

Test Four

1117) Schon-Egan

1 ♘xc6! wins a key pawn in view of 1...♕xc6? 2 ♗b5. (*1 point*)

1118) Mahesh Chandran-Vavrak

1 ♘c8! 1-0

White threatens mate and after 1...♖xc8 2 ♗xb7 Black's rooks are skewered. (*1 point*)

1119) Lin Zhigen-Hvistendahl

1 ♘f6+! 1-0

White wins the exchange on e8. (*1 point*)

1120) Izoria-Heimann

1 ♖xa6! 1-0

White's pawns decide after 1...♔xa6 (or 1...♖xd7 2 ♖a7+ ♔c8 3 ♖a8+ ♔b7 4 ♖ba1 followed by mate down the a-file) 2 ♔xc6 (threatening 3 ♖a1#) 2...♔a5 3 ♔c7 ♖gg8 4 b7 ♖b8 5 c5 ♔a6 6 c6 h4 7 ♔d6. (*2 points*)

1121) Samedov-Kirikova

1...♗xh3! 2 gxh3 (or 2 ♔g1 ♗xg2 winning material) **2...♕xh3+ 3 ♘h2** (similar and rather effective is 3 ♖h2 ♗xh2 4 ♘xh2 ♕xf3+) **3...♗xh2 4 ♖xh2 ♕xf3+ 5 ♔g1 ♖g6+ 6 ♖g2 ♖xg2+ 7 ♕xg2 ♕xd1+ 8 ♔h2 ♖f6** gave Black an overwhelming attack.

2 points for 1...♗xh3 and a further one if you spotted that the d1-rook would become loose.

1122) Kolev-Hernando Rodrigo

1 ♘h5! ♗d5 (Black is crushed after 1...gxh5 2 ♕h6 f6 3 ♖xe6, but there's no satisfactory defence in any case with 1...♗f5 failing to 2 ♕h6 ♗f8 3 ♕g5) **2 ♕h6 ♗f8 3 ♕g5** and White's threats down the long diagonal are decisive: **3...♗xe4 4 ♘f6+ ♔h8 5 ♘xe4+ ♕d4 6 ♗xd4+ cxd4 7 ♕f6+ 1-0**

1 point for 1 ♘h5 and a further one for seeing up to 3 ♕g5.

1123) Grivas-Hrisostomidis

1 ♖xh7+! ♔xh7 (or 1...♔g8 2 d6+ ♘c4 3 ♕h5 followed by mate) **2 ♕h5+ ♔g8 3 ♘e7# 1-0** (*1 point*)

1124) Pitl-Savchenko

1...♗f2! trapped the white queen: **2 ♕xf2 ♘d3+ 3 ♗xd3 ♕xf2 0-1** (*1 point*)

1125) Sokolov-Saric

1 ♘d7! (*2 points*) **1...♖d8?** (Black had to give up the exchange with 1...♖g6, even though the

ending should be winning for White after 2 ♘xf8+ ♗xf8 3 ♖xf5) **2 ♖h4+ 1-0**
It's mate after 2...♖h6 3 ♘f6+ ♔h8 4 ♖xh6#.

1126) Pucher-Gerard
1...♖xg2! (*2 points*) **2 ♖c8+** (or 2 ♕xg2 ♕xc1+ 3 ♔h2 ♕e3 with an extra pawn and some advantage) **2...♗xc8 3 ♕xg2 ♕xe5** saw Black pick up two pawns.

1127) Palliser-Burnett
1 ♗xg6!! hxg6 (after 1...♘xg6 2 ♘xg6 Black has nothing better than to transpose with 2...hxg6) **2 ♘xg6 ♘xg6 3 ♖xg6+ ♔h8** (and not 3...♔h7? 4 ♗f8!) **4 ♕h5 ♖h7 5 ♖g7!** ♖xg7 (the main point of White's whole combination is that 5...♕e8 fails to 6 ♖dxd7!: 6...♕xh5 7 ♖xh7+ ♔g8 8 ♖dg7+ ♔f8 9 ♖h8# or 6...♕xd7 7 ♖xd7 ♖xd7 8 ♗g5+ when White's queen and bishop combine with deadly effect; perhaps Black might have tried 5...♗e4, although after 6 ♖xe7 ♖xe7 7 ♗g7+ ♔g8 8 ♕g4 it's hard to believe that White's attack won't shortly net further material) **6 ♗xg7+ ♔g8 7 ♕h8+ ♔f7 8 ♕h5+ ♔g8** and now **9 ♗h6!** (rather than the game's horrible 9 ♖g1?) **9...♔h8 10 ♖g1** wins the black queen after **10...♕h7 11 ♗g7+ ♔g8 12 ♗xf6+.**
1 point for 1 ♗xg6, two more for 5 ♖g7 and a fourth point is available for seeing 9 ♗h6.

1128) Euwe-Reti
1...♗h3! (1...♗c5+ 2 ♔h1 ♗h3! also does the business) **2 ♕xa8 ♗c5+ 3 ♔h1** (or 3 ♖dd4 ♗xd4+ 4 ♖xd4 ♕e1#) **3...♗xg2+! 4 ♔xg2 ♕g4+ 5 ♔f1 ♕f3+ 6 ♔e1 ♕f2# 0-1** (*2 points*)

Test Five

1129) Von Herman-Tabatt
1 ♖fd1! ♕b5 (1...fxe4? fails to 2 ♖xc8+ ♖xc8 3 ♕xd7#) **2 ♘f6+! ♔e7 3 ♖xc8 ♖xc8 4 ♘xd7** gave White a crushing attack.
1 point for 1 ♖d1+ and a second for 3 ♖xc8.

1130) Pomar Salamanca-Liljedahl
1 ♘g5! (*1 point*) wins material down the long diagonal: **1...f6 2 ♗xb7 fxg5 3 ♕e3 ♘d7 4 ♕xe6+ ♔f8** (or 4...♕e7 5 ♕xe7+ ♔xe7 6 ♗xa8 ♖xa8 7 bxc3 with an extra exchange) **5 ♗xa8 ♕xa8 6 f3** and White went on to convert his extra exchange (Black cannot save both his knights).

1131) Ferguson-Wallace
1 ♖xg6! 1-0
White wins a piece in view of 1...♕xf2 2 ♖xg7+ and 3 ♖xf2. (*1 point*)

1132) Stadt-Roehrl
White wins Black's queen: **1 ♘g6+! ♘xg6 2 ♕xd6 1-0** (*1 point*)

1133) Alekhine-Reshevsky
1 ♖xb8+! ♔xb8 2 ♕xe5+! 1-0
Mate follows on the back rank after 2...fxe5 (or 2...♔a8 3 ♖a1+) 3 ♖f8+. (*2 points*)

1134) Morrison-Basman
1...♖xh2! 2 ♔xh2 ♖h8+ 3 ♔g1 ♖h1# 0-1 (*1 point*)

1135) Cebalo-Aleksic
1 ♘d6! ♕e7 (it's mate after 1...cxd6? 2 ♘a6+ bxa6 3 ♕c8#) **2 ♘dxb7 1-0**
Black swiftly finds himself defenceless on the queenside after 2...♘xb7 3 ♘a6+ ♚c8 (or
3...♚a8 4 ♕xc7! with a winning attack in view of 4...♕xc7 5 ♘xc7+ ♚b8 6 ♘a6+ ♚a8 7 ♖c8#)
4 ♘xc7.
1 point for 1 ♘d6 and a second if you realised just how fast the attack is after 2 ♘dxb7.

1136) Spraggett-Hernandez Garcia
1 ♘xa6+! *(1 point)* **1...♚a8** (or 1...bxa6 2 ♘c6+ and 3 ♘xc6 winning the black queen) **2
♘xc7+ 1-0**
White's attack is overwhelming after 2...♖xc7 3 axb6+ ♚b8 4 ♕a5.

1137) Svidler-Tiviakov
1 ♖xf7+! ♘xf7 2 ♘e6+ ♚g8 3 ♘xd8 wins a piece in view of 3...♘xd8 4 ♖a8. *(2 points)*

1138) Cnossen-Regniers
1...♕xf2+! 0-1
Back-rank mate follows after 2 ♖xf2 ♖a1+. *(1 point)*

1139) F.N.Stephenson-K.Neat
1 ♖xf6! gxf6 (White was ready with a double exchange sacrifice: 1...♘xf6 2 ♖xf6! gxf6 3
♕g4+ ♚h8 4 ♕g5 – shades of Lasker-Reshevsky) **2 ♕g4+ ♚h8 3 ♖xf6! ♘e5** (3...♘xf6 4 ♕g5
♖g8 5 ♗xf6+ ♕xf6 6 ♕xf6+ ♖g7 7 ♕xd6 sees White's extra queen run amok) **4 ♕f5 ♖g8** (or
4...♕d7 5 ♕xd7 – 5 ♕h5 is a very reasonable alternative – 5...♘xd7 6 ♖xd6+ ♚g8 7 ♖xd7
and White's bishops and d-pawn are far too strong) **5 ♖xd6! 1-0**
2 points for each played exchange sacrifice on f6 and a bonus point if you spotted 5 ♖xd6.

1140) Karpov-Csom
1 ♘f5!! 1-0
2 ♖h7+ and 3 ♕g7# is threatened, and 1...♘xd7 fails to 2 ♕h2+ ♚g8 3 ♕g3+ ♚f7 4 ♕g7#. *(3
points)*

Test Six

1141) Vanderbeeken-Flear
1...♕xc3! 0-1
Black wins a piece due to the pin down the d-file. *(1 point)*

1142) Palliser-Westra
1 ♕xg7! *(1 point)* 1...♖xf4? (a blunder, although after 1...♕xg7 2 ♘e6+ ♚e7 3 ♘xg7 ♖f7 4
♖xf7+ ♚xf7 5 ♘f5 gxf5 6 ♖h7+ ♚e6 7 exf5+ ♚d6 8 ♚b1 White's extra exchange should pre-
vail) **2 ♖h8+ 1-0**

1143) Dvirnyy-Pomaro
1 ♘xf7! ♕xf7 2 ♖xd6 wins a pawn. *(1 point)*

1144) Morris-Burton
1 b4! ensures that White remains a piece ahead after either 1...♕xb4+ 2 c3 ♕xd4 (2...♕b2?
loses to 3 ♕e5+ ♗e7 4 ♕xe7#) 3 ♗xd4 or 1...♗xb4+ 2 c3 gxf6 3 cxb4.
2 points for finding 2 c3.

1145) Gibson-Cork

1 ♘xb7! wins a key pawn since the a-pawn is unstoppable after 1...♘xb7? 2 a6. (*1 point*)

1146) Narayanan-Ikonnikov

1...♘g3+! 2 ♕xg3 f4 forced **3 ♕h3** (3 ♕e1 or 3 ♕f2 would have allowed mate after 3...♕xh2+! 4 ♔xh2 ♖h6+ 5 ♔h4 ♖xh4#) **3...♗xh3** with an easy win for Black.
2 points for 1...♘g3 and a further point for the queen sacrifice on h2.

1147) Szakolczai-Okara

1...♕xf2+! 0-1
Mate follows with 2 ♖xf2 ♖c1+ 3 ♖f1 ♗e3+ 4 ♔h1 ♖xf1#. (*2 points*)

1148) Bronstein-Ratner

1 ♘xe6! (*1 point*) **1...♖xd1** (White wins easily after this, but he also would have done after both 1...fxe6 2 ♖xd7 ♘xd7 3 ♕xe6+ ♕f7 4 ♖h8+! – *a second point for seeing this important follow-up* – and 1...♕e7 2 ♖h8+ ♔xh8 3 ♕h6+ ♔g8 4 ♕g7#) **2 ♘xf8 ♖xh1 3 ♔xh1 ♖xf8 4 ♕e7 ♔g7 5 ♕xb7 ♘c8 6 ♕d7 1-0**

1149) McNab-Gayson

1 ♖xg6+! hxg6 (or 1...♔f7 2 ♖xh7+ ♔e8 3 ♖gg7 with a mating attack) **2 ♗xg6 1-0**
Mate follows on h8. (*2 points*)

1150) Sareen-Palliser

1...♘xf2! (*2 points*) wins the exchange since **2 ♔xf2** failed to **2...fxg3+ 3 ♔xg3** (or 3 ♔e2 ♕f2+ 4 ♔d3 ♖f3+) **3...♕f2+ 4 ♔g4 ♖f4+** both winning the queen and forcing mate.

1151) Bologan-Vaganian

1 ♖xh7! 1-0
It's mate after 1...♔xh7 (or 1...gxf6 2 ♕xg6+ ♔f8 3 ♕f7#) 2 ♖h1+ ♔g8 3 ♕xg6 ♖e7 4 ♗xg7! ♖xg7 5 ♕e8#.
2 points for 1 ♖xh7.

1152) Negi-Hermansson

1 ♘xe6!! fxe6 (1...♕xe4 fails to 2 ♕xe4 ♗xe4 3 ♖c8+ and mate) **2 f7+ ♔d8** (or 2...♖xf7 3 ♘d6+ ♗xd6 4 ♕xe6+ ♗e7 – 4...♖e7 5 ♖c8+! ♗xc8 6 ♕xc8# – 5 ♕xf7+ ♔d8 6 ♖fd1+ ♘d7 7 ♕e6 with a crushing attack) **3 ♕g5+ ♖e7** (now Black is crushed, but it's mate after 3...♗e7 4 f8♕+ ♖xf8 5 ♖xf8#) **4 ♕e5 1-0** (*3 points*)

Test Seven

1153) Berbatov-Suuronen

1 ♗xf7+! wins the black queen: **1...♔e7 2 ♗c5+ ♔xf7 3 ♕xd8 1-0** (*1 point*)

1154) Repkova-Vlkovic

1 ♘xh7! wins a pawn in view of 1...♖xh7? 2 ♕g6+ ♔f8 3 ♕xh7. (*1 point*)

1155) Akatova-Nebolsina

1...♖xa3! 2 ♖xa3 (White also loses a rook after 2 bxa3 ♘f5) **2...♘c2** forked White's rooks and left Black a piece ahead after **3 ♖a7+ ♔e8 4 ♖a4** (or 4 ♖b1 ♗d4+) **4...♘xa1**.
1 point for 1...♖xa3 and a second if you spotted the check on d4.

1156) Lukovnikov-Bezgodova
1...♖xf2! 0-1
Black emerges a piece ahead after 2 ♕xf2 ♕xe5+ 3 ♕g3 ♕xa1. (*1 point*)

1157) Ehlvest-Illescas Cordoba
1 dxc6! ♘xc6 (White's main point is that 1...♗e4 2 ♖xa7!! ♖xa7 3 c7 sees the c-pawn queen)
2 ♖xb1 and White went on to convert his extra pawn. (*1 point*)

1158) Brown-Hardman
1 ♗xh7+! 1-0
White emerges the exchange ahead in an ending after 1...♔xh7 2 ♕xd5 ♘xd5 3 ♖xc6. (*1 point*)

1159) Debbage-Palliser
1...♘xg5! (otherwise 2 ♖h1 paralyses Black on the kingside, leaving White with a free rein on the queenside) **2 hxg5 ♕xg5+ 3 ♔h1** (and not 3 ♔f2?? ♕g3#) **3...♕h4+ 4 ♔g1 ♕g3+ ½-½**
Neither side can avoid the perpetual. (*2 points*)

1160) Weller-Clarke
1 ♗xh7+! ♔xh7 2 ♕d3+ ♔g8 (the game's 2...f5 should have led to mate with 3 exf6+ ♔g8 4 h7+ ♔f7 5 ♕g6#) **3 ♘xe6** threatens 4 h7# and thereby forces Black to give up his queen, either immediately or after 3...♕a5+ 4 b4 ♕xb4+ 5 c3.
1 point for 1 ♗xh7+ and a second for 3 ♘xe6.

1161) Cmilyte-Atalik
1...♕g4! 2 ♕xg4 (or 2 ♖e1 ♘f2+ 3 ♔g1 ♕xe2 4 ♖xe2 ♘h3+ 5 ♔h1 ♖f1+ 6 ♗g1 ♘xg1 with an extra piece) **2...♖xf1+ 0-1**
Black is a rook up after 3 ♗g1 ♘f2+ 4 ♔h2 ♘xg4+. (*2 points*)

1162) Rotlewi-Rubinstein
1...♖xc3!! 2 gxh4 (neither would 2 ♗xb7 ♖xg3 3 ♖ac1 ♖h3 4 ♖c2 ♗f2! nor 2 ♗xc3 ♗xe4+ 3 ♕xe4 ♕xh2# have saved White) **2...♖d2! 3 ♕xd2 ♗xe4+ 4 ♕g2 ♖h3! 0-1**
Mate follows on h2. (*3 points*)

1163) Evans-Larsen
1...♖f1+! (*2 points*) **2 ♖xf1** (it's mate too after 2 ♔xf1 ♕f5+ 3 ♖f3 – or 3 ♔g1 ♕c5+ 4 ♔h1 ♘f2+ 5 ♔g1 ♘h3+ 6 ♔h1 ♕g1+ 7 ♖xg1 ♘f2# – 3...♖xd1+ 4 ♔e2 ♘c3+! (*a bonus point for this*) 5 bxc3 ♕c2+ 6 ♔e3 ♕d2+ 7 ♔e4 ♖e1+ 8 ♔f5 ♕d5+ 9 ♔f4 ♕e5#) **2...♕c5+ 0-1**
Black mates after 3 ♔h1 ♘f2+! 4 ♖xf2 ♕c1+.

1164) Spassky-Tal
1...♗xh2+! 2 ♔xh2 ♖h5+! (much stronger than 2...♘g4+ 3 ♔g3!) **3 ♔g1** (or 3 ♔g3 ♘e4+ 4 ♗xe4 ♕h4+ 5 ♔f3 ♕xe4+ 6 ♔g3 ♕h4#) **3...♘g4! 0-1**
There's no good defence to the mate threat (beginning 4...♖h1+ 5 ♔xh1 ♕h4+).
1 point for 1...♗xh2+ and a further two for 2...♖h5+.

Test Eight

1165) Hindle-Horton
1 ♕d8+! 1-0
Mate follows with 1...♗xd8 2 ♖xd8#. (*1 point*)

1166) Kynoch-Hogg
1 ♗xf7+! ♔xf7 (or 1...♔d8 2 ♘e5 followed by either a crushing 3 ♘c6+ or 2...♗b7 3 ♘xd7) **2 ♘g5+ ♔e8 3 ♕e6+ 1-0**
It's mate after 3...♔d8 4 ♘f7#.
1 point for 1 ♗xf7+ and a second if you spotted the mate.

1167) Neave-Bryson
1...♕xg2+! 2 ♔xg2 ♘f4+ 0-1
Black will emerge a rook ahead after 3 ♔g1 ♘xd3. (*1 point*)

1168) Ballon-Meenakshi
1...♖xb2! 2 ♕xb2 ♗xc3 3 ♕c2 ♗xd2 wins two very useful minor pieces for a rook. (*1 point*)

1169) Irizanin-Sarenac
1...♖xa2! 0-1
It's mate down the a-file. (*1 point*)

1170) Rozentalis-Preuss
1...♘xf2! (*1 point*) wins the exchange: **2 ♕d2** (or 2 ♔xf2 e5) **2...e5 0-1**

1171) Palliser-Howell
1...♖xc3! (*1 point*) **2 ♕xc3 ♖e2 0-1**
White can only avoid mate on g2 by giving up his queen.

1172) Valmana Canto-Eggleston
1 ♗xg6! hxg6 (or 1...♘xd1 2 ♕xh7#) **2 ♖xd4 ♘xf1 3 ♕f6+ 1-0**
Mate follows after 3...♔h7 4 ♖d3.
1 point for 1 ♗xg6 and a further one if you spotted 3 ♕f6+.

1173) Zheleznov-Vovk
1...♗a2+! 2 ♔c1 ♕xc2+ 3 ♔xc2 ♗b3+ 4 ♔b1 ♗xd1 5 ♖xd1 left Black the exchange ahead for insufficient compensation. (*2 points*)

1174) Hunt-Howell
1...♖xe4!! 2 ♖xe4 (or 2 ♕c8+ ♔f3 3 ♖f1+ ♔e2 and the f- and g-pawns decide) **2...♕b6+ 3 ♔h1 ♕f2 4 ♕g1 ♔h3! 0-1**
Mate follows after 5...g2+ or 5 ♕xf2 gxf2.
2 points for 1...♖xe4 and a further two if you saw through to 4...♔h3.

1175) Spraggett-Llaneza Vega
1 ♘xg6! ♔xg6 (otherwise White simply wins material, such as with 1...♖g8 2 ♕xh5 ♗f7 3 ♗xg7 ♔xg7 4 ♘dxf4) **2 ♕xh5+!** (*3 points*) **2...♔xh5?** (better is 2...♔h7 3 ♘xf4 with only an extra pawn and some attacking chances for White) **3 ♘xf4+ ♔g5 4 h4+ ♔g4 5 ♔h2 1-0**
Mate follows with 6 ♗h3#.

1176) Smeets-Bu Xiangzhi
1...♘d5! (or 1...bxc2+ 2 ♔xc2 ♘d5!, transposing after 3 exd5) **2 exd5 bxc2+ 3 ♔xc2 ♖xa2+** and Black's counterattack is strong enough to force a draw: **4 ♔b1 ♖a1+! 5 ♔xa1** (5 ♔c2 ♖a2+ repeats) **5...♕xc3+ 6 ♔b1 ♕b3+ 7 ♔c1 ♕c3+ 8 ♔b1 ♕b3+ 9 ♔a1 ♕c3+ ½-½**
2 points for 1...♘d5 and a bonus one for 4...♖a1+.

Test Nine

1177) Bernstein-Capablanca
1...♕b2! 0-1
White loses his rook after 2 ♕e1 (or 2 ♖c2 ♕b1+ 3 ♕f1 ♕xc2) 2...♕xc3. (*1 point*)

1178) Smallbone-Cliffe
1 g3! (*1 point*) **1...♗xg3 2 ♖g1** and White's extra piece was decisive.

1179) Donner-Stephenson
1...♖xh2+! 2 ♔xh2 ♕xf2+ 3 ♔h1 g3 0-1
It's either mate on h2 or with 4 ♘f3 g2+ 5 ♔h2 g1♕+ 6 ♔h3 ♕gg3#. (*2 points*)

1180) Cooper-Smith
1 ♖xa5! 1-0
With 1...♕e4+ Black attempts to avoid the check on c7, but after 2 ♗e2 he must remain a piece down in view of 2...♘xa5? 3 ♘d6+. (*1 point*)

1181) Ivanchuk-Van Wely
1 ♖e8+! ♔g7 (Black loses his queen immediately after 1...♖xe8 2 ♕xc7, but she cannot be saved in any case) **2 ♘e6+! 1-0**
In view of 2...fxe6 3 ♖e7+ winning the queen and the game. (*2 points*)

1182) Lehtinen-Kaiju
1 ♘f6+! 1-0
White wins the exchange on e8. (*1 point*)

1183) Kramnik-Svidler
1 ♗xf7+! 1-0
White's connected passed pawns decide after 1...♔xf7 (or 1...♔d7 2 e8♕+ ♖xe8+ 3 ♗xe8+ ♔xe8 4 ♖xh7 with an easy win) 2 d7. (*2 points*)

1184) Onischuk-Kravtsiv
1 ♘h7+! ♔e8 (Black's queen is lost after 1...♘xh7 2 ♗xe7+, while 1...♔g8 runs into 2 ♘f5 ♕b7 3 ♕xg6) **2 ♘f5! 1-0**
White wins at least a piece after 2...gxf5 3 ♕xg7.
1 point for 1 ♘h7+ and a second if you found 2 ♘f5.

1185) Coleman-Simms
1 ♘xf7! 1-0
White wins a rook in view of 1...♔xf7? 2 ♕xe6+ ♔f8 3 ♕e7+ ♔g8 4 ♕xd8+ ♔f7 5 ♖e7#. (*1 point*)

1186) Taylor-Mirabile
1 ♗xh6! ♔g8 (White forces mate after 1...♗xh6 with 2 ♕xf8 ♕c1 3 ♖e3 ♘g7 4 ♘g5#) **2 ♗xg7 ♔xg7** (or 2...♘xg7 3 ♖h8+!) **3 ♖h7+! ♔xh7 4 ♕xf8 ♘g7** (White has a mating attack too after 4...♕c1 5 ♖e3) **5 ♘g5+ ♔h6 6 ♘xf7+ 1-0**
Mate follows on h8.
1 point for 1 ♗xh6 and a further two if you found 3 ♖h7+.

1187) Lisitsin-Ragozin

1 ♗h7+!! ♚xh7 (Black's cause isn't helped by 1...♚h8 2 ♘g5) **2 ♘g5+! ♚g8** (after 2...hxg5 3 ♕h5+ ♚g8 4 ♕xf7+ ♚h7 5 ♕h5+ ♚g8 6 hxg5 Black must give up his queen to prevent mate with 7 g6 and 8 ♕h7#, while 2...♚g6 is swiftly mated by 3 h5+! ♚xg5 4 ♗c1#) **3 ♘xf7 ♕b8 4 ♘xh6+! gxh6 5 ♕g4+ ♚h8 6 ♖f7 1-0**

Mate follows after 6...♖g8 7 ♕h5.

2 points for 1 ♗h7+ and a further point for 4 ♘xh6+.

1188) Alekhine-Prat

1 ♕h5+!! ♘xh5 2 fxe6+ ♚g6 3 ♗c2+ ♚g5 4 ♖f5+ ♚g6 (or 4...♚h4 5 ♖e4+ ♘f4 6 ♖exf4#) **5 ♖f6+ ♚g5 6 ♖g6+ ♚h4 7 ♖e4+ ♘f4 8 ♖xf4+ ♚h5 9 g3 1-0**

There's no defence to 10 ♖h4#.

Just 1 point for 1 ♕h5+, but three if you calculated through to mate.

Test Ten

1189) Palliser-Davies

1 ♘xd5! (*1 point*) **1...♕d8** (not the best defence, but in the case of 1...exd5 2 ♗xd7+ and 3 ♕xb7 Black would have been quickly destroyed) **2 ♕c3** and the rook on h8 dropped off.

1190) Bonilla Guzman-Michelmann

1...fxg1♘+! 0-1

Black is a piece up with a crushing attack after 2 ♚e1 (the main point of this Albin trap is that 2 ♖xg1 ♗g4+ wins White's queen) 2...♕h4+ 3 ♚d2 ♘c6 4 ♗c3 ♗g4. (*1 point*)

1191) Arluck-Benjamin

1...♗xg2+! 2 ♚xg2 ♖xe3 3 fxe3 ♘f5 saw Black's extra queen shortly prove decisive. (*1 point*)

1192) Katte-Zweschper

1...♘xe3! picks up two pawns after **2 fxe3** (or 2 ♕b3 ♘xf1 winning the exchange) **2...♕xe3+** and 3...♕xd3. (*1 point*)

1193) Granados Gomez-Larino Nieto

1 ♗xb7! (*1 point*) wins a pawn since the a-pawn queens after 1...♘xb7? 2 a6.

1194) Navara-Ponomariov

1 ♚e4! 1-0 (*1 point*)

White just needs to avoid 1 ♚xf4?? because 1...♖xf5+! 2 ♚xf5 would be an embarrassing stalemate.

1195) Milman-Rukavina

1 ♖xf4! 1-0

After 1...exf4 Black loses his queen to 2 ♕d4+ ♚f8 3 ♕f6+! ♚e8 4 ♗c6+.

1 point for 1 ♖xf4 and take a second if you saw as far as 4 ♗c6+.

1196) Meier-Saltaev

1 ♖c7+! ♚d4 2 ♖c5 1-0

The threat to capture on d5 wins a rook. (*1 point*)

1197) Pashikian-Yegiazarian
1...♕g1+! 2 ♔xf3 ♗c6 0-1
White's queen is lost after 3 ♕xc6 ♕h1+. (*2 points*)

1198) Portisch-Berger
1 ♘xh7!! ♔xh7 2 ♖h5+ ♔g7 3 ♗e5+ f6 4 ♖g5! 1-0
The key sting in the tail. Black cannot satisfactorily defend g6.
3 points if you saw all the way through to 4 ♗g5.

1199) Sammalvuo-Smeets
1 ♗d8!! ♘xd8 (it's mate after 1...♖d7 2 ♖xg7+ ♔xg7 3 ♕g5+ ♗g6 4 ♕f6+ ♔g8 5 ♖h8#, while
White wins further material in the event of 1...♔e8 2 ♖7h2) **2 ♖xg7+! ♔xg7 3 ♕g5+ ♔f7 4
♖h8 1-0**
There's no defence to 5 ♕f6#.
2 points for 1 ♗d8 and take a further two if you found 4 ♖h8.

1200) Palliser-Dineley
1 bxc3! ♕b2+ 2 ♗d2! (the star move preventing Black's queen from escaping via c3)
2...♕xa1 3 ♕g5 g6 4 ♕f6! gxh5 5 ♗h6 ♕xa2+ 6 ♘e2! 1-0
Now it's mate after 6...♕xe2+ 7 ♔g3 h4+ 8 ♔h3, but White had to avoid 6 ♔g3? in view of
6...h4+! 7 ♔xh4 (or 7 ♕xh4 ♕e6) 7...♕xg2.
Take two points for 1 bxc3 and a further two if you initially found 6 ♘e2.